D1378409

Women Writing War

Interdisciplinary German
Cultural Studies

Interdisciplinary German Cultural Studies

Edited by
Irene Kacandes

Volume 24

Women Writing War

From German Colonialism through World War I

Edited by
Katharina von Hammerstein
Barbara Kosta
Julie Shoults

DE GRUYTER

ISBN 978-3-11-056972-8
e-ISBN (PDF) 978-3-11-057200-1
e-ISBN (EPUB) 978-3-11-057104-2
ISSN 1861-8030

Bibliographic information published by the Deutsche Nationalbibliothek
The Deutsche Nationalbibliothek lists this publication in the Deutsche Nationalbibliografie;
detailed bibliographic data are available on the Internet at http://dnb.dnb.de.

© 2018 Walter de Gruyter GmbH, Berlin/Boston
Cover image: World War I, 1914–18: a German Red Cross nurse equipped by the Bavarian
women's association (Bayerischer Frauenverein) © akg-images.

Printing and binding: CPI books GmbH, Leck

www.degruyter.com

Table of Contents

Katharina von Hammerstein, Barbara Kosta, and Julie Shoults
Introduction

Women Writing War:
From German Colonialism through World War I

"So, what is war?" Recent publications at the intersection of War Studies and Gender Studies have called into question the traditional scope of the term we use for large-scale collective violence (Sylvester 2011, 125).[1] Rather than defining war mostly in terms of top-down abstractions like inter- and intra-state power struggles between belligerent parties, armament, and organization of fighting forces, political scientist Christine Sylvester proposes thinking of war as an "experiential phenomenon," as "a subset of social relations of experience" (2012, 490, 483).[2] This approach expands the categories of those considered impacted by war beyond the realm of combat to include the "myriad more actors, all of whom experience the collective violence differently, depending on their location, level and mode of involvement, gender, moral code, memories and access to technologies" (2011, 125). This bottom-up definition of war as the experience of "ordinary people" (2012, 483, 484, 487, 502; 2013, 5, 9) does not consign "people" to collateral positions (2012, 490). On the contrary, it (re)orients the focus of war research from "war strategies, weapons systems, national security interests and the like" (2013, 4) to the deeply personal and individual in the experience of war – including the war experiences of "ordinary women" (2013, 39).[3]

While women immediately following World War I "were not accepted as central to the war story, which [...] focused on the sacrifice and heroism of the soldiers," as historians Ingrid Sharp and Matthew Stibbe observe in *Aftermaths of War* (2011, 12),[4] this recent turn on the part of International Relations' War Studies that advocates "going to ground, going to individuals" (Sylvester 2012, 495)

---

1 See also Sylvester, "Introduction: War questions for feminism and International Relations" (2013, 1–14).
2 Sylvester speaks of "war as an experience of many kinds – physical, psychological, social, technological and so on" (2012, 489).
3 For intersections of Gender and War Studies, see Linda Åhäll and Laura Shepherd (2012), Miranda Alison (2009), Cynthia Enloe (1989/2014 and 2000), Annica Kronsell and Erika Svedberg (2012) and Tina Managhan (2012), to name a few.
4 Even a 1994 exhibit curated by the Deutsches Historisches Museum in Berlin, titled *Die letzten Tage der Menschheit: Bilder des Ersten Weltkrieges* (The last days of humanity: Images of the First World War) focused solely on the experience of the war on battlefields, where soldiers fought and died. No mention of women was made (Rother 1994).

https://doi.org/10.1515/9783110572001-001

encourages us to examine women's involvement with war and their narratives about both theaters of war and the home front. Interestingly, the German term *Heimatfront* (home front) was, according to historian Karen Hagemann, introduced as a reference to the *Heimat* (homeland) for the first time during World War I. It was:

> coined, not coincidentally, at the beginning of the war by official German propaganda. As it became increasingly industrialized, the war depended more than ever before on the willingness of civilians at home, both male and female, to support the war effort, not just by making material sacrifices and participating in war relief and nursing but above all by working in war-relevant industry. The 'second front' at home was expected to provide a steady supply of men and material for the war on the first front, and at the same time to process losses both materially and mentally. (2002b, 8; see also 2002a, 20)

Considering these efforts on the home front to sustain the fighting on the battlefront, it is all the more important to examine the experiences and perspectives of civilians vis-à-vis the war machinery of the early 1900s. While the lines between home front and battlefield, however interdependent, may be more clearly drawn in the context of Germany during World War I, since none of the battles were fought on German soil, there was little differentiation between these two spaces in the colonies. The German colonies were viewed as an extension of the homeland and were built on ambitions to control new lands and resources, representing a power grab legitimized by discourses of disseminating German cultural values to indigenous populations perceived as "racially" inferior. It might be said that the Scramble for Africa segued into World War I, with both colonialization and the Great War tied to the desire to build and defend an empire.

Emphasizing the interconnectedness of World War I and German colonialism, literary critic Marcia Klotz points out in the volume *Germany's Colonial Pasts* (Ames et al. 2005), "The Great War itself can hardly be understood without recourse to colonial history, and not only because colonial rivalries played an important part in the events leading up to its outbreak" (Klotz 2005, 136). The relationship of World War I and the preceding colonial conflicts is thus finely tethered through aspirations and discourses of nation-building, heroic affect, feelings of national and cultural superiority, an ineffable desire to belong to a larger cause, and the bitter sense of loss and despondence. It should be noted that Klotz uses the term "Great War" as it is difficult to reference the first major European conflict of the twentieth century, 1914–1918, as "First World War" unless we are looking at it in a context that already assumes the Second World War. Considering the challenge around this anachronism and given the specific focus of the volume, we use the terms "Great War" and "World War I" interchangeably. The focus on the Great War and the colonial wars through women's accounts produces a lesser explored relationship than the oft-cited continuity between World War I and II, while simultaneously establishing an implicit relationship between all three of these historic events. Consequently, we refer to World War I, cognizant that the authors and artists discussed in this volume did not use this designation.

Recognizing the intricate relationship between the wars at the beginning of the twentieth century, the volume *Women Writing War* brings together and offers critical analyses of the perspectives of female authors and artists who produced a lexicon of images that responded to colonial wars and World War I. As the title suggests, *writing* here is understood very broadly to include all forms of cultural production. This focus on women writers and artists thus importantly expands the war canon dominated by male writers, and contributes to a fuller, more comprehensive understanding of the experience of war on many fronts. As Claire Tylee in *The Great War and Women's Consciousness* claims for the British context: "To recover women's literature of the past is to understand our 'memory' of the Great War better. It necessitates an understanding of how and why women's writing has been suppressed, and how 'memory' is created" (1990, 258–259). The same may be said of women's writings about colonial wars.

As is well known, Germany's involvement in European colonialism worldwide began, apart from episodic forerunners, after the unification of Germany in 1871. In the context of the Scramble for Africa among European powers at the 1884–1885 Berlin Conference, Germany acquired Togo, Cameroon, German East Africa and German Southwest Africa. Germany also controlled the colonies of German New Guinea and German Samoa in the South Pacific and the treaty ports of Kiaochow, Chefoo and Tsingtao in China. The occupation of territories led to Germany's military involvement in a number of colonial wars including the Boxer Rebellion against Western colonialism in China (1900), the Colonial War with the Herero and Nama in German Southwest Africa (1904–1908) and the Maji-Maji War in German East Africa (1905–1908).[5] At the time, German discourse framed these colonial wars as "Aufstände" (uprisings, rebellions), which linguistically shifted the blame for the conflicts onto the colonized locals – rebels or freedom fighters, depending on one's perspective – and exculpated the colonial invaders. The German *Schutztruppe* (colonial occupation troops called protection troops) also engaged in notorious "Strafexpeditionen" (punitive expeditions) to suppress the rebellious indigenous populations.

---

5 For German colonialism, see Conrad (2008), Kundrus (2003), Smith (1978), and Speitkamp (2005).

It is important to differentiate, however, between daily violence and violence resulting from actual colonial conflicts, as historian Sebastian Conrad insists (2008, 79). The colonizers also exercised their power through structural violence (see Galtung 1982), which included the infliction of corporal punishment by colonial masters and mistresses against native female and male farm workers and servants in private households. German and native women, whether as victims, perpetrators and/or bystanders, were directly or indirectly involved in both manifestations of violence.

At first, relatively few white, German women went to the colonies. Those who did go joined husbands who were administrators, settlers or missionaries. Rarely did an upper- or middle-class woman venture to the colonies alone with the exception of trailblazing women like Frieda von Bülow (1857–1909) who organized the first "Krankenstationen" (small hospitals) in 1887–1888, primarily for Germans in Zanzibar and German East Africa, and managed her own plantation and limestone quarry in 1893–1894. In *Reisescizzen und Tagebuchblätter aus Deutsch-Ostafrika* (Travelogues and diary pages from German East Africa, 1889) and numerous autobiographical newspaper articles, in addition to her colonial novels,[6] the ultimately conservative Bülow endorses the hierarchical colonial order based on national and "racial" differences and plays down the daily violence as a necessary evil, thus justifying for example, expeditions of the *Schutztruppe* to subdue local resistance and the infamously brutal administrative style of colonialist Carl Peters in the Kilimanjaro area.

German Southwest Africa, which is the focus of several articles in this volume, was the only actual settler colony with several thousand German immigrants. Starting in 1898, the women's branch of the Deutsche Kolonialgesellschaft (German Colonial Society) (see Kundrus 2004, 2005) recruited women in Germany, often from the lower-classes, to marry white, male German settlers in order to ensure white rather than black procreation and secure German rather than Southwest African culture in the colony (see Dietrich 2007, Kundrus 1997, Walgenbach 2005). As white mistresses on their farms and as members of the colonial elite, women enjoyed more independence and authority – at the expense of the native populations – than their female counterparts in the motherland. Consequently, German settler women – more so than missionary women – adopted the ideology of white "racial" superiority and sided with the system of colonial hegemony (see Mamozai 1982, 1989, 1990, Kundrus 1997, Dietrich 2007,

---

6 See Frieda von Bülow's *Im Lande der Verheißung* (In the promised land, 1899) and *Tropenkoller* (Tropical madness, 1896) and critical readings of Bülow's autobiographical and fictional works from and about German East Africa in Friederike Eigler (1998), Katharina von Hammerstein (2012) and Lora Wildenthal (2001), to name a few.

Walgenbach 2005) rather than engage in women's solidarity across ideologically constructed racial boundaries. "Race" trumped gender (see von Hammerstein 2014).

The so-called "Herero Aufstand" (Herero Uprising, referred to as the beginning of the German-Herero Colonial War and understood today as a genocide) started in January 1904.[7] Most scholarship on this colonial war has focused on the accounts of men in the *Schutztruppe*, in colonial administrations and missions. It is interesting to note that during and immediately following the German-Herero Colonial War, numerous German narratives explicitly produced white women as endangered by the alleged barbarism of the Herero enemy and as valiant supporters of the cultural and national values of the homeland. The loss of colonies between 1915 and 1918 was equated with the loss of both ideals and status. In contrast, Herero narratives focus on their loss of lives, (home)land and community. Katharina von Hammerstein, critically addresses these narratives to include the representations of both German female settlers and Herero women who experienced the genocidal war first hand.[8] The Herero women's songs document the atrocities committed against their people, adding a new dimension to the colonial story, and perform the labor of mourning the loss of men, women and children in their community. These representations stand in stark contrast to the youth literature that Maureen Gallagher investigates, a body of work whose purpose is to "educate" German adolescent girls about women's alleged heroic role as purveyors of the German race and culture at the colonial front. Far from the missionary ambitions that Cindy Brewer explores in Hedwig Irle's missionary publications that aim to produce an imagined harmonious community of interracial, spiritual colonial families, tropes of colonial authority dominate the narratives of settler women.

The impact of World War I rippled through the colonies and resulted in demonstrative utterances of allegiance. Women's representations from the distant colonies also reflected strong ideological ties to the "homeland." Marianne Bechhaus-Gerst and Livia Rigotti offer rare investigations into German colonial women's narratives on daily life, emancipation and loss during and after the war in German East Africa and Samoa. What emerges from the colonies as affect during World War I is a strong sense of nationalism and the burning desire to emotionally support and participate in the war effort from afar. The discourses of colonialism bled into notions of the superiority of German culture as a mission and an end.

---

7 For historical details, see Zimmerer and Zeller (2008) and Hull (2005).
8 For additional examples, see Smidt (1995), Krüger (2008), Alnaes (1981 and 1989).

In both Germany and in its colonies, the beginning of World War I, in the wake of the assassination of Austrian Archduke Franz Ferdinand and his wife Sophie, Duchess of Hohenberg in Sarajevo, was greeted with great optimism. Erich Maria Remarque's (1898–1970) novel *Im Westen nichts Neues* (*All Quiet on the Western Front*, 1929) is a salient reminder of the *esprit de corps* that young men shared as they marched blindly into unfamiliar territories to fight enemies they had never met. Yet, Remarque was not alone in his critique. A decade earlier, Hedwig Dohm (1831–1919), in her stingingly cynical 1919 antiwar testament "Auf dem Sterbebett" (On her deathbed), condemns the display of "ardent patriotism" at the start of the war and describes the crowds as "foolishly cheering on" (dümmlich jauchzend) the "millions of blossoming young people" to "gun down human beings that never did them any harm" and to "march themselves into their graves" (1919, 198–199). The population in Germany and Austria in 1914 certainly expected immediate victory. Women who were left behind watched from balconies as troops paraded through towns or bid men, young and old, farewell on quays as they assembled at train stations. In fact, the train stations often became the point of convergence between soldiers and female nurses who tended the wounded, aided the shell-shocked and fed soldiers in transit. Texts that narrativize or report on these encounters often discuss themes of comradeship between nurses and soldiers at the front, shifting gender norms, and women's growing sense of independence through their work. The diaries of nurses that Margaret R. Higonnet investigates in this volume feature vignettes of soldiers' experiences that nurses recorded and reflections on their own personal struggles and rewards. Higonnet identifies the leitmotif of nursing "as a form of combat" because of their proximity to the front and their fight to save lives. The title of Adrienne Thomas's (1897–1980) novel *Die Katrin wird Soldat: Ein Roman aus Elsass-Lothringen* (*Katrin Becomes a Soldier*, 1930) squarely places women on the "front" while serving behind the scenes. Also based on a diary, her novel provides an intimate view of women's work during World War I and the horrors of patching together the wounded in order to return them to battlefields.[9]

Indeed, women contributed substantially to the war effort as nurses, ambulance drivers, spies, reporters, workers in munitions factories[10] and as female au-

---

9 See Brian Murdoch (1992) and Walter Hinck (2009) for more on Thomas's novel. On German and Austrian women's work behind the lines as nurses and members of the women's auxiliary service, see, for instance, Regina Schulte (1997), Bianca Schönberger (2002), Helen Boak (2013), and Christa Hämmerle (2014).
10 For more on women's historical contributions to and experiences of World War I internationally, see for instance, Gail Braybon (1981), Margaret R. Higonnet, et al. (1987), Higonnet (2011),

thors and artists who, broadly speaking, narrativized, for the most part critically, the war experience in essays, literature, sculptures and etchings. Bertha von Suttner (1843–1914) heralded pacifism already in 1889, prior to major German colonial wars and World War I in her famous pacifist novel *Die Waffen nieder!* (*Lay Down Your Arms*); her outspokenness garnered her the Nobel Peace Prize in 1905, and had a lasting impact on gendered discourses of peace throughout the twentieth century, as Shelley Rose suggests. Suttner's message resounded during the Great War while bullets and poison gas targeted enemies. Other activists followed in her footsteps declaring socialism as the pathway to peace rather than feminism in its first wave. While these two camps were often divided, they did align, as Julie Shoults shows, in the work of Hermynia Zur Mühlen (1883–1951). Her narratives promoted socialism, feminism and pacifism simultaneously through both the male and female protagonists. Writing after World War I, these female authors produced stories that imagined the means to a better world.

Women thus vocalized either their protest or support of the war effort. Ricarda Huch (1864–1947) joined authors like Thomas Mann (1875–1955) in valorizing war and went so far as to justify its collateral damage, more specifically, the destruction of cultural monuments like the Cathedral of Reims, if it ultimately advanced the war effort. James Skidmore introduces Huch as a much overlooked but important contributor to the cultural discourses on war, nationhood and heroism. Similar to Huch, writers like Ina Seidel (1885–1974) saw women's sacrifices for the fatherland as the most sublime expression of femininity, which also often included the willingness to surrender their children for a noble cause. The pervasiveness of selling the war effort did not only come from the ranks of the cultural elite; adolescent literature, much like its colonial counterpart, represented young female protagonists working for the war effort. The literature that addressed girls and mobilized their imaginations as patriots was not limited to Germany, as Jennifer Redmann's comparative study of the wartime girls' *Bildungsroman* shows, but surfaces in other national contexts.

The counterpoint to these representations are the many female authors who gave voice to women who mourned the loss of loved ones as mothers, wives, daughters and sisters. Considering the tremendous casualties of the war, few households were left untouched by the devastation of World War I. Erika Quinn and Erika Kuhlman feature the experiences of war widows in letters, diaries and popular novels. Quinn examines bestselling novels that significantly

---

Margaret H. Darrow (2001), Susan R. Grayzel (2002), Alison S. Fell and Ingrid Sharp (2007), and Christa Hämmerle, et al. (2014). Ute Daniel (1997) and Karen Hagemann and Stefanie Schüler-Springorum (2002) focus on the German context in their texts.

highlight the experiences of the home front, thus bringing stories of suffering and loss to a wide readership and providing widows with a public and private space to mourn. These narratives were all the more important since the experience of widows beyond the rhetoric of heroic sacrifice was excluded from the public discourse in order to avoid deflating the war spirit. For Kuhlman, the circumstances of the war widows change the "affective temporality of the war" long after the ceasefire. Widows lived within the postwar tension of developing independence, facing concrete bureaucratic impediments to their well-being and serving as symbols of bereavement and loss writ large. In Germany, 533,000 war widows were reminders of the personal toll of war, of Germany's defeat, and of the traumatic wound that festered throughout the Weimar Republic, while changing the face of the public space through taking on the jobs that were left vacant (see Whalen 1984, 110).

The most renowned memorialization of mourning are the sculptures of Käthe Kollwitz (1867–1945), specifically "Mother with Her Dead Son" (1937/ 1938) and "Mourning Parents" (1932), which were inspired by the death of her own son, Peter, on the front. As Martina Kolb proposes, they also acknowledge the labor of mourning, both public and private. In her diary entry of 27 August 1914, Kollwitz anticipates the tragic consequences of war, when she writes: "Where do all the women who have watched so carefully over the lives of their beloved ones get the heroism to send them to face the cannon? I am afraid that this soaring of the spirit will be followed by the blackest despair and dejection" (Sheldon 1999, 58).[11] Kollwitz's oeuvre has become synonymous with women's suffering, often related to war, and is subsequently the subject of many scholarly investigations.[12]

A number of primary authors introduced in this volume wrote for audiences who experienced World War I and who were wary of another war during the years of German fascism. Cindy Walter-Gensler introduces the lesser known author and political activist Käte Kestien's (1898–1936) novel *Als die Männer im Graben lagen* (When our men lay in the trenches, 1935) as an evocation of the hardships, particularly for working-class mothers, during World War I in order to warn against the potential of a new war. This novel brings into focus the shortages, the rates of child mortality and the sheer exhaustion of women and mothers of the proletariat who provide for their families in the absence of men.[13] While scholars generally identify women's entry into the workforce (even if tem-

---

11 See the German original in Käthe Kollwitz's *Tagebücher 1908–1943* (2007, 158).
12 See, for example, Sara Friedrichsmeyer (1989), von Hammerstein (2015), Higonnet (2018), Ingrid Sharp (2011), and Claudia Siebrecht (2008).
13 For more on these shortages, see Belinda Davis (2000).

porary) as a liberating experience and as an indication of a positive advancement for women during wartime, Walter-Gensler is quick to point out in her essay that this was dependent on class, as lower-class women and single mothers often experienced this so-called independence as a burden rather than as a sense of liberation. Interestingly, historian Ute Daniel confirms that "[w]orking-class women were the first to express criticism of the war, and they did so most emphatically" (1997, 292). Exacerbated by postwar inflation, challenges to their living conditions continued to plague this social stratum of women in the aftermath of the war.

Women's representations of World War I across classes, generations and continents thus challenge the many male representations of the home as either a stable refuge from the war, outside of history, or as a site of betrayal that refuses men the possibility to restore their masculinity. The recurring anxiety of the loss of home in the popular imagination appears in Joe May's film *Heimkehr* (*Homecoming*, 1928) and in G.W. Pabst's film *Westfront* (1930) when the soldier on leave discovers his wife in bed with another man. These dramatic representations suppress the narratives of women's lives that literature and art by women made visible.

In *The Unwomanly Face of War: An Oral History of Women in World War II* (2017; Russian original 1985), 2015 recipient of the Nobel Prize in literature Svetlana Alexievich (born 1948) collected, as a "witness to witnesses who usually go unheard," Russian women's voices about World War II experiences. Already as a child Alexievich had recognized that most of what we hear about war is told by men and that "women's [war] stories are different" (Khrushcheva 2017, 40, 37). More than a century before Alexievich's public recognition for conveying women's war experiences, women were sharing their stories of war and conflict at the turbulent start of the twentieth century. Whether they told their stories to someone else, as Alexievich's subjects did, or wrote down the words themselves, they recorded "war as experience," to use Sylvester's term. In fact, as Agnès Cardinal, Dorothy Goldman and Judith Hattaway note in the introduction to their anthology *Women's Writing on the First World War*, during much of the twentieth century, "the tradition of war writing was seen as belonging to men: but for many women also the war was the catalyst for creating a unique perspective and for developing a public voice" (1999, 1). Although these voices were largely subsumed by those of men returning from the trenches, they have garnered more scholarly attention in recent decades.

Dorothy Goldman observes in the introduction to *Women and World War 1: The Written Response* that this "canon [of women's writings] is still being created" (1993, 5). Because they were allowed to fade into the background, women's texts are still today in the process of being excavated in archives, rediscovered and republished. Goldman's volume with Cardinal and Hattaway is an oft-cited anthology that places women's texts in the foreground.[14] And while their anthology is a significant contribution to the field and provides an international perspective, it is noteworthy that of the 69 texts included in their collection, only ten are by German-language writers, and most of these are quite short, encompassing only a page or two. Perhaps this is due to the lack of translations available, but it nonetheless underscores the omission of German women's voices on the topic. Yet, as our volume shows, a good number of women commented on their nation's war efforts and imperial and colonial ambitions through literary and non-literary texts and visual representations. Reviving these texts is the first step to supporting scholarly work across disciplines on women's writing about war. Historian Susan Grayzel incorporates "women's cultural productions or the representation of women in war literature generally" into her historical analysis of World War I, arguing, "Undeniably, the art, literature and other cultural artifacts produced by women during the war helped to determine the effects of the war upon women and of women upon the war" (2002, 4).

While women's war writings have increasingly received scholarly attention, the focus especially regarding World War I, has most often been on British authors[15] or on English-language texts in general,[16] such as in *Intimate Enemies: English and German Literary Reactions to the Great War 1914–1918* (Stanzel and Löschnigg 1993) and *The Literature of the Great War Reconsidered: Beyond Modern Memory* (Quinn and Trout 2001). Dorothy Goldman's volume *Women and World War 1* includes an important contribution about German women by Agnès Cardinal, "Women on the Other Side" (1993). She introduces readers to a broad range of texts by German and Austrian women, observing key themes

---

14 Other anthologies include Catherine Reilly's *Scars upon my Heart: Women's Poetry and Verse of the First World War* (1981), Nora Jones and Liz Ward's *The Forgotten Army: Women's Poetry of the First World War* (1991), and Trudi Tate's *Women, Men, and the Great War: An Anthology of Stories* (1995), all of which focus on English-language texts. Margaret R. Higonnet includes texts by women of various nations in *Lines of Fire: Women Writers of World War I* (1999). Gisela Brinker-Gabler's *Frauen gegen den Krieg* (Women against war, 1980) remains an important German-language anthology of women's writings, speeches, and conference proceedings, yet the title of the volume alone indicates that the texts included align with a specific ideology rather than represent broad viewpoints.
15 See, for instance, key texts by Sandra Gilbert (1983), Claire M. Tylee (1990), Sharon Ouditt (1994), and Angela K. Smith (2000). Further examples include Jane Potter (2005), Esther MacCallum-Stewart (2006), Nancy Martin (2012), Maria Geiger (2015), Kabi Hartman (2015), Argha Banerjee (2016), and Eszter Edit Balogh (2017).
16 See, for example, Dorothy Goldman, et al. (1995), Suzanne Raitt and Trudi Tate (1997), and Emma Liggins and Elizabeth Nolan (2017).

of survival and motherhood in these works.[17] The breadth of experience reflected in these texts supports Cardinal's argument that context is essential to understanding the many ways in which women experienced World War I, and, in the case of our collection, the colonial conflicts as well. Cardinal asserts, "Wherever they lived, Germans experienced the war [WWI] against the background of their own local brand of historical and cultural tradition, and it is clearly important that each individual experience, whether it found expression in factual accounts, fiction, poetry or polemic, be understood within its own intrinsic context" (1993, 33).

German women's writings have found greater representation in other scholarly studies, such as in Catherine O'Brien's *Women's Fictional Responses to the First World War: A Comparative Study of Selected Texts by French and German Writers* (1997). In "Zum Opfern bereit: Kriegsliteratur von Frauen" (Prepared to sacrifice: Women's war literature, 1997), Hans-Otto Binder focuses exclusively on texts published by German women between 1914 and 1918. While some scholars have chosen to provide close readings of individual texts,[18] others offer comparative perspectives,[19] cover a spectrum of texts to stress recurring themes prevalent in German women's writing about the war,[20] or they delve into archives to provide fresh perspectives through the analysis and incorporation of archival materials.[21] As the scholarship on women's war writings continues to expand, scholars offer more nuanced readings of women's oeuvres and challenge staid receptions of now well-known texts.[22] These developments over the past several decades have opened new and exciting avenues of exploration into women's war writings.

---

17 Cardinal's discussion includes novels (Bertha von Suttner, Käte Kestien, Clara Viebig), novellas (Claire Goll), diaries and memoirs (Jo Mihaly/Piete Kuhr, Anna Eisenmenger, Ada Schnee), fictional diaries (Adrienne Thomas), poetry (Berta Lask, Ricarda Huch), letters (Rosa Luxemburg), political writings (Clara Zetkin, Hedwig Dohm, Annette Kolb), plays (Ilse Langner), songs (Hedda Zinner) and artwork (Käthe Kollwitz).
18 See, for example, Friederike Emonds's examination of the concepts of *Heimat* and *Vaterland* in Ilse Langner's *Frau Emma kämpft im Hinterland* (Frau Emma fights in the hinterland, 1929) (1998) and Inca Rumold's *"Der Malik:* Else Lasker-Schüler's Anti-War Novel" (1998).
19 For instance, Caroline Bland analyzes the notion of sacrifice in World War I novels by Lily Braun and Clara Viebig (2007).
20 See, for instance, Patricia Marchesi (2004).
21 For example, Ulrike Tanzer (2013) and Dorothee Wierling (2013) both examine archival materials to offer new insights regarding the lives and works of Rosa Mayreder and Lily Braun respectively, in particular their evolving thoughts on the war, women's roles and pacifism.
22 See, for instance, Erika Quinn's "At War: Thea von Harbou, Women, and the Nation" (2017).

Most recently, the centennial of World War I has prompted an outpouring of scholarly work on the topic, including the literature that inspired it.[23] While many of these projects incorporate women's voices and gendered approaches, German-language texts by females are still largely missing.[24] Few works focus exclusively on German women. In "Building Home: The War Experience of German Women Writers 1914–1918" (2014), Silke Fehlemann defines three "waves" of fictional "home front" literature as women grew increasingly war-weary, and in their edited collection *Der Krieg und die Frauen: Geschlecht und populäre Literatur im Ersten Weltkrieg* (War and women: Gender and popular literature in the First World War, 2016), Aibe-Marlene Gerdes and Michael Fischer employ a broad definition of "literature," as the essays examine a variety of genres from novels and poetry to songs and photographs that are by or about women. Our volume builds upon these important scholarly developments.

Women Writing War: From German Colonialism through World War I makes a unique contribution to the multidisciplinary perspectives on the discourses and legacies of colonialism and the war. Rather than focusing exclusively on World War I or bridging the two world wars, this volume, as mentioned earlier, traces a trajectory leading from colonial conflicts to World War I and its aftermath and seeks to draw connections between the discourses of nationalism, colonial pursuits, gender and "race," while alluding to their continuation across time. The articles assembled here close a gap in international, gender-related War Studies by focusing specifically on women's voices from Germany and Austria and related colonies. Publishing this scholarship in English introduces many un(der)researched texts, some of which have been excavated only recently from archives, to audiences interested in issues of gender and war in a variety of disciplines beyond German and Austrian Studies.

The collection therefore provides a close-up and a deeper understanding of women's participation in war and examines how women thought about and represented war in the early 1900s and thereafter. It brings into dialog women's rep-

---

23 See, for example, Martin Löschnigg and Marzena Sokolowska-Paryz's *The Great War in Post-Memory Literature and Film* (2014), Santanu Das's *The Cambridge Companion to the Poetry of the First World War* (2016), and Lesley Milne's *Laughter and War: Humorous-Satirical Magazines in Britain, France, Germany and Russia, 1914–1918* (2017). This is just a brief sample of the recent works addressing World War I from new angles.

24 For instance, a special issue of *Studies in Twentieth and Twenty-First Century Literature*, titled *Writing 1914–1918: National Responses to the Great War* (Garfitt and Bianchi 2017), largely features male authors, and while *Women's Writing of the First World War* (Liggins and Nolan 2017), a special issue of *Women's Writing*, focuses explicitly on texts by females, they are all English-speaking authors.

resentations, reflections and assertions on war and the scholarly analyses of these texts in order to provide a more complex, polyphonic reading of gender and the experiences of colonial conflicts and World War I. What becomes clear when we examine the broad range of women's writings is that there is neither a universal – Germany-related – female war experience nor a universal war (her)story, but rather a multiplicity of viewpoints and constructions, influenced by the many markers of identity along with factors like geographical location at the time of conflicts, the experience of violence and loss, marital status, religious beliefs, cultural traditions, ideological convictions and political engagement. Clearly, the texts analyzed here contradict the bifurcated concept of distinctly gendered affects and purposes that aligns with the understanding of early twentieth-century men as active participants in the public sphere and of women as nurturers and emotional anchors in the private realm. The perception of the home front as a site of refuge and projected emotional fulfillment, which women were thought to provide, is often as blurred as the traditional line that divides non-combatants and combatants. Indeed, women's roles in the wars of the early twentieth century were extremely diverse and even contradictory. Women fought on many fronts. They were caretakers, victims and/or perpetrators. They rallied for one cause or another, endorsing or opposing collective violence. They enjoyed agency and authority and shared the burdens of loss on several levels.

Included in this volume are scholarly readings of works by well-known authors with differing assessments of war, such as the pacifist Bertha von Suttner, the historian, author and defender of the war Ricarda Huch, and the artist Käthe Kollwitz, who defended the war, before becoming a pacifist, as well as other canonical and non-canonical texts. The composition of this collection represents a striking array of standpoints to intentionally complicate narratives of war. Under investigation are girls' literature as a form of sentimental education in both the colonies and the motherland, the accounts of female colonial settlers and missionary women in German Southwest Africa, German East Africa and the German colony of Samoa in the South Pacific, and colonized Herero women in German Southwest Africa, as well as the spectrum of German women's representations of World War I in Europe. All of the works reflect a passionate engagement with the historical contexts from which they emerge. As becomes apparent from the texts critically examined here, women's cultural production related to the colonial wars and World War I draws on multiple genres to deal with the complexities of violence and crisis. Novels, novellas and autobiographical accounts such as diaries, letters and reports, oral history (songs, interviews), visual art, public lectures, and a variety of print media, including newspapers, magazines and journals provide generic frameworks to organize meaning.

Many of the texts demonstrate how deeply personal the experience of war is, especially in the case of autobiographical genres.

The contributors to *Women Writing War* represent a variety of disciplines and employ diverse theoretical approaches – ranging from historical and political contextualizations, German and comparative literary analysis informed by War and Human Rights Studies, postcolonialism, feminism, psychoanalysis and visual culture – as they critically relate to the intersection of war, gender and the many modalities of identity and sensibilities. These approaches are as varied as the plethora of topics explored, which provides this volume with a rich texture of both primary and scholarly voices. Recurring themes of the home, women's labor, mourning, motherhood and femininity, of violence and trauma, of victimhood, heroism and agency, and of witnessing and testimony surface in many essays that grapple with the horrors of the historical realities, in which the literature and art are situated. Moreover, the essays investigate how imperial discourses and colonial conflicts contributed to a persistent atmosphere of patriotic *Kriegsbegeisterung* (enthusiasm for the war) that eventually culminated in the outbreak of World War I. In addition to the blind reproduction of the ideologies that spurned conflict, critical interventions also emerged, especially with the increase in casualties and suffering.

While we could have organized the volume by the historical chronology of the events described or publication/production dates, by disciplines, by genres or by ideologies expressed, we chose instead to join the articles in thematic, dialogic clusters with the first group of essays taking up "Representations of Colonial Conflicts." In addition to mapping out and exploring the conflicts between German settlers and native peoples, the contributors juxtapose the drastically differing narrative constructs of the war experiences and reveal how the interplay of colonial and racist discourses led to dramatic and traumatic consequences when economic, ideological and political interests of the colonizers dominated the narrative. The essays in this section demonstrate how in eyewitness accounts of some white German women writers, the language used produces an enemy Other foreign to the German body politic. These representations resonate to some extent with themes in the literature of World War I and the postwar period. For example, Maureen Gallagher's examination of girls' literature bridges these historical periods and shows how gender, in this case, femininity, is constructed to promote a patriotic affect and sense of purpose. In the section "Views from the Colonies on WWI," Bechhaus-Gerst and Rigotti deal with notions of German superiority and national pride that ring from afar, pitting the German outposts against Entente enemies in the texts women authored. It is striking that the narratives investigated in these essays consistently express the dire wish for news about developments in Europe – always delayed, always uncertain. Shifting from the colonies to the German mainland, the section "Political Perspectives on Nationalism and WWI" analyzes nationalist sentiments in the works of several female authors who bring diverse perspectives to the war. Regardless of their pro- or antiwar stances, the examined narratives assert women's place in the political realm, challenging notions that politics should be left to men. The contributions in this section bring female political engagement – both fictional and nonfictional – to the forefront. The focus in "Constructing the Labor of War: Girls, Mothers and Nurses" is on literary models of femininity and how these textual role models simultaneously expanded and limited women's opportunities during wartime. The essays point out that women in various classes stepped into the public sphere to support their families and/or serve the nation. In the domestic sphere, girls knit and were taught thrift, in factories they produced weapons, and at the front they tended to the wounded. As in the analyses of literature from the colonies, the contributors highlight how historical fictions and autobiographical accounts provide rich insights into the formation of femininity in times of conflict and crisis. The collection of articles concludes with "Narratives of Loss and Grief in Art and Literature" in order to examine the lasting personal impact of World War I, as women coped with its repercussions far into the Weimar Republic. Significantly, the series of essays ends with Kolb's analysis of Käthe Kollwitz's work, which connects this volume on past wars to the present. Since 1993, a replica of her "Mother with Her Dead Son," referred to now as the Pietà – with certain Christian overtones – resides in the Neue Wache (New Guardhouse) in Berlin as Germany's central memorial for the victims of war and tyranny.

The themes that unite the essays under each subheading are certainly not limited to that section but rather reverberate throughout the volume, providing a form of prismatic multiperspectivity. Recurrent themes of community, nationalism and suffering, among others, thread through the various investigations of primary texts. The search for community and the intense need to belong to larger causes (national, cultural, emotional, professional, religious, or political) are especially heightened during the establishment of colonial rule, and times of belligerent upheavals and crisis. Whether this is a concrete community, such as the Herero women presented by von Hammerstein, who vocalize the decimation of their people, or the symbolic community of female mourners as Quinn and Kuhlman show, who find a voice in literature to cope with the trauma of loss, or the proletarian female protagonists that Walter-Gensler analyzes in Kestien's novel, who demonstrate solidarity in their wartime struggles to survive. Significantly, Higonnet brings into focus the community of nurses, engaged in combat against mortality statistics, who are much different than the various pacifists who form a "community of practice" that Rose discusses as working towards a common goal

of peace. The desire for community translates oftentimes into chauvinistic nationalism, a concept that surfaces repeatedly in narratives that underscore and
deliver the nation's ideological tenets. Patriotism, evoked so often during this
time, becomes the object of analyses as it intersects with notions of German superiority vis-à-vis European enemies and racialized Others. Gallagher and von
Hammerstein explore the relationship between nationalism and racism in narratives of German settler women, which informed their framing of most Herero as
treacherous and violent and led to their implicit support of the genocide in German Southwest Africa. In contrast, Brewer offers a reading of Irle's multiracial
Christian mission family as an idealized community, an antidote to violence,
and a model for a pre-World War I concept of peace based in religious beliefs.
Nationalism here calls for inclusivity based on a credo of assimilation with dominant cultural values. The works of Frieda Zieschank, who resided in Samoa during World War I, reflect nationalistic feelings that were magnified by distance
from the geographical motherland and emotional fatherland, which Rigotti
sees expressed in the sense of German superiority toward the islanders and
the occupying troops from New Zealand. Further illustrating the colonial perspective, Bechhaus-Gerst highlights Frieda Schmidt's nationalist competition
with the British in East Africa and her sense of humiliation when German nation-
als were stripped of their membership in the international colonial community
perceived as elite. While nationalism became a strident part of German sensibilities in the colonial arenas, the belief in Germany's early victory was sustained
by notions of the preeminence of German strength and culture, which Skidmore
attributes to Ricarda Huch's position. Huch's support of the war effort from the
home front is reinforced in German girls' literature of the time that Redmann discusses. In contrast to British girls who were called to public service, German girls
discursively were knitted into home and hearth and learned through stories they
read to tend the German soul. Even as nationalism was used to fire passions, it
also was used as a rhetorical weapon to instrumentalize and even silence widows' expressions of public mourning, which Quinn and Kuhlman explore. Alter-
nately, internationalists like Zur Mühlen strove to imagine a progressive community based on socialist ideals. Shoults argues that Zur Mühlen's
protagonists were employed as vehicles to criticize the persistent threat of nationalism to international solidarity and peace. A further example of reaching
across national borders is Kollwitz's memorial that Kolb discusses, which the artist purposely placed at an inclusive war cemetery in Belgium to commemorate
her son along with all fallen soldiers regardless of national belonging.

A topic that echoes throughout the spectrum of investigations is the immense suffering that war produces in the microcosm of the private sphere. A
number of essays explore how women authors represent mothers who try to pro-

tect children against life-threatening food shortages and describe the burdens of procuring a living under the shadow of death and destruction. The contributors highlight the epistemological disjuncture between the home and war fronts, characterized by awkward questions in several works about whether soldiers at the front actually have more to eat to sustain themselves and are thus better off than civilians coping with long lines to procure basic goods and services. Other questions that enter into the narrative landscapes studied here are: How do the struggles of working-class women compare to those of their upper-class counterparts? Is life more difficult for Germans in the colonies, cut off from news of the fatherland and unable to contribute to its war efforts? How do those left behind cope with the deaths of their beloved? Many of the women's war narratives that serve as a basis for analysis in this collection engage such questions, while other works question the very notion of sacrifice as heroic and/or honorable.

What aligns the essays about the literary and artistic works assembled in this volume are the women who wrote, sang, sculpted, drew and etched and processed the colonial conflicts and Great War. Women's reflections on war are in all cases manifestations of their claim to and demonstration of agency vis-à-vis very diverse audiences. Their works are testimonies, memorializations, interventions and attempts to make sense of their worlds turned upside down by collective violence. The essays critically address the array of views and themes represented in the various primary sources with attention to the intersecting complexes of "war" "women" and "writing," which makes for fruitful lines of inquiry across disciplinary boundaries and provokes methodologically nuanced scholarly approaches. For this reason, scholars of History, German Studies, Gender Studies, and War Studies will find valuable sources and resources and may discover cross-references that enrich their own scholarly inquiries. There is still much to be done as we continue to (re)discover diverse texts that capture a broader range of female experiences of war.

This volume ultimately sheds light on the manifold, gendered theaters of war, and on the many female voices and historical actors who contributed to, were affected by, and/or critiqued German war efforts. While engaged German or Austrian women writers and artists commented on their nations' imperial and colonial ambitions and the events of the tumultuous beginning of the twentieth century, Herero women expressed their experience as victims of German aggression. The impact of war on the various home fronts in Germany, Austria and overseas that resonates across the texts examined reminds us of how deeply entrenched discourses of cultural hegemony, exclusion and sacrifice are and how easily they can be mobilized to produce affects like hope, joy, fear, despair and hatred that emerge from a desire to belong and be recognized within one's imagined community. As Judith Butler argues: "War sustains its practices through acting on the senses, crafting them to apprehend the world selectively, deadening affect in response to certain images and sounds, and enlivening affective responses to others" (2010, 51–52). The literature and art, in some cases introduced for the first time, and critically discussed by our contributors make visible how femininity is enlisted for these different causes. At the same time the diverse contributions inspire questions about the pressures that these wars exerted on representations of gender in the early twentieth century and the impact of war on notions of an insulated private sphere. The span from German colonialism to World War I brings these explosive periods into relief and challenges readers to think about the intersection of nationalism, violence and gender and about the historical continuities and disruptions that shape such events. Considering that in present-day wars the number of directly or indirectly involved civilians outweighs the number of combatants, we maintain that there is a certain urgency in investigating women's war experiences in the past as presented in fictional and nonfictional writings.

Works Cited

Åhäll, Linda, and Laura J. Shepherd, editors. *Gender, Agency and Political Violence* (Palgrave, 2012).

Alexievich, Svetlana. *The Unwomanly Face of War: An Oral History of Women in World War II*. 1985. Translated by Richard Pevear and Larissa Volokhonsky (Random House, 2017).

Alison, Miranda. *Women and Violence: Female Combatants in Ethno-National Conflict* (Routledge, 2009).

Alnaes, Kirsten. "Going Through the War: Herero Women in Botswana." Paper presented at the ASAUK Symposium on Women in African Politics, University of London, 22 Sept. 1981. *Women in African Politics*, edited by Agneta Pallinder (African Studies Association of the United Kingdom Symposium on Women in African Politics, 22 Sept. 1981). 15 ms. pp.

Alnaes, Kirsten. "Living with the Past: The Songs of the Herero in Botswana." *Africa*, vol. 59, no. 3 (1989), pp. 267–299.

Ames, Eric, et al., editors. *Germany's Colonial Pasts* (U of Nebraska P, 2005).

Balogh, Eszter Edit. "Women's Testimonies of Their Changing Roles during the First World War in English and Hungarian Culture." *Intertextuality, Intersubjectivity, and Narrative Identity*, edited by Péter Gaál-Szabó (Cambridge Scholars, 2017), pp. 119–133.

Banerjee, Argha. "Memory and Remembrance: Women's Elegies of the First World War (1914–18)." *The Arts of Memory and the Poetics of Remembering*, edited by Abbes Maazaoui (Cambridge Scholars, 2016), pp. 3–20.

Binder, Hans-Otto. "Zum Opfern bereit: Kriegsliteratur von Frauen." *Kriegserfahrungen: Studien zur Sozial- und Mentalitätsgeschichte des Ersten Weltkrieges*, edited by Gerhard Hirschfeld (Klartext, 1997), pp. 107–128.

Bland, Caroline. "Sacrifice for the Nation?: World War One in the Work of Lily Braun (1865–1916) and Clara Viebig (1860–1952)." *Schwellenüberschreitungen: Politik in der Literatur von deutschsprachigen Frauen 1780–1918*, edited by Bland and Elisa Müller-Adams (Aisthesis, 2007), pp. 249–270.

Boak, Helen. "'Forgotten Female Soldiers in an Unknown Army': German Women Working Behind the Lines, 1914–1918." *Women's History Review*, vol. 23, no. 4 (2014), pp. 577–594.

Braybon, Gail. *Women Workers of the First World War: The British Experience* (Routledge, 1981).

Brinker-Gabler, Gisela, editor. *Frauen gegen den Krieg* (Fischer Taschenbuch, 1980).

Bülow, Frieda von. *Reisescizzen und Tagebuchblätter aus Deutsch Ostafrika* [1889]. Edited and with an introduction by Katharina von Hammerstein (Trafo, 2012).

Bülow, Frieda von. *Im Lande der Verheißung* (Reißner, 1899).

Bülow, Frieda von. *Tropenkoller: Episode aus dem deutschen Kolonialleben* (Fontane, 1896).

Butler, Judith. *Frames of War: When is Life Grievable?* (Verso, 2010).

Cardinal, Agnès. "Women on the Other Side." *Women and World War 1: The Written Response*, edited by Dorothy Goldman (St. Martin's, 1993), pp. 31–50.

Cardinal, Agnès, et al., editors. *Women's Writing on the First World War* (Oxford UP, 1999).

Conrad, Sebastian. *German Colonialism: A Short History*. Translated by Sorcha O'Hagan (Cambridge UP, 2008).

Daniel, Ute. *The War from Within: German Working-Class Women in the First World War*. Translated by Margaret Ries (Berg, 1997).

Darrow, Margaret H. *French Women and the First World War: War Stories of the Home Front* (New York UP, 2001).

Das, Santanu. *The Cambridge Companion to the Poetry of the First World War* (Cambridge UP, 2016).

Davis, Belinda. *Home Fires Burning: Food, Politics, and Everyday Life in World War I Berlin* (U of North Carolina P, 2000).

Dietrich, Anette. *Weiße Weiblichkeiten. Konstruktionen von 'Rasse' und Geschlecht in deutschen Kolonien* (transcript, 2007).

Dohm, Hedwig. "Auf dem Sterbebett (1919, nach dem Weltkrieg von 1914–1918)." *Erinnerungen an Hedwig Dohm: Jugenderinnerungen einer alten Berlinerin*, edited by Hedda Korsch (ALA, 1980), pp. 197–200.

Eigler, Friederike. "Engendering German Nationalism and Race in Frieda von Bülow's Colonial Writings." *The Imperialist Imagination: German Colonialism and Its Legacy*, edited by Sara Friedrichsmeyer, et al. (U of Michigan P, 1998), pp. 68–85.

Emonds, Friederike. "Contested Memories: *Heimat* and *Vaterland* in Ilse Langner's *Frau Emma kämpft im Hinterland*." *Women in German Yearbook*, vol. 14 (1998), pp. 163–182.

Enloe, Cynthia. *Bananas, Beaches, and Bases: Making Feminist Sense of International Relations*. 1989. 2nd ed. (U of California P, 2014).

Enloe, Cynthia. *Maneuvers: The International Politics of Militarizing Women's Lives* (U of California P, 2000).

Fehlemann, Silke. "Building Home: The War Experiences of German Women Writers 1914–1918." *"Then Horror Came Into Her Eyes…": Gender and the Wars*, edited by Claudia Glunz and Thomas F. Schneider (Vandenhoek & Ruprecht, 2014), pp. 69–95.

Fell, Alison S., and Ingrid Sharp, editors. *The Women's Movement in Wartime: International Perspectives, 1914–19* (Palgrave Macmillan, 2007).

Friedrichsmeyer, Sara. "'Seeds for the Sowing': The Diary of Käthe Kollwitz." *Arms and the Woman: War, Gender and Literary Representation*, edited by Helen M. Cooper, et al. (U of North Carolina P, 1989), pp. 205–224.

Galtung, Johan. *Strukturelle Gewalt: Beiträge zur Friedens- und Konfliktforschung* (Rowohlt, 1982).

Garfitt, Toby, and Nicholas Bianchi, editors. *Writing 1914–1918: National Responses to the Great War*, special issue of *Studies in Twentieth and Twenty-First Century Literature*, vol. 41, no. 2 (2017).

Geiger, Maria. "No Trench Required: Validating the Voices of Female Poets of WWI." *War, Literature, and the Arts: An International Journal of the Humanities*, vol. 27 (2015).

Gerdes, Aibe-Marlene, and Michael Fischer, editors. *Der Krieg und die Frauen: Geschlecht und populäre Literatur im Ersten Weltkrieg* (Waxmann, 2016).

Gilbert, Sandra M. "Soldier's Heart: Literary Men, Literary Women, and the Great War." *Signs: Journal of Women in Culture and Society*, vol. 8, no. 3 (1983), pp. 422–450.

Goldman, Dorothy, editor. *Women and World War 1: The Written Response* (St. Martin's, 1993).

Goldman, Dorothy, et al., editors. *Women Writers and the Great War* (Twayne, 1995).

Grayzel, Susan R. *Women and the First World War* (Routledge, 2002).

Hämmerle, Christa. "'Mentally broken, physically a wreck…': Violence in War Accounts of Nurses in Austro-Hungarian Service." *Gender and the First World War*, edited by Hämmerle, et al. (Palgrave Macmillan, 2014), pp. 89–107.

Hämmerle, Christa, et al., editors. *Gender and the First World War* (Palgrave Macmillan, 2014).

Hagemann, Karen. "Heimat – Front: Militär, Gewalt und Geschlechterverhältnisse im Zeitalter der Weltkriege." *Heimat—Front: Militär und Geschlechterverhältnisse im Zeitalter der Weltkriege*, edited by Hagemann and Stefanie Schüler-Springorum (Campus, 2002a), 13–52.

Hagemann, Karen. "Home/Front: The Military, Violence and Gender Relations in the Age of the World Wars." *Home/Front: The Military, War and Gender in Twentieth-Century Germany*, edited by Hagemann and Stefanie Schüler-Springorum (Berg, 2002b), pp, 1–41.

Hagemann, Karen, and Stefanie Schüler-Springorum, editors. *Heimat—Front: Militär und Geschlechterverhältnisse im Zeitalter der Weltkriege* (Campus, 2002).

Hagemann, Karen, and Stefanie Schüler-Springorum, editors. *Home/Front: The Military, War and Gender in Twentieth-Century Germany* (Berg, 2002).

Hammerstein, Katharina von. "Meine unhaltbar widerspruchsvolle Stellung zum Kriege": Käthe Kollwitz von Kriegsbefürwortung zu Kriegsgegnerschaft, 1914–1918." *Acta Germanica*, vol. 43 (2015), pp. 165–176.

Hammerstein, Katharina von. "'Rasse' ist Trumpf und sticht Geschlecht: Konstruktionen kolonialer Männlichkeiten in ausgewählten Werken von Frieda von Bülow." *Frauenphantasien: Der imaginierte Mann im Werk von Film- und Buchautorinnen*, edited by Renate Möhrmann (Kröner, 2014), pp. 274–296.

Hammerstein, Katharina von. "'Ein segensspendendes Werk zur Ehre der deutschen Nation': Vorschlag einer Lesart von Frieda von Bülows kolonial-nationalistischen Aufzeichnungen aus Deutsch-Ostafrika." Frieda von Bülow. *Reisescizzen und Tagebuchblätter aus Deutsch-Ostafrika*, edited by von Hammerstein (Trafo, 2012), pp. 9–54.

Hartman, Kabi. "Male Pacifists in British Women's World War I Novels: Toward an 'Enlightened Civilisation.'" *English Literature in Transition 1880–1920*, vol.58, no. 4 (2015), pp. 536–550.

Higonnet, Margaret R. "Girl Soldiers in World War I: Marina Yurlova and Sofja Nowosielska." *Children and Armed Conflict: Cross-Disciplinary Investigations*, edited by Daniel Thomas Cook and John Wall (Palgrave Macmillan, 2011), pp. 7–21.

Higonnet, Margaret R. *Lines of Fire: Women Writers of World War I* (Plume, 1999).

Higonnet, Margaret R. "Maternal Cosmopoetics: Käthe Kollwitz and European Women Poets of the First World War." *Becoming Modern*, edited by Santanu Das and Kate McLaughlin (Oxford UP, 2018), 197–222.

Higonnet, Margaret, et al., editors. *Behind the Lines: Gender and the Two World Wars* (Yale UP, 1987).

Hinck, Walter. "Adrienne Thomas: *Die Katrin wird Soldat:* Der Tod und das Mädchen." *Frankfurter Allgemeine Zeitung* (24 Mar. 2009). www.faz.net/aktuell/feuilleton/buecher/rezensionen/belletristik/adrienne-thomas-die-katrin-wird-soldat-der-tod-und-das-maedchen-1921836.html. Accessed 14 Feb. 2018.

Hull, Isabel V. *Absolute Destruction: Military Culture and Practices of War in Imperial Germany* (Cornell UP, 2005).

Jones, Nora, and Liz Ward, editors. *The Forgotten Army: Women's Poetry of the First World War* (Highgate, 1991).

Khrushcheva, Nina. "The Historian of the Soul: The Novel laureate Svetlana Alexievich extracts the human truth about life under Soviet rule." *The Atlantic*, vol. 320, no. 2 (Sept. 2017), pp. 36–40.

Klotz, Marcia. "The Weimar Republic: A Postcolonial State in a Still-Colonial World." *Germany's Colonial Pasts*, edited by Eric Ames, et al. (U of Nebraska P, 2005), pp. 135–147.

Kollwitz, Käthe. *Die Tagebücher 1908–1943*. Edited and with an afterword by Jutta Bohnke-Kollwitz (Random House, 2007).

Kronsell, Annica, and Erika Svedberg, editors. *Making Gender, Making War: Violence, Military and Peacekeeping Practices* (Routledge, 2012).

Krüger, Gesine. "Beasts and Victims: Women in the Colonial War." *Genocide in German South-West Africa: The Colonial War of 1904–1908 and Its Aftermath*, edited by Jürgen Zimmerer and Joachim Zeller, translated by Edward Neather (Merlin Press, 2008), pp. 170–192.

Kundrus, Birthe. "Die imperialistischen Frauenverbände des Kaiserreichs: Koloniale Phantasie- und Realgeschichte im Verein." Working Paper No. 3 (*Basler Afrika Bibliographien*, 2005). *Namibia Digital Repository*, namibia.leadr.msu.edu/items/show/153. Accessed 18 Jan. 2018.

Kundrus, Birthe. *Moderne Imperialisten: Das Kaiserreich im Spiegel seiner Kolonien* (Böhlau, 2003).

Kundrus, Birthe. "Weiblicher Kulturimperialismus: Die imperialistischen Frauenverbände des Kaiserreichs." *Das Kaiserreich transnational: Deutschland in der Welt 1871–1914*, edited by Sebastian Conrad and Jürgen Osterhammel (Vandenhoeck & Ruprecht, 2004), pp. 213–235.

Kundrus, Birthe. "'Weiß und herrlich': Überlegungen zu einer Geschlechtergeschichte des Kolonialismus." *Projektionen: Rassismus und Sexismus in der visuellen Kultur*, edited by Annegret Friedrich, et al. (Jonas, 1997), pp. 41–50.

Liggins, Emma, and Elizabeth Nolan, editors. *Women's Writing of the First World War*, special issue of *Women's Writing*, vol. 21, no. 1 (2017).

Löschnigg, Martin, and Marzena Sokołowska-Paryż, editors. *The Great War in Post-Memory Literature and Film* (DeGruyter, 2014).

MacCallum-Stewart, Esther. "Female Maladies? Reappraising Women's Popular Literature of the First World War." *Women*, vol. 17, no. 1 (2006), pp. 78–97.

Mamozai, Martha. *Komplizinnen* (Rowohlt, 1990).

Mamozai, Martha. *Schwarze Frau, weiße Herrin: Frauenleben in den deutschen Kolonien* (Rowohlt, 1989).

Mamozai, Martha. *Herrenmenschen: Frauen im deutschen Kolonialismus* (Rowohlt, 1982).

Managhan, Tina. *Gender, Agency and War: The Materialized Body in US Foreign Policy* (Routledge, 2012).

Marchesi, Patricia. "Boundaries, Borders, and Female Identity in German Women Writers of World War I." *Women & Language*, vol. 27, no. 2 (2004), pp. 51–57.

Martin, Nancy. "'The Rose of No Man's Land [?]': Femininity, Female Identity, and Women on the Western Front." *Journal of International Women's Studies*, vol. 13, no. 6 (2012), pp. 5–17.

Milne, Lesley. *Laughter and War: Humorous-Satirical Magazines in Britain, France, Germany, and Russia, 1914–1918* (Cambridge Scholars, 2017).

Murdoch, Brian. "'Hinter die Kulissen des Krieges sehen': Adrienne Thomas, Evadne Price – and E. M. Remarque." *Forum for Modern Language Studies*, vol. 28, no. 1 (1992), pp. 56–74.

O'Brien, Catherine. *Women's Fictional Responses to the First World War: A Comparative Study of Selected Texts by French and German Writers* (Peter Lang, 1997).

Ouditt, Sharon. *Fighting Forces, Writing Women: Identity and Ideology in the First World War* (Routledge, 1994).

Potter, Jane. *Boys in Khaki, Girls in Print: Women's Literary Responses to the Great War* (Clarendon Press, 2005).

Quinn, Erika. "At War: Thea von Harbou, Women, and the Nation." *Women in German Yearbook*, vol. 33 (2017), pp. 52–76.

Quinn, Patrick J., and Steven Trout, editors. *The Literature of the Great War Reconsidered: Beyond Modern Memory* (Palgrave, 2001).

Raitt, Suzanne, and Trudi Tate, editors. *Women's Fiction and the Great War* (Clarendon Press, 1997).

Reilly, Catherine, editor. *Scars upon my Heart: Women's Poetry and Verse of the First World War* (Virago, 1981).

Remarque, Erich Maria. *Im Westen nichts Neues* (Propyläen-Verlag, 1929).

Rother, Rainer, editor. *Die letzten Tage der Menschheit: Bilder des Ersten Weltkrieges* (Ars Nicolai, 1994).

Rumold, Inca. "*Der Malik*: Else Lasker-Schüler's Anti-War Novel." *Women in German Yearbook*, vol. 14 (1998), pp. 143–161.

Schönberger, Bianca. "Motherly Heroines and Adventurous Girls: Red Cross Nurses and Women Army Auxiliaries in the First World War." *Home/Front: The Military, War and*

Gender in Twentieth-Century Germany, edited by Karen Hagemann and Stefanie Schüler-Springorum (Berg, 2002), pp. 87–113.

Schulte, Regina. "The Sick Warrior's Sister: Nursing during the First World War." *Gender Relations in German History: Power, Agency and Experience*, edited by Lynn Abrams and Elizabeth Harvey (Duke UP, 1997), pp. 121–141.

Sharp, Ingrid. "Käthe Kollwitz's Witness to War: Gender, Authority, and Reception." *Women in German Yearbook*, vol. 27 (2011), pp. 87–107.

Sharp, Ingrid, and Matthew Stibbe. "Introduction: Women's Movements and Female Activists in the Aftermath of War: International Perspectives 1918–1923." *Aftermaths of War: Women's Movements and Female Activists, 1918–1923*, edited by Sharp and Stibbe (Brill, 2011), pp. 1–25.

Sheldon, Sayre P., editor. *Her War Story: Twentieth-Century Women Write about War* (Southern Illinois UP, 1999).

Siebrecht, Claudia. "The *Mater Dolorosa* on the Battlefield – Mourning Mothers in German Women's Art of the First World War." *Untold War: New Perspectives in First World War Studies*, edited by Heather Jones, et al. (Brill, 2008), pp. 259–291.

Smidt, Karen. "'Germania führt die deutsche Frau nach Südwest': Auswanderung, Leben und soziale Konflikte deutscher Frauen in der ehemaligen Kolonie Deutsch-Südwestafrika 1884–1920: Eine sozial- und frauengeschichtliche Studie." Dissertation (Otto von Guericke-Universität Magdeburg, 1995).

Smith, Angela K. *The Second Battlefield: Women, Modernism, and the First World War* (Manchester UP, 2000).

Smith, Woodruff D. *The German Empire* (U of North Carolina P, 1978).

Speitkamp, Winfried. *Deutsche Kolonialgeschichte* (Reclam, 2005).

Stanzel, Franz Karl, and Martin Löschnigg, editors. *Intimate Enemies: English and German Literary Reactions to the Great War 1914–1918* (C. Winter, 1993).

Suttner, Bertha von. *Die Waffen nieder! Eine Lebensgeschichte*. 1889. Edited by Sigrid and Helmut Bock (Verlag der Nation, 2006).

Sylvester, Christine. "Pathways to experiencing war." *Experiencing War*, edited by Sylvester (Routledge, 2011), pp. 118–130.

Sylvester, Christine. *War as Experience: Contributions from International Relations and Feminist Analysis* (Routledge, 2013).

Sylvester, Christine. "War Experiences/War Practices/War Theory." *Millennium—Journal of International Studies*, vol. 40 (2012), pp. 483–503.

Tanzer, Ulrike. "Feminism and Pacifism: Rosa Mayreder's Writings against War." Translated by Judith Beniston, *Austrian Studies*, vol. 21 (2013), pp. 46–61.

Tate, Trudi, editor. *Women, Men, and the Great War: An Anthology of Stories* (Manchester UP, 1995).

Thomas, Adrienne. *Die Katrin wird Soldat: Ein Roman aus Elsass-Lothringen* (Propyläen-Verlag, 1930).

Tylee, Claire M. *The Great War and Women's Consciousness: Images of Militarism and Womanhood in Women's Writings, 1914–1964* (U of Iowa P, 1990).

Walgenbach, Katharina. *"Die weiße Frau als Trägerin deutscher Kultur": Koloniale Diskurse über Geschlecht, "Rasse" und Klasse im Kaiserreich* (Campus, 2005).

Whalen, Robert Weldon. *Bitter Wounds: German Victims of the Great War, 1914–1939* (Cornell UP, 1984).

Wierling, Dorothee. *Eine Familie im Krieg: Leben, Sterben und Schreiben 1914–1918* (Wallstein, 2013).

Wildenthal, Lora. *German Women for Empire, 1884–1945* (Duke UP, 2001).

Zimmerer, Jürgen, and Joachim Zeller, editors. *Genocide in German South-West Africa: The Colonial War of 1904–1908 and Its Aftermath.* Translated by Edward Neather (Merlin Press, 2008).

Representations of Colonial Conflicts

Katharina von Hammerstein

"Who Owns Hereroland?"

Diverse Women's Perspectives on Violence in the German-Herero Colonial War

Introduction and research focus

"After all, I don't think that all these small incidents can have provided sufficient grounds for the dreadful uprising of the blacks."[1] Thus conclude the reflections of the white, German settler Else Sonnenberg (1876–1967) about the beginning of the German-Herero Colonial War (1904–1908),[2] which she experienced in early 1904, in the former colony of German Southwest Africa, today's Namibia (2004, 53). The "incidents" that Sonnenberg dismisses as "small" in her 1905 autobiographical account *Wie es am Waterberg zuging: Ein Beitrag zur Geschichte des Hereroaufstandes* (What happened at the Waterberg: A contribution to the history of the Herero uprising) refer to the discrimination and defrauding of Herero[3] by German colonists and authorities, whose actions resulted in the significant loss of Herero land and cattle to German settlers and companies. For the Herero these so-called "incidents" were hardly "small"; indeed they contributed to the Herero's call to arms in January 1904.[4] Herero women supported the defense of their land and cultural identity, expressed in the song *Ehi rOvaherero* or "Who owns Hereroland? We own Hereroland," which was sung to spur on Herero combatants during battle (Anz 1981, 657; Henrichsen 1994, 15, 22–23). The subtitle of Sonnenberg's book refers to this armed conflict as the "Herero uprising," a turn of phrase used in Germany at the time and in much of German historiography since then. Yet the term uprising is misleading, especially when combined with the adjective "dreadful" (Sonnenberg 2004, 53), as it suggests that the en-

---

1 All translations from German into English are my own unless otherwise stated.
2 This colonial war officially ended in 1907, but the prisoner of war camps continued into 1908. Because combat and camps cannot be separated, I follow Joachim Zimmerer in setting the period of war from 1904 to 1908 (2008, 58).
3 The Herero refer to themselves as Ovaherero and Omuherero, as in Otjiherero the prefixes "ova" and "omu" indicate plural and singular forms. In agreement with most international scholarship on this topic, I use the term Herero for singular and plural nouns and adjectives. I thank Dr. Jekura U. Kavari, Head of the Otjiherero Section of the Department of Language and Literature Studies at the University of Namibia, Windhoek, for his clarification.
4 See the letter of 6 March 1904 from Samuel Maharero, Paramount Chief of the Herero, to Theodor Leutwein, Governor of German Southwest Africa (cit. Okupa 2006, 163–164).

https://doi.org/10.1515/9783110572001-002

suing war resulted from an arbitrary act of aggression solely on the part of the Herero, against which Germans merely defended themselves. Anthropologist Larissa Förster points out that her present-day Herero interviewees never refer to this belligerent interaction as an "uprising," "revolt" or "rebellion," but as *ovita* (Otjiherero for battle) (2010, 123) or *orlog* (war) implying violence on both sides. Thus, Sonnenberg's testimony, on the one hand, and the accounts of Herero witnesses, on the other, offer examples of incompatible perceptions of what constituted violence and what triggered counter-violence between ethnic groups in colonial contexts.

German colonial violence fits the definition of violence as a form of "needs deprivation," a concept developed by Johan Galtung, founder of international peace and conflict studies (Galtung and Fischer 2013, 47). "Violence [as] needs deprivation" can be understood more precisely as preventing someone from accessing what is necessary to achieve their full human potential (Winter 2012, 200). Galtung differentiates between three categories of violence: "direct violence" (physical, visible), "structural violence" (systemic, invisible), and "cultural violence" (discursive), which legitimizes the first two forms (Galtung and Fischer 2013, 46). When direct violence is collective, we call it war. According to international relations scholar Christine Sylvester's bottom-up definition of war, the term refers not merely to organized military operations, but to the experience of "ordinary people" (2012, 483, 484, 487, 502; 2013, 5, 9), including "ordinary women" (2013, 39). The "ordinary" Herero and German women discussed in this chapter sang, recounted and wrote about their war experiences in distinctly differing ways and (re)presented distinctly differing perspectives.[5]

International historical and literary scholarship on the German-Herero Colonial War has concentrated predominantly on texts by and about white, German males[6] – officers, administrators, settlers – as authentic witnesses and fictional characters.[7] By contrast, my investigation shifts the focus to the voices of "ordinary women" on both sides of the conflict: first, the under-researched autobio-

---

5 For critical inquiries into other white German women's perspectives on the German-Herero Colonial War in fiction and self-writings in the early 1900s, see the articles by Maureen Gallagher and Cindy Brewer in this volume.
6 See critical publications by Helmut Bley (1971), Horst Drechsler (1984), Horst Gründer (1985), Isabel Hull (2005), Reinhart Kößler (2015), Jeremy Sarkin (2011) and Jürgen Zimmerer/Joachim Zeller (2008) to name a few historians, and Medardus Brehl (2007) and Stefan Hermes (2009), among others, as literary scholars.
7 For male fictional characters, see, for example, the novels by Giselher Hoffmann (1994), Gerhard Seyfried (2003) and Uwe Timm (1978). Female characters can be found in more recent literature by female authors such as novels by Andrea Paluch (with Robert Habeck, 2004) and Patricia Mennen (2011) and the play by Jackie Sibblies Drury (2014).

graphical publications of the three white, German settler women, Else Sonnenberg, Helene von Falkenhausen (1873–1945) and Margarethe[8] von Eckenbrecher (1875–1955),[9] and second, extremely rare documents, that for the most part have eluded scholarly attention in the global North, of black Herero oral history.[10] These include *omatjina* (songs sung by women; sg. *outjina*) and interviews conducted with female Herero survivors recorded in the 1970s (Alnaes 1981 and 1989) as well as interviews with descendants conducted between 1999 and 2004 (Förster 2010) and in 2007 (Erichsen 2007 and 2008[11]).

Undertaking for the first time a textual, rather than a historical or anthropological analysis of the material, I draw from theoretical approaches developed in a variety of disciplines: 1) sociologist Galtung's three categories of violence; 2) political scientist Sylvester's concept of "war as experience" mentioned above; 3) philosopher Judith Butler's concepts of precariousness and precarity – her terms for the general and individual state of vulnerability – that inform her critique of the practice that "under conditions of war, some human lives are [considered, KvH] worthy of protection while others are not" and can be destroyed with impunity (2010, 18); and 4) anthropologist and Doctor Without Borders Didier Fassin's genealogy of classical definitions of witness inspired by philosopher Giorgio Agamben: *superstes* (first-hand victim of atrocities testifying based on

---

8 In accordance with the cover of her book *Was Afrika mir gab und nahm* (What Africa gave me and took from me, 1907), I spell the author's first name Margarethe. On some of her works, her name is spelled Margarete.

9 For critical studies on literature by white, German women settlers about the German-Herero Colonial War, see Karen Smidt (1995, 131–146) and Lora Wildenthal (2001, 151–156) as well as Maureen Gallagher in this volume; for Sonnenberg, see Otto Pfingsten (2004) and Uwe Krebs (2012); for Eckenbrecher, see Katharina Gerstenberger (2000, 64–99) and Rosa Schneider (2003, 74–76, 226–238).

10 For studies, mostly in history and anthropology, on Herero perspectives on the German-Herero Colonial War, see Norwegian Kirsten Alnaes (1981 and 1988), German Ernst Dammann (1987), Gesine Krüger (1999 and 2008) and German-American Katharina von Hammerstein (2016, 2017), Dutch Jan-Bart Gewald (1999), Namibian-Swiss Dag Henrichsen (1994), and Namibian Annemarie Heywood (1992), Brigitte Lau (1995) and Effa Okupa (2006). Anthropologist Alnaes and historian Krüger focus specifically on texts by and about Herero women's war experience.

11 In the project called "What the Elders Used to Say" (2007), interviews with mostly male and a few female descendants of the Herero – and other ethnicities – were conducted by Alex Kaputu and Casper Wulff Erichsen, translated from Otjiherero into English by interpreters and compiled by Erichsen. While Erichsen published a study entitled *"What the Elders Used to Say"* (2008) referencing some of the interviews, I quote here from the actual originals archived at the National Archives of Namibia at Windhoek, Namibia. For cultures of remembering the German-Herero Colonial War among both present-day German-speaking and Herero Namibians, see Förster (2010).

what s/he has experienced), *testis* (third-party observer of atrocities testifying on the basis of what s/he has seen), *histor* (removed in time from atrocities and testifying based on what s/he has heard from others) and *auctor* (the author-ity using testimony in the contest of a public initiative) (2012, 204–209, 215).

Employing this theoretical lens, I explore select written and oral war testimonies by white German and black Herero women *superstites*, *testes* and *histores* about the German-Herero Colonial War. The focus on representations of their experiences of, perspectives on, and participation in direct, structural and cultural violence includes related images of victimization as well as indicators of agency, attributions of value or lack thereof placed on the lives of disparate human populations, and ways of creating narratives of the war in Germany and/or Southwest Africa. This inquiry concentrates on accounts of women's war experiences in the first phase of the German-Herero Colonial War in 1904, while acknowledging that it was followed by a second phase that played out in concentration camps and recognizing that the Nama, Damara and San peoples were also heavily affected. After providing a historical and discursive context, I begin with an examination of the three German texts *en bloc* before turning to the Herero material. Comparisons between women's accounts of war are drawn in the latter part of the study.

Historical and discursive context: The German-Herero Colonial War

In the interest of understanding better the multiple perspectives on the German-Herero Colonial War, I sketch this lesser known colonial power struggle and women's fate in it. Of particular relevance for my inquiry is Galtung's definition of "structural violence as *social injustice*" (1969, 171): "*structural violence* connotes inequalities built into established patterns of social relationships, so that not only are resources 'unevenly distributed,' but also '*the power to decide over the distribution of resources*'" (Cocks 2012, 222 citing Galtung 1969, 171). One possible reaction to the "needs deprivation" caused by "structural violence" is "direct violence" (Galtung and Fischer 2013, 47). In the former colony of German Southwest Africa the relevant resources around 1900 were land, cattle and water. After the European colonial powers assigned this territory to Germany at the Berlin Conference of 1884–1885, the "patterns of social relationships" between the semi-nomadic native populations and the rapid influx of white, German, male and female settlers and traders were "established" in such a way that "the power to decide over the distribution of [all three, KvH] resources" moved increasingly into the hands of the German colonists. The Herero were the most powerful local tribe owning large herds of cattle and controlling vast grazing grounds. Having initially collaborated with the Germans, they soon saw their livelihood threatened due to substantial land, water and cattle robbery and brutal abuses by Germans, whose actions were protected by the colonial legislation, administration and military. In January 1904, the Herero responded to the "structural violence" that caused their "needs deprivation" with "direct violence," killing 123 white Germans, including four women. Contrary to rumors that the white press spread about supposed Herero abuses of white women (see Smidt 1995, 142–144; Zimmerer 2008, 42) and purported in the war reports of Margarethe von Eckenbrecher (2000, 111, 142) and Helene von Falkenhausen (1905, 185), German women were generally spared physical violence.[12]

After initial tactical successes, many Herero withdrew to the water-rich Waterberg region – mentioned in Sonnenberg's title – with their cattle and entire families in expectation of peace negotiations (see Moses Maharero in Erichsen 2007). Approximately 35,000 Herero men, women and children were assembled. Instead of conducting peace talks, the technically far superior German *Schutztruppe*[13] attacked the Herero on 11 August 1904, in the Battle of Waterberg. The Herero call it the *ovita yOhamakari*, referring to the historic water hole where they spent their last peaceful night in their own territory, which even the Germans called "Hereroland." This battle was a turning point in the armed conflict that the German General in charge, Lothar von Trotha, would term a "race war"[14] against "nonhumans" (Dannhauer 1904, 1). Literally tens of thousands Herero men, women and children fled east into the Omaheke, part of the Kalahari desert, to escape German troops. The experience of this traumatic historical moment is represented, among other sources, in the Herero *outjina*, the song "The Flight" analyzed below. With the German troops in pursuit, armed and unarmed Herero of both sexes and all ages were randomly shot dead, poisoned at the rare water holes, or died of thirst, starvation and exposure trying to reach the British Protectorate Bechuanaland, today's Botswana. Herero survivors caught in the territory that was declared German were taken to concen-

---

12 The four exceptions were deemed accidents.

13 *Schutztruppe* [literal transl.: protection force] is a euphemism used in the colonial era for the German colonial occupation troops.

14 Lothar von Trotha Papers, no. 315, p. 40; similarly von Trotha to von Schlieffen, 4 October 1904, Bundesarchiv Berlin, R 1001, no. 2089, pp. 5–6, cited and translated by Hull (2005, 59). I thank the historians Effa Okupa, Jürgen Zimmerer and Isabel Hull for their excellent archival work and English translations of German documents.

tration camps[15] where many died and/or suffered – along with other black ethnicities – from disastrous nutritional, housing and medical conditions, forced labor and mistreatment, including the rape of women and little girls. In total, approximately 65,000 out of 80,000 Herero (~ 80%) and 10,000 out of 20,000+ Nama (~ 50%) men, women and children were killed between 1904 and 1908.[16] This was the twentieth century's first genocide, as later defined by the 1948 United Nations' Convention on the Prevention and Punishment of the Crime of Genocide and as recognized in the 1985 UN Whitaker Report.[17] It was finally acknowledged as such by the German Foreign Office in 2015, but not yet by the German parliament.

The two leading figures in the German-Herero conflict – Samuel Maharero as Paramount Chief of all Herero and General Lothar von Trotha as Commander of the German *Schutztruppe* – chose diametrically opposed approaches to the treatment of women on both sides. Numerous eyewitness accounts by both Herero and Germans document that the Herero chiefs under Maharero's leadership explicitly decided to target only German men, because they were perceived as responsible for the Herero's "needs deprivation," as Galtung would call it, and to "spare the lives of all German women and children" as well as of all missionaries, British and Dutch (Daniel Kariko in Silvester and Gewald 2003, 100[18]; see also German governor Leutwein, cit. Silvester and Gewald 2003, 101; Zimmerer 2008, 42). According to the testimony of a Dutch female settler living in Omaruru, Herero Chief Michael Tysesita [or Tjiseseta], assured her, "we are not making war on women and children" (Silvester and Gewald 2003, 101; see also Krüger 2008, 176). In Judith Butler's terms, the "precarity" of white German women's lives was

---

15 The term "concentration camp" was first used by the British for camps for men, women and children in the context of the 1900 Boer War in Transvaal.

16 Historians agree that the exact numbers are uncertain, see Hull (2005, 88–90), Lau (1995, 43–46), Okupa (2006, 191–192), and Zimmerer (2008, 62).

17 See article 2 of the 1948 Convention on the Prevention and Punishment of the Crime of Genocide, according to which "genocide means any of the following acts committed with intent to destroy, in whole or in part, a national, ethnical, racial or religious group, as such: (a) Killing members of the group; (b) Causing serious bodily or mental harm to members of the group; (c) Deliberately inflicting on the group conditions of life calculated to bring about its physical destruction in whole or in part [...]" (United Nations 1948). The 1985 Whitaker Report lists among the examples of genocide "the German massacre of the Hereros in 1904" (paragraph 24).

18 For conflicting scholarly views on the creation of the British *Report on the Natives of South West Africa and Their Treatment by Germany*, also called *Blue Book* (1918, annotated reprint by Silvester and Gewald, 2003) and its usage in contexts ranging from British negotiations for the Treaty of Versailles to the Southwest African People's Organization (SWAPO), see Silvester and Gewald (2003, XV–XXXVII) and briefly Hull (2005, 48).

respected; they were considered human beings worthy of protection and, in many cases, escorted to safety. Else Sonnenberg's report on how Herero leaders protected her and her infant son Werner attests to this policy (2004, 74, 108 – 110).

By contrast, German racist hardliner General von Trotha stressed repeatedly in his correspondence with the German High Command in Berlin and in his notorious extermination order of October 1904, cited at length as the ultimate document proving his intent to commit genocide,[19] that he would not help Herero women and children who asked German troops for water. He asserted that "accepting [Herero] women and children, who are mostly ill, is an eminent danger to the [German] troops [...]. I think it better that the [entire Herero, KvH] nation perish rather than infect our troops and affect our water and food. [...] They must now die in the desert [...]. This uprising is [...] the beginning of a race war" (footnote 14). "Race,"[20] not gender, age or qualification for combat, was the decisive factor in von Trotha's determination that Herero civilian lives, including those of women and children, were not worth protecting.

Constructions of war experiences by three white German settler women

In 1903, women made up approximately 19 % of the white German population of about 3,000 (65% of the total white population) in German Southwest Africa (Smidt 1995, 430).[21] Many of them, like Margarethe von Eckenbrecher, Helene von Falkenhausen and Else Sonnenberg,[22] were wives of white German settlers

---

19 Lothar von Trotha, Proclamation, 2 October 1904, copy J. No. 3737, Bundesarchiv Berlin, R 1001, no. 2089, p. 7, cited and translated by Hull (2005, 56) and Zimmerer (2008, 48).

20 I put "race" in quotation marks because, unlike traditional discourse around 1900, I follow those who view "race" as a social construct and thus a relational rather than biological category.

21 Due to the war, a census was not taken in 1904 (Smidt 1995, 430).

22 The lives of the three authors have not been explored much by scholarship, see footnote 9. Margarethe von Eckenbrecher, née Hopfer (1875 – 1955) from Bernburg, Germany was a trained teacher. She married painter Themistoklas von Eckenbrecher in 1902 and emigrated with him to German Southwest Africa. After their farm near Omaruru was partly destroyed by the Herero in early 1904, the family returned to Germany where Margarethe's teaching supported the family. Following the couple's divorce in 1913, Margarethe returned with her two sons to the colony where she again worked as a teacher in Windhoek. Her popular autobiography (1907) was published in eight editions until 1940; the author expanded on her memoirs in the latter editions. Helene von Falkenhausen, née Nitze (1873 – 1945) from Weißenburg, Germany came to Southwest Africa when her father emigrated there in 1894. She also worked as a teacher in Windhoek and

and/or traders. Historical and sociological scholarship on gender and "race" under German colonialism suggests that around 1900 some members of the presumed "inferior sex" were eager to escape constricting class and gender relations in the German motherland and seek positions of authority as members of the presumed "superior race" in the African colonies (see Gouda 1993; Mamozai 1989; Walgenbach 2005; Dietrich 2007; Bechhaus-Gerst 2009). At the beginning of the German-Herero Colonial War in 1904, when direct violence on the part of the Herero also entered the political and military dynamics, the asymmetric colonial power relations between white colonizers and black colonized in Hereroland were temporarily reversed, and male as well as female settlers' sense of white German superiority had to yield, for a short time, to black Herero control.

Falkenhausen, Sonnenberg and Eckenbrecher published – as both *superstites* (victims of atrocities testifying on the basis of what they have experienced) and *testes* (observers of atrocities testifying based on what they have seen) – autobiographical reports about their traumatic war experiences, which included losing their husbands (Sonnenberg 2004, 73–74, Falkenhausen 1905, 184), small children (Falkenhausen 1905, 215) and/or property (all three). The titles of their publications reflect the authors' identities as German women, as colonial settlers in Southwest Africa and as witnesses to the "Herero uprising": Sonnenberg's *Wie es am Waterberg zuging: Ein Beitrag zur Geschichte des Hereroaufstandes* (1905); Falkenhausen's *Ansiedlerschicksale: Elf Jahre in Deutsch-Südwestafrika 1893–1904* (The fate of settlers: Eleven years in German Southwest Africa 1893–1904; 1905), "Ein Farmerheim im Hereroland" (A farmer's home in Hereroland, 1907) and *Bei den Hereros: Erzählung aus den Aufständen Südwestafrikas* (Among the Herero: A tale from the uprisings in Southwest Africa, 1914); and Eckenbrecher's *Was Afrika mir gab und nahm: Erlebnisse einer deutschen Ansiedlerfrau in Südwestafrika* (What Africa gave me and took from me: Experiences of a German settler woman in Southwest Africa, 1907) and "Padleben in Südwestafrika" (Life on the path in Southwest Africa, 1907).

While German men's reports about the beginning of the German-Herero Colonial War focus on combat and the development of the armed conflict, the three

---

married trader and farmer Friedrich Ernst Alexander Konrad Freiherr von Falkenhausen in 1899. After he was killed by the Herero in January 1904, she returned to Germany and lost one of her children to illness on the way. She worked as a teacher in Germany, made an unsuccessful attempt at living again in Southwest Africa and South Africa, and eventually died in Germany. Else Sonnenberg, née Träger (1876–1967) from Wendeburg, Germany married Gustav Sonnenberg in 1903 and arrived with him in Southwest Africa in March of the same year. They ran a country store near the Waterberg where Else gave birth to their son in October. In January 1904, Gustav was murdered by one of their workers. Else returned to Germany.

women authors contextualize their personal recollections of war as the experiences of "ordinary people" (Sylvester) by including colorful sketches of everyday, intercultural prewar life on German-owned farms and at country stores. Their testimonies combine images of exotic and beautiful Africa with the violence and horrors of war and thus create a contrast that expresses all the more a sense of personal loss due to the direct violence blamed on the Herero.

All three authors describe German Southwest Africa before the war as a rough but fascinating and cherished natural paradise waiting to be developed by hardworking, moral and kind white, Christian, German men and their equally diligent, thoughtful and compassionate Christian wives. Both men and women are depicted as working towards the personal and national goal of cultivating the land and civilizing its native people, who are perceived as a primitive, "uncultured Negro tribe" "not capable of developing the country" (Sonnenberg 2004, 37, 94) – much along the lines of the French concept of *mission civilisatrice* and the British understanding of the white man's burden. The narratives follow the tradition that postcolonial critics of German literature Sara Friedrichsmeyer, Sara Lennox and Susanne Zantop call the German colonial "legend of the benign, superior German colonizer[s]" among their – mostly – loyal native subjects (1998, 25, see 20). The transformation of "free," arid space into fertile ground is understood as proof of "racial" and cultural superiority (22). Falkenhausen, for example, muses, "There lies a particular appeal in forcing a previously wild country into a state of culture" (1905, 149, see 1907, 33 and Sonnenberg 2004, 44). The verb "force" (zwingen) alludes to the element of violence in the process of converting natural wilderness and domesticating attitudinal wildness to culture and civilization.

In binary constructions of alleged cultured and civilized German Selves, these narratives of war divide the Herero into two stereotypes of Others characterized as less civilized: either amiable, docile, loyal, childlike, oftentimes Christianized servants who do not question the colonial order, or defiant, haughty, deceitful, treacherous pagans whose images of pride and resistance foreshadow the upcoming rebellion early in the reports. A social and political colonial hierarchy prior to January 1904, predetermined the German structural violence that was taken by the historical Herero as cause for war. This same hierarchy is presented by the German women authors as a multiracial coexistence "in the most beautiful peace" under rightful German supremacy, as a kind of idyllic *pax Germanica* characterized by the colonizers' "benefaction" (Sonnenberg 2004, 61, see 49). Falkenhausen's title "Ein Farmerheim im Hereroland" (A farmer's home in Hereroland) alludes to the Germans making themselves at "home" on Herero land and thus taking possession of it.

The passages describing prewar colonial bliss contain noteworthy silences. The authors rarely mention direct violence by Germans against Herero, although scholarship has established that cases of direct violence by Germans were frequent, not least against native women, as the incidents of rape and the arbitrary killing in 1903 of Louisa Kamana, daughter-in-law of Chief Zacharias Zeraua of Otjimbingwe, suggest. The fact that the German court allowed her German murderer to get away without severe punishment attests to another one of the injustices that fueled the Herero's decision to go to war in January 1904 (Silvester and Gewald 2003, 94–96).

Another more subtle silence about the causes of the war may be found in prewar images that Eckenbrecher, Sonnenberg and Falkenhausen attentively provide and the overriding omission as insignificant of what Galtung would call "structural violence" and what we, in postcolonial hindsight, easily identify as the build-up of tensions leading to the "direct violence" called war: the Germans' transfer of "the best [Herero] land" to "big [German] corporations" (Eckenbrecher 2000, 63), "the division of the [Herero's] land into reservations which would leave them with relatively small areas" (Falkenhausen 1905, 168), and the trading and lending business that earned German settlers and traders significant profits (151; Sonnenberg 2004, 35). The traders encouraged the Herero to purchase German goods on credit for which they charged fees, which were in some cases extortionate and to be paid in kind. Falkenhausen and Sonnenberg write in relative detail about the effects a change in colonial legislation regarding the payment of debts had on Herero-German relations, but conclude that "the natives ha[d] nothing to fear from the [German] traders" (Sonnenberg 65) and thus dismiss the Herero perspective. Notably, both authors use practically the same wording: "forcible debt collections" (Falkenhausen 1905, 168) and "bare-knuckle collection of claims" (Sonnenberg 2004, 52) vis-à-vis the Herero described as dilatory; both reports mention the Herero's fear that "their entire property would be taken" (Falkenhausen 168), that "their land would be taken away and all villages would become the property of white people and would be sold without their [the Herero's] consent" (Sonnenberg 52). Yet, Falkenhausen and Sonnenberg agree that while "these conditions and regulations alarmed the Herero [...], they were not the cause of the uprising" (Falkenhausen 168, see Sonnenberg 53 cited at the beginning of my essay). Both explicitly deny this causality, even though Sonnenberg tells of secret meetings of Herero leaders planning "to shake off the German rule" (52). Similarly, Falkenhausen observes that the Herero leadership wished to "shake off the foreign rule; but knew that they were no match for the Germans and therefore held back their people" (169). This almost identical vocabulary in the two war reports indicates that they fed from and contributed to the same prewar discourse in the German Southwest African colonial community and later shared the same interpretation of the causes for the war.

According to the new regulation "Legal Transactions and Disputes of Nonnatives with Natives," debt obligations by "natives to nonnatives [would, KvH] expire within one year" (Zimmermann et al. 1904, 7: 163). This pressured the Herero to pay off debts quickly or else face confiscation of collateral such as land or livestock, often significantly below market value. This regulation became effective on 1 November 1903, and clearly contributed to the Herero taking up arms two months later against its beneficiaries. The white women's writings reject this connection.

Unlike the settler/trader wives, missionary wife Hedwig Irle (1857–1938) complains in her 1911 publication *Unsere schwarzen Landsleute in Deutsch-Südwestafrika* (Our black compatriots in German Southwest Africa) about this legally supported "great injustice" carried out by unscrupulous traders at the Herero's expense (73).[23] By contrast, Sonnenberg and Falkenhausen interpret the regulation as a burden on the white traders who now had to collect the Herero debts sooner and more forcefully (Sonnenberg 2004, 53). They comment on cases of "unbelievable defraudation" of the Herero (Falkenhausen 1905, 148) and use verbs like "robbed" and "plundered" to illustrate some German traders' ruthless actions (Sonnenberg 2004, 35), which they play down as exceptions to the rule (Falkenhausen 1905, 148, see 166, 168, 208). In fact, the authors are eager to distance their husbands and themselves from such disgraceful "business practices" and emphasize, in contrast, how "popular" their husbands had been with the local people (Falkenhausen 1905, 148, 165; see Sonnenberg 2004, 61). Falkenhausen blames the Herero's rapid impoverishment – within only two decades of German colonialism – not on any wrongdoing on the part of Germans or any systemic discrimination they introduced, but on what she describes as the Herero's own undisciplined consumerism, deliberate tardiness in paying their debts, their conceited arrogance and tradition of "a free people" and altogether on their unwillingness to submit to "no ruler other than their own" (1905, 168–169). This interpretation frames the Herero's desire to govern themselves as unjustified obstinance. It furthermore ignores the fact that the Herero were unfamiliar with the concepts of debts, interest or private possession of land as opposed to collective land claims.

So, while the white settler women's reports demonstrate a certain sensitivity to the injustices done to the Herero and to the Herero's subsequent "bitterness"

---

23 For Hedwig Irle's presentation of German-Herero relations, see Cindy Brewer's article in this volume.

against German rule (Sonnenberg 2004, 52, 53; Falkenhausen 1905, 168), the authors do not acknowledge the economic and social hardships caused by colonial hierarchy as "structural violence" in the sense of Galtung's definition of "needs deprivation." Rather, subscribing to a racist social Darwinist perspective, they perceive German prewar colonial domination as a natural right of the fittest over the weaker, of the more advanced *Kulturvolk* over the less advanced *Naturvolk*. Their writings exhibit a disregard for the natives' experience of oppression under German rule and an obliviousness to their own participation as white women in perpetuating colonial oppression.

According to Falkenhausen, Eckenbrecher and Sonnenberg, the beginning of the "Herero uprising" came as a complete surprise to the entire German colonial community and constituted not counter-violence, but an unwarranted act of Herero aggression against utterly innocent, peace-loving, unsuspecting Germans. Using adjectives like "mildtätig" (charitable) and "milde" (lenient) (Sonnenberg 2004, 40), Germans are represented as non-aggressive, kind and caring masters and neighbors whom none of the Herero would "wish any harm" (68). Falkenhausen claims, "[E]ven the whites who had lived among [the Herero] for many years had not the slightest idea of their intentions" and "were not in the least concerned about an uprising" (1905, 169). Looking back at 1904, one and two years later, when most of their works were published, the narrators admit that their husbands and other white male fellow settlers were blind to any serious "danger" the native population may have presented, while the women sensed "ominous signs of trouble" (Sonnenberg 2004, 61–70). Sonnenberg, who owned a store and farm with her husband near the Waterberg, points out that the Herero now purchased food and weapons on credit in an "almost crazy shopping spree" (63); and Eckenbrecher notes a colder and more provocative behavior in some Herero men and hidden warnings by some Herero women (2000, 105–111, see also Sonnenberg 2004, 61, 65, 76, 96). The authors express their outrage regarding the perceived betrayal on the part of the Herero, most of whom they characterize as thankless, undeserving and deceptive.

Caught in a paternalistic colonial world-view and in denial of their own role in any structural violence that may have brought about the German-Herero war, the white settlers' descriptions of the actual war focus almost exclusively on the direct violence the Herero exerted. Such a skewed perception, according to Galtung, is a common phenomenon because "[p]ersonal [or direct, KvH] violence *shows*. [...] Structural violence is silent, it does not show" (173). Political scientist Joan Cocks elaborates further that "beneficiaries of structural violence misrecognize themselves as victims and misrecognize the stone thrower as the original sinner who brought violence to paradise" (2012, 222).

Applying this image to our three authors' war narratives, scenes of a German-dominated "paradise" are contrasted with scenes of Herero "stone throwing" and the fear and chaos resulting from it. The horrors of war are illustrated in episodes depicting the German settler women fending for themselves and their children after their husbands are either called away to military duty (Eckenbrecher) or killed as "victims on the altar of the fatherland" (Sonnenberg 2004, 75; see Falkenhausen 1905, 184). Helene von Falkenhausen's report stresses her unique position as "the [white] woman [...] who was hit by the Herero" with a "kirri" (club) and suffered a head wound when the "orloogh" (war) broke out (175–177). The contradictory narration of her survival represents the confusion of the moment and simultaneously creates a dramatic effect: she writes that the local Herero intentionally spared her and that they wanted to kill her (177) and that she saved her and her children's lives solely by fleeing to the nearby mission (179–180).[24] Sonnenberg's traumatic eyewitness account of her husband being beaten to death on their farm and their home being pillaged, resembles a cinematic nightmare in slow motion:

> There – three terrifying thuds from the bedroom, a short muttering – I tumbled [...]. Dashing inside, I saw Ludwig [a Herero farmhand, KvH] holding the heavy stone hammer, his face dreadfully disfigured, and screaming "Otjurumbu backoka" (the white man is dead) as he rushed out of the house. [...] There lay my faithful husband. [...] The room was silent for a few seconds. I was alone with him. – He could not be dead! [...] Here came the hordes of raiders racing to the boxes and suitcases, dragging away our linen and clothes. One smashed the window. How fast that would go! – Now they came closer to where I was sitting on the bed. I raised my hand in defense, my lips moved, but I could not make a sound. [...] I heard loud screaming. Oh God, this was the nurse with the child in her arms. [...] In terrible fear for my child, I dashed out of the window. How they rampaged! It sounded like the howling of wild animals. Can human beings screech so dreadfully? Where was I? I looked around for help, and my gaze fell on the women in their pagan outfits lugging away our things [...]. How come the men had all these guns? Where would I be safe? This is when Tapita came up to me crying, embracing me and pulling me away. [...] We were fleeing, dragged by Tapita. [...] I was trembling and incapable of defending myself. (2004, 73–74)

This vivid scene communicates the narrator's emotional shock through verbalizing visual and auditive sensations and flashes of thoughts. The Self appears as both observing *testis* and experiencing *superstes* in a position of extreme vulnerability. The white woman's safety depends on her Herero child servant Tapita.

---

24 See Maureen Gallagher's analysis in this volume of the respective visual construction depicting Helene von Falkenhausen as a white, German woman under attack by black Herero men (Figure 2).

The girl's innocence and humanity is highlighted as an exception to the behavior of the adult Herero collective. The Herero men are described as violent, nonhuman "animals" (see also Falkenhausen 1905, 186) similar to Falkenhausen's representation of the Herero as a "blood-thirsty mob" (178). When the Herero women do not aid the German women, Sonnenberg depicts them as greedy looters and Falkenhausen portrays them as threatening creatures with "fury-like faces," a "devilish expression" and "bestial character" (176 – 177, 182). In either case, they are constructed in opposition to the author's self-image as human, even humane, and victim.

Contrary to her actual war experience, Falkenhausen misrepresents "news of the terrifying atrocities committed against [white, German, KvH] men *and* women" (185, my emphasis; see 181, 187 – 188 and Eckenbrecher 2000, 111, 142). Margarethe von Eckenbrecher, too, alludes to the alleged rape of German women by Herero men, when she emphasizes repeatedly: "In cold blood, I would have shot first my child and then myself rather than fall into the hands of these monsters," whom she decries as "black devils" (114, 134). As in Falkenhausen's report, the sexual undertone in Eckenbrecher's also incites the condemnation of the Herero among her German readers by implying that for a white woman surviving honorably under reversed inter"racial" power relations would be unthinkable.[25]

By contrast, Else Sonnenberg communicates through her narrative that she was not sexually assaulted while under Herero control, demonstrating that surviving honorably was in fact possible. She recounts how she and her newborn son Werner survived the Herero "uprising" thanks to her young Herero servants Tapita and Moritz, the protection of Christian Herero community elders, and the local Herero Chief David (74, 81, 107 – 108). She describes how she treks to safety in an oxcart for almost six weeks between February and April 1904, together with the Waterberg missionary family Eich "amidst the Herero with their wives, children and cattle" (94). The diary format that makes up the latter part (81 – 108) of Sonnenberg's otherwise retrospective narrative enhances the immediacy of her firsthand account. Dramatically, it conveys a fear for her life among "twenty thousand" Herero "in the midst of war, in the headquarters of the chiefs" (108). And yet, while Falkenhausen and Eckenbrecher paint sharp pictures of Herero insidiousness and brutality in contrast to German honesty and heroism in both literal and figurative black and white fashion, Sonnenberg's representa-

---

25 Missionary wife Hedwig Irle, on the other hand, insists several years later in *Wie ich die Herero lieben lernte* (How I learned to love the Herero, 1909) that according to her experience no Herero man would intentionally harm white women (124). For Irle's perspective on the German-Herero Colonial War, see Brewer's article in this volume.

tions of German-Herero, white-black, female-male and female-female relationships display nuances and some ambivalence. To be sure, her report also constructs images of peaceful, benevolent, white colonization versus the destruction and war attributed to the Herero. But her partly resentful, partly culturally sensitive presentation reflects not merely her own war experience, but also recognizes the prewar and war experiences of the Herero: their criticism of German settlements (17), their girls' and parents' fear of rape by white men (31), their fear of white brutality (69), some Herero's hesitation to join the "uprising" (69, 83), their fear on the trek (106), their combatants killed in action (102, 107, 109) and their dead in the desert (44). Sonnenberg even evokes a certain feeling of compassion in her German readers when she wonders in hindsight whether Tapita and Moritz also perished in the Omaheke, like so many others (114), or whether they survived like the few black and "mixed-race" orphans who were taken in by missionary Eich and his wife (44, 114). Importantly, Sonnenberg highlights how Paramount Chief Samuel Maharero twice personally protected her and her baby boy (109, 110). She thereby contradicts the image of the Herero as savage women- and child-killers popularized elsewhere. And still, despite her *de facto* protection by the Herero whose provisions of food and oxen for her cart she acknowledges, Sonnenberg ascribes her "fortuitous, miraculous rescue from the hands of the enemy" not to the Herero, but, like Falkenhausen and Eckenbrecher, to the German *Schutztruppe* (113, see 112; Falkenhausen 1905, 201; Eckenbrecher 2000, 146).

Historian Gesine Krüger bases the popularity of eyewitness war reports of the abandoned wives and endangered widows, in part, on their presentation of the white, German woman as a victim – as opposed to the widespread constructions of black, Herero women as beasts (2008, 178). Contrasting pure, white, female, German innocence versus the violence of hideous, black, male, Herero had a strong appeal because the German woman had already been constructed in prewar German discourse in and about German Southwest Africa as the epitome of colonial Germanness, as savior of German culture in the rough colony far from home (Walgenbach 2005; Dietrich 2007). Since 1898, shiploads of German women had been recruited and "imported" to German Southwest Africa as brides for German colonists to prevent them from getting involved with black local women, from adapting to native cultures and producing "bi-racial" children who might claim German citizenship. Narratives about the victimization of women settlers so central to the success of the colony as a whole fed into the topos of the helpless white, German woman threatened by Herero men stylized as demonic aggressors (e. g., Eckenbrecher 2000, 114, 134). This construction then effectively served in historical reality as justification for the Germans' genocidal revenge on the Herero.

It must be mentioned that the female characters in the narratives of Eckenbrecher, Sonnenberg and Falkenhausen also exhibit agency in both content and language. The authors complement images of endangered and fearful German women with illustrations of their admirable courage and initiative during the war. Eckenbrecher recounts how she helped the wounded, ran her farm in the absence of her husband, carried stones in a military defense effort (2000, 129–131) and participated in discussing military strategy vis-à-vis the peaceful Damara people (134, 136). Sonnenberg illustrates how she walked through the wilderness to get help for her trekking party (2004, 111). All three narrators elaborate on how they tried to ensure their children's survival. Most importantly, however, the authors' agency lay in the act of writing and publishing itself. Communicating their war experiences to a public audience, they contributed to the colonial war discourse in the German motherland.

Considering the three authors' deliberate step into the controversial public debate about the war, it is noteworthy that none of them mention General von Trotha's extermination order of 2 October 1904 (footnote 19), that was widely discussed in the German press. It is true, their reports center on events prior to October 1904, yet the texts were published in 1905, 1907 and 1914. In fact, the retrospective narratives that build up from German peace to Herero war are constructed in a teleological fashion that foreshadows and implicitly endorses the historical events that followed the authors' actual war experiences in early 1904: the inhumane massacre at the Waterberg, the pursuit into the Omaheke desert, and the internment of Herero combatants and civilians including women and children in concentration camps later in the same year. The authors were aware of these developments by the time of publication as we see in Sonnenberg's report (2004, 114). Their texts articulate the desire for revenge in the strongest terms and call for the Herero's punishment without "mercy" or "pity" (Eckenbrecher 2000, 149, see 148, 150; Sonnenberg 2004, 82, 90–91, 93, 113; Falkenhausen 1905, 187) "until German rule will firmly establish its foothold" in German Southwest Africa (Sonnenberg 2004, 93). In so doing, they justify to their German audience the murderous atrocities of the *Schutztruppe* as necessary acts of self-defense in the interest of *re*-claiming what is presented as legitimate German ownership of and dominance in Hereroland. Eckenbrecher goes so far as to project the intention of a "race war" onto the Herero by claiming to quote one of their captains: "'Our cause is the struggle of one race against the other. No one can go against their blood'" (2000, 122). She may well have perceived the war as a *mutually* intended "race" war, yet historical research proves, as we have seen, that the Herero fought a war over resources against German male opponents, not against the German nation or white "race." We see here the discursive proximity between Falkenhausen's, Sonnenberg's and Eckenbrecher's rhetorical call for direct German violence against the Herero and von Trotha's concept of a merciless "race war" against "nonhumans" (see above).

Against the backdrop of Butler's fundamental thesis that in war people often differentiate "between lives worth [... protecting, KvH] and lives worth destroying – [...] between valuable and grievable lives on the one hand, and devalued and ungrievable lives on the other" (2010, 22), it becomes clear that in the war reports of Eckenbrecher, Falkenhausen and Sonnenberg the differentiation between valuable and devalued lives is not an issue of friend and foe, but an issue of "race." Applicable is then also Butler's observation that in war certain populations – such as those of another "race" – are considered "'lose-able' [...] since, in the twisted logic that rationalizes their death, the loss of such populations is deemed necessary to protect the lives of 'the living'" of the beholder's own group (31) or "race." With particular respect to colonial violence, Butler criticizes, "whereas the self-defense of the colonizer is given infinite capacity to justify acts of violent destruction, any effort on the part of the colonized to defend life and land are taken as evidence of 'inherent' violence" (xxv). "Under such conditions it becomes possible to think that ending life in the name of defending life is possible, even righteous" (xxx). The mass extinction of "lose-able" Herero lives would then be perceived by the three colonial authors discussed here as the price to be paid to gain and maintain a thriving German colony.

Similar to Butler but without explicitly referring to "race," Galtung also links violence and war to "the idea of sharp and value-loaded dichotomies" and "the distinction between the Chosen and Unchosen; let us call them Self and Other"; "[a] steep gradient is then constructed, inflating, even exalting the value of Self, deflating, even debasing the value of Other" (Galtung and Fischer 2013, 51). Galtung continues: "Any Self Other gradient can be used to justify violence against those lower down on the scale of worthiness" (57). Like Butler, Galtung criticizes attributing different value to different human lives: "When Other is not only dehumanized but has been successfully converted into an 'it', deprived of humanhood, the stage is set for any type of direct violence, blaming the victim. [...] Extermination becomes not only psychologically possible but a duty" (51). He views the sharp distinction between Self and Other as rooted in "the ideology of nationalism": "Killing in war is now done in the name of the nation comprising all citizens with some shared ethnicity" (52). All this is applicable to the writings of Sonnenberg, Falkenhausen and Eckenbrecher: they "inflate" the German Self and "deflate" the Herero Other, endorse a hierarchical "scale of worthiness" for life, and devalue, demonize and dehumanize the Herero. They advocate German direct violence, which is justified as a measure of self-defense that also advances the national(ist) project of colonialism.

Let us return to Galtung's "concept of 'cultural violence' – the intellectual justification for direct and structural violence through nationalism, racism, sexism and other forms of discrimination and prejudice in education, the media, literature" (Galtung and Fischer 2013, 12) – and to his observation that "*[c]ultural violence makes direct and structural violence look and feel right*, or at least not wrong" (39, 42). In this light, we must read the three German women's autobiographical war reports, which transmit "discrimination and prejudice" via literature to the German public and make German colonial violence "look and feel right," as contributions to the dominant narrative of colonial imperialism in general and to cultural violence against the Herero in particular. Documenting their experiences during and after the war may initially have served as a therapeutic means of processing their trauma, as missionary Eich is said to have recommended to Sonnenberg (2004, 77). Publishing their reports, however, represents a political step impacting their German *polis*. In line with the uncanny connection between the white women's emancipatory agenda and colonial racism around 1900, the three authors' textual contributions to colonial war discourse made them, as the title of sociologist Martha Mamozai's standard work *Komplizinnen* (Women accomplices, 1990) suggests, active and public accomplices to the white man's national project of hegemonic colonialism, the privileges of which the white woman colon(ial)ist happily shared.

Constructions of war experiences by women in Herero oral history

The German-Herero Colonial War created a stark contrast between German and Herero women in terms of perspectives, interests and experiences of "ordinary people," to return to Sylvester's term. Yet, there are also striking similarities in their textual documentations of experiencing, witnessing and participating in violence, of suffering traumatic losses of children and other loved ones, and of flight, chaos and powerless victimhood. Similar also is the women's demonstration of agency by creating war narratives within and for their respective Herero and German communities in an effort to come to terms with the war that turned their worlds upside-down.

Searching for testimonies of Herero women's war experiences, we must carefully differentiate among: 1) war accounts *about* Herero women by contemporary *testes* – e.g., in German and Herero missionaries' and doctors' reports about rape or mass mortality in the concentration camps, descriptions by German and German-affiliated troops or the German press (see Krüger 2008 and 1999), 2) war stories told by Herero descendants *about* their foremothers (see Erichsen

2007; Förster 2010), and 3) and central to my investigation, actual first-hand tes-timonies *by* surviving Herero women *superstites* (see Alnaes 1981 and 1989; Dam-mann 1987). In the latter two categories, we rely on Herero oral history: inter-views and songs as well as stories that were handed down from generation to generation. In the early 2000s, Larissa Förster interviewed mostly male Herero about the German-Herero Colonial War, because women were seldom recom-mended to her (2010, 139). Importantly, she stresses that "the role of women in passing on knowledge about the war must not be underestimated," since her male interviewees – *histores*, in Fassin's typology of witnesses, who are re-moved in time and have heard about atrocities from others – often revealed their mothers, grandmothers or great grandmothers as the sources of their war stories (2010, 119, 137).[26]

In the 1970s, Kirsten Alnaes conducted extremely rare interviews with actual Herero *superstites*, many of them women, who survived the death trek through the Omaheke desert as children in the latter part of 1904 and 1905. According to their eyewitness accounts, in early "1904 the Herero women played a strongly supportive role against the Germans; they took part in the decision to start the war; they fought on the battlefield; and they supported the men during the flight to what was then the [British, KvH] Bechuana Protectorate" (Alnaes 1981, 1, see 7–9, 14). Alnaes was told, "during the meeting when the decision was taken to start the war, it was the women's ululation which tipped the balance in favour of starting the war despite disagreement within the council" (8). Regarding wom-en's role and agency in actual battle, "[a]n old woman, who herself survived the battle of Hamakari [at the Waterberg, KvH], told how the women rallied be-hind the men, egging them on to fight: 'The women were among the bullets. They shouted and ululated'" (8). The evidence of Herero women chanting and actively participating "among the bullets" in what Galtung calls "direct violence" is cor-roborated by German first lieutenant Stuhlmann's diary entry about Herero com-bat tactics: "In the third line stand the women who encourage the men with shouts and sensual songs."[27] Recorded not in Otjiherero but by a German theo-

---

26 Regarding references to foremothers as sources of war stories, see also Herero descendants Moses Maharero, Jololine Mbahahiza Katjatenja and Matuipi Uahova [Felicity] Ruhumba in Erik-sen's archived collection of interviews "What the Elders Used to Say" of 2007.

27 National Archives of Namibia [NAN], Private Accessions A.109, Stuhlmann, "Tagebuch mein-er Kriegserlebnisse in Süd-West-Afrika 1904 und 1905 als Oberleutnant der Schutztruppe" (Diary of my war experiences as first lieutenant of the *Schutztruppe* in Southwest Africa, 1904 and 1905, 62, cit. Krüger 2008, 178; see also Krüger 1999, 116). For the role of Herero women in this war and their perception by German soldiers as both "unleashed beasts thirsting for revenge" and "un-fortunate victims of war," see Krüger's entire chapter "Die besondere Rolle von Frauen im Here-

logian is the Herero women's praise song "Who Owns Hereroland? We Own Hereroland" cheering on their warriors (Anz 1904, 657; see Henrichsen 1994, 15; Krüger 2008, 178, and 1999, 116). The slogan captures the women's desire to defend Herero grazing land, which was their home and source of livelihood (cattle), economic power and political recognition in the region and thus the foundation of their collective cultural identity.

Only very few of the oral texts about the war that Herero women produced are available for research (Krüger 2008, 180) and accessible in languages other than Otjiherero.[28] While the rare interviews with *superstites* reveal individual memories of their collective experience of war and genocide, their songs were by design performed "in situations with ritual overtones when kinsfolk and friends join together. [...] The songs about their difficulties are sung on communal occasions and are dependent upon the interchange [...] between lead singer and audience, who together create the song" (Alnaes 1989, 292). Songs women sing are called *omatjina* (sg. *outjina*) and those by men *omihiva* (sg. *omuhiva*) (Krüger 1999, 292).

Konstanze Tjiposa sang the following *outjina* about flight in 1954 in Omaruru, then South-African controlled Southwest Africa, today independent Namibia. Ernst Dammann, who published it, assumes that it refers to the expulsion of Herero from a particular village in 1904:

Our village *hiyee, hiyee*	our village
Our village left,	our village
[...].	
The werf[29] was ousted, *hiyee*.	our village
It was scattered.	our village
Clap [your hands]!	our village
The werf was ousted.	our village
Let us flee, let us flee!	our village. (Dammann 1987, 264–265)

---

ro-Krieg" (The notable role of women in the Herero War, 1999, 116–122) and her article "Beasts and Victims: Women in the Colonial War" (2008).

28 For women's contribution to Herero oral history on the German-Herero Colonial War, see Alnaes, "Going Through the War" (1981) and "Living with the Past" (1989) and Krüger's chapter "Erinnerungen—Formen der Kriegsbewältigung in der oralen Literatur" (Memories—forms of coming to terms with war in oral literature, 1999, 290–297) and Krüger, "Beasts and Victims" (2008). For voices of descendants, see Erichsen (2007 and 2008) and Förster (2010).

29 Most of the semi-nomadic Herero lived in werfs, multi-generation family compounds including a kraal, several pontoks (cabins), a holy fire and a fence of dried thornbush around the dwelling. They moved in and out of such settlements depending on the movement of their cattle.

In simple brush strokes repeating basic facts rather than providing intricate details, this song paints the picture of the war experience of many Herero fleeing from their homes under pressure from German troops. The twofold exclamation "Let us flee!" underscores the fear and sense of urgency. The participles "left," "ousted" and "scattered" relate the loss of land, family and collective roots, an overall sense of disorientation and the destabilization of the villagers' former cultural identity as a consequence of the forced displacement of the Herero from Herero land within Hereroland. The steady refrain "our village" and the auditive as well as physical (hand clapping) interchange between the individual singer and her audience and chorus represent both the longing for the old communal life before the war and genocide and the creation of a new collective identity that emerges out of the ashes of past losses. The song thus indicates agency in that it contributes to creating a postwar sense of belonging based precisely on the shared experience of war and the memory of a prewar community.

Another *outjina* entitled "The Flight," sung by an old woman who survived the war in the Botswanan exile (Alnaes 1989, 278) and recorded and translated by Alnaes in the 1970s, also focuses on the Herero's need to frantically flee after being attacked. The singer's employment of direct speech between Samuel Maharero and his wife Johana brings to life the historical turn when the German *Schutztruppe* under von Trotha, rather than beginning peace talks, encircled and attacked the Herero at the Waterberg. Their one and only escape route was eastward through the Omaheke desert.

> Herero person, where are you going?
> Herero person, where are you going?
> They have prepared [...]
> There is shooting by the thornbush of Mujema
> They are running
> They have guns
> Give me my stick [gun] [...]
> They are going to fight the war.
> They are going to shoot TUUUUUUUUUUH! [the sound of the gun] They are running with guns under their arms [...]. 'You all prepare, let us go. Johana, let us go and drink from the shallow waterholes [in the Omaheke, KvH].' [...] TUUUUUUUUUUH! [...] 'Johana, carry the child on your back, [...] Johana, come, we must go!' – 'The child, my child, where has it gone? It has fallen [has been killed]. [...] I am not going to take that horse, it will throw me off! [...] Samuel, hear the guns [...]. People are distraught; the child has lost its mother, the mother has lost her husband, the lambs have gone to suckle the goats.' – 'Let us go, we must go [...].' TUUUUUUUUUUH! They shoot. (Alnaes 1989, 279)[30]

---

30 See interpretations by Alnaes (1989, 279–280, see a slightly different translation in 1981, 9) and Krüger (1999, 293–295, and 2008, 170–171).

Although an eyewitness performs the song, it does not reflect an actually observed encounter between the leading Herero couple, but rather captures the general confusion and fear generated by the unexpected, sudden need to flee during the war. It exemplifies the Herero's vulnerability independent of gender, age and involvement in combat by focusing on one single "Herero person" who notices the German attack and on one single high-ranking woman who reacts to the disintegration of order and normalcy around her and to the loss of her "fallen" child, small enough to be carried "on her back." The child, however, represents the entire generation of young Herero who perished.

As in Sonnenberg's description of her husband's murder (2004, 73–74), the Herero woman's song zeroes in on the traumatic historical and personal moment that changed everything: a wife and mother realizes the precarity of her "child" that she can no longer protect and the precariousness of her entire "people" whom the Herero leadership can no longer defend. Similar to the German female settlers' autobiographical narratives (and particularly Sonnenberg's diary format) that create for their German readers the illusion of unmediated witnessing of the war, the *outjina's* dramatic dialog recreates for the Herero audience even years later the immediacy of the traumatic experience of 1904. The ever more pressing "Let us go, we must go" relates the same sense of urgency as the equally emotionally charged "Let us flee, let us flee!" in the *outjina* interpreted above. In "The Flight," the male speaker and leading historical figure, Samuel Maharero, stands for decisive, practical action in the face of disaster: "Give me my stick" and "You all prepare, let us go." The song's focus, however, is on the female speaker's personal helplessness, fear and concern for individual human beings: "child," "mother" and "husband" referred to not merely according to their age and gender, but according to their family ties and thus according to the emotional, social and economic importance to those closest to them. Demonstrating the war experience of random killings and observing that many a child and mother "has lost" their family support, the song foregrounds the social collapse and personal pain on the side of the Herero and their collective shock at realizing that Herero lives have lost all value, or in Butler's terms, their precariousness, in the eyes of the German enemy troops.

In "The Flight," the interplay between individual and collective war experience is created by the use of the individual names of Johana, Samuel and "my child," on the one hand, and "you all," "people" and "we" on the other. The song furthermore bridges past and present. Sung to a post-genocidal Herero audience, it activates their collective memory. The mere mention of the "shallow waterholes" triggers images of suffering and death in the listeners who know that the majority of Herero refugees died because the Omaheke (Otjiherero for *sandveld*) could not provide enough water for tens of thousands of "distraught people" and their cattle, and that when they desperately approached the rare water holes many were ambushed by hidden German troops (see "The Water-hole," cit. Alnaes 1989, 280 – 282).

Unlike the war accounts of Sonnenberg, Falkenhausen and Eckenbrecher, which explicitly describe and condemn the Herero enemies, the Herero songs center mostly on the Herero's own war experience of fear, loss, chaos and displacement from Hereroland. Through the mere use of personal pronouns, the Herero "we" and the German "they," the latters' identities remain anonymous, "The Flight" evokes the two sides of the conflict. "Their" violent omnipresence is vividly expressed through their catastrophic "shooting" (highlighted by the onomatopoetic leitmotif "TUUUUUUUUUUH!") and its devastating result: the many "fallen," "distraught" and "lost" Herero human beings. Reversing the contrast of peace-loving Germans and brutal Herero in the three German settlers' narratives, "The Flight" depicts the Germans in the role of aggressors determined to "fight the war" with (modern) "guns," while the Herero, not even defending themselves but thinking only of escape, are cast in the role of objects of "their" direct violence. However, similar to the impressions on the senses in Sonnenberg's account, here, too, the sound of war conveys the woman's experience of horror and victimization.

Drawing a connection between Germany's first and second genocide, Alnaes concludes, "To the Herero the war against the Germans and the flight across the Kalahari desert was an experience of holocaust-like dimensions" (1989, 291). In "The Flight," the overall disruption of the natural order is succinctly symbolized by the unnatural phenomenon of lambs suckling goats; this can be attributed solely to the circumstances of extreme, existential needs deprivation, to use Galtung's definition of violence again.

The extremity of circumstances is accentuated by two related themes in Herero oral history about the historic flight: tales of women cutting their breasts to save starving children by feeding them their blood and references to the competition between men and children for women's breast milk:

> 'The milk for the babies became water for the men,' as one woman put it. Another inform-
> ant, an old woman who had herself fled through the desert, described how the men asked
> their wives to suckle them: 'I have the seeds of new offspring [sic] in my loins. Leave that
> child behind and give me your breast to suck.' However, none of the survivors whom I [Al-
> naes] asked had actually seen this happen. (Alnaes 1981, 8 – 9; see 1989, 275, and Förster
> 2010, 138)

As eyewitnesses did not confirm these occurrences, I concur with Gesine Krüger who interprets the image of the breast as a metaphor for the essential source of "life and hope" (Krüger 2008, 184, see 1999, 291), which had come under attack.

Similar to the descriptions of female courage in the German women's narratives, we see in the Herero women's oral histories constructions of heroines who denied themselves water and, on the one hand, sacrificed their children to help male combatants survive and, on the other hand, rescued young children. The song called "The Waterhole" specifically refers to "the wife of Hijakame" who collected and cared for small, "newly weaned" children who had survived the flight, but wandered around alone because their families were dead or dispersed (see Alnaes 1989, 281, 283–284; Krüger 2008, 184, and 1999, 295). Praised are actions that benefit the community by ensuring the survival of (parts of) the Herero tribe and the continuity of Herero culture. Postwar songs about Herero women's "heroic deeds" may have helped "re-establish order in the face of chaos" (Krüger 2008, 185).

In later Herero generations, stories of victimized women who "were abused […] sexually and otherwise [and] beaten" by Germans (Moses Maharero in Erichsen 2007) were complemented by those of brave Herero women whose legacy has contributed to resurrecting a sense of both collective and female pride. Matuipi Uahova [Felicity] Ruhumba recounts in 2007, how Herero men resisted the Germans, and how "the women fought back, too" (in Erichsen 2007). Another woman whose husband was shot is said to have "kept burn[ed]-out firewood of the holy fire in Ovamboland" until she returned from the camps (Kaipindwa Veseeivete in Erichsen 2007). Descendant Elrike Christian Zeraua proudly recounts how his grandmother Rupertine acted as "de facto leader of the Ovakwendata clan," using her "knowledge and skills of being a teacher [… as] the weapon […] to save her family," including rescuing her son from being hanged by the Germans "so that I can be here today" (in Erichsen 2007). Herero women are thus celebrated as representatives of solidarity in the German-Herero war, as saviors of Herero traditions and as guarantors of present-day Herero lives.

Conclusion

This examination of diverse Herero and German women survivors' narratives of the beginning of the German-Herero Colonial War in 1904 – based on rare, un(der)researched voices and in some cases made available relatively recently to English- or German-speaking audiences by feminist, postcolonial or human rights scholars – has expanded the scope of perspectives on this war and genocide and on women's roles in it.

Parallels and differences between the textually documented traumatic war experiences of "ordinary" (Sylvester) Herero and German women have become clear. Their accounts highlight their exposure to atrocities, threats to their lives, and their need to flee. Regarding the war's impact on their identity, the German autobiographies discussed here emphasize individual suffering, while the Herero oral songs and stories stress communal losses. Although the German settlers and traders were factually intruders on Herero land, by 1904 each side perceived the Other as the aggressor and the Self as the victim being ousted from their property and homes in "Hereroland." Each set of narratives shows women as both victims and perpetrators passively and actively involved in forms of "direct, structural and/or cultural violence" – in Johan Galtung's terminology – in the context of this colonial war. The reports by both Germans and Herero highlight the heroic deeds of women; we can further observe that both tried to claim agency by disseminating their war stories to their respective communities, thereby helping advocate contrary perspectives on the traumatic events.

A sense of powerlessness is also common to all of the women's war narratives studied here. The white narrators' repeated usage of adjectives like "machtlos" (powerless; Sonnenberg 2004, 64, 110) and "ohnmächtig" (unconscious; Falkenhausen 1905, 175, 176), both deriving from the German noun for the lack of "Macht" (power), indicate the authors' feeling of having lost control over their destiny. At first glance, this, too, seems parallel to the Herero women's songs and stories, which highlight their inability to protect their children and fellow Herero when they collectively faced mass death and diaspora captured in the unanswered question "Herero person, where are you going?" in "The Flight."

Yet there are profound differences between the narratives of the white German and black Herero women. It was precisely the European notion of the uneven colonial power distribution between the two groups, rationalized by the hierarchical concept of "race," that determined the difference in their exposure to violence, their treatment as "precarious" human beings worthy of protection or not, and thus differences in how their war experiences and narrations were constructed and evaluated. The fact is, in this colonial conflict, which many Germans, including the settler women, considered a "race war," Judith Butler's observation, that in war the lives of certain populations are defined *a priori* as less valuable and therefore not worth preserving, did not apply to white German women and children but did apply to all Herero independent of gender, age and involvement in combat, merely on the grounds of their ethnic affiliation. Despite the settler women's certainly harrowing individual experiences of temporarily having to surrender white German power, assumed as natural, to black Herero control, these women were not physically targeted and in the end could return to a supportive homeland at peace in the German motherland. They felt invited to contribute on the side of the powerful winners of the war to writing colonial history as we see in Sonnenberg's book title *Ein Beitrag zur Geschichte des Here-*

roaufstandes (A contribution to the history of the Herero uprising, 1905). Their texts provide today's researchers with rich material and food for thought about the complex *liaison dangereuse* between racism and white women's interest in emancipating themselves, in enjoying relative independence and authority at the expense of non-whites in colonial settings. Accordingly and with few exceptions, Margarethe von Eckenbrecher, Helene von Falkenhausen and Else Sonnenberg constructed in their war reports representatives of peace and war, good and evil, valuable lives and condemned lives along "racial" lines. Doing so, they committed acts of "cultural violence" (Galtung) against Herero in particular and black Africans in general.

So, while the German settler women's war stories tell tales of white women suffering because they lost their husbands and their dream of building a successful existence as members of the white colonizing elite in a German-dominated Southwest Africa, the colonized Herero women's texts tell of genocide, perpetrated in order to make that very dream of Germans "owning Hereroland" come true. Herero women found themselves on the losing, powerless side of the war and would not recover economically or culturally or "own Hereroland" for the major part of an entire century of oppression, first under German colonial and then South African apartheid rule. Their voices – not about "racial" differences, but about white people exerting violence and black people being subjected to violence – were long suppressed in the historiography of the German-Herero Colonial War, dominated as it was by the victors and related holders of white power. Yet, Herero women – and men – maintained agency across generations. Their songs and storytelling about the cataclysmic war and genocide have served over the past century as an important form of bearing witness, sustaining Herero cultural identity and building Herero postwar community. They have helped empower Herero descendants to regain public voices and agency despite their people's history of victimization. Herero – and other – oral and written testimonies have been passed on in many cases by female *superstites* (victims of atrocities) and *testes* (observers of atrocities) and told by *histores* (who heard about and recorded atrocities much later). Only on the basis of such testimonies have present-day Herero political activists or *auctores* (Fassin's term for those endowed with the author-ity to utilize records of atrocities for public initiatives) been able to apply some pressure on the German government to acknowledge the Herero genocide, written and sung about by Herero and German women in similar, but yet in entirely different fashions.

Works Cited

Alnaes, Kirsten. "Going Through the War: Herero Women in Botswana." Paper presented at the ASAUK Symposium on Women in African Politics, University of London, 22 Sept. 1981. *Women in African Politics*, edited by Agneta Pallinder (African Studies Association of the United Kingdom Symposium on Women in African Politics, 22 Sept. 1981). 15 ms. pp.

Alnaes, Kirsten. "Living with the Past: The Songs of the Herero in Botswana." *Africa*, vol. 59, no. 3 (1989), pp. 267–299.

Anz, Wilhelm. "Gerechtigkeit für die Deutschen in Südwestafrika!" *Die christliche Welt*, vol. 18, no. 28 (Marburg 7 July 1904), p. 657.

Bechhaus-Gerst, Marianne, and Mechtild Leutner, editors. *Frauen in den deutschen Kolonien* (Ch. Links, 2009).

Bley, Helmut. *South-West Africa under German Rule* (Heinemann, 1971).

Brehl, Medardus. *Vernichtung der Herero: Diskurse der Gewalt in der deutschen Kolonialliteratur* (Fink, 2007).

Butler, Judith. *Frames of War: When Is Life Grievable?* (Verso, 2010).

Cocks, Joan. "The Violence of Structures and the Violence of Foundings." *Revisiting Johan Galtung's Concept of Structural Violence*, edited by Yves Winter. Special volume of *New Political Science*, vol. 34, no. 2 (June 2012), pp. 221–227.

Dammann, Ernst. *Was Herero erzählten und sangen: Texte, Übersetzung, Kommentar*, edited by Dammann (Dietrich Reimer, 1987).

Dannhauer, Otto. "Brief aus Deutsch-Südwestafrika." *Berliner Lokalanzeiger*, vol. 358 (2 Aug. 1904), pp. 1–2.

Dietrich, Anette. *Weiße Weiblichkeiten: Konstruktionen von "Rasse" und Geschlecht in deutschen Kolonien* (transcript, 2007).

Drechsler, Horst. *Aufstände in Südwestafrika: Der Kampf der Herero und Nama 1904 bis 1907 gegen die deutsche Kolonialherrschaft* (Dietz, 1984).

Drury, Jackie Sibblies. *We Are Proud To Present a Presentation About the Herero of Namibia, Formerly Known as Southwest Africa, from the German Sudwestafrika, between the Years 1884–1915* (Bloomsbury, 2014).

Eckenbrecher, Margarete von. "Padleben in Südwestafrika." *Deutsch-Südwestafrika. Kriegs- und Friedensbilder: Selbsterlebnisse geschildert von Frau Margarete von Eckenbrecher, Frau Helene von Falkenhausen, Stabsarzt Dr. Kuhn, Oberleutnant Stuhlmann* (Wilhelm Weicher, 1907), pp. 1–20.

Eckenbrecher, Margarethe von. *Was Afrika mir gab und nahm: Erlebnisse einer deutschen Ansiedlerfrau in Südwestafrika 1902–1936.* 1907 (8th ed., Mittler & Sohn, 1940; reprint: Peter's Antiques/Superprint, 2000).

Erichsen, Casper W. *"What the Elders Used to Say": Namibian Perspectives on the Last Decade of German Colonial Rule* (Meinert, 2008).

Erichsen, Casper W. "What the Elders Used to Say: Oral History Project 2007." Compilation of interviews conducted by Alex Kaputu and Erichsen. National Archives of Namibia. Findaid 2/102. AACRLS. 196.

Falkenhausen, Helene von. *Ansiedlerschicksale: Elf Jahre in Deutsch-Südwestafrika 1893–1904* (Reimer, 1905; reprint: Peter's Antiques/Superprint, 1995).

Falkenhausen, Helene von. *Bei den Hereros: Erzählung aus den Aufständen Südwestafrikas* (Verlag der Adler-Bibliothek, 1914).

Falkenhausen, Helene von. "Ein Farmerheim im Hereroland." *Deutsch-Südwestafrika. Kriegs-und Friedensbilder: Selbsterlebnisse geschildert von Frau Margarete von Eckenbrecher, Frau Helene von Falkenhausen, Stabsarzt Dr. Kuhn, Oberleutnant Stuhlmann* (Wilhelm Weicher, 1907), pp. 21–33.

Fassin, Didier. *Humanitarian Reason: A Moral History of the Present* (U of California P, 2012).

Förster, Larissa. *Postkoloniale Erinnerungslandschaften: Wie Deutsche und Herero in Namibia des Kriegs von 1904 gedenken* (Campus, 2010).

Friedrichsmeyer, Sara, et al. "Introduction." *The Imperialist Imagination: German Colonialism and Its Legacy*, edited by Friedrichsmeyer, et al. (U of Michican P, 1998), pp. 1–29.

Galtung, Johan. "Violence, Peace, and Peace Research." *Journal of Peace Research*, vol. 6, no. 3 (1969), pp. 167–191.

Galtung, Johan, and Dietrich Fischer. *Johan Galtung: A Pioneer of Peace Research* (Springer, 2013).

Gerstenberger, Katharina. *Truth to Tell: German Women's Autobiography and Turn-of-the-Century Culture* (U of Michigan P, 2000).

Gewald, Jan-Bart. *Herero Heroes: A Socio-Political History of the Herero in Namibia 1890–1923* (James Currey / David Philip / Ohio UP, 1999).

Gouda, Frances. "Das 'unterlegene' Geschlecht der 'überlegenen' Rasse: Kolonialgeschichte und Geschlechterverhältnisse." *Geschlechterverhältnisse im historischen Wandel*, edited by Hanna Schissler (Campus, 1993), pp. 185–203.

Gründer, Horst. *Geschichte der deutschen Kolonien* (Schöningh, 1985).

Hammerstein, Katharina von. "The Herero: Witnessing Germany's 'Other Genocide.'" *Sites: Contemporary French & Francophone Studies*, vol. 20, no. 2 (2016), pp. 267–286.

Hammerstein, Katharina von. "Kriegs-Schau-Platz Omaheke: Multiple Perspektiven auf den Völkermord an den Herero." *Acta Germanica*, vol. 45 (2017), pp. 29–44.

Henrichsen, Dag. "'Ehi rOvaHerero': Mündliche Überlieferungen von Herero zu ihrer Geschichte im vorkolonialen Namibia." *WerkstattGeschichte*, vol. 3, no. 9 (1994), pp. 15–24.

Hermes, Stefan. *'Fahrten nach Südwest': Die Kolonialkriege gegen die Herero und Nama in der deutschen Literatur (1904–2004)* (Königshausen & Neumann, 2009).

Heywood, Annemarie, et al., editors. *Warriors Leaders Sages and Outcasts in the Namibia Past: Herero Sources for the Michael Scott Oral Records Project 1985–6* (Meinert, 1992).

Hoffmann, Giselher. *Die schweigenden Feuer: Roman der Herero* (Peter Hammer, 1994).

Hull, Isabel V. *Absolute Destruction: Military Culture and Practices of War in Imperial Germany* (Cornell UP, 2005).

Irle, Hedwig. *Unsere schwarzen Landsleute in Deutsch-Südwestafrika* (Verlag des Missionshauses, 1911).

Irle, Hedwig. *Wie ich die Herero lieben lernte* (Bertelsmann, 1909).

Kößler, Reinhart. *Namibia and Germany: Negotiating the Past* (U of Namibia P, 2015).

Krebs, Uwe. *Auf den Spuren der Else Sonnenberg: Unterwegs in Namibia, 100 Jahre nach dem Herero-Aufstand: Ein Bildband mit Originalzitaten aus ihrem Tagebuch 'Wie es am Waterberg zuging'* (Uwe Krebs, 2012).

Krüger, Gesine. "Beasts and Victims: Women in the Colonial War." *Genocide in German South-West Africa: The Colonial War of 1904–1908 and Its Aftermath*, edited by Jürgen Zimmerer and Joachim Zeller, translated by Edward Neather (Merlin Press, 2008), pp. 170–192.

Krüger, Gesine. *Kriegsbewältigung und Geschichtsbewußtsein: Zur Realität, Deutung und Verarbeitung des deutschen Kolonialkriegs in Namibia 1904 bis 1907* (Vandenhoeck & Ruprecht, 1999).

Lau, Brititte. "Uncertain Certainties: The Herero-German War of 1904." 1989. *History and Historiographie—4 Essays in reprint*, edited by Annemarie Heywood (DISCOURSE/MSORP, 1995), pp. 39–52.

Mamozai, Martha. *Komplizinnen* (Rowohlt, 1990).

Mamozai, Martha. *Schwarze Frau, weiße Herrin: Frauenleben in den deutschen Kolonien* (Rowohlt, 1989).

Melber, Henning, editor. *Namibia, Kolonialismus und Widerstand* (Informationsstelle Südliches Afrika, 1981).

Mennen, Patricia. *Sehnsucht nach Owitambe* (Blanvalet/Random House, 2011).

Okupa, Effa. *Carrying the Sun on our Backs: Unfolding German Colonialism in Namibia from Caprivi to Kasikili* (LIT, 2006).

Paluch, Andrea, and Robert Habeck. *Der Schrei der Hyänen* (Piper, 2004).

Pfingsten, Otto. *Das Schicksal der Else Sonnenberg im Herero-Aufstand: Das Geschehen 1904 in Deutsch Südwestafrika* (Uwe Krebs, 2004).

Sarkin, Jeremy. *Germany's Genocide of the Herero* (James Currey, 2011).

Schneider, Rosa B. *"Um Scholle und Leben": Zur Konstruktion von "Rasse" und Geschlecht in der kolonialen Afrikaliteratur um 1900* (Brandes & Apsel, 2003).

Seyfried, Gerhard. *Herero* (Eichhorn, 2003).

Silvester, Jeremy, and Jan-Bart Gewald, editors. *Words Cannot Be Found: German Colonial Rule in Namibia: An Annotated Reprint of the 1918 Blue Book* (Brill, 2003).

Smidt, Karen. "'Germania führt die deutsche Frau nach Südwest': Auswanderung, Leben und soziale Konflikte deutscher Frauen in der ehemaligen Kolonie Deusch-Südwestafrika 1884–1920: Eine sozial- und frauengeschichtliche Studie." Dissertation (Otto von Guericke-Universität Magdeburg, 1995).

Sonnenberg, Else. *Wie es am Waterberg zuging: Ein Beitrag zur Geschichte des Hereroaufstandes*. 1905. Reprint: *Wie es am Waterberg zuging: Ein Originalbericht von 1904 zur Geschichte des Herero-Aufstandes in Deutsch-Südwestafrika*. With a foreword by Prof. Dr. Uwe Ulrich Jäschke (Uwe Krebs, 2004).

Sylvester, Christine. *War as Experience: Contributions from International Relations and Feminist Analysis* (Routledge, 2013).

Sylvester, Christine. "War Experiences/War Practices/War Theory." *Millennium—Journal of International Studies*, vol. 40 (2012), pp. 483–503.

Timm, Uwe. *Morenga*. 1978 (Deutscher Taschenbuch Verlag, 2000).

United Nations. *Convention on the Prevention and Punishment of the Crime of Genocide* (Geneva, 9 Dec. 1948). www.hrweb.org/legal/genocide.html. Consulted 16 Sept. 2017.

Walgenbach, Katharina. *"Die weiße Frau als Trägerin deutscher Kultur": Koloniale Diskurse über Geschlecht, "Rasse" und Klasse im Kaiserreich* (Campus, 2005).

Whitaker, Benjamin. *Revised and updated report on the question of the prevention and punishment of the crime of genocide* (United Nations Economic and Social Council Commission on Human Rights Sub-Commission on Prevention of Discrimination and Protection of Minorities, 2 July 1985). www.preventgenocide.org/prevent/UNdocs/whi taker/. Consulted 16 Sept. 2017.

Wildenthal, Lora. *German Women for Empire, 1884–1945* (Duke UP, 2001).

Winter, Yves. "Violence and Visibility." *Revisiting Johan Galtung's Concept of Structural Violence*, authored by Andrew Dilts, et al. Special volume of *New Political Science*, vol. 34, no. 2 (June 2012), pp. 195–202.

Zimmerer, Jürgen. "War, Concentration Camps and Genocide in South-West Africa: The First German Genocide." *Genocide in German South-West Africa: The Colonial War of 1904–1908 and Its Aftermath*, edited by Zimmerer and Joachim Zeller, translated by Edward Neather (Merlin, 2008), pp. 41–63.

Zimmerer, Jürgen, and Joachim Zeller, editors. *Genocide in German South-West Africa: The Colonial War of 1904–1908 and Its Aftermath*. Translated by Edward Neather (Merlin Press, 2008).

Zimmermann, Alfred (until 1905), editor. *Die Deutsche Kolonial-Gesetzgebung: Sammlung der auf die deutschen Schutzgebiete bezüglichen Gesetze, Verordnungen, Erlasse und internationalen Vereinbarungen mit Anmerkungen und Sachregister: Auf Grund amtlicher Quellen und zum dienstlichen Gebrauch herausgegeben* (Mittler, 1893–1910).

Cindy Patey Brewer
Christian Love and Other Weapons

The Domestic Heroine of the Multiracial Colonial Mission "Family" as an Antiwar Icon in Hedwig Irle's Mission Memoirs

Shortly after the end of the German-Herero War (1904–1907), during which roughly 80,000 of the approximately 100,000 Herero people were exterminated by the German army in the former colony of German South-West Africa,[1] Hedwig Irle's (1857–1938) 1909 mission memoir, *Wie ich die Herero lieben lernte* (How I learned to love the Herero), appeared in print. Her brother, Dr. Konsistorialrat Gustav von Rohden, wrote the introduction in which he compares the missionary efforts to convert the Herero tribes to Christianity with the colonial war to suppress the Herero uprising: "We sympathize, that the Herero resisted the inward conquest through Christian love as much as they resisted the outward subjugation via German weapons" (Irle 1909, 3).[2] Rohden's comparison between Christian love and German weapons is striking but not surprising when one considers that missionaries have long imagined themselves as Christian soldiers, fighting and sometimes dying on the mission battlefield.

This romantic view of the missionary warrior has roots in the New Testament[3] and asserted itself in mission literature of all varieties, appearing in the most fanciful poetic forms as well as in the most mundane mission reports. This icon of religious valor fueled public support for the missions among European Christians at home and impassioned many a young person to venture out into the mission fields abroad. During the initial fervor of Germany's colonial period, 1885–1918, mission and colonial supporters touted a partnership of church and state in colonizing foreign lands and Christianizing the natives.[4] In this con-

---

1 This number is difficult to ascertain, most historians estimate somewhere between 60,000 and 100,000 Herero killed. See Bley (1968, 150–151), Oermann (1999, 102) and Krüger (1999, 63).
2 This and all subsequent translations from German originals are mine.
3 Ephesians 6:13–17.
4 In Europe in the latter half of the nineteenth century, there was great enthusiasm among missionaries for collaboration between religious and secular entities in colonizing Africa. Christianity, commerce, and civilization became catchwords for missionaries, politicians, and settlers alike, even though in practice these objectives rarely worked well together (see Hastings 1994, 283–293 and Porter 1985). In Germany in 1893, we see similar expectations, for example, in the magazine *Kreuz und Schwert*. But here the magazine already adds a qualifier to their support: "The new magazine wanted to be a support to government, so long as it used wholesome

https://doi.org/10.1515/9783110572001-003

text, images of the German colonial soldier and the Christian missionary seemed at times to conflate into one and the same masculine ideal. Thus, it is not surprising that some scholars of Germany's colonial period have likewise made little distinction.

A review of literature examining missionaries and war in a colonial context reveals an almost exclusive attention to empirical history and a skeptical assessment of missionaries.[5] The postulation that missionaries simply reproduced the values of the colonizer remained the prevailing paradigm among scholars from the 1960s through the 1990s.[6] German theologian and historian Nils Oermann noted this phenomenon, explaining that missionaries are presented as "puppets or as silent assistants for the colonial authorities [...,] a homogeneous group which possessed a political agenda dominated by self-interest or no political agenda at all" (1999, 20). While such assumptions still remain, a growing body of evidence by scholars of History, Anthropology, and Cultural Studies has appeared demonstrating the myriad ways in which missionaries could be at cross purposes with colonizers.[7]

While historians have attempted to answer the question of missionary complicity with colonial oppression by examining what various missionaries actually did during the German-Herero War – and here the answers are in no way monolithic[8] – my focus is different. As a scholar of literature and thus textual constructions, I am interested in how missionaries, particularly women, re-imagined the ideal Christian soldier in the wake of colonial violence. While German General Lothar von Trotha pursued his plan to exile or exterminate the entire Herero nation and German colonial newspapers and literature offered up justifi-

---

means to bring order to the territories overseas, and thereby blaze a path for Christianity" (1 January 1893, 1).

5 For discussion of this tendency among scholars, see the introduction to *Gendered Missions* edited by Huber and Lutkehaus (2002).

6 See, for example, Drechsler (1966), Loth (1963), Gründer (1999), and Paczensky (1991).

7 See van der Heyden's and Becher's volume, *Mission und Gewalt* (Mission and violence, 2000), which features a more nuanced collection of essays on the topic. See particularly Irving Hexham's essay entitled "Violating Missionary Culture" cautioning scholars against the tendency to read mission literature with an eye toward a particular theory.

8 Rhenish Mission historian and former missionary Gustav Menzel acknowledges the mission was, at the very least, a "passive participant in colonial oppression" (1978, 248). Nils Oermann notes differing opinions among the missionaries about the German-Herero War and notes that some missionaries, who were initially sympathetic toward the colonial authority, became pro-African after witnessing the atrocities committed by these authorities (1999, 100–109).

cation for these policies with tales of Herero atrocities,[9] what counter-narratives appeared among the missionaries, that subset of German colonists most familiar with the Herero people, their culture, and their motives for rebellion? More specifically, what narratives did missionary women contribute, what images did they evoke, what alternative did missionary women offer for the culture of hyper-masculine militarism so popular in imperial Germany and also in the mission narratives of the day?

A broad examination of all missionary writings about the German-Herero War is beyond the scope of this chapter, however Hedwig Irle's two memoirs of her time among the Herero offer a rare opportunity to learn how a female missionary perceived the war.[10] Hedwig was the wife of Protestant missionary Johann Jakob Irle and one of the few missionary women in colonial German South-West Africa who wrote and published. She was also intimately familiar with the Herero people, having lived among them for nearly 14 years (1890–1903) until her malaria illness forced a return to Germany just months before the Herero uprising. Her first book, *Wie ich die Herero lieben lernte*, was published in 1909, and was followed two years later by her second book, *Unsere schwarzen Landsleute in Deutsch-Südwestafrika* (Our black compatriots in German South-West Africa). Both books contain much about day-to-day missionary life among the Herero people and, since they were published after the German-Herero War, include discussions of the war and its aftermath.

The writings of missionary women have seldom attracted scholarly attention, and this is particularly true of Hedwig Irle's works. Though a search for her husband, Jakob Irle, will yield dozens of articles, analysis of Hedwig Irle's writing is scant to non-existent. There appear to be no publications (scholarly or otherwise) that focus specifically on Hedwig Irle, no biographies, no assessments of her work. When her writings are mentioned, it is typically just a footnote in the accounts of mission historians.

In my anaylsis of Hedwig Irle's memoirs, I am less concerned with historical events and more interested in a missionary woman's discourses within the context of colonial war. Literary historian Marcia Klotz offers a useful model for my project. In her article, "Memoirs from a German Colony: What Do White Women

---

9 For German women settlers' published reports on the beginning of the German-Herero War, see Katharina von Hammerstein, and for representations of girls in this war in German girls' literature, see Maureen Gallagher (both in this volume).

10 Mission historian Vera Mielke has noted that writings of missionary women differed significantly from the writings of missionary men. Women, in particular, rarely commented on the political events, focusing instead on the day-to-day life in the mission (2000, 399). Irle is an exception to this, discussing the German-Herero War from both a personal and political perspective.

Want?,," Klotz analyzes discourses on race and gender in the colonial setting "reading these memoirs not as 'evidence' of some preexisting factual history that lies outside the texts themselves, but rather as gendered articulations of a discourse that both constitutes and responds to German imperialism" (1994, 160). Whereas Klotz is interested in discourses by colonial women generally, my analysis of Irle's missionary memoirs provides a unique and contrastive perspective. While participating in a rhetoric that still constitutes German imperialism from a religious perspective, Irle's writings also undercut many assumptions used to justify colonial domination. Furthermore, I argue that Irle's memoirs represent a gendered articulation reflecting a departure from the hyper-masculine discourses of war so typical of Wilhemine Germany toward the promotion of a rhetoric of cultural accommodation. Rather than agrandizing aggression or defense, Irle advocates welcoming the cultural Other into one's private sphere. In spite of her brother's use of the military conquest metaphor in the introduction to her mission memoirs (quoted above), Hedwig Irle's own writings do not at all employ the missionary as soldier metaphor. For her, the missionary hero is neither soldier nor even male. Instead, she is the antithesis – female, domestic and decidedly antiwar.

What follows in this chapter, then, is a close reading of Irle's memoirs about the German-Herero War within the larger cultural and historical context of gendered missionary ideals. A brief analysis of the cover page *Kreuz und Schwert im Kampfe gegen Sklaverei und Heidentum* (Cross and sword in the fight against slavery and heathendom), a Catholic mission magazine from the same time period, will frame my analysis and provide cultural reference points for the discourses in Irle's writings. It should be noted, however, that *Kreuz und Schwert* had no direct relationship to Hedwig Irle other than the magazine's focus on Christian missionary work in Africa. As a Protestant, Irle did not publish in this magazine, nor is it likely that she read it. Nevertheless, it is useful here for the following reasons. First, the magazine was unusual in that it was expressly designed to address issues at the intersection between missionary work and the German colonial government, thus serving as a focal point for larger discourses on Christian women and colonial war. Second, the magazine spans the same years that Irle was serving as a missionary in Africa and later publishing her memoirs, years in which wars in the colonies and growing numbers of women in the missions were changing the discursive landscape. Images on the cover of the magazine can serve as paradigmatic examples of these changing discourses influenced directly by women and war in the colonial context, discourses that crossed denominational and territorial boundaries and mirrored the discourses in Irle's memoirs.

Gendered icons of the colonial mission

The ubiquitous soldier-missionary was not a metaphor that Irle employed in her memoirs, but it was the predominant metaphor for missionary work at the beginning of Irle's time in Africa. It takes a particularly interesting form on the cover page of *Kreuz und Schwert* (fig. 1), which features two images corresponding to the title. The cross is represented by a missionary priest on the left side and the sword is represented by a German colonial officer on the right. Twenty-five years after its debut, the editor of this magazine admits somewhat apologetically that the original title sounded "rather warlike" but explains it as a war of words, "Indeed, the task was to preach a crusade" (October 1916, 2). Despite this ex post facto explanation, the German colonial officer on the title page, eyes forward, drawn sword and German flag planted triumphantly in African soil, seems to suggest a less metaphorical crusade and appears as a strange counterpart to the priest. Set side by side, the two heroes conflate into one ideal: the patriotic missionary soldier, conquering foreign lands and subduing the so-called "heathen" souls.

Figure 1: "Cross and sword in the fight against slavery and heathendom," *Kreuz und Schwert*, July 1897

Significant changes to the cover and title of the Catholic magazine occurred in 1906, when two of Germany's African colonies were engaged in the brutal suppression of native uprisings, the Herero rebellion in German South-West (1904) and the Maji Maji rebellion in German East Africa (1906–1907). Apparently, the image of the battle-ready colonial soldier had lost its appeal in the wake of real violence in the colonies. The reading public in Germany had already heard much of the German-Herero War and the ongoing Maji Maji conflict and this may have been the impetus for *Kreuz und Schwert* to adopt a new name and do away with the image of soldier (fig. 2). The new title, *Kreuz und Charitas im Kampfe gegen die Barbarei und Heidentum* (Cross and charity in the fight against barbarism and heathendom), strikes me as somewhat ambiguous, as it is not entirely clear who the perpetrators of barbarism are, the indigenous people or, perhaps, the colonial officer now banished from the cover. An editorial article in the first issue under the new title explained that times have changed and "the activities of the sword have lost interest for us" (January 1906, 1). While there is nothing in the magazine itself directly indicating that the removal of the colonial officer had anything to do with the brutality of the German colonial soldiers, the timing remains suspicious. This is not to say that the magazine withdrew its support for the colonial government; on the contrary, articles published after the title change continued to offer support for the troops.[11] It is, however, noteworthy, that as the German colonial troops in armed conflict increased their prominence as a heroic icon in Christian mission literature appears to have waned.

Kreuz

und

Charitas

im

Kampfe gegen Barbarei und Heidentum.

Figure 2: "Cross and charity in the fight against barbarism and heathendom," *Kreuz und Charitas*, January 1906

---

11 See, for example, "Die katholischen Missionen in Südwest Afrika" (The Catholic missions in Southwest Africa) (*Kreuz und Charitas*, February 1906, 65–66) which expresses Catholic missionary support for the German troops and criticizes Protestant missionaries for being less supportive.

The 1906 cover redesign was more than a shift away from images of war and weapons of violence. The new design also represented a gendered shift away from the masculine ideal of the missionary soldier so popular in the previous decades. An entirely new type of iconic ideal emerged, a missionary heroine in a domestic setting. This female missionary mirrored the corresponding image of the priest, the two characters cast in surprisingly egalitarian roles of reconciliation and peace, each with head bent to the left, each with arms identically angled, and each attesting to be intermediaries for God. While the priest's robe, beard and halo cast him as Christ figure, the missionary woman poses as a Madonna with child. The missionary woman stands in front of a Chinese home signaling the magazine's expanded support for missions beyond Africa, but also signaling the increasing numbers of women in the mission ranks. Catholic and Protestant women alike were joining the missions in record numbers both at home and abroad. New mission fundraising societies in Europe, run primarily by and for women, were being founded at rates thirty times that of previous decades (see Haller-Dirr 1999, 148). Missionary work in general was getting a new face and that face was female. Still condescending towards their potential converts, this new pair of icons nevertheless abandoned all suggestions of a militaristic crusade, replacing it with a more domestic and familial representation of missionary work.

As the new gendered paradigm mapped itself onto the historical tradition of missionary work as a strictly masculine domain, it was the image of domestic feminine charity that replaced the masculine image of war and conquest. No longer are the native homes distant background images on foreign landscape. Now they move into the foreground, where the female missionary heroine stands center stage in a private and familial setting. As we see on the cover of *Kreuz und Charitas* (fig. 2), her contact with the native inhabitants is less symbolic and more direct. While the priest performs religious rites, the female missionary's role is, quite literally, hands on. Unlike the priest, she is touching and blessing the Chinese woman, and this touch and blessing is reciprocated, forming a circle of touches between the missionary, the woman, the child and the infant. The scene suggests an intimacy that is clearly familial, constituting a multiracial mission "family" based on religious – not biological – bonds. These shifts away from masculine symbols of violence are particularly relevant to Hedwig Irle's memoirs, which gave a voice to the new domestic heroine of the colonial mission.

As I move through my analysis of Irle's mission memoirs, I will trace the two related but mutually exclusive discursive icons represented by the image of the conquering colonial soldier and the domestic female missionary who displaces him in mission literature. The authoritative colonial soldier stands as public enforcer of boundaries and as a symbol of violence and war. The domestic female missionary stands in direct opposition to the colonial soldier. She has neither weapons nor political authority. Her heroism is as understated as her actions, which are to touch the Other and allow them to touch her in return. In doing so, the domestic missionary creates a cultural bridge between black and white, African and European. This is the heroic feminine ideal Irle constructs in her narratives, the white missionary at the center of her African Christian family as defined above. Threatening her power of familial influence in the colonies is the colonial soldier, sword drawn and German flag waving.

Narratives of domestic bliss: The new heroine of the multiracial mission "family"

The dominance of the masculine colonial soldier or, alternatively, the feminine domestic missionary is at stake in Hedwig Irle's narratives – exclusion vs. inclusion, war vs. peace. While Irle acknowledges a natural impulse to be fearful, to react defensively, and to exclude the Other by force, her texts about colonial German South-West Africa advocate Christian love and accommodation. For Irle, this was much more than a public position to be preached from the pulpit, it was personal morality to be practiced in the domestic sphere. Irle's two memoirs, focusing primarily on the religious and familial life of the mission station, thus serve as the ideal venue for representing the white, female domestic missionary in action.

Irle's 1909 book, *Wie ich die Herero lieben lernte*, is a collection of short narratives originally published individually in mission magazines or colonial newspapers.[12] Organized in rough chronological order, each chapter depicts aspects of Irle's experiences in German South-West Africa beginning with her first days among the Herero and ending with a heart-wrenching farewell fourteen years later. Breaking out of this organization are chapters describing events during and after the German-Herero War.[13] Because each chapter may or may not bear any thematic relationship to the previous chapter and contains no transition to the next, the effect can be jolting. The central chapters, describing epi-

---

12 Rhoden notes this in the foreword to Irle's book, but there is no indication exactly where and when these were published previously. Since authors of individual articles in mission or colonial newspapers are typically not listed in library catalogues and databases, these are extremely difficult to find.

13 Irle left the colony a few months before the Herero uprising, but she and her husband were intimately familiar with the circumstances leading up to the war and remained in contact via letters with missionaries and Herero converts throughout the war and afterwards.

sodes in the war, erupt from within otherwise placid narratives about daily life in the mission (see chapters 7–10).

Her 1911 book, *Unsere schwarzen Landsleute in Deutsch-Südwestafrika*, describes more general aspects of Herero culture, history, and economy. Though this book may also represent a compilation of sorts, the chapters are more thoughtfully organized and include transitions relating one chapter to the next. This volume spans a broader time period, relating, among other things, a brief history of missionary work in South-West Africa from 1844 onward. The book includes three chapters specifically on the German-Herero War and its aftermath, discussing its impact on Herero culture, religion, and economy (chapters 4, 5, and 14).

Both books reflect perceptions of the native African populations that are typical of the day and, at first glance, strike the reader as very similar to other colonial narratives. Irle, for example, makes racialized assertions, that the natives are naturally "prideful, deceptive, beggarly, dirty and lazy" (1911, 60). Cultural historians and scholars of literature looking for instances of racist colonial rhetoric, condescension, and prejudice are sure to find plenty of examples. As it is common practice to examine colonial era discourses from this standpoint, it is also easy to overlook the ways in which Irle's memoirs break the mold. Notably, and despite their popularity, military metaphors for a missionary "conquest" are not found anywhere in Irle's two books beyond her brother's introduction. The ideal missionaries in Irle's memoirs are not crusaders. While the masculine heroic soldier represents an impulse to exclude and conquer, the domestic missionary heroine in Irle's memoirs learns to resist that impulse in favor of breaking down barriers, be they political, cultural, or linguistic.

Perhaps it is to be expected that Irle's answer to the colonial war is Christian missionary work, but less obvious is her belief that this is best done by accommodating the Herero people in her own domestic and familial space. This is something that Irle had to learn and, at first, she felt beleaguered: "In the beginning, so many new and unusual things *besiege* one. The German customs and practices have absolutely no place here; everything must be learned anew" (1909, 7, my emphasis). Significantly, Irle's stories about her first encounters with the native Other are depicted as a series of invasions and attacks in which she must discipline herself to not react defensively. When first meeting the Herero Chief Kukuri, she is initially repulsed by his size, his appearance, his smell, and his mostly naked body smeared with fat. When he attempts to greet her with a polite kiss, she reacts defensively and jerks her head back frightened. But she quickly recognizes this as a mistake and is relieved when he is not offended (1911, 163).

This first experience is followed by others in which she characterizes herself as one besieged by the Herero. They enter her house without knocking, stay all day, appear suddenly in rooms where she does not expect them, fill her home until she feels she cannot move about without bumping up against "half-naked heathens" (1909, 8). She describes her feelings of fear and her initial instinct to fortify herself against them by locking the door and forbidding entrance into her home. But when she asks her husband if she can at least lock the door when he is gone, he advises strongly against it, emphasizing the need to accommodate the Herero:

> No, definitely do not do that. The people will think you do not love them. They will be frightened away and will not come nearly so much to the mission house, and that would be regrettable. [...] The more time one spends with the natives, the more insight one gains into their life and their way of thinking, and one gains influence with them. (1909, 9)

Irle's husband accentuates the importance of coming to know and understand the Herero, their way of life and their way of thinking. Irle takes his words to heart and this becomes her personal creed as a missionary from that time forward, welcoming the Herero into her home and including them as part of her mission family.

Missions stations in South-West were organized around the mission house, church and school built upon farmland owned or managed by the mission. The Herero built their thatched huts round about the mission station and these mission communities became centers for Herero life. Irle learned their language and attended to their needs with food, clothing, medicine, advice, and comfort. She reports taking in young Herero girls and training them like her own daughters to cook, clean, sew, and become proficient in the European domestic arts. Indeed, she writes that she considered these domestic duties to be her "primary task as a missionary's wife in Africa" (1909, 23). In this role, Irle served as a "mother" to the entire mission family.

Over the years of shared domesticity, Irle's initial fear and distress in the presence of the Herero is transformed into trust, security, friendship and love. She informs her readers:

> Many in Europe think the Herero are just crude and cruel savages, and yet not only the missionaries, but all the white people could travel safely through the land before the uprising, in a way that you would not even dare to do in Germany. No naked wild-looking heathen with his Kirri, his club, in his hand would ever even try to just frighten a white woman [...] And then, consider the Christians! [...] we have experienced such deep feeling from some of our parish members, such sacrificing love as is rarely found in Germany. (1909, 124)

Twice in this passage, Irle compares life among the Herero to life in Germany and deems life with the Herero preferable. Passages like these attempt to disabuse readers of the common notion that the native inhabitants are inherently danger-ous and warlike. Irle even goes so far to suggest that, in spite of their more civi-lized appearance, Europeans may actually pose the greater threat. She empha-sizes that the "wild" appearance of the Herero belies their peaceful nature, a general attribute she ascribes to Christian and non-Christian Herero alike.

Accentuating this point further, Irle portrays the singular love of the Herero congregation as profound. Writing about her departure from South-West fourteen years later, Irle describes the pain of leaving her beloved Herero behind. Even leaving her daughter, son-in-law and grandchild was not as heart-breaking as leaving their black congregation:

> We were mute with grief, and we held each other and looked into each other's eyes that were darkened by tears. But the hardest of all was already behind us, when we had to tear ourselves away from the black congregation that my husband had gathered in over 30 years of faithful work. [...] With many tears and deep sorrow the people clung to us at our departure and many could not be comforted. (1909, 123–124)

This scene reflects the ideals represented by the domestic missionary heroine on the cover of *Kreuz und Charitas* (fig. 2). Indeed, the multiracial Christian family, with Irle and her husband at the center, is bound together in reciprocal love and affection, touching and blessing one another. This image stands in direct oppo-sition to the stories of violence and war that permeated the press at the time of the book's publication (see Gallagher and von Hammerstein in this volume).

Irle's description of mutual familial affection is idealized in her narrative, but appears to be genuine nonetheless. Similar experiences are recounted in countless missionary narratives. It should be noted, however, that relationships bound by genuine affection do not preclude racial or cultural prejudice which may continue to persist. Indeed, Irle's narrative also mirrors the hierarchical ar-rangement of the missionary images from *Kreuz und Charitas*, depicting a rela-tionship of parent to child. Irle accommodates Herero culture, but the expecta-tion remains that African members of the mission family should eventually adopt European customs along with the Christian faith. Nevertheless, there ap-pears to be no coercion here. The Irle family relationship with Chief Kukuri lasted 30 years with many testaments to their mutual affection before Kukuri decided to become Christian. This was and is to be interpreted by readers past and present as evidence that even a willfully independent non-Christian could be included within Irle's familial sphere.

A hostile review of *Unsere schwarzen Landsleute* in the colonial press gives us an indication of how German colonists reacted to such notions of inclusivity.

The title alone was vexing enough for some readers, who could not stomach the idea of the Herero as "our compatriots," most particularly after the German-Herero War, when the book appeared in print. Literary critic Hans Bertold wrote a scathing, if polite, review published in the *Deutsche Kolonial-Zeitung* (1912):

> It is just unfortunate that the author assumes that understandable but nevertheless inexcusable one-sided mission standpoint, namely a position that those in settler circles will greet with the sharpest protest. I don't believe an Englishman would have found success if he wrote a book for Englishmen entitled "Our Black Compatriots." The term "black compatriot" has no rightful standing, not from a legal standpoint nor from the standpoint of race. (186)

The idea that blacks might have any claim (legal, racial or otherwise) to a status commensurate with white German citizens in the colony was, for Bertold, unthinkable. Statements like Bertold's clearly point to the division between missionary and settler.

Despite her own racial and cultural prejudices, Irle represented a progressive and disruptive element. This, however, is not to say that the Irle family's attitudes incited or encouraged rebellion. More likely, as with most missionaries, Irle advocated obedience to colonial law. However, published after the defeat and almost complete decimation of the Herero by the German *Schutztruppe* (protections troops), her books challenged the rhetoric of the conquerors. The most disruptive aspect of Irle's memoir, the reason her books stirred such a vehement response in the colonial press, is that the image of the blissful multiracial mission family – with the white domestic missionary at the center – undercut Germany's self-justifying war narrative.

If, as Irle attested, the Herero were not the murderous, deceitful creatures depicted in most colonial-era fare, but, instead, were part of the human family and "our compatriots" in the colony, then the German-Herero War of suppression and annihilation could no longer be articulated as a heroic narrative of self-defense. From that alternate viewpoint – that so-called "understandable but nevertheless inexcusable mission standpoint" – the German-Herero War was, on the part of the Germans, a fundamentally immoral act of betrayal against their own people (i. e., their Herero compatriots). The war must then be articulated as a brutal narrative about the economically strong preying on the economically weak, an argument Irle puts forward in *Unsere schwarzen Landsleute* (73). Worse, it was exposed as a narrative of colonial filicide, in which the fatherland abused his Herero sons, raped his Herero daughters, stole their land and livelihood, and ultimately sentenced them to death for attempting a defense. Indeed, this is how Irle tells the story of the German-Herero War: not as a disinterested account of some distant "savage" tribe, but as a personal narrative about Irle's dearest friends and loved ones – men, women and children, who become the victims of unimaginable brutality at the hands of the German colonial army.

Narratives of violence: The colonial soldier destroys the multiracial mission family

With the outbreak of war, the heroic masculine icon, the colonial soldier, came into violent conflict with the multiracial mission family, sweeping Irle's Christian "sons and daughters" into a stream of violence so powerful, that no one could impede the course of destruction. The poignancy of Irle's war narratives stems directly from her personal relationships with the victims. In both books, Irle reports on the wartime fates of black Christians with familiar names – Petrine, Ottlie, Eliphas, Wilhelmine and more. By narrating the war in terms of personal relationships and individual families, Irle takes a distinctly feminine – in the traditional sense of domestic – approach. Whereas German men – journalists and missionaries alike – were more likely to report on military strategy, battles and casualties, Irle's version of the German-Herero War is a distinctly domestic narrative, about individual fathers, mothers, sons and daughters. The disintegration of the multiracial mission family was an almost immediate result of the war:

> Our parish was completely scattered and, when the Germans drove them [the Herero] into the waterless desert, horrific misery descended upon them. Countless starved or died of thirst. Many parents did not know where their children were and the children wandered aimlessly about without parents. (1909, 79)

The stories of congregations dispersed, families separated and children lost surely tore at the hearts of mission supporters in Germany. In the mind of her audience, the orphaned Herero children would be seen as a metaphor for Irle's own "mission children." The African Christians were violently separated from their European missionary "parents" and lost to wander the desert alone. As Irle's war narratives unfold, the long-term viability of the multiracial mission family becomes doubtful.

In the chapter entitled "Eine christliche Hererofamilie im Glück und Unglück" (A Christian Herero family in joy and sorrow) in *Wie ich die Herero lieben lernte*, Irle narrates the particularly wrenching story of Eliphas and his wife Wilhelmine, who were among Irle's closest Herero friends. Eliphas was the youngest son of Chief Kukuri and, as a Herero of social standing, a particular target of the Germany army, even though he had no role in the uprising. Irle takes pains to articulate the way in which this Herero family represented the best European Christian ideals. She describes their education, their cleanliness, their diligence, their well-mannered children, their European-style house, Eliphas's preaching talent, and Wilhelmine's enviable ability on the sewing machine. This was a family mission-minded readers could identify with and view as one of their own, and thus it was particularly disturbing when they were hunted, murdered and enslaved.

Irle constructs this war narrative in relationship to the familial mission community that was lost by the time she wrote about it. She explains that, at first, Eliphas's family was among the lucky ones, who in spite of extreme hardship, managed to stay together in the scorching desert, "but what a difference compared to the peaceful familial bliss in the mission station!" (1909, 79). Each episode in Eliphas's story is narrated as part of a series of attempts to return to the mission. In fact, Eliphas's family was one of the first to heed the call to return and surrender, trusting in the German government's promise of safety for those who did not participate in the rebellion. Ultimately, however, they were betrayed. When Eliphas hears of the execution of his brother, he no longer trusts the colonial authority's promises. His hunch proves accurate:

> [Eliphas] sent his wife and children and fled with his oldest son into the mountains. The Germans took his second oldest son, Willibald, with them, so that he could show them his father's hiding place. Willibald led them astray in order to save his father. He succeeded and Eliphas escaped. Willibald, however, was executed for this by the soldiers. When the father heard that his son had to die for his sake, it broke his heart. (1909, 79)

Eliphas's narrow escape and the execution of his young son are narrated without adornment or editorial commentary. But the straightforward narration of events implicates the guilty nonetheless. As Irle learns of the fates of her Herero loved-ones, she writes, "our hearts trembled over all the grief contained in that long list of the dead comprising those very people who had been our congregation members" (1909, 70–71). Again, the impact of the war is stated in relationship to the loss of the multiracial family – her lost congregation. The "peaceful familial bliss," the idealized marker of the prewar mission family, is no more. Even the white domestic heroine of the mission is displaced; the mission station is burned to the ground. Standing in the place of this lost Christian community is the victorious colonial soldier, German flag waving over the African landscape, and sword bloodied by violence against innocents.

All of Irle's war narratives are tragic and marked by the faithful valor of Christian martyrs. In this way, Irle's narrative participates in the tradition of the Christian hagiography. Eliphas is cast as a suffering saint, enduring all for Christ's sake. Grieving over his son's murder, exiled from his country, separated forever from his children and from his dying wife, Eliphas remains true to his faith. He sends his sincerest love and affection by letter to his former teacher, Jakob Irle. Hedwig Irle paraphrases his letter attesting that "in all this misery, he still sets his hopes upon God, the Lord, and will not depart from Him" (1909, 80). Mission magazines were full of these stories recounting the courage and faith of missionaries and native converts alike. Irle's audience would recognize Eliphas, his family, and other Herero Christians as their own martyrs for the faith. And it would tear at their souls to know that German sons in the colonial army were participants in such atrocities. Missionary reports on the war, the destruction of mission stations, and the brutality of the German army provoked protest in Germany and the colonial soldier fell out of favor among mission supporters as an icon of heroism. While he was victorious on the battlefield and certainly garnered recognition among colonists as a defender of white European interests, as an icon of masculine valor in mission literature, he seemed to fade.

Looking back on the German-Herero War of 1904–1907 and its consequences for the Herero people and the Christian missions in German South-West Africa, Irle depicts significant changes. First, various tribes, each with their distinctive culture and language, are shuffled together and scattered across the country as captives in German work camps. Like other tribes, the Herero are stripped of their culture and identity. Irle laments this postwar state of affairs in language that strikes the modern reader as almost postcolonial in sentiment:

> The current [1911, C.B.] chiefs are so called foremen, set in place by the German government and without power. Their priests have no more sacrificial sites where they can perform their rituals. They have forfeited their independence; their social mores and their laws have lost their meaning; one can no longer speak of a Herero culture. They must even accept the language of their conquerors. (1911, 74)

While Irle, as a missionary, surely does not regret the loss of their "superstitions," she understands what this spiritual loss means to the Herero in the context of their entire cultural devastation. They have no rights, no property, no hope. The mission stations are destroyed or abandoned. The villages are flattened and the schools are empty.

In a fashion so typical of believers, Irle seeks out reasons to hope, despite the overwhelming feelings of desolation. She reports that in the camps, the beaten-down Herero seek desperately for something to cling to and are more willing to listen to the missionaries. For Irle, this in no way justified the war, nor the losses incurred.[14] Irle notes one other tragic consequence of war that has partic-

---

14 In contrast, some missionaries made statements that were unambiguous in their endorsement of war: "As the Lord had to punish Israel, he had to make the natives in German

ular relevance for the Christian missions in German South-West Africa. She writes:

> Since then, mission life has been structured entirely differently. Missionaries can no longer gather together the free people into a congregation, instead they must go after them, wherever they are scattered in the land, some here some there, where they reside as servants and workers for white people. One can no longer construct the old patriarchal relationship of the missionary to his congregation, and that is certainly regrettable. (1909, 112)

Irle laments the loss of a mission station as a gathering point, around which the Herero built their villages and constructed their Christian community. Without the station, the "patriarchal relationship between the missionary and his congregation" was likewise lost. How could the multiracial mission family be built without a shared domestic space in which to construct it? Irle's multiracial family with the domestic missionary heroine at the center was utterly destroyed by the war and Irle expresses realistic doubt as to whether it could ever exist in the same way again. In fact, the colonial authority tried to prevent these centers of Herero solidarity and cultural life from reemerging after the war by denying missionaries the use of lands they had farmed for over 60 years (see Bley 1968, 255–256). The prospects of reestablishing such a familial relationship between missionary and congregation seemed hopeless.

Yet, whatever barriers to a familial mission congregation may have existed after the German-Herero War, the idealized image of that multiracial mission family with its domestic heroine persisted. Among Irle's publications is a 32-page booklet entitled *Die schwarze Johanna* (The black Johanna). The date of publication is unknown, except that it was part of a larger series that appeared in the years after 1905 and thus after the Herero uprising of 1904. The cover features an image of a missionary "mother" presiding in the midst of her multiractial and multicultural "family" (fig. 3). I will not include a detailed analysis of the booklet's content, since the narrative does not touch directly on the German-Herero War, but some aspects of this book are significant for my line of argument. First, the protagonist, Johanna Maria Gerste (Uerieta Kazahendike, 1837–1936), was the first Herero to be converted to Christianity. She asked for baptism after living several years in the home of missionary Carl Hugo Hahn and his wife Emma Sarah Hahn, neé Hone. Thus, Johanna was a product of Irle's domestic missionary ideal, having been mentored in Christian and European domestic val-

---

South-West Africa feel his arm in order to make them realize that they were walking the wrong path" (qtd. in Oermann 1999, 109).

ues by Emma.[15] Second, the familial image on the cover (fig. 3) that complements the domestic conversion story is precisely *not* an image of the black Johanna, as one might expect given the title of the booklet and the focus of the narrative. Instead, it is an image of the white missionary heroine, presumably Emma Hahn. Once again, in the wake of war, the iconic image of the domestic missionary heroine emerges.

As a Madonna with child, this protestant white heroine constitutes a near mirror image of the missionary woman on the cover of *Kreuz und Charitas* (fig. 2), including the one hand reaching out to touch and bless one of her flock. The heroine's attitude is familial and intimate and the figures form a similar circle of touches, uniting them into one multiracial family. In the wake of newspaper and mission reports about the wars between German troops and the Herero, this picture strikes the viewer as surprisingly serene. There are no symbols of war, no signs of revolt, no weapons of any kind. Instead, symbols of domesticity abound. Directly behind the heroine is a wagon and, further back, we see the round mud and thatch homes of the Herero. On the bottom center, a Herero man rests his arm on tools for domestic use, pots to carry water or food. The Herero are not depicted in European clothing (typically a visual sign of their Christian faith), but are wearing their traditional attire, the women wearing their elaborate head adornments. In spite of their indigenous garb, they are depicted as peaceful, quite different from what readers at that time had come to expect in images of the "uncivilized heathens" of Africa. While the composition remains hierarchical and the message Eurocentric, there is no suggestion of a "conquest." This scene is entirely a woman's domain. The men, along with any symbols of masculinity, take a back seat. Hugo Hahn himself, first patriarch of the Rhenish Mission, is seated and his dark suit allows him to blend in with the Herero such that one hardly notices him. Even among the Herero, it is the women who dominate, standing taller with their headdresses. The Herero men sit on the ground or stand behind women and children. More than ever, this image represents the feminization of missionary work and the banishment of masculine symbols of war.

The white domestic missionary woman stands in direct opposition to contemporary militaristic narratives of conquest and suppression. Even as the German colonial soldier dominated the real battlefield – enforcing racial division in

---

15 Protestant missionaries have told Johanna Maria Gerste's story many times over the decades and each rendition is slightly different. Historian Glen Ryland offers a discussion of various versions within the changing sociopolitical context of the Rhenish Mission Society from 1904 to 1936, but was possibly unaware of Hedwig Irle's version of Johanne Maria Gerste's story and thus does not include it in his analysis.

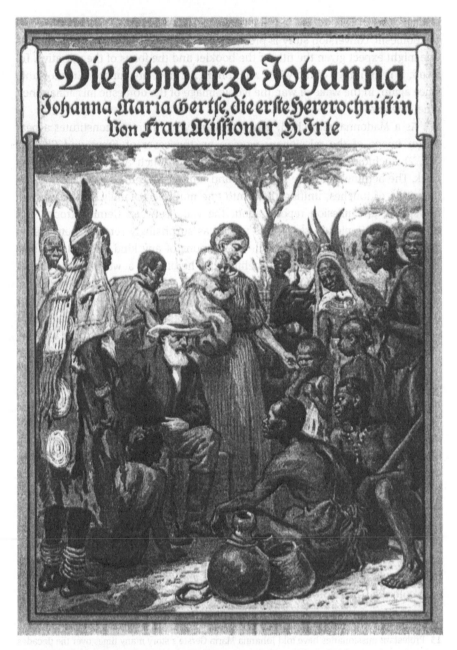

Figure 3: Cover of *Die schwarze Johanna* (Black Johanna) by Hedwig Irle (no year)

the colonies and destroying the shared domesticity of a multiracial mission family – he faded out of mission lore as a heroic symbol. In my surveys of both Catholic and Protestant mission literature, the German colonial soldier may appear in mission literature after the German-Herero War but nowhere does he rise to the status of a heroic ideal. The image of the domestic missionary woman at the center of a multiracial Christian family, however, persisted long after the possibilities of achieving such an ideal in the real world had been curtailed. The domestic white missionary woman existed in real life long before the war, but it was the context of war itself that casted her into the foreground of public discourse as an antiwar icon of mission heroism. Her image symbolized the hope that black and white could live peacefully together in the colonies (notably with white missionaries at the helm). The more racial conflict in the colonies, the greater the distress of war, the more she became the symbol of a longed-for peace.

Even as late as 1916, and in the midst of World War I, after the loss of Germany's colony in South-West Africa, and when Europe's enthusiasm for missionary work had started to wane, the multiracial Christian family reappeared as a full-page drawing in *Kreuz und Charitas* (fig. 4). The image has a very curious caption: "A colonist family's Christmas celebration in Africa." As an image of a colonist family, it is certainly not a typical one.[16] It strikes me as surprisingly egalitarian for its time. Whether this depicts a missionary family or not (we assume so given its presence in a mission magazine), the white couple does not take up the center of the picture. Instead the Christmas tree is central, a symbol for a family who puts Christian faith at the center. Beyond this, every member of the family is dressed in European clothing and every white member of the family is paired with a black member. The white father teaches a black child. The white daughter tries to get the attention of an older black "sister," who is preoccupied reading. A white baby is held up by a black "mother" so that she can see the tree. And finally, the white mother goes about her domestic duties and is paired in conversation with two black men. Though she is not in the center and her back is turned, this is clearly her domain; she orchestrates it, she presides, and her husband sits and attends to a child. Standing just outside, and thus somewhat excluded, are two African men attired in more traditional African clothing. These likely represent outsiders curious about this Christian family. In every way, this in an idealized image of the multiracial mission family.

---

16 The typical colonist family was more likely to look like Margarethe von Eckenbrecher's family photo taken about 1903 and reprinted in Helmut Bley's book on South-West Africa (1968, plate 17). In that photo, the white German family relaxes at the table and a black servant boy holding a tray of food stands apart like a prop in the exotic scenery. For Eckenbrecher's account of the beginning of the German-Herero War, see von Hammerstein in this volume.

Weihnachtsfeier einer Kolonistenfamilie in Afrika.

Figure 4: "A colonist family's Christmas celebration in Africa," *Kreuz und Charitas* 1916, 43

Conclusion

Perhaps it could be argued that the recurring image of the multiracial mission family (with the domestic white female missionary at the center) is more a construct of mission lore than a representation of reality on the ground at the beginning of the twentieth century. Certainly, in Hedwig Irle's case, we can assume she has given us an idealized picture of the missionary colonial life. But as a recurring representation of an ideal, the image of the multiracial mission family achieved symbolic status within the visual and narrative discourses surrounding women in the colonial mission. In the examples discussed here, this ideal emerged in the discursive context of the German-Herero War, where it functioned as both idealized antidote to violence and, alternatively, as the marker of all that could be lost. It constituted a reaction against the violence and exploitation of German imperialism even as it reconstituted German imperialism in a religious context as a benevolent but hierarchical Christian family. It also marks a feminization of mission rhetoric in which domestic femininity supplants the hyper-masculine militaristic discourse so popular in the period leading up to World War I.

Works Cited

Bertold, Hans. "Unsere schwarzen Landsleute in Deutsch-Südwest Afrika." *Deutsche Kolonial Zeitung*, vol. 29 (23 Mar. 1912), pp. 186–188.

Bley, Helmut. *South-West Africa und German Rule 1894–1914* (Leibniz Verlag, 1968).

Drechsler, Horst. *Südwestafrika unter deutscher Kolonialherrschaft: der Kampf der Herero und Nama gegen den deutschen Imperialismus (1884–1915)* (Akademie Verlag, 1966).

Gründer, Horst. *Christliche Mission und deutscher Imperialismus, 1884–1914* (Schöningh, 1982).

Haller-Dirr, Marita. "Das Unternehmen Mission sucht Investoren." *Helvetia Franciscana*, vol. 28, no. 2 (1999), pp. 133–164.

Hastings, Adrian. *The Church in Africa, 1450–1950* (Claredon Press, 1994).

Hexham, Irving. "Violating Missionary Culture: The Tyranny of Theory and the Ethics of Historical Research." *Mission und Gewalt: Der Umgang christlicher Missionen mit Gewalt und die Ausbreitung des Christentums in Afrika und Asien in der Zeit von 1792 bis 1918/19*, edited by Ulrich van der Heyden and Jürgen Becher (Franz Steiner, 2000), pp. 193–206.

Huber, Mary Taylor, and Nancy Lutkehaus, editors. *Gendered Missions: Women and Men in Missionary Discourse and Practice* (U of Michigan P, 2002).

Irle, Hedwig. *Die schwarze Johanna: Johanna Maria Gerste die erste Hererochristin* (Jugend- und Volksschriften-Verlag, no year).

Irle, Hedwig. *Unsere schwarzen Landsleute in Deutsch-Südwestafrika* (Bertelsmann, 1911).

Irle, Hedwig. *Wie ich die Herero lieben lernte* (Bertelsmann, 1909).

Klotz, Marcia. "Memoirs from a German Colony: What Do White Women Want?" *Eroticism and Containment: Notes from the Flood Plain*, edited by Carol Siegel and Ann M. Kibbey (New York UP, 1994), pp. 154–187.

Kreuz und Charitas im Kampfe gegen die Barbarei und Heidentum: Nachrichten vom Arbeitsfeld der katholischen Missionen. Missions-Gesellschaft Mariens (1906–1925).

Kreuz und Schwert im Kampfe gegen Sklaverei und Heidentum: Missions- und Unterhaltungsblatt für die Mitglieder des Afrika-Vereins Deutscher Katholiken (1893–1906).

Krüger, Gesine. *Kriegsbewältigung und Geschichtsbewußtsein: Realität, Deutung und Verarbeitung des deutschen Kolonialkriegs in Namibia; 1904 bis 1907* (Vandenhoeck & Ruprecht, 1999).

Loth, Heinrich. *Die christliche Mission in Südwestafrika: Zur destrukiven Rolle der Rheinischen Mission beim Prozess der Staatsbildung in Südwestafrika 1842–1893* (Akademie-Verlag, 1963).

Menzel, Gustav. *Die Rheinische Mission* (Verlag der Vereinigten Evangelische Mission, 1978).

Mielke, Vera. "Unterstützung und Bekämpfung von Gewalt durch Missionarinnen in China 1842 bis 1918." *Mission und Gewalt: Der Umgang christlicher Missionen mit Gewalt und die Ausbreitung des Christentums in Afrika und Asien in der Zeit von 1792 bis 1918/19*, edited by Ulrich van der Heyden and Jürgen Becher (Franz Steiner, 2000), pp. 397–411.

Oermann, Nils Ole. *Mission, Church and State Relations in South West Africa under German Rule (1884–1915)* (Franz Steiner, 1999).

Paczensky, Gert von. *Teuer Segen: Christlich Mission und Kolonialismus* (Albrecht Knaus, 1991).

Porter, Andrew. "'Commerce and Christianity': The Rise and Fall of a Nineteenth-Century Missionary Slogan." *The Historical Journal*, vol. 28, no. 3 (1985), pp. 597–621.

Ryland, Glen. "Stories and Mission Apologetics: The Rhenish Mission from Wars and Genocide to the Nazi Revolution, 1904–1936." *Symposia*, vol. 5 (2013), pp. 17–35.

van der Heyden, Ulrich, and Jürgen Becher, editors. *Mission und Gewalt: Der Umgang christlicher Missionen mit Gewalt und die Ausbreitung des Christentums in Afrika und Asien in der Zeit von 1792 bis 1918/19* (Franz Steiner, 2000).

Maureen O. Gallagher

Girls, Imperialism and War in Women's Writing from the German-Herero War and WWI

This essay addresses the gendered performance of female heroism in German novels for girls published between 1910 and 1916. Featuring young, unmarried female protagonists, these texts set during the colonial wars in German Southwest Africa (1904–1907) – conflicts that ultimately led to the deaths of over 60,000 Herero and Nama people in what is generally considered the first genocide of the twentieth century – place white German girls at the center of the action. The brave heroines are not only endangered by the colonial uprising but are sometimes even called upon to take up arms against the colonized African Other. In contrast, novels written a mere handful of years later and set during World War I present a decidedly more passive model of heroism, with white German girls doing their patriotic duty through traditionally feminine occupations like nursing, cooking, knitting, and child-rearing.[1] In this essay I will show how the colonial racial context of the conflict in German Southwest Africa (present-day Namibia) allowed for more fluid gender borders. With white women central to German colonial discourse as a means of ensuring the survival of white Germandom, young female characters in German colonial texts by women participate directly in the defense of their bodies and the colony. Absent this racial context, heroines in WWI novels are assigned more submissive roles.[2]

---

1 Jennifer Redmann makes similar observations regarding WWI novels for German girls in her essay in this volume, providing a transnational comparison, whereas my focus is on interrogating literary models from two separate German wars.

2 Of course, World War I had its own racial context, on both its colonial and European fronts, but this does not become a topic in the German media until after the war, when the French deployment of colonial soldiers in the Rhineland leads to sensationalized news coverage about crimes including the alleged mass rape of white women. This came to be known as the "Schwarze Schmach am Rhein" (Black horror on the Rhine). However, these concerns are not addressed in girls' literature at the time.

https://doi.org/10.1515/9783110572001-004

Wartime heroism in girls' colonial novels

In the decades leading up to both the German-Herero War and World War I, the literature that Wilhelmine girls read was strongly formulaic.[3] Germany's achievement of near-universal literacy by the 1890s and the improvement of print technology in the late nineteenth century ensured that there was a wealth of affordable and available literature written for and marketed directly to young people (Schenda 1976, 38). The publishing world became extremely specialized, with publishers focusing on particular gender and age groups in the works they produced, a phenomenon known as book market segmentation.[4] Having found their niche, publishers hewed to relatively narrow models and produced hundreds of almost interchangeable books. Books featuring adolescent female protagonists set in the contemporary world, the "Backfischbuch," as it was known, generally featured the coming-of-age story of a teenage protagonist who grows up, learns to tame her wild impulses and do her duty to her family, and eventually marries.[5] These novels show girls performing generally traditional roles as they transition from girlhood to womanhood and learn to conform to societal gender regimes, abandoning childish independence and tomboyishness in favor of feminine duty and domesticity in the interest not only of their families but also of the nation; in her 2013 study of Wilhelmine girls' literature, literary critic Jennifer Askey calls this "emotional nationalism."

The anomalous white German heroines of texts set during the colonial conflicts in German Southwest Africa are allowed to break the mold and take up arms against the Black[6] Herero in wartime because of the unique significance assigned to white women and the white female body during the colonial encounter. Using postcolonial theory, I offer a reading of five novels, three set during the

---

3 For more on reading material for girls in this period see Gisela Wilkending, "Mädchenliteratur" (Girls' literature, 2003).

4 For more on this phenomenon see Lynne Tatlock's edited volume, *Publishing Culture* (2010), in particular Jennifer Askey's and Jana Mikota's essays.

5 The term "Backfisch" refers to fish that were caught too young and are therefore only good for baking (*backen*). For more on the *Backfischbuch* as a genre for girls, see Gallagher, "*Kränzchen*" (2014).

6 Throughout this chapter I will capitalize the word "Black" when referring to people or characters who are part of the African diaspora. Though not universally approved by style manuals, this usage is widely in use as a marker that Black is more than a color and to give it parity with the stylistic treatment of national, ethnic, and tribal groups, as journalism professor Lori Tharps has argued in a *New York Times* editorial. She quotes W.E.B. Du Bois from a 1929 letter to the editor of *Encyclopaedia Britannica* calling "the use of a small letter for the name of twelve million Americans and two hundred million human beings a personal insult" (2014).

German-Herero War and two during WWI, to show how these divergent models of female heroism relate to the symbolic role of women in the German colonial enterprise, a racialized symbolism lacking from the Great War context. The novels under consideration are Valerie Hodann's *Auf rauhen Pfaden: Schicksale einer deutschen Farmerstochter in Deutsch-Südwest-Afrika* (On rough paths: The fortunes of a German farmer's daughter in German Southwest Africa, 1910), Elisa Bake's *Schwere Zeiten: Schicksale eines deutschen Mädchens in Südwestafrika* (Difficult times: Fortunes of a German girl in Southwest Africa, 1913), Henny Koch's *Die Vollrads in Südwest: Eine Erzählung für junge Mädchen* (The Vollrad family in Southwest: A story for girls, 1913–1914),[7] Else Ury's *Nesthäkchen und der Weltkrieg* (Nesthäkchen and the World War, 1916), and Marie von Felseneck's *Trotzkopfs Erlebnisse im Weltkrieg* (Trotzkopf's experiences during the World War, 1916). The texts from Hodann, Bake, and Koch are three of approximately half a dozen novels featuring young female protagonists set in colonial Namibia, and they are the only ones to feature the German-Herero War prominently. The relative lack of colonial novels for girls forms an illustrative counterpoint to the dozens of war novels for girls that appeared in the opening years of World War I (Wilkending 2003, 259). The Great War texts from Felseneck and Ury are two typical examples of the genre, particularly interesting because they feature beloved protagonists from series books and were widely read.

My approach is informed by Ann Laura Stoler and Frederick Cooper's injunction to examine metropole and colony as a single sphere of influence (1997, vii–viii). The colonies were not merely controlled and exploited by the metropole but instead exerted their own reciprocal influence. Here I take up the significant role the colonies play in the metropolitan imaginary and how fiction about unmarried women and their participation in the wars against the Herero and Nama peoples reflects the complicated matrix of sex, gender, and race relations during

---

7 Koch's novel was first published in the illustrated girls' magazine *Das Kränzchen* between 1913 and 1914 and appeared as a stand-alone volume with Union Deutsche Verlagsgesellschaft in 1916. During her career Henny Koch (1854–1925) wrote thirty novels, primarily targeting a young female audience, including *Die Traut* (Traut, 1905), *Irrwisch* (Imp, 1907), and *Ein tapferes Mädchen* (A brave girl, 1914). Her books were often serialized in the bourgeois illustrated girls' magazine *Das Kränzchen*, and many of them also feature young women who live or travel abroad. Koch also worked as a translator of American literature, publishing the first German translation of *Huckleberry Finn* in 1890. Little biographical information has yet been unearthed about Elisa Bake (1851–1928). She lived in Hamburg and was active as an author and translator from the 1890s to the 1920s, with her high point of activity between 1911 and 1913. I have found no biographical information about Valerie Hodann (1866–1939), other than a handful of additional literary titles and that she was the life-partner of little-known dramatist Theodor Walther (1861–1927).

the time of German colonialism. I draw on critical race theorist Kimberlé Crenshaw's concept of intersectionality for understanding how social and cultural categories like race and gender interact. To fully understand different models of wartime female heroism it is necessary to examine the way that race, gender, and national identity work together and change in significance in relation to each other at particular historical moments.

The case of Germany and German colonialism reflects what scholars of other colonial traditions have noted about the symbolic role that white European women – and a particular model of traditional female identity – play in the understanding and propagation of colonialism. For example, Anne McClintock, a scholar of English and Gender Studies, has argued that the cult of domesticity and "gender dynamics were, from the outset, fundamental to the securing and maintenance of the imperial enterprise" (1995, 7). At the same time this domesticity is part of the regulation of sexual morality to ensure racial purity; as anthropologist Ann Laura Stoler puts it: "Who bedded and wedded whom in the colonies [...] was never left to chance" (2002, 47). The ellipsis I have placed in Stoler's quote covers the absence of Germany from her list of colonial empires – France, England, Holland, and Iberia; significant feminist and historical research, however, has shown the applicability of Stoler's comment to the German imperial enterprise. Social scientists Katharina Walgenbach, Anette Dietrich, Robbie Aitken, and Lora Wildenthal have all shown how gender and sexual identities were policed and contested in the German colonies and colonial discourse in this period.

German efforts to regulate this "bedding and wedding" relied on the presence of white women in the colonies. They were seen as the bearers of Germanness and the only means to propagate white families in colonial spaces; as Wildenthal notes, "women's ability to sustain racial purity was the basis for their political participation in colonialism" (2001, 6). German colonial organizations sent single women to the colonies to marry white German male settlers to prevent interracial relationships and the creation of biracial children. Men who "went native" (German: *verkaffern*) showed, according to Walgenbach, how "porous and vulnerable" the boundary between Black and white could be, and "here gender discourses gained a particular relevance, for the stabilization of this precarious border was delegated to German women, the so-called 'culture bearers'" (2004, 174).[8] In this schema German women served as symbolic border

---

8 "Hier erhalten Geschlechterdiskurse eine besondere Relevanz, denn die Stabilisierung der prekären Grenzen wird an deutsche Frauen als so genannte 'Kulturträgerinnen' delegiert." All translations are my own.

guards of the German nation; this coincides with the observation by Wildenthal that racial segregation and racial hierarchies became more pronounced as women settled in the colonies in greater numbers (2001, 33).[9]

Colonial novels for young female readers feature young women protagonists in German Southwest Africa who represent the last stand in the defense of the German colonial order, and these figures are then used as a justification for genocidal violence against the Herero and Nama peoples. Drawing on historian Helmut Bley and his understanding of the importance of violence in maintaining German rule in Africa, German Studies scholar David Kenosian observes, "The story of German colonialism in Southwest Africa must be understood within the context of the history of violence as a political praxis" (1997, 182). According to legal scholar Harald Sippel, those who wrote the laws governing the German colonies "apparently presupposed during the composition of the colonial laws the fiction of the complete separation of the colonizers and the non-white colonized" (1995, 134).[10] Under this legal framework it was necessary to enforce strict divisions between "Eingeborene" (natives) and "Nichteingeborene" (non-natives), even though these divisions were, as Albert Gouaffo, a Germanist trained at the University of Dschang in West Cameroon, explains, only a fiction: "Geographically and hierarchically separate ways of living between colonizers and colonized could only be partially realized" (2008, 28).[11] Robbie Aitken's *Exclusion and Inclusion* (2007) meticulously documents the competing national, racial, class, and legal discourses at play in efforts to ban or eliminate mixed race marriages in German Southwest Africa. This fiction of colonizers and colonized starkly divided along racial lines was enforced by violent means if necessary and is the reason the white heroines in the novels by Koch, Bake and Hodann risk their lives during the military colonial conflicts in German Southwest Africa in defense of the colonial racial order.

German colonial novels for girls feature active protagonists who transgress boundaries and are placed at the front lines of the German colonial wars against the Nama and Herero. Relatively few examples of young adult literature set in German Southwest Africa were written for girls or with girl protagonists, making

---

9 For autobiographical accounts of the beginnings of the German-Herero Colonial War by female German settlers, see Katharina von Hammerstein in this volume. For the perspective on racial relations in German Southwest Africa through the lens of a female German missionary, see Cindy Brewer in this volume.

10 "war bei der Ausarbeitung des Schutzgebietsgesetzes offenbar von der Fiktion der völligen Separation zwischen den Kolonisierenden und den farbigen Kolonisierten ausgegangen."

11 "Die geographisch und hierarchisch getrennte Lebensweise zwischen Kolonisierenden und Kolonisierten konnte nur begrenzt realisiert werden."

these texts particularly significant for understanding the relationships between race and gender in the German colonial imaginary.[12] The German colonies as portrayed in these novels seemingly give young women *Spielraum* or latitude to behave in ways that would not be appropriate in the metropole. The repertoire of femininity is expanded to allow for heroines who wear men's clothing, ride horses, and carry weapons all while still maintaining their femininity. Erika, the protagonist of Hodann's *Auf rauhen Pfaden*, wears masculine clothing (corduroy trousers made "from the same practical material that the members of the *Schutztruppe* wore") and accompanies her brothers around the farm on horseback (1910, 53).[13] Ernestine from *Schwere Zeiten* is similarly described using masculine language; early in the story her uncle refers to her as "the brave little lad" (Bake 1913, 61).[14] Koch's Hanna Vollrad is often called by the masculine name Hänsel by her father, who jokes to the missionary and fellow settlers that he has four sons, rather than three sons and a daughter. However, in spite of their rough and tumble behavior and appearance, traditionally viewed as masculine or tomboyish, all three heroines are presented as dutiful daughters who play an important role in ensuring their family's fortune and survival in colonial Africa. The colonial setting allows for a wider, less marked range of acceptable feminine behavior.

Under the logic of German colonial thought, white women like Erika, Ernestine, and Hanna serve a de facto role of ensuring the survival of white Germanness, a fact that is particularly clear when the heroines are threatened during scenes of racialized and sexualized violence. When the rebellion of the Herero against German colonial rule begins, Hodann's Erika is left alone and helpless on her family's farm and is threatened with violence by family servant Kornelius. The racialized component of the scene is clear, with Erika appealing in vain to her white privilege as a defense against the attack of a Black man: "Have you forgotten how you are supposed to treat the daughter of the white chief?" (Ho-

---

12 Other novels for girls that feature young female protagonists in the colonies include Käthe van Beeker's *Heddas Lehrzeit in Süd-West* (Hedda's apprenticeship in Southwest, 1909) and, to a lesser extent, Agnes Sapper's *Werden und Wachsen* (Becoming and growing, 1910), which features a female character who moves to Southwest Africa as a newlywed with her colonist husband; she is not, however, the main or only protagonist of the story. I discuss these works together with Hodann's, Bake's, and Koch's works in my article "Fragile Whiteness" (2016) for how they construct images of fragile white femininity in colonial spaces.
13 The full description of Erika's masculine appearance reads: "Sie ritt nach Herrenart, hatte Kordhosen an von demselben praktischen Stoff, wie ihn die Schutztruppler trugen, einen breitrempigen Hut auf dem welligen Haar, der dem frischen Gesichtchen entzückend stand, braune, feste Stiefelchen, und über der weißen Batikbluse eine dicke, weiße Wolljacke."
14 "der tapfere, kleine Kerl."

dann 1910, 122).[15] As he tries to seize Erika, Kornelius also explicitly references her whiteness, calling her a "proud white girl" (127).[16] The novel does not overtly state that Kornelius intends to sexually assault Erika, but it can be inferred based both on Erika's response – an avowed intention to commit suicide rather than "fall living into the hands of these devils" – and the description of the scene (119).[17] The image of Kornelius's dark hand menacingly reaching for Erika's white robe, a symbol of her racial and virginal purity, while shouting "Now you are mine!" presents Black male sexuality as threatening to white women (127).[18]

Heroine Ernestine from *Schwere Zeiten* is placed in a similar scene of racialized and sexualized violence. Having heard news of the outbreak of fighting that would later lead to full-scale war, Ernestine's male relatives depart to bring in the livestock, leaving Ernestine, her mother, and sister without male protection. It thus falls to Ernestine to defend them against an attack. Having urged her mother and sister to flee and arming herself with a shotgun, Ernestine, confronted with the Herero described as having "hideous faces with bulging lips, predator teeth, and malicious expression," shoots, ultimately killing one of them (Bake 1913, 98).[19] The exaggerated racial stereotypes dehumanize the men standing before Ernestine and serve as a justification for her use of violence.

Koch's Hanna, on the other hand, is not endangered in quite the same way as the other heroines. However, she, too, takes up arms against the Herero when threatened, an act that is coded as both brave and masculine. When her father and brother leave her alone in the house, she is scared, but takes heart when her father entreats her to not act like a girl but instead "show that you have marrow in your bones and the blood of the Vollrads in your veins" (Koch 1916, 157).[20] When a German soldier comes to the door of her father's house bearing news of the outbreak of the Herero uprising, Hanna knows it falls on her to carry the message to her father and brothers and resolves to show that "Vollrad girls

---

15 "Wißt Ihr nicht mehr, wie Ihr der Tochter des weißen Häuptlings zu begegnen habt?"
16 "stolzes, weißes Mädchen."
17 "lebend würde sie nicht in die Hände dieser Teufel fallen." See the almost identical statement in Margarethe von Eckenbrecher's autobiography about surviving the beginning of the German-Herero Colonial War (114, 134) and von Hammerstein's analysis of this account in this volume.
18 "Jetzt bist Du mein!"
19 "die scheußlichen Gesichter mit den wulstigen Lippen, den Raubtierzuahnen und den tückischen Ausdruck."
20 "Nur jetzt kein Frauenzimmergetu! Zeig, dass du Mark in den Knochen und Vollradsblut in den Adern hast."

fear as little as Vollrad boys do" (161).[21] As she prepares to leave, Herero men come to the door; Hanna takes her father's rifle and shoots through a crack in the door. The effort of shooting at the men – who are characterized as making a noise like the "howling of wild animals" in response – all but saps Hanna's resolve and she sinks to the ground in resignation, until she realizes the men have fled. When she alerts her father to the danger of the coming war, he praises her efforts by saying, "such a brave Hänsel. You really are half boy!" (165).[22]

The protagonists Ernestine, Erika, and Hanna offer Wilhelmine adolescent female readers models of active wartime heroism; they participate directly in the major conflict of the day and behave in ways that are coded not only noble, selfless, and self-sacrificing but also brave. These three heroines show the fluidity of gender norms, able to be simultaneously masculine and feminine. The descriptions of Ernestine's and Hanna's attackers as animals and grotesquely sketched predators and the repeated invocations of Erika's whiteness remind the reader of the racial and colonial motivations behind their acts of heroism. The female bodies serve as the symbolic boundary of race and nation, so that white girls and women must be willing and able to protect themselves at all costs.[23] Both of these scenes mark the climax of their respective texts. Ernestine's armed defense of her father's homestead forms the frontispiece of the novel in a striking color illustration (see figure 1). After being rescued from her attackers, Erika returns to Germany, the "African tomboy" transformed into a "well-mannered young woman" (Hodann 1910, 174).[24] She later returns to Southwest Africa as the bride of a German soldier, seemingly understanding her place in the colonial hierarchy and prepared to propagate white Germanness in Africa.

These three novels vividly illustrate the way that women and their presence in the colonies were used to justify genocidal violence. The scenes in which Erika, Ernestine, and Hanna fight off the Herero precede frank discussions of the necessity of ridding Southwest Africa of its indigenous inhabitants using social Darwinist language. Early in Hodann's text Erika questions the necessity of

---

21 "Vollradsmädel fürcht' sich nit, so wenig wie die Vollradsbuben."

22 "So 'n tapferer Hänsel! Bist doch ein halber Bub!"

23 Both of these scenes also call to mind Hans Grimm's story "Wie Grete aufhörte ein Kind zu sein" (How Grete stopped being a child) from his 1913 *Südafrikanische Novellen* (South African novellas), a subject I treat more fully in the dissertation chapter from which this paper is drawn, as well as my article "Fragile Whiteness." See also Sara Lennox's essay on this topic (2005).

24 The full quote reads, "Es überraschte sie angenehm, daß aus dem afrikanischen Wildfang, als den sie Erika von ihrem letzten Besuch her in Erinnerung hatte, und der in ihrem stillen Heim das unterste zu oberste gekehrt hatte, eine gesittete junge Dame geworden war."

Figure 1: The frontispiece of Elisa Bake's *Schwere Zeiten* (1913) depicts a scene where heroine Ernestine shoots a Herero man who is pursuing her.

colonial violence, refusing to participate when her family decides to hunt down the natives who have been rustling cattle, insisting, "I would never shoot at a man unless driven to by the direst of emergencies!" (1910, 74).[25] Erika's refusal to bear arms against the Herero is constructed as almost leading to her undoing, as she is nearly driven to suicide to preserve her sexual and racial purity. The danger that Erika was subjected to is then used as a justification for taking the lives of the Herero and Nama people to purge the land for the German settlers: the text ends by declaring "the lesser race had to perish" in order for the territory to become truly German (221).[26] Bake's *Schwere Zeiten* is similarly cavalier about the deaths of the Herero and Nama people: "Forced into the desert, sweltering and thirsting, the Hereros perished! A people 60,000 strong was, for the most part, wiped out – not through the sword so much as through the elements of this powerful land, into which civilization shall be brought by German pioneers" (1913, 116).[27] Nature rather than the Germans is blamed for the deaths of tens of thousands. When Hanna's father returns from the war he describes the campaign to his daughter, dwelling on the "thousands upon thousands" of Herero men, women and children driven into the desert to perish (Koch 1916, 246). In a quavering voice she asks, "Did we have the right to do that?" to which he provides the social Darwinian justification that the Germans had the "right of the fittest and more hard-working" (Koch 1916, 246).[28]

These scenes draw on a common pool of portrayals of violence in colonies after the Herero uprising and subsequent violent conflicts between German colonial troops and the native populations of Namibia.[29] Violence against women was a minor but recurring theme in these depictions, such as in Helene von Fal-

---

25 "Ich würde nie auf einen Menschen schießen, wenn mich nicht die äußerste Not dazu zwänge!"
26 The longer quote reads, "Einer nur kann herrschen. Neben den reichen Land- und Viehbesitzern war kein Raum für die deutsche Entwickelung; so musste die geringere Rasse untergehen. Erst durch diesen blutigen Krieg ist die Kolonie deutsches Land geworden."
27 "In die Wüste gedrängt, verschmachtend und verdurstend, kamen die Hereros um! Ein Volk von 60000 Köpfen wurde, zum größten Teile, vernichtet – nicht sowohl durch das Schwert, als durch die Naturgewalten des mächtigen Landes, in das die Zivilisation durch deutsche Pioniere gebracht werden sollte." For authentic voices of female Herero survivors about their flight into the Omaheke desert, see von Hammerstein in this volume.
28 "Hatten wir dazu ein Recht?"; "das Recht des Tüchtigeren und Fleißigeren." There follows a long speech of colonialist discourse about the need for German expansion abroad to spread culture and "Sitte."
29 On the representation of the Herero uprising and subsequent wars in Southwest Africa, see the chapter on "Feldzugberichte" in Sibylle Benninghoff-Lühl (1983); on pages 107–111 she discusses firsthand accounts of the colonial wars.

kenhausen's 1905 *Ansiedlerschicksale: Elf Jahre in Deutsch-Südwestafrika 1893 – 1904* (Fate of settlers: Eleven years in German Southwest Africa). In this memoir Falkenhausen describes a life-threatening attack she faced following her husband's death in the conflict.[30]

When we compare the illustrations (figures 1 and 2) of the attacks on the historical Helene von Falkenhausen and the fictional Ernestine, we see the latter constructed as a much more active heroine. The images of the two female figures bear a superficial resemblance to one another; both are petite, clad in white dresses that accentuate their white skin color and their thin and shapely figures, with short or upswept dark brown hair. The second illustration has as its focal point the helpless figure of Falkenhausen, the moment before she is attacked; in the first illustration it is the Herero men who are the victims, with one contorted in pain as Ernestine's shot strikes him. While the second illustration shows the terrified face of Falkenhausen, the first features Ernestine at an oblique angle; the visual center of the image is instead the pistol she fires. In both cases, the oblique angle enhances the impression of the colonial order off balance due to the revolt of the Herero. That the only color image in the book (the frontispiece) depicts Ernestine in the act of saving the colony through her bravery and action shows the centrality of this scene not only to the action of the plot but in illustrating the importance of German women and the defense of their sexual and racial purity to German colonialism.

The paratextual elements of the source volume for this illustration of Falkenhausen's attack demonstrate how gender is used as a justification for the racial violence in Germany's war against the Herero and Nama. Falkenhausen's memoir is unillustrated; the illustration above was created for the 1908 collection of soldier and officer memoirs from the wars in Southwest Africa, *Deutsche Reiter in Südwest* (German cavalry troopers in Southwest), compiled by Friedrich von Dincklage-Campe. That the editor of *Deutsche Reiter in Südwest* felt the need to commission this illustration and place it at the very beginning of the publication speaks to the symbolic importance of white German women and threats of violence against them to the volume. Though the book consists of almost five hundred pages of war memories by men, female colonists provide the discursive frame for the volume. Attached to the foreword is the illustration depicting Falkenhausen's attack, and the final two pieces in the collection are by or about women. The first is a short piece by Falkenhausen written after her attack as she recuperates and makes the decision to take shelter in a military base to en-

---

30 Falkenhausen discusses the attack in chapter fifty-one of her memoirs (209 – 215). For an analysis of Helene von Falkenhausen's war account, see von Hammerstein in this volume.

Figure 2: This illustration from *Deutsche Reiter in Südwest* (1908) depicts a scene from Helene von Falkenhausen's 1905 memoir where she describes being assaulted by Herero natives.

sure her and her children's safety, and the second is a piece about German nurses written by a male military officer. The book ends with a tribute to the nurses who "always did their duty gladly and joyfully": "Hats off to the women who shared the joy and suffering of war with us as loyal companions!" (Dincklage-Campe 1908, 480).[31] Though Falkenhausen was over thirty years of age and pregnant with her third child at the time of her attack, the trim, fashionably-dressed woman in white in the illustration could pass for a teenager. Her arms held above her in a protective gesture, she has sunk to her knees with a terrified look on her face, helpless in front of the armed men towering over her. The book thus begins with an image of white German womanhood threatened by the violence of Black African men, offering a justification for the military conflict, which fills the next 450 pages of the book. The final two pieces of writing then offer further reassurance of the justness and necessity of German military action by portraying women who are safe and protected and filling their proper role by nurturing and caring for white men in the colonies.

Hodann's, Bake's, and Koch's novels, as well as the volume *Deutsche Reiter in Südwest,* provide evidence for the trenchant observation of Margaret Higonnet et al. that "war must be understood as a *gendering* activity, one that ritually marks the gender of all members of a society, whether or not they are combatants" (1987, 4). The portrayal of Falkenhausen as victim and the flowery description of a German nurse contrast with girl heroines Erika and Ernestine and point toward the representation of women in war that later dominates Great War writing for girls.

Heroines in girls' literature from World War I

The contrast between the colonial heroines and those of WWI texts written only a few years later can be attributed then to what might be called the post-colonial – in the temporal sense – context of the Great War itself. Germany's former colonial possessions were officially redistributed among the Entente powers under the terms of the Treaty of Versailles (1919), but Germany lost its colonies relatively early in the conflict, most of them occupied by Japanese, British or French forces already in 1914–1915, the only exception being German East Africa, where General Paul von Lettow-Vorbeck and his Askari (primarily Sudanese) sol-

---

31 "Dies ist eine von den vielen Schwestern, die stets gern und freudig ihre Pflicht erfüllt haben zu unseren Besten. [...] Hut ab vor den Frauen, welche als treue Kameradinnen mit uns des Krieges Leid und Freude geteilt haben!"

diers fought until the bitter end of the conflict in 1918.[32] Contemporary media show a shift in national attention away from Germany's colonial possessions; for example teachers' manuals and curricular guides drastically downplay Germany's role as an imperial power to present Germany instead as the victim of European imperialism, the target of envy on the part of empires like France and England.[33] Under these circumstances, the symbolic importance of women in colonialism recedes, and WWI literature for young female readers reconfigures gender and notions of heroism. In short, compared to the colonial tomboys, these narratives lack strong, active female heroes who join in the fight.

World War I saw the mass mobilization of young people for war.[34] Parents, teachers, clergy, and officials sought to engage young people in the war effort and awaken them to their patriotic duty through school curriculum, books, and other media. Certainly this was a gendered and gendering endeavor. In a collection of German children's school writings and drawings about the war, *Das Kind und der Krieg* (The child and the war, 1916), we find the words of a boy who has been instructed to write sentences that feature opposites (such as "Fire is hot – water is cold"). Drawing on the omnipresent war, the anonymous boy formulates a sentence that succinctly illustrates gendered German mobilization efforts: "Boys are brave, girls are docile" (Schach 1916, 45).[35] During World War I, German boys and girls thus received different messages about war mobilization and their patriotic duty that relied on a bifurcated understanding of gender identity.[36] Stories aimed at boys (which, of course, were also read by girls) generally showcased battlefield heroism or disobedience, such as boys running away to enlist without parental consent.[37] As the anonymous boy's remark in *Das Kind und der Krieg* shows, men and women, boys and girls, were seen as opposites, both able to serve the nation but in different ways based on their supposed natures and abilities, boys with their bravery and girls with their docility.

---

32 Michelle R. Moyd has written a history of the Askari, their complicated motivations for fighting with the German army, and their daily life under German colonial rule (2014).

33 Germany's self-presentation as a victim of European imperialism during World War I is discussed more fully in "'A World of Enemies': Gender, War Mobilization, and Colonialism in German Young Adult Literature from WWI," chapter six of Gallagher (2015, 206–238).

34 Andrew Donson (2010) and Jeffrey Verhey (2000) address the question of mass mobilization of German adults and German youth for the war in their respective publications.

35 "Jungens sind tapfer, Mädchen sind zahm."

36 For more on how gender was understood in Wilhelmine Germany, in particular within the bourgeois women's movement, see Catharine Dollard, "Marital Status" (2006) and Nancy Reagin (1995).

37 Donson (2004) has written about the character of most boys' literature from the war years.

A similar contrast exists between the brave heroines and the docile heroines depicted in colonial and Great War literature respectively. Anglo-American girls' fiction from this period shows girls actively participating in the war, traveling to the front and coming into contact with Europe's battlefields, yet their German counterparts remain bound to the home front.[38] German literature for girls written and published during World War I portrays the war as a totalizing force that touches every aspect of life and culture, but these novels eschew the portrayals of girls who undertake brave and daring adventures that are found in English-language fiction (Redmann 2011, 11). Instead German girls' novels portray girls as vital to the war effort through their embrace of traditional gender roles, by rolling bandages, baking cookies, or knitting socks for the troops. Through their performance of this traditional femininity, girls become symbols of national renewal.

The titles of German girls' WWI literature reflect contemporary understandings of the importance of the war and girls' role in it: *Deutsche Mädel in großer Zeit* (German girls in great times, Else Hofmann, 1916), *Im heiligen Kampf* (In the holy battle, Sophie Kloerß, 1915), *Daheim in großer Zeit* (At home in great times, Emily Albert, 1915). These texts portray girls rising to the occasion of times that were constructed as great and becoming dutiful, responsible young women once the war breaks out. Tosia Eschenhorst from Marga Rayle's *Majors Einzige im Kriegsjahr* (The major's only daughter during the war, 1915) goes from looking forward to her summer holidays and gossiping with her school friends to devoting long days to war work, including child care, knitting socks, and cooking. Isolde from *Die unsere Hoffnung sind* (Those who are our hope, Helene Christaller, 1916) is initially flighty and unfocused, having finished school without the requisite grades to become a teacher. During the war, however, she focuses on supporting her family, adopts a war baby, and finally becomes engaged to a soldier. Ruth from *Morgenrot* (Dawn, Bertha Clement, 1916), the youngest and very artistic daughter of her family, must exert herself in new ways and take over her older sister's duties in caring for her mother and the household. Examples of such literary texts are numerous, with several dozen produced during each year of the war, but here I will focus on two typical examples of girls who grow up in wartime, addressing what happens when the heroines of two of the most popular girls' series from Wilhelmine Germany go to war.

---

38 Jennifer Redmann addresses this contrast in a comparative essay (2011).

In her novel *Nesthäkchen und der Weltkrieg* (1916), by far the most popular of the ten *Nesthäkchen* books when it was published, Else Ury[39] portrays the ways in which children were mobilized for the Great War. The text, the fourth in what would become a ten-volume series, centers on Annemarie Braun, the youngest of three children of a Berlin doctor. Ury shows how all three Braun children imbibe patriotic sentiment in school that they in turn pass on to their elders. The Braun children are zealous in their duty, teaching their grandmother how to behave, encouraging her not to hoard food, to obey the bread ration cards, and to turn in copper kettles to be used in munitions manufacturing. It takes the efforts of all three children to convince their grandmother to exchange her gold for paper money, explaining to her the necessity of sacrificing for the fatherland. Grandmother eventually relents and accedes to the children's requests: "She never would have thought she would ever give up her hoarded gold. But the intelligent, patriotic woman had realized that it was necessary to put the welfare of the people ahead of the welfare of the individual. 'Yes, yes, the world is all turned around, and now the old learn from the young,' she said [...]" (Ury 1916, 135 – 136).[40] With their patriotic spirit awakened by their teachers and what they read and experienced of the war, Annemarie and her brothers are able to influence their elders and help further the war effort. In this way Ury herself participated in youth mobilization, providing girl readers of Wilhelmine Germany with a patriotic heroine to emulate.[41]

---

39 Else Ury (1877–1943) was one of Wilhelmine and Weimar Germany's most famous authors of children's and young adult literature. She began her publishing career in 1906 and continued until she was ejected from the Reichsschrifttumskammer (Reich Literature Chamber) in 1935 because of her Jewish origins. She published almost forty books during her career and was particularly well-known for her *Professors-Zwillinge* (The professor's twins) and *Nesthäkchen* series, the latter of which was made into a German TV miniseries in the 1980s. Her writing earned her substantial amounts of money, enough to allow her to purchase a vacation home in Krummhübel she christened Villa Nesthäkchen. She resisted pressure from her brothers to emigrate to England after the Nazis came to power, and she remained in Germany to care for her ailing mother. She was deported and died in Auschwitz in 1943.

40 "Nie hätte sie gedacht, dass sie das gehütete Gold aus freien Stücken abliefern würde. Aber die kluge und vaterlandsliebende Frau hatte inzwischen erkannt, dass es notwendig war, das Wohl des einzelnen dem wohl der Gesamtheit hintenan zu setzen. 'Ja, ja, die Welt ist jetzt umgekehrt, die Alten lernen von den Jungen,' sagte sie."

41 Even though *Nesthäkchen und der Weltkrieg* was initially so popular, it was out of print for sixty years after World War II. Because of its nationalistic content, the Allies placed it on a list of forbidden books in 1945 and it was only reprinted in the spring of 2014. It was also the first *Nesthäkchen* book to have been translated into English: *Nesthäkchen and the World War*, trans. Steven Lehrer (2006). Lehrer has since published translations of the third novel in the series, *Nesthäkchen in the Children's Sanitarium* (*Nesthäkchen im Kinderheim*). In "Rilla and Anne-

Even though thirty years had elapsed since the original publication of Emmy von Rhoden's *Der Trotzkopf*, Marie von Felseneck drew on the enormously popular girls' novel for her unauthorized sequel, 1916's *Trotzkopfs Erlebnisse im Weltkrieg*.[42] In her 1885 text, Rhoden chronicled the teenage years of a defiant young woman, Ilse Macket. Rhoden's novel is a typical *Backfisch* story and remains one of the most well known German girls' novels, continuously in print since its release. Felseneck picks up where Rhoden left off, with defiant Ilse reformed after a stint in a boarding school and engaged to Leo Gontrau. Their plans to wait a year to announce their engagement, while Leo serves in the foreign service and Ilse moves to Munich with her aunt and uncle to study painting, are abruptly disrupted by the outbreak of WWI.

Although Rhoden's novel already showed Ilse's transformation into a calm, dutiful, marriageable young woman, Felseneck rewrites the character so that the war completes the process of maturity that began for Ilse in *Der Trotzkopf*. The protagonist puts aside her disappointment at the need to delay her marriage when Leo enlists and chooses to selflessly engage in war work with her aunt Lotte instead of continuing her artistic studies. She tirelessly engages in traditional female occupations during the war, volunteering at the village school, nursing the sick and injured, and sewing and knitting for the troops. At the end of *Trotzkopfs Erlebnisse im Weltkrieg* she tells her mother and Leo: "I have learned to appreciate, perhaps with more difficulty than other girls, that it is only work, honest work, that gives life value" (Felseneck 1916, 245).[43] She has lost her childish selfishness and learned to be orderly, calm, self-controlled, patient, and dutiful. There are clear similarities between Felseneck's Trotzkopf, and Rhoden's Nesthäkchen as the war transforms her, too, from a tomboy into a proper young lady. At the beginning of *Nesthäkchen und der Weltkrieg*, the protagonist loathes knitting, but she perseveres and soon begins joyfully churning out socks and other knitted goods to aid in the war effort. She furthermore takes in a "war baby," an orphan from East Prussia, and raises it until foster parents can be found. In a sense, the war domesticates both protagonists, as Trotzkopf

marie," an essay comparing Ury's Nesthäkchen character to Lucy Maud Montgomery's Rilla Blythe, I argue that Ury's work is more complicated than it appears at first glance and actually contains elements that both support and undermine contemporary nationalist discourses.

42 Marie von Felseneck, pseudonym of Marie Luise Mancke (1847–1926), was a prolific author of young adult literature, writing dozens of books for girls between 1890 and her death. Popular titles include *Durchgerungen* (Fortitude, 1890), *Königin Luise* (Queen Luise, 1897), *Drei Freundinnen* (Three friends, 1903), and *Landwehrmanns Einzige* (Landwehrmanns' only daughter, 1915).

43 "...das habe ich einsehen gelernt, vielleicht schwerer als andere Haustöchter, dass nur Arbeit, ehrliche Arbeit das Leben uns wert machen."

and Nesthäkchen abandon their wild tomboy ways to engage in feminine tasks like handiwork and nurturing. While initially reluctant, both heroines in the end whole-heartedly embrace these small acts of self-sacrifice as they learn to subsume their own desires for the greater good of the national war effort.

Felseneck glorifies female sacrifice in her novel and emphasizes women's symbolic role as an inspiration to men on the battlefield over any more tangible contributions to the war effort. During a typhus outbreak Ilse volunteers to care for the sick children, sacrificing her own beloved Christmas celebrations at home and putting her health in jeopardy. She conceives of this as her patriotic duty and minimizes the importance of her actions: "If I were a man, I would be out there in the trenches, but since I am only a woman, it is my duty here at home to act like my brothers out there in the field and not value my own life too highly [...]" (Felseneck 1916, 147).[44] Felseneck only briefly acknowledges the material contributions of women to the war effort in the role of nurturers and nurses; instead she more strongly highlights the symbolic importance of women to German nationalism and the war effort. Ilse's uncle Kurt says to Lotte: "My dear wife [...] if all German women think like you and Ilse, then in this sign we must conquer" (108).[45] This phrase, a translation of the Latin *In hoc signo vinces*, with its connection to early Christianity and the Roman emperor Constantine I, emphasizes the symbolic role of the German woman as a standard-bearer in WWI. Lotte and Ilse become symbols in the eyes of Kurt and Leo, the inspiration and motivation for fighting the war, a role that trumps any contribution women can make to the war effort with their physical labor.

Felseneck's text, like other works of this period, constructs women and girls who are vital to the war effort through their acceptance of traditional gender roles and behaviors. Historical women undertook enormous amounts of paid and unpaid labor during World War I, filling the positions vacated by able-bodied men to ensure the smooth running of the national war machine and the homefront economy.[46] By contrast, literary texts overwhelmingly portray women and girls contributing to the war effort through traditionally female virtues such as duty, patience and sacrifice, and through traditionally female handcrafts like knitting. In a collection of essays published in 1916 by a school inspec-

---

44 "Wäre ich ein Mann, so läge ich draußen in Schützengraben, da ich aber nur ein Weib bin, so ist es meine Pflicht, hier in der Heimat es meinen Brüdern draußen im Felde gleich zu tun und mein eigenes Leben nicht zu hoch einzuschätzen [...]"
45 "Mein geliebtes Weib [...] wenn alle deutschen Frauen denken wie du und Ilse, dann müssen wir in diesem Zeichen siegen."
46 For more on gender and labor history from World War I see the works of Ute Daniel (1997), Young-Sun Hong (1992), and John Horne (2000).

tor named J. Radtke, one young girl writes on the topic "How we girls serve the fatherland"[47]:

> We live now in a very earnest time. A world of enemies has arisen against us. Thousands of men and boys have rushed out to protect our beloved fatherland. We girls also gladly place our weak powers in the service of the fatherland [...] Even thriftiness is now a weapon. (1916, 18)[48]

Like Felseneck, the girl who wrote these words minimizes the importance of actual women's practical work by describing the weakness of women's powers and thereby does not offer a challenge to the patriarchal social structures that prioritized men and their contributions. Instead she emphasizes how women and girls can serve their country through traditional female activities like frugal shopping, knitting, or making gifts to send to the troops at the front.

The characters of Ilse Macket and Annemarie Braun exemplify the gendered mobilization of German girls during what they perceived as the Great War. The use of familiar characters like Trotzkopf and Nesthäkchen show the reactionary politics of wartime writing including that by women authors. While writers repeatedly emphasize the immense impact of the war and show its transformational effect on German society, the ideological focus remains on the traditional and conservative. The need for the spiritual renewal of the nation allegedly can be met only if the youth adopt traditional gender roles. This gendered mobilization and call for a return to the traditional was presented as necessary to prepare youth for the changed world in which they lived. WWI writing presents the war as a massive force that has the ability to sweep away the evils of modern industrial society and allow for a return to a supposedly simpler, better time. This rhetoric echoes that of colonial literature that viewed places like German Southwest Africa as spaces for the renewal of the German nation. Both call for a return to a mythic time in the German past that likely never existed, an expression of dissatisfaction with contemporary times.[49]

---

47 "Wie wir Mädchen dem Vaterlande dienen."

48 "Wir leben jetzt in einer sehr ernsten Zeit. Eine Welt von Feinden hat sich gegen uns erhoben. Tausende von Männern und Jünglingen sind hinausgeeilt, unser geliebtes Vaterland zu schützen. Auch wir Mädchen stellen gern und freudig unsere schwachen Kräfte in den Dienst des Vaterlandes. [...] Auch die Sparsamkeit ist jetzt eine Waffe."

49 As Catherine Dollard has shown, there was much debate in Wilhelmine Germany about the role of women. Even though marriage rates and female employment rates remained relatively consistent until World War I, many in society spoke of a crisis and feared an erosion of the traditional family and traditional gender roles (see Dollard, *Surplus Woman* 2009).

Conclusion

The figures of Ernestine, Erika, Hanna, Ilse, and Annemarie offer a spectrum of wartime female identity for young readers, and an intersectional analysis of them reveals the importance of race in impacting portrayals of gender in wartime German identity in the early twentieth century. All these heroines are presented as heroic, but their heroism takes different forms – active and passive, brave and domestic, masculine and feminine. Ernestine, Erika, and Hanna are in some ways anomalies when viewed alongside other *Backfisch* book protagonists, but when they are compared to the portrayal of WWI heroines the explanatory power of the colonial context becomes clear. The heroines of colonial novels for girls reveal the symbolic significance of women under German colonialism; they take up arms against the Herero (portrayed as aggressors) to defend the colonial racial order, the bodies of unmarried women and girls as the last stand of defense. The heroines of WWI texts, on the other hand, advocate a less militaristic and more traditionally feminine form of heroism. Women are depicted as standard-bearers and symbols of domesticity and comfort, inspiration and motivation for the men on the front. WWI novels therefore show girls and women engaged in traditional female occupations like nursing, child-rearing, and housekeeping. Comparing Ernestine, Erika, and Hanna to Annemarie and Ilse reminds us of the importance of not losing sight of the racial and colonial contexts of German identity in the early twentieth century, and it shows that while the colonies were physically distant from mainland Germany, they play an important role in the metropolitan imaginary. Studying the roles and opportunities afforded to women in wartime thus also serves to cast some light on the long shadow of colonialism in German literature and culture.

Works Cited

Aitken, Robbie. *Exclusion and Inclusion: Gradations of Whiteness and Socio-Economic Engineering in German Southwest Africa, 1884–1914* (Peter Lang, 2007).
Albert, Emily. *Daheim in großer Zeit* (Levy und Müller, 1915).
Askey, Jennifer Drake. *Good Girls, Good Germans: Girls' Education and Emotional Nationalism in Wilhelminian Germany* (Camden House, 2013).
Askey, Jennifer Drake. "A Library for Girls: Publisher Ferdinand Hirt & Sohn and the Novels of Brigitte Augusti." *Publishing Culture and the "Reading Nation": German Book History in the Long Nineteenth Century*, edited by Lynne Tatlock (Camden House, 2010), pp. 155–178.
Bake, Elisa. *Schwere Zeiten: Schicksale eines deutschen Mädchens in Südwestafrika* (Gmelin, 1913).

Benninghoff-Lühl, Sibylle. *Deutsche Kolonialromane 1884–1914 in ihrem Entstehungs- und Wirkungszusammenhang* (Verlag des Übersee-Museums, 1983).

Bley, Helmut. *South-West Africa under German Rule* (later reprinted as *Namibia under German Rule*). Translated by Hugh Ridley (Heinemann, 1971).

Christaller, Helene. *Die unsere Hoffnung sind* (Thienemann, 1916).

Clement, Bertha. *Morgenrot: Eine Erzählgung aus dem Großen Krieg für Mädchen* (Loewes, 1916).

Cooper, Frederick, and Ann Laura Stoler, editors. *Tensions of Empire: Colonial Cultures in a Bourgeois World* (U of California P, 1997).

Crenshaw, Kimberlé. "Demarginalizing the Intersection of Race and Sex: A Black Feminist Critique of Antidscrimination Doctrine, Feminist Theory and Antiracist Politics." *University of Chicago Legal Forum*, vol. 1989, no. 1 (1989), pp. 139–167.

Daniel, Ute. *The War from Within: German Working-Class Women in the First World War.* Translated by Margaret Ries (Berg, 1997).

Dietrich, Anette. *Weiße Weiblichkeiten: Konstruktion von "Rasse" und Geschlecht im deutschen Kolonialismus* (transcript, 2007).

Dincklage-Campe, Friedrich von, editor. *Deutsche Reiter in Südwest: Selbsterlebnisse aus den Kämpfen in Deutsch-Südwestafrika* (Bong & Co., 1908).

Dollard, Catherine. "Marital Status and the Rhetoric of the Women's Movement in World War I Germany." *Women in German Yearbook*, vol. 22 (2006), pp. 211–235.

Dollard, Catherine. *The Surplus Woman: Unmarried in Imperial Germany, 1871–1918* (Berghahn, 2009).

Donson, Andrew. "Models for Young Nationalists and Militarists: German Youth Literature in the First World War." *German Studies Review*, vol. 27, no. 3 (Oct. 2004), pp. 579–598.

Donson, Andrew. *Youth in the Fatherless Land: War Pedagogy, Nationalism, and Authority in Germany, 1914–1918* (Harvard UP, 2010).

Eckenbrecher, Margarethe von. *Was Afrika mir gab und nahm: Erlebnisse einer deutschen Ansiedlerfrau in Südwestafrika 1902–1936.* 1907 (8th ed., Mittler & Sohn, 1940; reprint: Peter's Antiques/Superprint, 2000).

Falkenhausen, Helene von. *Ansiedlerschicksale: Elf Jahre in Deutsch-Südwestafrika 1893–1904* (Reimer, 1905). *Nineteenth Century Collections Online*, tinyurl.galegroup.com/tinyurl/5chijX. Accessed 1 Oct. 2014.

Felseneck, Marie von. *Trotzkopfs Erlebnisse im Weltkrieg* (Weichert, 1916).

Gallagher, Maureen. "Fragile Whiteness: Women and Girls in German Colonial Fiction, 1900–1913." *Women in German Yearbook*, vol. 32 (2016), pp. 111–137.

Gallagher, Maureen. "The *Kränzchen* Library and the Creation of Teenage Identity." *Detectives, Dystopias, and Poplit: Studies in Modern German Genre Fiction*, edited by Bruce B. Campbell, et al. (Camden House, 2014), pp. 207–226.

Gallagher, Maureen. "Rilla and Annemarie: Gender, Nationalism, and Books for Young People on Both Sides of the First World War." *L.M. Montgomery and War*, edited by Andrea McKenzie and Jane Ledwell (McGill-Queen's UP, 2017), pp. 146–164.

Gallagher, Maureen. "Young Germans in the World: Race, Gender, and Imperialism in Wilhelmine Young Adult Literature." Dissertation (University of Massachusetts, 2015).

Gouaffo, Albert. "Beziehungsgestaltung in kolonialer Situation: Literarische Kolonialdiskurse zwischen Herrschaft und Gegenseitigkeit: Ein Beispiel aus der Kolonialliteratur zu Kamerun." *Acta Germanica*, vol. 36 (2008), pp. 21–29.

Grimm, Hans. "Wie Grete aufhörte ein Kind zu sein." *Südafrikanische Novellen* (Rütten und Loening, 1913).

Higonnet, Margaret, et al., editors. *Behind the Lines: Gender and the Two World Wars* (Yale UP, 1987).

Hodann, Valerie. *Auf rauhen Pfaden: Schicksale einer deutschen Farmerstochter in Deutsch-Südwest-Afrika* (Dietrich, 1910).

Hofmann, Else. *Deutsche Mädel in großer Zeit* (Fock, 1916).

Hong, Young-Sun. "The Contradictions of Modernization in the German Welfare State: Gender and the Politics of Welfare Reform in First World War Germany." *Social History*, vol. 17, no. 2 (Winter 1992), pp. 251–270.

Horne, John. "Labor and Labor Movements in World War I." *The Great War and the Twentieth Century*, edited by Jay Winter, et al. (Yale UP, 2000), pp. 187–228.

Kenosian, David. "The Colonial Body Politic: Desire and Violence in the Works of Gustav Frenssen and Hans Grimm." *Monatshefte*, vol. 89, no. 2 (Summer 1997), pp. 182–195.

Kloerß, Sophie. *Im heiligen Kampf* (Union, 1915).

Koch, Henny. *Die Vollrads in Südwest: Eine Erzählung für junge Mädchen* (Union, 1916).

Lennox, Sara. "Race, Gender, and Sexuality in German Southwest Africa: Hans Grimm's *Südafrikanische Novellen*." *Germany's Colonial Pasts*, edited by Eric Ames, et al. (U of Nebraska P, 2005), pp. 63–75.

McClintock, Anne. *Imperial Leather: Race, Gender, and Sexuality in the Colonial Contest* (Routledge, 1995).

Mikota, Jana. "For the Love of Words and Works: Tailoring the Reader for Higher Girls' Schools in Late Nineteenth-century Germany." *Publishing Culture and the "Reading Nation": German Book History in the Long Nineteenth Century*, edited by Lynne Tatlock (Camden House, 2010), pp. 179–210.

Moyd, Michelle R. *Violent Intermediaries: African Soldiers, Conquest, and Everyday Colonialism in German East Africa* (Ohio UP, 2014).

Radtke, J. *Themen und Aufsätze zum Weltkrieg* (Hirt, 1916).

Rayle, Marga. *Majors Einzige im Kriegsjahr* (Meidinger, 1914).

Reagin, Nancy. *A German Women's Movement: Class and Gender in Hanover, 1880–1933* (U of North Carolina P, 1995).

Redmann, Jennifer. "Doing Her Bit: German and Anglo-American Girls' Literature of the First World War." *Girlhood Studies*, vol. 4, no. 1 (Spring 2011), pp. 10–29.

Rhoden, Emmy von. *Der Trotzkopf: Eine Pensionsgeschichte für erwachsene Mädchen* (Weise, 1885).

Sapper, Agnes. *Werden und Wachsen: Erlebnisse der großen Pfäfflingskinder* (Gundert, 1910).

Schach, Max. *Das Kind und der Krieg: Kinderaussprüche, Aufsätze, Schilderungen und Zeichnungen* (Eckart, 1916).

Schenda, Rudolf. *Die Lesestoffe der kleinen Leute: Studien zur populären Literatur im 19. und 20. Jahrhundert* (Beck, 1976).

Sippel, Harald. "'Im Interesse des Deutschtums und der weißen Rasse': Behandlung und Rechtswirkungen von 'Rassenmischehen' in den Kolonien Deutsch-Ostafrika und Deutsch-Südwestafrika." *Jahrbuch für afrikanisches Recht*, vol. 9 (1995), pp. 123–159.

Stoler, Ann Laura. *Carnal Knowledge and Imperial Power: Race and the Intimate in Colonial Rule* (U of California P, 2002).

Tatlock, Lynne, editor. *Publishing Culture and the "Reading Nation": German Book History in the Long Nineteenth Century* (Camden House, 2010).

Tharps, Lori L. "The Case for Black with a Capital B." *New York Times* (18 Nov. 2014). www.ny times.com/2014/11/19/opinion/the-case-for-black-with-a-capital-b.html?_r=0. Accessed 23 Feb. 2018.

Ury, Else. *Nesthäkchen und der Weltkrieg* (Meidinger, ca. 1916).

Ury, Else. *Nesthäkchen and the World War.* Translated by Steven Lehrer (iUniverse, 2006).

van Beeker, Käthe. *Heddas Lehrzeit in Süd-West* (Loewe, 1909).

Verhey, Jeffrey. *The Spirit of 1914: Militarism, Myth, and Mobilization in Germany* (Cambridge UP, 2000).

Walgenbach, Katharina. "Rassenpolitik und Geschlecht in Deutsch-Südwestafrika." *Rassenmischehen – Mischlinge – Rassentrennung: Zur Politik der Rasse im deutschen Kolonialreich*, edited by Frank Becker (Steiner, 2004), pp. 165–183.

Wildenthal, Lora. *German Women for Empire, 1884–1945* (Duke UP, 2001).

Wilkending, Gisela, editor. *Mädchenliteratur der Kaiserzeit: Zwischen weiblicher Identifizierung und Grenzüberschreitung* (Metzler, 2003).

Wilkending, Gisela. "Mädchenliteratur von der Mitte des 19. Jahrhunderts bis zum Ersten Weltkrieg." *Geschichte der deutschen Kinder- und Jugendliteratur*, edited by Reiner Wild (Metzler, 1990), pp. 220–250.

Views from the Colonies on WWI

Marianne Bechhaus-Gerst
Woman on the Edge of Time

Frieda Schmidt and the Great War in East Africa

This article investigates the impact of World War I and its aftermath on *white*[1] German women living in the German East African colony. I explore what happens when the colonial order, colonial imaginations and fantasies fall apart, and in which way the transitional period of German (post)colonialism between 1913 and 1919 influenced or changed gender, class and RACE relations and constructions.[2] Since my investigation focuses on the experience and perspective of only one woman, Frieda Schmidt (1890–1986), the answers given might not be representative, but her accounts may serve as a sort of microstudy that represents an approach to an underresearched topic. We still do not know much about the lives of ordinary, civilian *white* people, especially about women, during the period indicated and about how these lives were affected by the war. This academic void is difficult to fill because of the scarcity of written records. It seems all the more necessary to work with any material we can find in the archives that has not yet been considered. My main perspective is that of an Africanist specializing in the history of German-African encounters in the (former) German colonies on the African continent as well as in Germany. Although I approach the archival material with rather traditional tools of historical research such as critical textual analysis, my theoretical and methodological background can be found mainly in postcolonial and critical whiteness theories and postcolonial discourse analysis.

---

1 I use *white* in italics to emphasize its being a marked socio-political category and to make it more vulnerable. I use capital letters for RACE and its derivatives to indicate that I am not referring to a biological category "race" but to racialized groups, conceptions, social, political and economic categories and constructions of inequality as well as mostly asymmetrical forms of power. Lower cases with quotation marks are found when I refer to fantasies of biological purity of "race."

2 Shortly after the beginning of World War I the Germans started to lose their African colonies Togo, Cameroon, and German Southwest Africa one by one to the European enemy nations who were better equipped for an overseas war. Only German East Africa was defended until the war ended. With the Peace Treaty of Versailles of 1919 it became evident that Germany would not be regaining control over their former territories. Thus, although people might not have been aware of it at the time, the period between 1913 and 1919 was a transitional period between colonialism and – temporal – postcolonialism for Germany.

https://doi.org/10.1515/9783110572001-005

The leading questions touch on two fields of research, which so far have rarely been studied jointly, i.e., the subject of *white* women in the colonies and the consequences of World War I on the German colonies in general, and on the lives of *white* women living there in particular. In recent years numerous ground-breaking studies of the manifold roles and constructions of *white* women in the German colonies have appeared.[3] These were much overdue, since for a long time German colonialism had been primarily regarded as a man's project. That this perception stood for the continued existence of fantasies regarding colonial masculinity finally became obvious.[4] As systematic studies have shown, *white* women constituted an essential part of Germany's colonial project at home and in the colonies. For many women, migration to the colonies was associated with upward social mobility. Having settled overseas, *white* women were victims as well as perpetrators. They used violence against the colonial subjects to enforce a RACIAL hierarchy that was imagined to be natural. *White* women were responsible for the stabilization of *white* hegemony and the establishment of Germanness in the overseas territories. Finally, they were the guarantors for "racial purity," for the continued existence of an imagined "white race." So, women were the representatives as well as the cornerstones of a colonial order that was negotiated around concepts of RACE, class and gender.[5]

The African theaters of war have not yet captured the attention of historians in a comprehensive or adequate way. Most of the existing studies are either based on personal memoirs of high-ranking German officers and other war veterans or focused on the military aspects and proceedings of battles and actions. A few groundbreaking works study the African military personnel under different aspects; however, comprehensive discussion of the literature is beyond the scope of this essay.[6] Important in this context are the rather few studies that focus on civilians who lived and worked in the colonies and who were plunged

---

3 Martha Mamozai's pathbreaking book *Schwarze Frau, weiße Herrin: Frauenleben in den deutschen Kolonien* (Black women, white mistress: Women's life in the German colonies) was published as early as 1989 and was one of the first studies which focused on the German colonial context.
4 Different studies deal with various aspects of "colonial masculinity": See, e.g., Mrinalini Sinha (1995) or for the German colonial context Maß (2006).
5 Some of the respective studies focus on the constructions of *white* women in the context of discourses about and constructions of RACE, class and gender in colonial Germany (Dietrich 2007; Walgenbach 2005). These works have been especially informative for my approach to Frieda Schmidt. Other studies (e.g., Bechhaus-Gerst and Leutner 2009) give a more general overview of the colonial encounter between German and indigenous women in the colonies as well as in Germany.
6 See, e.g., the discussion in Pesek (2010, 16–24).

into a severe crisis by the outbreak of the Great War (Steinbach 2008). Even less attention has been paid to the imprisonment and internment of Germans in the colonies, be it military personnel or civilians. Very few investigations focus on British and German prisoners of war and internees in East Africa (e. g., Steinbach 2014; Pesek 2011). None of these studies addresses specifically how German women were affected by the war and how they dealt with internment and the breakdown of colonial society. Fortunately, an important research gap will soon be addressed by a pathbreaking, not yet published, dissertation on prisoners of war and civilian internees from the German colonies during the Great War (Murphy 2015).[7]

Since my investigation examines the effects of war on dimensions of what has been termed the colonial order, Michael Pesek's book *Das Ende des Kolonialreichs: Ostafrika im Ersten Weltkrieg* (The end of the colonial empire: East Africa in World War I, 2010) is particularly relevant because it focuses on colonial orders and their representations. Pesek even defines the battlefield as an "agonal theater of colonial orders" (2010, 36). But although the frequently invoked colonial order serves as a kind of departure here, it must be noted that this order was never a fixed concept. This vagueness also pertains to academic studies of the many aspects of colonialism where the label "colonial order" is frequently used without clear definitions.[8] It can encompass the economic and political spheres but more often refers to orders of RACE, class and gender – as it does here – that had to be continuously negotiated in the colonial encounter. Thus, it is important to note that there was no homogeneous colonial order under German colonial rule, and especially in the political sphere it was always precarious (Pesek 2010, 30). I will return to the precariousness of this order later in my essay. Another aspect Pesek identifies concerns the necessary two perspectives when discussing colonial order(s). On the one hand, the colonial order(s) could be regarded as belonging to the sphere of representation, as imaginations and fantasies conjured up by the colonial mind (2010, 31–33).[9] On the other hand, these imaginations and fantasies had an impact on the daily lives of the colonizer as well as the colonized. For the colonized this impact quite often was devastating, and sometimes deadly.

From the perspective of the *white* German woman Frieda Schmidt, whose writings I consider here, the colonial order with regard to RACE, class and gender is easy to define: It is the way things were supposed to be, it is the allegedly nat-

---

7 I thank Mahon Murphy for granting me access to the manuscript of his PhD thesis.

8 As the academic works, which use the term "colonial order," are too numerous to list here, see Pesek, 2010 and 2011 for a discussion of this term.

9 On the subject of colonial imaginations see also Zantop (1997).

ural order of the world in which she planned to live. And it is through the falling apart of this imagined order during wartime that we learn what exactly it consisted of in the mind of an ordinary middle-class *white* German woman.

The sources

My study investigates unpublished letters, journal entries and other writings of Frieda Schmidt, née Kleböhmer, a young woman who lived in German East Africa between 1913 and 1920.[10] The most important source is a special form of private journal, which Frieda and her husband Gottfried started in April 1914, after their daughter, Kätchen, was born.[11] The journal entries directly address Kätchen and tell her about everyday life in the colony and about her development from baby to toddler, as well as about the events surrounding the outbreak of the war and its aftermath. Frieda's entries alternate with her husband Gottfried's until he was captured by the British in 1916, and subsequently deported to Ahmednaggar, India. For the years 1917/1918 only entries written by Frieda can be found. Additionally, a bundle of letters written by Frieda during the war and addressed to her family in Germany has been preserved. Due to censorship regulations imposed by the British most of the letters are not especially informative but mainly reassure her loved ones at home of her well-being and health. Fear of possible consequences if the journal would have fallen into enemy hands might also have been the reason why Frieda tore out several pages of the journal in midsentence. Since Frieda took over her husband's duties as the manager of the Mwule plantation[12] for a short period of time during the war, she was also responsible for entries in the "cash book" for the Mwule plantation. This "cash book" provides interesting insight into Frieda's attempts to find her own way of making the plantation profitable in difficult times and to work her way into an area of expertise of which she had no prior knowledge.

---

10 Frieda Schmidt's papers, as well as those of her husband Gottfried, are kept at the municipal archive of Bad Salzuflen (henceforth StadtA BS), inventory N III. They are part of the personal papers of Käte Husemann, née Schmidt, daughter of Frieda and Gottfried Schmidt. The papers comprise 53 record files and 450 photos. I am currently preparing a detailed study of the Schmidt family's life in German East Africa and Ahmednagar/India. So far there has been only one study of the Schmidts' life in Africa, which was published as a three-part series in a local historical journal (Göke 1997, 93 – 118; 1998, 65 – 91; 1999, 105 – 118).

11 Kätchen is a term of endearment or nickname for German Käte. Usually the nickname is used for children, Käte for grownups.

12 The Mwule Rubber Plantation was located at kilometer 63.7 along the Usambara railway line, which connected the port of Tanga at the Indian Ocean and the interior of German East Africa.

Introduction to the protagonist Frieda Schmidt

Frieda Schmidt was born in 1890 in a small village in the northeastern part of present-day North Rhine-Westphalia. She was the fifth of eight children.[13] The family was not particularly well off, although her father had a clock and watch-maker business. Their already difficult financial situation deteriorated during the war when the family's property was threatened by foreclosure.

Frieda received a basic elementary education, which consisted of eight years of classes for those who could not afford the tuition for secondary education. In general, the situation of middle-class women at the end of the nineteenth and early twentieth century was precarious. Demographically there was a surplus of women which led to a comparatively large number of unmarried women with no education to speak of.[14] Most professions were not open to middle-class women, whose options to support themselves were restricted to working as a governess, a lady's companion or teacher. This rather bleak perspective also pertained to Frieda who turned to offering private needlework lessons and working as a nanny to support herself. In Germany, her chances of marrying well were slim. Her brother Hermann Kleböhmer, who worked as an engineer in the German colony Cameroon, offered a way out of these discouraging prospects. In Cameroon, Hermann had met Gottfried Schmidt from Kiel, a German town on the Baltic Sea. He was looking for favorable plantation sites on behalf of several German trading and plantation companies. A wife was missing from Gottfried's life, and after a short, written introduction by her brother, he started courting Frieda by writing letter after letter for nearly two years before finally meeting her in person when he returned to Germany for a visit. This was by no means exceptional for this time period, especially for men living and working in the colonies where *white* women were in short supply. Proposing to a woman one had barely met during a short home leave was the norm. Gottfried did not hesitate to inform Frieda that she did not correspond to his ideal of female beauty. He favored taller women, but as he wrote, "kisses and cooing do not prove love; love is begotten and proven through deed and hard work."[15] Frieda's papers do not reveal whether Gottfried was her ideal type of a man, but there can be no doubt why she accepted his marriage proposal and followed him to German East Africa, today's Tanzania, Rwanda, and Burundi. Marrying Gottfried brought

---

13 StadtA Bad Salzuflen BS, Findbuch N III, 28 (Genealogie der Familien Kleböhmer und Schmidt).

14 On the topic of this surplus of women, see, for example, Nipperdey (1866–1918, 21).

15 "Mit Küssen und Kosen giebt man keinen Liebesbeweis; Liebe will durch Tat und Arbeit gezeugt und bewiesen sein" (N III 13, 29–30). All translations of German sources by the author.

about an unhoped-for advancement in social status. He had been offered a position as a plantation manager in German East Africa and willingly accepted it. His contract came with a salary of 6,000 Marks for the first year, 7,000 for the second and 8,000 for the third, with the option of an additional contract extension.[16] Compared to the average income of an office staff member in either the public or private sector in Germany, which for many was between 1,800 and 2,400 Marks per year (Pierenkemper 1983, 69–92), this was quite a lot of money and must have appealed to a young woman of uncertain economic circumstances. Additionally, the contract came with a house and complimentary health care. There was also the possibility of clearing the debts on Frieda's family home with the help of Gottfried's salary.[17] This marriage seemed to be the perfect solution for everyone involved. Frieda reached the Indian Ocean port Tanga, German East Africa, on 30 April 1913 and married Gottfried the next day.

Frieda and her husband settled into their new home on the Mwule rubber plantation like other German couples did under similar circumstances. Gender roles as well as class and RACE constructions were considered clearly defined and were regarded as essentially non-negotiable. Accordingly, the couple started their new life with the prospect of leading a comfortable life amongst the colonial upper class. Frieda took command of house and garden, and exactly one year after her arrival in Tanga, she gave birth to daughter Kätchen. Gottfried managed the plantation and oversaw about 200 African workers, the majority of whom had to tap rubber.

The outbreak of World War I from Frieda's perspective

There is no doubt that – from the German perspective – the war fundamentally changed the "natural" order of things, meaning the colonial RACE as well as gender relations and constructions. Frieda and her husband were unenthusiastic when it became obvious that the war would not spare the colonies.[18] On 6 August 1914 Frieda noted in her diary that while travelling home from a doctor's appointment a railway official warned her about the war reaching East Africa. Admittedly this was terrifying news, but she still hoped that these prospects

---

16 StadtA BS N III 35 contains an employment contract which presumably served as a model for Gottfried's contract.

17 StadtA BS N III 13, 248–249.

18 Steinbach also points to a less than enthusiastic atmosphere in German East Africa (2008, 189–190)

would not come true.[19] German East Africa was surrounded by British, Belgian and Portuguese colonies better equipped for what was regarded an intra-European war. Living in the northern part of the colony, Frieda feared the English, whose colonial army was based a little more than a stone's throw away in Kenya.

The outbreak of the war brought about considerable changes in the content of Frieda's diary addressed to her young daughter, Kätchen. Up to this point it had been full of endearing stories about the little girl's development, life on the plantation and the family's social life with German compatriots. On the first pages the narrative is characterized by a light tone suitable for a story to be told to a little girl. Throughout the diary Frieda tried to retrieve that tone, but at the same time she starts commenting on war-related events in East Africa. The diary now functioned as an outlet for thoughts and feelings difficult to express otherwise or to be preserved for posterity. There is nothing childlike about Frieda's summary of the complex events in the European war theater and the declaration of war by the British in August 1914. Her writings show that Frieda, along with many compatriots in Germany and the colonies, was adamant in her belief that Germany's wartime enemies had "ganged up" against her beloved fatherland because of envy and jealousy of the country's economic achievements and power.[20] She was convinced that they would not have dared to attack Germany without the support of one another. Although it is evident that the Germans found themselves confronted with a number of formidable enemies, Frieda presented herself as belligerent and willing to join forces with other "German East Africans," at least verbally. But rallying calls were soon silenced by the realization that the war affected everybody's life in a fundamental way. A last batch of letters and postcards from Germany arrived on 1 August 1914. Subsequently shipping traffic was disrupted and, according to her diary, worries about the loved ones at home and at the front come to dominate Frieda's thoughts and emotions.[21]

Renegotiating RACE relations

Frieda and her husband Gottfried agreed that having to live and work with Africans was an enormous burden. Gottfried was troubled by his workers as well as by the general situation in the colony where Africans were putting up resistance

---

19 StadtA BS N III 3, 37.
20 StadtA BS N III 3, 38–39.
21 StadtA BS N III 3, 38–39.

against forced labor in different ways. "Those who have lived among the natives for some time," he wrote in his diary, "will never vote for the abolishment of chain and 25."[22] At first, Frieda's own concerns about having to deal with Africans centered on her female sphere of control. She was convinced that her so-called "boy" was not able to look after Kätchen. She wrote in her diary that after leaving her daughter in his care for only five minutes he brought her back with a bloody nose and lips. She was quite positive about her servant's inability to act responsibly.[23]

Although contact with other German families required considerable effort and was therefore infrequent, it was never seriously considered that Kätchen could seek and find playmates among the numerous African children living on the plantation. Frieda mockingly commented on a photograph of African children, which she put into the diary: "These little nigger-watotos will soon be your playmates." But Gottfried quickly added: "Well, better not!"[24]

After the beginning of WWI, presumed certainties concerning the relationship between the colonial masters and their subjects quickly unraveled. For Frieda, as for other Germans in East Africa, there was the sudden fear that with the outbreak of the war the colonial subjects would turn against their *white* masters.[25] Frieda's main causes of concern were the Maasai. The Schmidts had employed armed Maasai as guardians of the plantation's maize fields against wild animals. Frieda now feared that the Maasai would not hesitate to shoot their masters instead of boars.[26] The fact that the majority of Maasai settled in British East Africa intensified her anxieties. Her concerns were not unfounded: In his book on East Africa during World War I, Pesek describes the case of the German settler Anna Rau, who was murdered by her African workers (2010, 241). After her husband was conscripted, Rau encountered conflicts with her servants. As was her custom, she wanted to solve the conflict with the *kiboko*, the hippo-hide whip, but this time her servants simply took off never to return. Without protection Rau was easy prey for the plantation workers who had constantly been maltreated with the utmost brutality and who had been denied their wages more often than once.

---

22 StadtA BS N III 13, 222. Twenty-five was the usual number of lashes with the kiboko, the hippo-hide whip, as punishment.
23 StadtA BS N III 13, 62.
24 StadtA BS N III 13, 27. "Solch kleine Niggerwatotos werden nun bald Deine Spielgefährten sein. – Na, lieber nicht." *Watoto* is the Kiswahili plural form of *mtoto* (child).
25 For reports on this fear of rebellions, see, for instance, Steinbach (2014, 269).
26 StadtA BS N III 3, 37.

Frieda bought a Browning pistol to defend herself and her child against possible burglars and complained in her writings that the servants had lost all respect for their mistress.[27] Her sense of being isolated in a hostile environment increased when a longtime servant escaped with a considerable amount of Frieda's cash (Göke 1998, 88).

When the British colonial army reached Amani in the Usambara Mountains, where many German women and their children had been evacuated – among them Frieda and Kätchen –, Frieda was horrified to realize that only two Europeans were accompanied by about 100 Indian, "Nubian" and other African soldiers. She commented that, fortunately, they were properly dressed and the European officers were draconic in penalizing any criminal behavior. Thieves were executed on the spot. But similar strict regulations were issued concerning the Germans – "now that we are prisoners."[28] With non-European Askari presenting bayonets fixed all around her, she had to surrender her Browning pistol to the British, and with it her only means of self-defense.[29] Frieda thus had to cope with a radical loss of status. What had been constructed as some sort of *white* solidarity among colonizers of different European nationalities before the war was no longer valid. Mahon Murphy notes that the Germans experienced "a severe racial role reversal that fundamentally changed their position in colonial society" (2015, 16). *White* supremacy now became attached to nationality (see 14), and Frieda had the wrong one. Not only was she controlled by the victorious British, but these British did not hesitate to treat her like any non-*white* colonial subject. At least this was her impression. And beyond being upset about the arrival of the British and the loss of German territory, Frieda ranted in her private writings about the fact that the British colonial army consisted mainly of non-European, non-*white* soldiers who seemed to be everywhere and who had the power to control her every move (see 14). It was completely incompatible with German colonial RACIAL concepts to establish non-*white* soldiers as masters of *white* people and perceived as the utmost form of humiliation. Although the German East African colonial army included some officer's ranks open to African soldiers, they were never allowed to command or control *white* officers or civilians.[30]

---

27 StadtA BS N III 13, 49.

28 StadtA BS N III 3, 91–93.

29 StadtA BS N III 3, 91–93.

30 Compliance with what was perceived as the "natural racial order" was of utmost importance to many Germans. This became even more evident when right after the war French and British victorious powers dispatched non-*white* soldiers as part of the occupational army on German

Renegotiating gender constructions

Unlike a number of other German women who went to the colonies, Frieda did not mention any emancipatory ambitions before the war, but the critical economic situation on the plantation after Gottfried's conscription challenged her role as mistress of house and garden.[31] As we learn from Frieda's diary, war service was a frustrating experience for her husband. Due to British blockade tactics, there was a shortage of weapons and ammunition so that German men were often left unarmed. Gottfried and other German civilians had to wait for a blockade runner to bring a supply of weapons. Because of this situation Gottfried was called up to serve in the colonial army called "Schutztruppe" (colonial protection troops) as late as 1 May 1915. The first blow to his self-esteem was that he was deemed unfit for active duty; the second blow was that he was assigned a position with the coast guard with three other men equipped only with outdated rifles. Their assignment was to observe and not to act.[32]

Frieda was happy that Gottfried was stationed within travel distance, and although his quarters could not compare to their house on the plantation, Gottfried tried his best to uphold the standards they were used to. Frieda and Kätchen visited him there for days at a time, pretending everything was no different than before.[33] But the change had occurred and had an effect on their well-rehearsed gender roles. Reduced more or less to a passive role in an obviously perilous situation, Gottfried explored other options. On the one hand, he became a proficient cook and homemaker at his coastal station; on the other hand, he tried to compensate for his imposed inactivity with diatribes against their European opponents in the war. "God shall punish England! The world can exist without England," he ranted in his own diary. The Russians were "pigs," the Italians "lousy wops" – empty words by a man whose masculinity was suddenly in question.[34]

Gottfried Schmidt was taken prisoner by Indian soldiers on 17 July 1916. With his capture, his fantasies concerning an active involvement in the defense of colony and home came to an end. Capture and imprisonment by the British was a disempowering experience which has been extensively described in scholarship

---

soil. German propaganda termed this experience, which *white* Germans found extremely humiliating, "Die schwarze Schmach am Rhein" (The black horror on the Rhine).
31 For changes brought about by the lack of *white*, German men after they had been called up, see, for example, Daniel (1989); Kundrus (1995); Grayzel (1999 and 2002).
32 StadtA BS N III 3, 67–79.
33 StadtA BS N III 3, 64.
34 StadtA BS N III 3, 72.

about POWs of the European war theaters.[35] Like many of his compatriots in East Africa, Gottfried was transferred to a British prison camp in Ahmednaggar, India. There he and the other POWs had to re-define their perception and construction of masculinity. They were not allowed to work, so boredom became the biggest problem besides the often bemoaned verminous accommodation. What can be termed as colonial order of masculinity might have brought about the emasculation of the colonized man. In this particular situation of war imprisonment and of forced inactivity, it was the former colonizer who underwent a process of emasculation and feminization.[36] Even before being transported to India, we can observe Gottfried's obsession with food and food preparation. The symbolic content of this obsession is twofold. It does not merely represent the adoption of female activities; the substantial quantity and quality of food distributed by the British seemed to be symbolic of the preservation of a higher status for *whites* and thus of the colonial hierarchy even though Germans were de facto on the losing side of the war. This might explain Gottfried's lengthy description of corned beef, butter, white bread, biscuits, and tea with milk and sugar distributed by the British. It seems to have been important for Gottfried to document that, at least in this respect, the British still regarded the Germans as equals.[37]

Left to fend for herself and her daughter, Frieda tried to take control of her life. We know of such developments in many settings where women had to take over positions of authority at home while their men were defending their countries at the front.[38] According to her diary, Frieda had a hard time developing her own perspective in this situation. Her first impulse was to run, and she sought shelter with the widow of another German planter. But the two women did not get along and Gottfried convinced her to return to the plantation and to serve as his proxy. It was in the couple's best financial interest to fulfill their contractual obligations to their employer. So, Frieda returned home and took control of the plantation. Within a short period of time, she seemed to have become a proficient manager – officially a deputy manager with a separate contract – who even initiated a fundamental change in the economic basis of the plantation by relying more and more on maize instead of rubber. Much maize was plucked, processed and sold. Virgin soil and fallow land were prepared for sowing.[39] For the first time in her life Frieda personally generated a considerable income to

---

35 See, e.g., Rachamimov (2002 and 2006); Stibbe (2012); Feltman (2015).
36 See, e.g., Rachamimov 2006 on transgender performances among POWs in Russia and on the new opportunities this exceptional situation brought about.
37 StadtA BS N III 13, 346. See also Steinbach (2014, 277).
38 See footnote 30.
39 StadtA BS N III 3, 56 and 80. N III 36, 247 and 259.

support her small family. It could not have been easy for Gottfried to watch his wife take over the "male" part of their marital equation while he was condemned to passivity. It sounds a little patronizing when he writes how proud he is of her achievements.[40] For a short period, the war and Gottfried's absence – due to being first enlisted and then captured by the British – were empowering experiences for Frieda. Traditional gender constructions which she had accepted upon marrying Gottfried unraveled and were turned upside down. During this period of the war, Frieda acquired a certain agency accompanied by an awareness of autonomy in making decisions even in difficult situations. German women were allowed to travel freely to and from their homes, the homes of acquaintances, and the Amani Research Institute, the botanical lab that functioned as a milk distribution center during the war and refuge for Germans.[41] In between her obligations as plantation manager Frieda travelled to Amani several times for visits but also expecting deportation by the British. When Frieda returned to the Mwule plantation from one of her visits in July 1917, she seemed to have made the conscious decision not to take up production again, because it would only have helped the British enemy.[42]

Class and status

In the course of the Great War in East Africa, most of the *white* German women and children in the colony ended up becoming interned or were held on parole by the British. Frieda called the place of their "internment" a concentration camp, in reference to the camps installed by the British during the Boer War in South Africa between 1900 and 1902.[43] This naming explicitly evokes images of horror and torture because British concentration camps in South Africa had the reputation of being particularly heinous. This reputation seems to have been used by the British to create a climate of fear among the women "interned" in East Africa. According to Frieda's diary, she and other female acquaintances had to pack up their meager belongings several times because their transport

---

40 StadtA BS N III 13, 29.
41 The institute was founded in 1902 by the Germans as a biological-agricultural research center but expanded into other areas of tropical research in the following years. When the British arrived at Amani on 20 July 1916 the institute and the surrounding area were full of German refugees and the botanical lab was functioning as a milk distribution center (see Conte 2002, 234–246).
42 StadtA BS N III 3, 132–138.
43 StadtA BS N III 3, 91 and 92.

to South Africa was allegedly imminent,[44] yet, it never happened. The German discourse on the alleged maltreatment of German internees and prisoners at the hands of the British impacted the perception of her subjective reality. In March 1916, it became obvious that the British advancement into the North of German East Africa would inevitably lead to the British taking possession of the Mwule plantation. Frieda's husband Gottfried made the necessary arrangements for the evacuation of his family to the Amani Research Institute in the Usambara Mountains.[45] The institute covered a vast area and was well-known for its favorable climate which would also allow Frieda to properly recover from a previous illness. Every attempt was made to transfer status, style and privacy by all means and as completely as possible; therefore Gottfried had commissioned a portable house made of corrugated metal which was transported to Amani by train. In the end, an even better solution was found. Gottfried's status allowed him to pressure the institute's administration into reserving two rooms in the institute's bowling alley with *en suite* bathroom and toilet for his family. The rooms were spacious enough to accommodate all of the family's furniture as well as household goods (Göke 1998, 87).[46] At Amani, Frieda and her daughter met other evacuees, and for a short time it seemed possible to transfer and re-establish the accustomed colonial order of things in the new surroundings of the institute. In fact, this rather comfortable situation did not initially change fundamentally when the British arrived on 20 July 1916. Contrary to Frieda's recorded perception of being imprisoned, the women were more or less free to leave the Amani station and travel or even return to their homes. Otherwise it would not have been possible for Frieda to return to the Mwule plantation and to take over managing functions while being officially interned by the British. But the discourse on being interned by the enemy was different, and Frieda insisted in her diary that the British tormented her mercilessly.[47]

Frieda's attempts to keep up appearances by transferring the comforts of plantation life to Amani could not conceal the inexorable loss of social and economic status. The British blockade policy had effectively impeded the import of articles, goods and food products demanded by the Germans in East Africa as well as the export of the plantation's products. Even more difficult to deal with was the shortage of money that became evident soon after the war reached East Africa. In anticipation of a general shortage, Gottfried and other Germans

---

44 StadtA BS N III 3, 130, 141–142.
45 See footnote 41.
46 StadtA BS N III 13, 53–55. Murphy speaks of a particular German space which was created in the camps (2015, 14).
47 "[..] bis auf's Blut gequält" (StadtA BS N III, 140).

started to hoard staple foods with the little cash they had left.[48] After Gottfried left and was later imprisoned, and even more so after Frieda and everyone else completely abandoned work on the plantation, the financial situation deteriorated. There was no income and Frieda had to subsist on the sale of personal property or take out loans with acquaintances.[49] Finally, she hit rock bottom and had to turn to the detested British administration, declaring bankruptcy in order to qualify for a monthly loan. According to her diary, Frieda experienced this as a second imprisonment. Giving up her freedom, as she wrote, and being at the mercy of the enemy nation seemed to have been the worst wartime experience for this German woman. Even after she applied for support, the British kept her waiting for more than two months until they granted her a meager loan. This may have even further enhanced her sense of humiliation at the hands of the victors.

Being destitute had bearings on several levels with regard to the colonial order of things. Having no money meant not being able to employ a "sufficient" number of African servants. The number of servants was the utmost symbol of having successfully climbed the social ladder and of one's status within the colonial society. Frieda thought of herself as modest in her wartime demand for three servants, consisting of a "boy," a dhobi (washerman) and a water carrier.[50] By the end of 1918, she had no servants at all, and Frieda bitterly complained that she herself had to do all of her washing and all of the household chores.

There are further indicators of the economic and social decline Frieda experienced during World War I. One is the steady decrease in number and quality of Christmas or birthday presents prepared for Kätchen. Frieda gave detailed accounts of these events and which gifts were given by whom. Most of the presents were self-made toys and clothes, but there were enough of them as Frieda proudly records. In April 1918, however, she described "the saddest holiday, I ever went through," when she noted that she did not have any presents for Kätchen at Christmas 1917, although her daughter had been so well-behaved.[51] The other indicator concerns the clothes Frieda was able to provide for herself and her daughter. Early photographs show her as a well-dressed young woman with an equally well-dressed child. As the war progressed, Frieda lacked the funds to stock new dresses, nor were there sufficient supplies in the colonies. In April 1918, she noted that they had been wearing long pinafore dresses made

---

48 StadtA BS N III 3, 40.
49 See, e.g., StadtA BS N III 28.
50 StadtA BS N III 3, 140.
51 StadtA BS N III 3, 141.

of unbleached cotton cloth for quite some time; shoes and stockings were in disrepair, underpants were full of holes. Although Frieda tried to remain optimistic, she was convinced that her mother should not know about her miserable circumstances.[52] The war had completely dashed all hopes and fantasies of upward social mobility and a more comfortable and well-off life in the colonies.

Epilogue

At the beginning of this essay, I posed the question of what happens when the colonial order, colonial imagination and fantasies fall apart. Frieda Schmidt's writings show that the Great War fundamentally changed what she had imagined as the natural order of things. Alleged certainties concerning the colonized were shattered. The German colonizers suddenly had to realize that the devoted colonial subject, the devoted servant was nothing but a figment of the colonial mind. The same holds true for the colonial construction of *white* complicity, i. e., the alliance between colonizers of different European nationalities, and the social status attached to being a *white* colonial mistress. At the same time, conventional gender constructions unraveled or were even reversed.[53] If only for a brief moment, new possibilities in terms of gender roles presented themselves to Frieda but also to her husband Gottfried.

I chose the title "Woman on the Edge of Time"[54] for this short insight into the life of a *white* German colonial woman at a time of crisis owing to the effects of World War I. The notion of an edge implies that there is an abyss, and for Frieda the loss of what was important in her life – a well-off husband, economic security, social status, a new home in the colony, and, however short-termed, agency – equaled falling into an abyss. For her and her small family, the changes unleashed by the outbreak of the Great War were permanent and devastating. Frieda, Kätchen and Gottfried did not meet again. Mother and daughter returned to Germany in April 1919. There were no financial reserves whatsoever, and their meager possessions could be carried in a little suitcase. Frieda's ambitious expectations regarding economic wealth and social status had not come true. Gottfried was finally allowed to leave India at the beginning of 1920. On a stopover in

---

52 StadtA BS N III 3, 141.
53 Pesek poses it as a question, "The colonial order upside down?" (2011).
54 I chose the title *Woman on the Edge of Time* in reference to and in honor of Marge Piercy's 1976 eponymous novel.

Egypt, where he and 700 so-called "Ahmednagaris" had to wait for their transport to Europe, he caught the Spanish flu and died on 1 February 1920.

In 1947, a now grown-up Käte, Frieda's and Gottfried's daughter, took up the
diary started by her parents in order to complete it with her own memories of
their time in colonial East Africa during the Great War and beyond for her son
Hinrich.[55] Frieda was still alive and supported the endeavor by contributing to
the "lively picture" Käte wanted to convey. History had repeated itself, insofar
as Käte had been widowed during World War II just as her mother had been
in the aftermath of World War I. Bearing in mind that Kätchen had only been
born in May 1914, and was five years old in 1919, it is impossible to determine
who exactly contributed which memory to this last chapter of the "diary" nearly
thirty years after Frieda and Kätchen returned from East Africa to Germany. The
narrative clearly seems to reflect either the perceptions of the small child Käte
during the war or her mother's romanticized retrospective view on an actually
traumatic experience. In any case, Käte as the actual writer of this last chapter
creates a paradisiacal past where the friendship with a little German boy, who
would later become her son's godfather, meant everything. The East African
landscape and scenery is depicted as overwhelmingly beautiful, and the
Amani Research Institute, which Frieda had described as a prison, is remembered by her daughter as one big adventurous playground for her and her friend.
The African landscape is more or less devoid of Africans. Käte describes African
villages and their residents as if they were part of a human zoo only to be visited
on special occasions with special performances specifically for the *white* German
visitors. African drums and dances, colorful cloths and hairstyles, an Indian
shop where everything was available for Europeans – these are the components
of a (post)colonial fantasy that Käte projects in her reminiscences. Therefore, at
least in retrospect of the subsequent generation, the colonial order was constructed as still intact and the hideous British enemies of World War I emerge
as responsible for the German "expulsion from paradise."[56]

Works Cited

Bechhaus-Gerst, Marianne, and Mechthild Leutner, editors. *Frauen in den deutschen Kolonien*
(Christoph Links, 2009).
Conte, Christopher A. "Imperial Science, Tropical Ecology and Indigenous History: Tropical
Research Stations in Northeastern German East Africa, 1896–1914." *Colonialism and the*

---

55 StadtA BS N III 3, 151–173.
56 StadtA BS N III 3, 157.

Modern World: Selected Studies, edited by Gregory Blue, et al. (M. E. Sharpe, 2002), pp. 234–246.

Daniel, Ute. *Arbeiterfrauen in der Kriegsgesellschaft: Beruf, Familie und Politik im Ersten Weltkrieg* (Vandenhoek & Ruprecht, 1989).

Dietrich, Anette. *Weiße Weiblichkeiten: Konstruktionen von "Rasse" und Geschlecht im deutschen Kolonialismus* (transcript, 2007).

Feltman, Brian K. *The Stigma of Surrender: German Prisoners, British Captors, and Manhood in the Great War and Beyond* (U of North Carolina P, 2015).

Göke, Robert. "Im langen Schatten des Kilimanjaro: Die Eheleute Gottfried und Frieda Schmidt aus Schötmar auf einer Plantage in Deutsch-Ostafrika während der Endphase der Kolonialzeit (Teil 1–3)." *Jahrbuch Bad Salzuflen* (1997), pp. 93–118; (1998), pp. 65–91; (1999), pp. 105–118.

Grayzel, Susan. *Women and the First World War* (Longman, 2002).

Grayzel, Susan. *Women's Identities at War: Gender, Motherhood, and Politics in Britain and France during the First World War* (U of North Carolina P, 1999).

Kundrus, Birte. *"Kriegerfrauen": Familienpolitik und Geschlechterverhältnisse im Ersten und Zweiten Weltkrieg* (Christians, 1995).

Mamozai, Martha. *Schwarze Frau, weiße Herrin: Frauenleben in den deutschen Kolonien* (Rowohlt, 1989).

Maß, Sondra. *Weiße Helden, schwarze Krieger: Zur Geschichte kolonialer Männlichkeit in Deuitschland 1918–1964* (Böhlau, 2006).

Murphy, Mahon. "Prisoners of War and Civilian Internees Captured by British and Dominion forces from the German Colonies during the First World War." PhD thesis (Department of International History of the London School of Economics, 2015).

Nipperdey, Thomas. *Deutsche Geschichte 1800–1918.* Vol. 2 (1866–1918), vol. 2/1, Arbeitswelt und Bürgergeist (C.H. Beck, 1990).

Pesek, Michael. "The Colonial Order Upside Down? British and Germans in East African Prisoner-of-War Camps During World War I." *Hybrid Cultures – Nervous States: Britain and Germany in a (Post)Colonial World*, edited by Ulrike Lindner, et al. (Rodopi, 2011), pp. 23–41.

Pesek, Michael. *Das Ende des Kolonialreichs: Ostafrika im Ersten Weltkrieg* (Campus, 2010).

Piercy, Marge. *Woman on the Edge of Time* (Fawcett Crest, 1976).

Pierenkemper, Toni. "Die Einkommensentwicklung der Angestellten in Deutschland: 1880–1913." *Historical Social Research*, vol. 8, no. 3 (1983), pp. 69–92.

Rachamimov, Alon. "The Disruptive Comforts of Drag: (Trans)Gender Performances among Prisoners of War in Russia, 1914–1920." *The American Historical Review*, vol. 111, no. 2 (2006), pp. 362–382.

Rachamimov, Alon. *POWs and the Great War: Captivity on the Eastern Front* (Berg, 2002).

Schmidt Papers. Municipal archive of Bad Salzuflen (StadtA BS), inventory N III.

Sinha, Mrinalini. *Colonial Masculinity: The 'Manly Englishman' and the 'Effeminate Bengali' in the Late Nineteenth Century* (Manchester UP, 1995).

Steinbach, Daniel. "Defending the Heimat – The Germans in South-West Africa and East Africa during the First World War." *Untold War: New Perspectives in First World War Studies*, edited by Heather Jones, et al. (Brill, 2008), pp. 179–208.

Steinbach, Daniel. "Power Majorities and Local Minorities: German and British Colonials in East Africa during the First World War." *Germans as Minorities in World War I*, edited by Panikos Panayi (Ashgate 2014), pp. 263–288.

Stibbe, Matthew. "Gendered Experiences of Civilian Internment during the First World War: A Forgotten Dimension of Wartime Violence." *Gender and Conflict since 1914: Historical and Interdisciplinary Perspectives*, edited by Ana Carden-Coyne (Palgrave Macmillan, 2012), pp. 14–28.

Walgenbach, Katharina. *"Die weiße Frau als Trägerin deutscher Kultur": Koloniale Diskurse über "Rasse" und Klasse im Kaiserreich* (Campus, 2005).

Zantop, Susanne. *Colonial Fantasies: Conquest, Family, and Nation in Precolonial Germany, 1770–1870* (Duke UP, 1997).

Livia Rigotti
World War I in Samoa as Reported by Frieda Zieschank in the German Colonial Magazine *Kolonie und Heimat*

Focussing on the Samoa Islands in the Pacific, the texts under discussion in the following analysis offer a rare perspective on the outbreak of World War I and its consequences. On 30 August 1914, New Zealand troops occupied the Samoan islands that were a German colony at this time. In contrast to the German colonies in Africa, historical research seldomly considers the so-called "South Sea Colonies" and the fact that German women lived in these South Pacific territories is typically overlooked. One of these women, Frieda Zieschank reported in detail her experience of the war from this peripheral spot of the world and published her impressions in books as well as in articles in the popular colonial magazine *Kolonie und Heimat* (Colony and homeland).[1] Apart from some brief comments by a few German nurses, Zieschank's texts remain the only known published sources offering a German woman's perspective on the effects of World War I in Samoa and the national feeling from the distant colony. Her texts serve as a unique historical source, and because they provide much more information than Zieschank probably intended, the following investigation offers a close reading of her publications that aims to inspire further analysis conducted in the context of Gender Studies, War Studies, Colonial Studies and other approaches.

Historical background and source base

"... like a miracle of creation – like a precious jewel – like a bright emerald – lifted to light from the deep sea by the good hand of God – it lies there, wreathed by a white shimmering reef: Samoa!" (Zieschank 1923, 49).[2] With these impassioned words Frieda Zieschank describes her temporary home in Samoa in the early 1900s in her novel *Ein verlorenes Paradies* (A lost paradise).

German interest in the Pacific Islands began in the 1850s, with German traders concentrating first on whaling, then on trading the most precious product of

---

1 The dates of Zieschank's birth and death are unknown.
2 All quotations from Zieschank are my own translations.

https://doi.org/10.1515/9783110572001-006

the region, *copra,* (the dried flesh of the coconut), which grew in importance (Gründer 2002, 44–45). The German government was willing to protect these economic interests, and apart from that, land possessions in the Pacific proved to be attractive strategic locations for naval bases. Following the German colonization of the northeastern part of New Guinea with the Bismarck Archipelago, the northeastern Solomon Islands, the Caroline Islands, Palau, the Mariana Islands, the Marshall Islands and Nauru, the German flag was hoisted in Apia, the capital of Samoa, on 1 March 1900 (Mückler 2012, 75–76).

From 1889 to 1899 Americans, British and Germans jointly ruled the Samoan Islands with little collaborative success owing to their differing interests. In the Tripartite Convention of 1899 Britain abandoned its claim to Samoa; Germany in return agreed to give up its claim to Tonga and a big part of the Solomon Islands. The United States and the German Empire divided up the Samoan islands, and Germany acquired the larger share of the territory with Upolu and Savai'i (Mückler 2012, 75–76). The German colonial administration of Samoa reached a sudden end when New Zealand officially took possession on 30 August 1914, one day after ground troops arrived. Samoa therefore became the first German territory to be occupied by allied forces during World War I.[3]

These events are rarely considered when the outbreak and consequences of World War I are reviewed. One reason is Samoa's peripheral location and its rather minor historical importance. Contemporaneous witnesses, in fact, already showed little interest in these Pacific colonies with their poor connection to the motherland, when compared to German possessions in Africa. The population of Samoa was nearly cut off from the outside world and communication with the motherland was extremely complicated: mail from Germany had to travel around the world for 42 days before it reached Samoa, and the islands were not accessible per cable until the end of the German colonial administration. Since the tropical climate was considered harmful to the health of Europeans, Samoa was – like the other Pacific colonies – never considered an area of settlement, which meant that only few Germans lived there. On 1 January 1913, the reporting date of the last official statistics published before the outbreak of World War I, only 222 German men and 63 German women lived in Samoa (Reichskolonialamt 1914, 34–35). Therefore, it is not surprising that the source base for investigating the period of German colonialism in the South Pacific is much less compared to that of the German colonies in Africa. Especially rare are historical sources with

---

[3] For details of World War I in Samoa see Hiery (2002, 832–836; 1995, 154–182) and Meleisea (1987, 102–125).

female authorship, as only very few women wrote about their "South Sea experience."

One of these women was Frieda Zieschank who followed her husband to Samoa in 1906, where he worked as a doctor in colonial service. Zieschank lived with her husband in Apia where she gave birth to two children and they remained there for ten years. She took care of her family and the household but was able to delegate many tasks to her servants. In her free time, she enjoyed helping her husband during surgery or accompanying him to visit patients, especially when he was called to a birth (Zieschank, 1918, 21; Loosen 2014, 239–241).[4] Zieschank documents this period of her life in several publications; she is the only German woman to publish a book about her stay in Samoa (*Ein Jahrzehnt in Samoa* / A decade in Samoa, 1918). Five years later, she published a colonial novel that also reflected her experience in Samoa, titled *Ein verlorenes Paradies* (A lost paradise). Furthermore, she wrote three extensive articles that were printed in the colonial magazine *Kolonie und Heimat*, the periodical of the *Frauenbund der Deutschen Kolonialgesellschaft* (Women's League of the German Colonial Society), henceforth referred to as the *Frauenbund*.[5]

The *Frauenbund* was founded in 1907, with the intent to increase the interest of young women in colonial topics and to support, both spiritually and financially, their move to the colonies. Supporting the settlement of young German women was thought to facilitate the creation and expansion of German family life in the colonies and was considered a means to prevent sexual relations between German men and indigenous women. Regardless of how dubious the intentions of the *Frauenbund* must appear from today's perspective, the women of the early twentieth century were obviously enthusiastic about them: the association recruited 1,000 members in the first three months of its existence. According to historian Birthe Kundrus, *Kolonie und Heimat* quickly became the most popular German colonial magazine, and in 1910, three years after the first issue, it had 100,000 subscribers (2003, 12 n34). The magazine attracted enthusiastic readers both in the homeland and in the colonies – also in Samoa as the source material shows (Loosen 2014, 105–106). Readers in the metropole and in the periphery valued the magazine as a connection to places across the sea. For example, a German nurse Auguste Hertzer stationed in colonial New Guinea, wrote in her diary that reading *Kolonie and Heimat* felt like shaking hands with her dear old friends overseas (diary fragment without date, between May

---

4 Loosen is now publishing under the name Rigotti.
5 For details of the *Frauenbund* and *Kolonie und Heimat*, see Walgenbach (2005, 83–110) and Loosen (2014, 98–106).

1891 and January 1893). Corresponding to the objectives of the *Frauenbund, Kolonie und Heimat* was oriented toward the national conservative line. Frequent subjects were the contributions of women to the colonial project and the challenges they faced in their daily lives in the colonies. With these texts, the magazine helped to create a specific role model (Walgenbach 2005, 83). After the outbreak of World War I, *Kolonie and Heimat* appeared in a shortened form as the so-called "war issues."

Zieschank's reports appeared in some of these issues. She wanted to present her readers with "an accurate description" of wartime in Samoa (1918/19b, 12.1, 6). Her goal was to report her experiences in a "plain and simple" manner, without exaggerations and embellishments, so she started a series of articles titled "Zwei Kriegsjahre in Samoa" (Two war years in Samoa). The headline suggests that the story was taken from Zieschank's diary; the story is subdivided by the dates of her entries. The text was issued in ten parts within the twelfth year of *Kolonie und Heimat* (1918/1919) and was published in nearly identical form in the second half of her book, *Ein Jahrzehnt in Samoa*, which adds two concluding chapters. Together with the six-part article series, "Heimwärts durch die englische Kontrolle" (Homewards through English control) that was published in *Kolonie and Heimat* that same year (1918/1919a), these publications are outstanding historical sources, as they are among the very few surviving descriptions of the events of the war in Samoa by German female authors and none describes their experiences in as much detail as Zieschank.

Particularly interesting is the role the author ascribes to herself and other women during these events. What role model(s) does she create in her texts? What relationship does she establish through her writings to her homeland as a "Kolonialdeutsche" (colonial German)? What effects did the isolated setting have on her perception of the events of war? Does the author position herself as a patriot in her texts, and what does that mean for her? Last but not least, what effect on her readers does she likely intend to achieve?

This investigation, which provides a more descriptive discussion about one unique source rather than a literary and theoretically informed analysis, argues that Zieschank reveals more of the historic discourse than she probably intended with her so called "plain and simple" reports (1918/19b, 12.1, 6). In particular, the great importance of sacrifice in the context of war is a characteristic feature of her writings that deserves a closer look. Zieschank's texts also illustrate how important a concept the enemy is for the creation of national identities, as for example Anette Dietrich stresses (2007, 53). This already becomes evident in her first article concerning the outbreak of war.

The outbreak of war and the occupation of Samoa

Zieschank begins her reports with the 1914 assassination of the Austrian Arch-duke Franz Ferdinand in Sarajevo. She writes that the news left the Germans in Samoa "distressed and indignant" but she considers the effect not "as deeply felt as in the homeland" (1918/19b, 12.1, 9; see also, 1918, 117–155). She apologetically adds that in remote Samoa nothing has an immediate effect on the colonial inhabitants, because all overseas news arrives weeks later. According to Zieschank, there is no apprehension in Samoa of the serious consequences of the assassination and, because no actual newspapers are available, everybody continues their normal life "unsuspecting and peaceful" (1918/19b, 12.1, 9). Only when the rumor of a German mobilization reaches Zieschank on the evening of 31 July 1914, do "horrible days of nervousness and uncertainty" begin (1918/19b, 12.1, 9). Here the reader sees, for the first time, a recurring motif in Zieschank's texts – her sadness that, in this remote colony, she has to be content with rumors. She experiences the anxiety of waiting for news as a heavy burden (1918/19b, 12.1, 9; 12.4, 7; 12.9, 7).

Even as the order for mobilization was announced in Apia on 3 August 1914, local Germans were apparently still uncertain about who the enemy was (1918/19b, 12.1, 9). When information reached Samoa that not just Russia, but also France and the United Kingdom, had declared war on Germany, Zieschank describes the sense of horror and contrasts it with the presumed atmosphere in Germany:

> Here it was, the dreadful, unthinkable! We stared at each other in horror, unable to speak a word for minutes. Everyone probably saw the picture of the precious homeland before his inner eye, the homeland to which something so dreadful had happened. Oh you, having stood at home in the roaring racket of the mobilization, you can't imagine what effect that had on us on our lonely island. We heard no emphatic speeches, read no flaming essays, didn't see anything of Young-Germany's cheering enthusiasm for war. We just saw the horrible ghost that arose before us. (1918/19b, 12.1, 9)

According to Zieschank, concerns for the homeland dominated the mood of the Germans in Samoa because the colony was isolated from the enthusiast war rhetoric, which overcame Germany. Shortly after the outbreak of the war, the new radio tower in Apia started to work and, from that point on, up-to-date news was finally available in Samoa and eager support for the war subsequently spread at once to the colony. Zieschank writes:

> And a spark of the huge fire of enthusiasm for war in Germany had now also reached us lonesome people and caught fire. Yes, also in us, in every German, the holy fire burned.

> Then came the victory of Liège. Oh, proud cheering! What marvellous luck to be German! But beside this there grew a burning pain, not to be there. (1918/19b, 12.1, 9)

Zieschank's effusive patriotic language expresses her profound identification with Germany, made more compelling through the geographical distance. Wanting to make up for not being in Germany during this important event, the constant declaration of her strong love for her fatherland seems to compensate for her very limited possibilities to contribute and participate in her nation's victories.

In the period immediately after the outbreak of the war, the only sign of Germany's involvement in a war was the newly conscripted German security team that patrolled the colony. It was forbidden to leave on any lights after nine p.m. that could be seen from the harbor. The settlers of other, now enemy, nations, were allowed to retain all of their liberties, as well as their weapons. Zieschank reports that it was difficult for German settlers all of a sudden to see the British as enemies since they had lived together many years in harmony (1918/19b, 12.1, 9; see also 1923, 221 and Hiery 2002, 650 – 651).

According to Zieschank, everyone – regardless of their nationality – worried about Samoa's destiny and wondered whether British or French troops would arrive. On 29 August 1914, warships were at last sighted on the horizon. An Australian-New Zealand armada took possession of Samoa: the ships were Australian, the troops came from New Zealand (Hiery 2002, 832). Zieschank writes that she involuntarily laughed when she saw the fleet because the enemy forces seemed excessive for the occupation of small Samoa: "This honor that the enemy paid us!" (1918/19b, 12.2, 6). In Zieschank's opinion, the caution the enemy boats displayed vis-à-vis the Germans when searching for mines in the harbor was extremely exaggerated: "Oh God, we harmless, helpless people and mines!" (1918/19b, 12.2, 6). Indeed, the German population of Samoa had no chance to defend itself, so the German governor had no other choice but to surrender the colony to the New Zealanders without resistance, after which he was removed from the island as a prisoner of war (Hiery 2002, 833). From the very beginning, Zieschank depicts the occupying forces as ridiculous figures: "The surrounding area of the town was swarming with English troops, most of them very young boys from New Zealand. In dense, disordered mobs they closed the roads, holding their rifles with the fixed bayonets in a clumsy way" (1918/19b, 12.2, 7). Zieschank calls the occupying forces from New Zealand "Tommies" and decries their military discipline. She claims that they were not even able to handle their rifles and seemed to be afraid of them instead (1918/19b, 12.4, 6). The trenches the soldiers dug were so small that not even children could take cover in them. Mockingly, she describes the soldiers' clothes as made from a heavy loden fabric that was completely inappropriate for the warm Samoan climate. During their exhausting work on the trenches, the men saw no other solution than to take off their clothes, which led a horrified Zieschank to comment:

> They simply removed [...] their clothes, and on the beach road of Apia you had the outrageous sight of a white naked man digging up the ground, dressed in a lava-lava [Samoan loincloth]. The Tommies lack every sense to which a white man owes his reputation to the colored people. (1918/19b, 12.4, 6)

In Zieschank's eyes, the New Zealanders, by wearing the scant lava-lava, discredited themselves still further by reducing the supposed appropriate distance between the colonized and colonizing population that the German colonial press constantly demanded. She uses every opportunity to represent to her readers the occupying forces as incompetent and dim-witted. For instance, she claims, "The pupil of the most modest German village school has ten times more general knowledge than the 'educated' New Zealander" (1918/19b, 12.4, 6). The negative picture she constructs of the enemy troops allows her to present the Germans as clearly superior. Here it becomes evident that Zieschank had passed through the fluid border between patriotism and nationalism: while patriotism is usually defined as love for one's country, mostly accompanied by the wish to contribute to the public interest, nationalism devalues other countries and their inhabitants (Schubert and Klein 2011, headwords "Nationalismus" and "Patriotismus").[6] In this context, the term "culture" and the concept of being cultured as opposed to "primitive" also play an important role.

Following the dominant understanding of gendered roles in Germany at that time, Zieschank, as a white German woman colonist, felt responsible for promoting German culture in the colony. The colonial press constantly emphasized that German women were "bearers of an important cultural mission" (Trägerinnen einer wichtigen Kulturmission), as for instance social scientists Katharina Walgenbach and Anette Dietrich point out (Walgenbach 2005, 119, 125–130; Dietrich 2007, 83; Loosen 2014, 178–180). Zieschank derides the soldiers from New Zealand as an affront to civilization and their defense of culture as an oxymoron: "They fight for Great Britain, they fight for culture! The New Zealander for culture and against Germany! You have to know these people to acknowledge the grotesquery!" (1918/19b, 12.4, 6). The assertion that war served as a defense of cultural values was a popular propaganda slogan of all warring countries, especially during World War I. Not just the German side felt entangled in a war of beliefs, they

---

6 For the historical changes in the terms "patriotism" and "nationalism," see Kronenberg (2013, 135–140).

claimed that the triumph of their own culture was for the benefit of humanity as a whole (Bremm 2013, 24–36). Zieschank's report is a typical expression of this discourse, in which the author obviously sees no inconsistency between her propagandistic way of writing and the self-declared goal of describing the events in Samoa in "a plain and accurate fashion" (1918/19b, 12.1, 9).

Despite her constant criticism of the occupying forces, Zieschank remarks that the soldiers from New Zealand did not riot immediately after they landed, and the Germans remained in their homes undisturbed (1918/19b, 12.4, 7). After a few days of occupation, all German public officials resigned their posts because they did not want to work as "servants of the occupation service" (Hiery 2002, 833). On 12 September 1914, they learned of their impending journey to New Zealand as prisoners of war. Two wives accompanied their husbands voluntarily, according to Zieschank (1918, 128). She reports that the Germans found it difficult to say farewell, but, since they were certain that the war would not last long, they arranged to meet each other for Christmas.

The importance of sacrifice for the homeland

While Zieschank hoped for a quick end to the war, she initially felt lonely in Samoa and longed for her homeland (1918/19b, 12.4, 7). More importantly, she stressed again and again her yearning for the opportunity to make sacrifices for her fatherland (1918/19b 12.4, 7; 12.5, 6; 1918/19a 12.33, 6). She describes her own "burning impatience" and the enthusiastic cheering among other Germans, when, on 14 September 1914, German warships unexpectedly appeared. Despite the expectation of battles, in which her husband would partake, and the probable destruction of her home, her enthusiasm remained unbridled: "Even if the farewell was bitter, we were still allowed to make a sacrifice for the fatherland at last!" (1918/19b, 12.5, 6; see also 1923, 215). Initially, however, Zieschank's only contribution was to pack her husband's suitcase to prepare for his departure and to help the German nurses sew a Red Cross flag. As the Germans "did not doubt for one second" that the German ships came to "free Samoa" (1918/19b, 12.5, 6), the disappointment was enormous when they left for unknown reasons. While the author describes her expectations of the military conflict's certain victory in detail, she remains nearly mute about the German warship's disappearance: "I can't speak about the misery of this hour, it hurts too much" (1918/19b, 12.6, 6; see also 1923, 215).

Zieschank notes a growing lack of discipline among the New Zealand soldiers as time passed (1918/19b, 12.6, 6) and repeated conflicts between the soldiers and their superiors: the colonel in charge even had to request a warship to support him against his own troops (1918/19b, 12.7, 6). This description of the alleged powerlessness of the commanders served Zieschank in two ways: she first wanted to cast the New Zealand military forces in an ambiguous light and, second, to impress upon her readers back home that their lack of discipline constituted a threat to the Germans in Samoa. She reports that on Christmas Eve, her house came under siege by about 30 enemy soldiers who demanded alcohol (1918/19b, 12.7, 6). While her husband talked to the men, the author, together with her small son and his nanny, secretly ran to a neighbor's house for help. When they returned, her husband had already diplomatically settled the conflict. All in all, the Germans did not have much to complain about the occupying forces acting cruelly; Zieschank herself admits: "We personally didn't experience any truly frightening moments apart from that dreadful Christmas Eve" (1918/19b, 12.6, 6). In a further text, she expresses shame for not having to suffer more terrible effects of the war in Samoa. As a kind of overcompensation, she depicts the comparatively small sacrifices she had to make during the occupation as immensely difficult. Measured against the tragic consequences of the outbreak of war for all those who did not live in the insular security of a South Sea colony, Zieschank's descriptions of the "silent suffering" of the Germans in Samoa seems disproportionate to the suffering that occurred in Europe (1918/19b, 12.9, 6):

> Now I want to talk about this, how nearly every one of us has suffered emotionally out here, although I know that no one who has been at home [in Germany, L.R.] during this time is able to sympathize with me at all. Or is there anyone in the homeland who can understand that we looked in despairing rage at our sumptuous roasts, the wonderful big hams, knowing that at home shortages reigned, that a scrap was measured for each person? At home, everyone helped on the whole, albeit it was just by saving and sparing. Even that was refused us, our saving would not have been useful for the homeland. Excluded! We were excluded from our holy people's community (Volksgemeinschaft)! (Zieschank 1918/19b, 12.9, 6; see also 1918/19a, 12.32, 6)

As this passage demonstrates, being a valued member of the community was measured by the sacrifices that were "allowed" to be made for the homeland. Zieschank's concept of sacrifice resonates with the feeling of national solidarity that French author and scientist Ernest Renan stresses in his famous speech given at the Sorbonne in March 1882: "A nation is a large, supportive community, built by the feelings for the sacrifices one made and is willing to make" (qtd. in Kronenberg 2013, 41). For Zieschank, this conversely meant that being denied the possibility of making a sacrifice equalled exclusion from the community, of which she wanted so dearly to be part:

At home, all forces moved for the fatherland in these hard times and we couldn't do anything, nothing at all, not even make the smallest sacrifice. We felt like outcasts. [...] Proud post-victory euphoria at home and we had to swallow bitter humiliation. [...] Anyhow we felt lonely, lonely. (1918/19b, 12.4, 7, see also 1918/19a, 12.32, 6)

This feeling of loneliness and isolation dominated Zieschank's experience of war so much so that it is taken up again in her 1923 colonial novel *Ein verlorenes Paradies* set in Samoa; here, too, the protagonists complain about their isolation and the resulting powerlessness (213). The loneliness in the South Sea colonies was often discussed in times of peace, but the events of war in the German mother country apparently intensified these feelings: "You were cut off from your tribe, a scattered leaf" (Zieschank 1923, 220). Zieschank recalls the "longing for the community of people in hard times of need" the "bitterest thing you can imagine" and claims it was harder to bear than the longing for loved ones who were far away (1918/19a, 12.32, 6).

As confirmed by historian Joseph Hermann Hiery, the Germans in Samoa had to continue to abide by the rules of the occupying forces: they had to comply with a curfew in the evening and were not allowed to turn on a light at night. To change their place of residence they needed written permission, even when it was just for one night. Every German was obliged to register in the capital, Apia, once a week. Even minor violations of these rules were severely punished (Hiery 2002, 834; Zieschank 1918, 1918/19b, 12.6, 6 and 1918/19a, 12.33, 6).

Moreover, during the British occupation, the Germans in Samoa were not allowed to receive mail from other countries or to send any, so they did not receive any messages about the well-being of their relatives back in Germany (Hiery 2002, 834; Loosen 2014, 576). They did not know whether male relatives had been killed in action or how their children, who often lived in Germany, were faring. Zieschank regards the bitter isolation and imposed restrictions on communication, that were stricter in Samoa than in any other South Sea colony, as "senseless, contemptible cruelty" (1918/19a, 12.36, 7; see also 12.32, 6 and 1918/19b, 12.9, 6). She had left her mother and two of her children in Germany and tried desperately to hear from them. When, at Christmastime in 1915, she pleaded with the censor to at least tell her whether her relatives were still alive, he answered apathetically that news of somebody's death would have been communicated. However, even that would often not happen, Zieschank writes (1918/19b, 12.9, 6).

Furthermore, the Germans were not allowed to read any German newspapers, so they could only follow the events of war in Europe through English newspapers, which they distrusted. Zieschank regarded the propaganda they contained against "Huns and Barbarians," as well as the caricatures of the German emperor, as hurtful (1918/19b, 12.9, 6). Still, she stresses: "But in spite of the many humiliations we had to endure, the many invectives against Germany and the lies we had to hear, we never doubted the final victory of Germany and that in our beloved Samoa the German flag would be hoisted again" (1918/19b, 12.9, 7). For her, as a colonial German, winning back the South Sea colonies was, of course, a central goal of the war, as can also be seen in other sections of her texts. The reporting in English newspapers was not only frustrating for Zieschank, she also gained satisfaction from reading between the lines about the "angry admiration" of the English for the German enemy and their talent for organization (1918/19b, 12.9, 6). Twice, German newspapers found their way to Samoa. They reached the colony only in fragments, and they were six months old, but they were handed around like a treasure among the settlers. This hunger for news was more acute than the hunger for bread and meat in the homeland, Zieschank claims, though this must be understood in the context of her desire to sacrifice (1918/19b, 12.9, 7; 1918/19a, 12.32, 6) in order to emphasize her sense of belonging to the German national community.

Apart from the experience of isolation and the desire to participate in the war effort, German colonists experienced the constant danger that every German man might suddenly be transported as a prisoner to New Zealand and this fear was "nerve-wracking" (Zieschank 1918/19b, 12.9, 7). Indeed, more and more civilians followed the public officials into prisoner of war camps. In no other South Sea colony were so many people arrested, a fact that is generally seen as a symptom of the exceptionally despotic rule of the inexperienced British military administrator, Colonel Robert Logan (Hiery 1995, 157 and 2002, 833 – 834; Meleisea 1987, 106). Thus, for many German women, the worst change the British occupation brought was a long separation from husbands, who were taken as prisoners. Prisoner of war Rudolf Berking wrote many letters of complaint about the prison camp and also made many requests in the name of his fellow prisoners to the General Governor of New Zealand, Lord Liverpool, hoping that he could end their desperate situation.

In November 1917, Berking pointed out that six of the prisoners had been separated from their families for 25 months and eight of them for more than 19 months. He stressed that the children and wives of the prisoners were the real victims of this situation, and again he begged that the prisoners might return to Samoa (Berking to Liverpool, Motuihi Island, 23 November 1917, ANZ (W), IT1 275, Ex 29/17(1)). The requests were futile, and the women saw their husbands again long after the war had ended (Headquarters/Auckland Military District to the Director of Personal Services/N.Z. Military Forces, 29 November 1918, ANZ(W), IT1 275, Ex 29/17(1)).

To Zieschank's great delight, her husband escaped arrest; he was able to pass himself off as a prisoner of war in order to be transported to Germany (1918/19b, 12.10, 6), at least this is *one* version of her story, which will be explained below.

The different versions of the homeward journey

In May 1916, Zieschank was allowed to travel back to Germany together with her young son on neutral ships via America, which did not enter the war until April 1917, and neutral Scandinavia. Although it was difficult for Zieschank's family to say farewell to Samoa, she expresses great enthusiasm for permission to travel home: "So it was true, we were really allowed to go home during wartime? We were allowed to help and to suffer?" (1918/19b, 12.10, 6; see also 1918/19a, 12.32, 6). Again, Zieschank stresses her patriotic readiness to make sacrifices and does not tell the reader about any possible fears, sorrows or doubts regarding the journey to her war-affected homeland. Her German friends in Samoa would have envied the family because of their exit permit and many asked them to give messages to their relatives in Germany. Two German companies even handed annual reports to the author and, fearing the customs officers, she learned them by heart (Zieschank 1918/19b, 12.10, 6).

Zieschank's account of her journey homeward, which started in Pago-Pago together with other Germans from different South Sea colonies, appeared as a series of articles published as "Zwei Kriegsjahre in Samoa." She wanted to share some touching moments with German readers, like when an orchestra at the pier in Honolulu played "Deutschland, Deutschland über alles" (Germany above all) for the German passengers as the ship left the harbor: "Light tears were running down our faces, we hadn't been allowed to hear this for nearly two years!" (Zieschank 1918/19b, 12.11, 6).

Upon sighting the European mainland on 20 June 1916, Zieschank relates being very moved to arrive in "poor, war-affected" Europe (1918/19b, 12.11, 7). Even more emotional is the description of her arrival in her homeland at the end of her series of articles: "And then our feet touched German soil, our eyes in tears greeted the land! Homeland, precious, much longed-for homeland, we greet you!" (1918/19b, 12.11, 7).

Although Zieschank described her experience beginning with the outbreak of the war followed by her arrival in Germany in *Kolonie und Heimat* in 1918, the first article of a new series called "Heimwärts durch die englische Kontrolle" (Homewards through English control 1918/19a, 12.32, 6) appeared 21 issues later in 1919. Here, too, the subtitle indicates that the series is based on Frieda Zieschank's "Tagebuchblätter aus Samoa in der Kriegszeit" (Diary from Samoa in wartime), but here the author tells a different story. As the title suggests, the focus is on the homeward journey, this time depicted as a great adventure. The author casts herself center stage, portraying herself as a brave, clever and cunning woman, who outwitted the British enemy. At the same time, she endeavors to make clear that she was motivated by her love of country and her husband; she tells the story of how she helped him flee to Germany, so he could report for a mission as a reserve medical officer in the Navy. Most likely, Zieschank desired to declare her patriotism publicly. At the beginning of this series of articles, Zieschank describes a visit to German friends in Samoa, who are very happy about their purchase of a new gramophone. Together they triumphantly find out that the gramophone is a German product, although it is labelled as a British one. They play "God Save the King" but sing the text of the hymn of the German Emperor "Heil dir im Siegerkranz" (Hail to you in the victor's wreath) until they become hoarse (Zieschank 1918/19a, 12.33, 6). As in the episode quoted above about "Deutschland, Deutschland über alles," the mention of patriotic songs importantly demonstrates the author's allegiances and asserts her national identity.

The reader then becomes familiar with the details of the plan for the homeward journey. While Zieschank, as a woman, was allowed to travel home freely, her husband had to be smuggled through British control from Samoa to Germany. Only a few accomplices were initiated into the plan, among them, Klinger, the dormant partner of the Zieschank plantation, who agreed to take care of their possessions after their departure. The author cites him with the following words that very much resemble her own: "[...] greet the homeland for me. And tell everyone at home that nobody here doubts the German victory and that the Empire is strong enough to hoist the German flag here again!" (Zieschank 1918/19a, 12.33, 6). Corresponding to this patriotic conviction, Klinger approved of Zieschank's escape plan. They had decided that after Frieda Zieschank's departure, her husband would start a journey through Samoa. On this trip, he would pretend to have a fatal riding accident (1918/19a, 12.33, 6; 12.35, 6–7). To that end, the author's husband later informed her that he shot his horse and pushed it off the cliff into the sea. He also made sure that Samoans passing nearby would hear his cry and find the sun-helmet in the bushes. He then hid in the woods, shaved his long beard, changed his clothes and waited until loyal Samoans and "half-castes" rowed him at night into the American part of Samoa (1918/19a, 12.35, 6–7).

Zieschank describes being troubled by another problem: she wanted to take the few thousand marks with her from Samoa that she had hidden in a jar in the grounds of her garden. She needed the money to pay the accomplices who organized her flight to Pago-Pago and to buy tickets. The occupying forces only allowed her to carry 2,000 marks at the most, so Zieschank searched for a suitable method to smuggle the money (1918/19a, 12.32, 6; 12.33, 6–7; see also 1918/19b, 12.10, 6). She describes in detail how she found a way after various considerations and experiments. In the end, she hid the notes and some pieces of gold in a canteen made of aluminium, fixed it with liquid plaster, poured in some hot paraffin to seal it and filled the bottle with cold tea (1918/19a, 12.33, 7). Zieschank stresses that German customs officers would probably have found her hiding place but she believed that New Zealanders were incapable of discovering it: "these former dockers, waiters and hunters of rabbits?" (1918/19a, 12.33, 7; see also 12.32, 6). When her plan succeeds, she proudly reports how a German captain, whom she met in the American part of Samoa, admired her for her cleverness: "Yes, the women, the women, even out here in the South Sea they dupe the men with their sharpness! [...] I'll be damned, you have taken care of things very well and smuggled a decent amount out of the claws of the British!" (1918/19a, 12.34, 7).

Zieschank recounts how she organized the escape of her husband from Pago-Pago. It was her job to convince a befriended "half-caste" to let some oarsmen transport her husband from the German part of Samoa to Pago-Pago. Different from the preceding articles, here Zieschank portrays herself as a "strong woman," who moved self-confidently among men of status, such as the German consul and the German captain; she even played the card game "Skat" with them, and succeeded in realizing her plans (1918/19a, 12.34, 6–7; 12.35, 6). After her husband's lucky escape, the couple travelled together to San Francisco, U.S.A. To be on the safe side, Zieschank pretended to travel alone while her husband travelled incognito as "Mr. Neals" from Auckland (1918/19a, 12.35, 7). From San Francisco, the couple took the train eastwards. In order to cross the Atlantic to Europe, they found a Los Angeles businessman who agreed to have the author's husband travel with him as his secretary: the couple did not want to arouse any suspicion of being together (1918/19a, 12.33, 7). After all, there was a risk that the true identity of her husband could be discovered. Zieschank recounts with great relief: "We made it! Out of the territory of the hated Union Jack at last!!!" (1918/19a, 12.37, 6).

According to this series of articles, Zieschank not only triumphantly disclosed the secret of her husband's identity to her fellow passengers, but also experienced some surprises herself after they safely arrived in Christiana, Sweden: a supposedly deaf and dumb Spanish passenger turned out to be "a good German," and the butler of a Swedish countess on board was in reality her own German husband. The countess accompanied him to Germany "with the most cold-bloodedness right under the noses of the English," Zieschank delights (1918/19a, 12.33, 7). The author presents this clever and beautiful countess as another brave female role model (1918/19a, 12.36, 6; 12.37, 6): "What a cargo of patriotism, yearning, courage and cunning was carried in such an ocean steamer at this time!" (1918/19a, 12.37, 6). Zieschank ends the account of her adventure by reminding the readers that she herself exhibited a significant amount of "patriotism, yearning, courage and cunning" as an accomplice in the escape of her husband.

However, the question remains how this version of her description of the journey can be aligned with the preceding one. Assuming that both series of articles describe Zieschank's personal experience, allegedly based on her diary entries, there are numerous inconsistencies. Although the dates of her departure from Samoa and her itinerary line up in both texts, from Pago-Pago onwards the author reports different dates for her stopovers. In the first series of articles, Zieschank mentions that her small son was traveling with her, in the second one she does not. Significantly, it is obvious that she refers to her husband as "Kurt" in the second text, although it is known from different sources that his name was Hugo.[7] Also in her book *Ein Jahrzehnt in Samoa*, Zieschank tells readers that she and her child were traveling alone to Germany via America, while her husband initially had to stay in a prisoner of war camp in Somes Island, New Zealand before he could come home (1918, 155).

The difference in the versions could be explained by the dates of publication; maybe the author only risked telling the whole truth about the homeward journey of her husband after the official end of the war, which falls *between* the two series of articles and *after* the publication of her first book. An argument for this is that she dropped a hint about the smuggled money in the first text ("Well, I knew how to help myself, but at the moment I am not allowed to give any details," 1918/19b, 12.10, 6), while she reports the successful fraud in the second text, in a very detailed fashion (1918/19b, 12.33, 7). However, if Zieschank wanted to tell the "true story" of the homeward journey of her husband after the end of the war, it remains unclear why she would give different dates for her itinerary and a different name for her husband; after all, he could be easily identified from her authorship and was no longer in need of being disguised.

Alternatively, we can hypothesize that the author just enjoyed publishing another series of articles in *Kolonie und Heimat*, this time one in which she could let her imagination run wild, presenting herself (or rather the female first-person narrator) in a heroic, adventurous role during World War I. After the end of the

---

7 For example: Adressbuch für Deutsch-Neuguinea, Samoa, Kiautschou. Nach amtlichen Quellen bearbeitet, Berlin 1913 (Directory for German New Guinea, Samoa, Kiautschou. Based on official sources, Berlin 1913), and different letters by Hugo Zieschank in MESC(AU): S15-IG86-F15.

war and the final loss of her beloved colony of Samoa, it may have been a patriotic pleasure for her to tell a story in which the Germans deceived the "simple" British officials. Whether Zieschank herself or the editorial staff of *Kolonie und Heimat* had the idea of writing that these articles were based on Frieda Zieschank's "Tagebuchblätter aus Samoa in der Kriegszeit" (Diary from Samoa in wartime) remains unclear. Surely their alleged authenticity would have increased the interest of readers.

Conclusion

In the end, it is irrelevant how the author's husband travelled back to Germany and whether the "cunning female accomplices" who aided in the escape in the second series of articles are fictitious or real because at issue is the type of representation. Zieschank's texts reveal the role she ascribed to white German colonial women in World War I Samoa: they are portrayed as supporting their white German husbands and their fatherland bravely and selflessly, always ready to make sacrifices. Zieschank used the special historical circumstances to demonstrate female power, and the female characters in her texts all fulfill this ideal.

The source texts that have been under consideration in this chapter show that the author, different from what she claims at the beginning of the first series of articles, did not merely report the events in Samoa, but rather, wanted to communicate specific messages again and again in her text. First of all, she wanted to show that despite their isolation, the Germans in Samoa were true patriots who suffered as a result of not being able to provide active support to their fatherland in a time of war. Zieschank claimed that to endure this isolation and the forced idleness was a larger sacrifice for the colonial Germans than ever could be imagined in their homeland. Even as a woman, the author presented herself as an equal to all other Germans in terms of patriotic readiness to make sacrifices. She stressed that within the realm of possibilities, the colonial Samoan Germans tried to serve the fatherland in the war, for instance, by a skillful and daring flight to their homeland or giving assistance to such a plan. In contrast to the colonial Germans, the New Zealand occupying forces were presented as clearly inferior to the Germans in military, intellectual and cultural capabilities. Zieschank did not get tired of repeating that no German in the South Sea ever doubted Germany's final victory. Last, but not least of course, Zieschank held the opinion that Samoa should become a German colony again. With this orientation, Zieschank's texts conform to the habitus of *Kolonie and Heimat*: they were not only flanked by advertisements for colonial novels and equipment for the tropics, but also by appeals to send dogs as helpers at the front and, most importantly, by proclamations that every German should sign the war loans. One of these slogans in the journal was, "*You*, too, should help so your people survive!" (1918/19b, 12.2, 6): every single person – man or woman – should make a contribution to the fatherland in these hard times. Frieda Zieschank's texts show how she aligned herself with this patriotic discourse as she longed to become a full member of the *Volksgemeinschaft*, the "people's community."

In the end, the most important contribution Zieschank made in support of her fatherland at war was probably that she wrote her nationalistic, anti-British texts and presented them to a broad readership. She remained true to this agenda in her subsequent publications: in the conclusion of *Ein Jahrzehnt in Samoa*, she still proclaimed her certainty of a German victory: "After this war, no power in the world will dare to come close to Germany!" (1918, 160). She vigorously demanded in her texts that the German government not give up claim to the South Sea colonies (1918, 157). In 1924, in the last pages of her colonial novel, *Ein verlorenes Paradies*, after a sideswipe at the last imperial cabinet whom she held responsible for the shameful end of the war (1923, 227), Zieschank implicitly announced the return of the "Teutons": at the end of the book the protagonist is deported from Samoa together with 300 other Germans, but she draws energy from the certainty of the following vision of the future: "Now once again a strong pure wave subsides back from a sun-drenched country! But it will return again and again – the high tide of Germanic power, driven by the Germanic's soul longing for the sun!" (1923, 230).

Frieda Zieschank, then, was not just a white, German, colonial woman, who reported the outbreak and course of World War I from a remote corner of the world. She exemplifies the continuing discourse of the colonial mission during the Weimar Republic and the belief that the story of German colonialism was hardly finished.

Archives

ANZ(W) = Archives New Zealand (Wellington/New Zealand)
IT = Island Territories Department
MESC(AU) = Ministry of Education, Sports and Culture; Culture Division; Archives Unit
    (Apia/Samoa)

Works Cited

Adressbuch für Deutsch-Neuguinea, Samoa, Kiautschou. Nach amtlichen Quellen bearbeitet
    (Paetel, 1913).

Bremm, Klaus-Jürgen. *Propaganda im Ersten Weltkrieg* (Theiss, 2013).

Dietrich, Anette. *Weiße Weiblichkeiten: Konstruktionen von "Rasse" und Geschlecht im deutschen Kolonialismus* (transcript, 2007).

Gründer, Horst. "Die historischen und politischen Voraussetzungen des deutschen Kolonialismus." *Die deutsche Südsee 1884–1914*, edited by Hermann Joseph Hiery (Schöningh, 2002), pp. 27–58.

Hertzer, Auguste. *Diary Fragments (May 1891 – January 1893)*, in private possession.

Hiery, Hermann Joseph. "Die deutsche Verwaltung Samoas 1900–1914." *Die deutsche Südsee 1884–1914*, edited by Hiery (Schöningh, 2002), pp. 649–676.

Hiery, Hermann Joseph. "Der erste Weltkrieg und das Ende des deutschen Einflusses in der Südsee." *Die deutsche Südsee 1884–1914*, edited by Hiery (Schöningh, 2002), pp. 805–854.

Hiery, Hermann Joseph. *The Neglected War: The German South Pacific and the Influence of World War I* (U of Hawaii P, 1995).

Kronenberg, Volker. *Patriotismus in Deutschland: Perspektiven für eine weltoffene Nation* (Springer VS, 2013).

Kundrus, Birthe. *Moderne Imperialisten: Das Kaiserreich im Spiegel seiner Kolonien* (Böhlau, 2003).

Loosen, Livia. *Deutsche Frauen in den Südsee-Kolonien des Kaiserreichs: Alltag und Beziehungen zur indigenen Bevölkerung, 1884–1919* (transcript, 2014).

Meleisea, Malama. *The Making of Modern Samoa: Traditional Authority and Colonial Administration in the History of Western Samoa* (Inst. of the Pacific Studies of the Univ. of the South Pacific, 1987).

Mückler, Hermann. *Kolonialismus in Ozeanien* (Facultas, 2012).

Reichskolonialamt, editor. *Die deutschen Schutzgebiete in Afrika und der Südsee 1912/13: Amtliche Jahresberichte, Statistischer Teil* (Mittler, 1914), pp. 34–35.

Schubert, Klaus, and Martina Klein. *Das Politiklexikon: Begriffe – Fakten – Zusammenhänge* (Dietz, 2011).

Walgenbach, Katharina. *Die weiße Frau als Trägerin deutscher Kultur: Koloniale Diskurse über Geschlecht, "Rasse" und Klasse im Kaiserreich* (Campus-Verlag, 2005).

Zieschank, Frieda. *Ein Jahrzehnt in Samoa (1906–1916)* (E. Haberland, 1918).

Zieschank, Frieda. *Ein verlorenes Paradies* (E. Haberland, 1923).

Zieschank, Frieda. "Heimwärts durch die englische Kontrolle: Tagebuchblätter aus Samoa in der Kriegszeit." *Kolonie und Heimat*, vol. 12, no. 32, 1918/19a, p. 6; vol. 12, no. 33, 1918/19a, p. 6–7; vol. 12, no. 34, 1918/19a, p. 6–7; vol. 12, no. 35, 1918/19a, p. 6–7; vol. 12, no. 36, 1918/19a, p. 6–7; vol.12, no. 37, 1918/19a, p. 6.

Zieschank, Frieda. "Zwei Kriegsjahre in Samoa: Tagebuchblätter." *Kolonie und Heimat*, vol.12, no. 1, 1918/19b, p. 9; vol. 12, no. 2, 1918/19b, p. 6–7; vol. 12, no. 4, 1918/19b, p. 6–7; vol. 12, no. 5, 1918/19b, p. 6; vol. 12, no. 5, 1918/19b, p. 6; vol. 12, no. 6, 1918/19b, p. 6; vol. 12, no. 7, 1918/19b, p. 6–7; vol. 12, no. 8, 1918/19b, p. 6; vol. 12, no. 9, 1918/19b, p. 6–7; vol. 12., no. 10, 1918/19b, p. 6; vol. 12, no. 11, 1918/19b, p. 6–7.

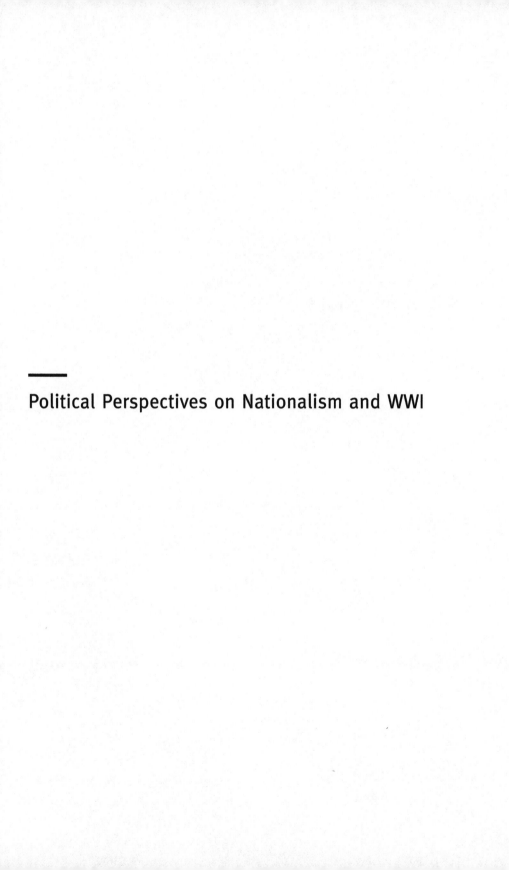

Political Perspectives on Nationalism and WWI

Shelley E. Rose
Bertha von Suttner's *Die Waffen nieder!* and the Gender of German Pacifism

In 1977, former West German Chancellor Willy Brandt penned the preface to a re-print of *Die Waffen nieder!* (*Lay Down Your Arms*, 1889), contending, "[e]very reader must answer for him or herself whether [Bertha von Suttner (1843–1914)] was a pacifist politician or – as is often said – a literary talent and likable dreamer" (vi).[1] Then-President of the Socialist International, Brandt's statement not only reflects debates about Suttner's identity as an author, pacifist, activist, and woman, but also the often deep divisions between peace activists and for-mal party political space in Germany. The question of Suttner's gender as a co-founder of the *Deutsche Friedensgesellschaft* (German Peace Society, DFG) also became a critical reference point for German pacifists who struggled to un-derstand the failure of pacifist agendas in party platforms during the Weimar Re-public and in post-1945 West Germany. As the female author of one of the most successful nineteenth-century pacifist *Tendenzromane* (political novels) and first female recipient of the Nobel Peace Prize in 1905, Suttner's gender identity re-mains at the center of disagreements over whether or not she compromised the concept of peace in German politics. That is, her political and social status as a woman reinforced preconceived notions that peace is an implicitly feminine concept and therefore incompatible with the masculine realm of party politics.

Over 200,000 copies of the 1889 novel *Die Waffen nieder!* were sold by the time Suttner died on 21 June 1914, making her one of the most well-known women to write about the experience of peace, militarism, and war by the begin-ning of World War I. Germanist Regina Braker argues in "Bertha von Suttner as Author," "*Die Waffen nieder!* was the most widely read fictional exposition of an antiwar message in the quarter century before 1914" (1991, 74). *Die Waffen nieder!* displays how *Kriegsbegeisterung* (war enthusiasm) permeated everyday life in nineteenth-century Europe, particularly in Germany. A fictional autobiography of Austrian aristocrat Martha (Althaus) von Tilling, *Die Waffen nieder!* details Martha's two marriages, family relationships, and experience of being widowed twice, against the background of nationalist and militaristic society. The novel's time frame spans four European conflicts: the Italian War (1859), the Second Schleswig War (1864), the Austro-Prussian War (1866) and the Franco-Prussian War (1870–1871). Suttner's graphic battlefield descriptions (for which she con-

---

1 All translations from German into English are my own unless otherwise stated.

https://doi.org/10.1515/9783110572001-007

sulted with veterans) are a hallmark of her style in *Die Waffen nieder!*. The author makes her intention for these descriptions clear in the final pages of the novel during a conversation between Martha and her son, Rudolph. When Rudolph muses that *Die Waffen nieder!* might be painful to read, Martha responds, "I hope so. If that pain should only awake in a few hearts an energetic hatred against the source of all the misery here described, I shall not have put myself to the torture in vain" (427).[2]

This historical investigation contextualizes the paradox of *Die Waffen nieder!*: the novel is a study in nineteenth-century gender relationships and the power of hyper-masculine militarism, yet its publication, and subsequent use as a key text for the organized peace movements in Germany and Austria before and after World War I, led to deep gender and political divisions in attitudes on war and peace still evident today. Despite the novel's appeal as a founding text of the German Peace Society in 1892, Suttner's deliberate critique of masculine militarism throughout her novel, and the moral peace which she advocated during her lifetime, seemed to reinforce nineteenth-century assumptions about the concept of peace as a feminine idea. As a result, *Die Waffen nieder!* has garnered significant attention from literary scholars, pacifists, and politicians. Suttner's political legacy in Germany as a female author and pacifist, however, remains understudied by historians.

I demonstrate the value of gender analysis for understanding the historical impact of *Die Waffen nieder!* and its subsequent use by twentieth-century German pacifists and politicians within the broader framework of Germany's political landscape.[3] In this essay, I first engage the rich multidisciplinary scholarship on Suttner and her novel, *Die Waffen nieder!*. Second, I offer a gender analysis of *Die Waffen nieder!*, by focusing on Suttner's representation of war through political scientist Christine Sylvester's theoretical framework of "war as experience," which she defines, pertaining to any war, as "the physical and emotional connections with war that people live [...]" (2013, 5). Finally, I explore the contention of scholars and activists that Suttner's complicated legacy as a co-founder of the German Peace Society rendered twentieth-century pacifist political agendas ineffective in German politics. Here I consider both individual and organized paci-

---

2 All citations and English quotes from *Die Waffen nieder!* are from *Lay Down Your Arms: The Autobiography of Martha von Tilling* (1914), which was translated by T. Holmes, unless otherwise stated.

3 Here I rely on historian Kathleen Canning's understanding of gender as "a category of social analysis that denotes the relational character of sexual difference" (2006, 4). That is, scholars cannot understand nineteenth-century gender relationships without studying the roles of both men and women, as well as masculine and feminine stereotypes of militarism and peace.

fists in twentieth-century Germany – such as Carl von Ossietzky, Lida Gustava Heymann and Anita Augspurg, as well as more recent activists like Elly Bommersheim, Walter Baumhauer and Elisabeth Brändle-Zeile who created a trajectory to Petra Kelly and the Green Party around 1980 – as members of a "community of practice" (Eckert and McConnell-Ginet 1992, 464) which emerged in the penumbra of party politics and was bound by common references, such as *Die Waffen nieder!*, and its goals for the future of peace politics.[4]

The volume *Women Writing War* calls for scholarly attention to gendered experiences of war, which Bertha von Suttner clearly addresses in *Die Waffen nieder!*. The relative success of Suttner's novel has led to both accolades and criticism. Suttner's goals for *Die Waffen nieder!* and her choice to publish under her own name reveal a keen understanding of her position in nineteenth-century European society that is not fully explored in the current scholarship. Literary scholarship on *Die Waffen nieder!* obscures the importance of its complex gender relationships by focusing primarily on literary analysis or the role of the novel as a rallying cry for the organized peace movement. In Germany, for example, *Die Waffen nieder!* is perhaps best known for Suttner's stark critiques of nineteenth-century *Kriegsbegeisterung*.

Suttner's novel and personal activism provided the foundation for a pacifist community of practice in German politics in the 1890s which continued into the twentieth century. Indeed, literary scholar Charlotte Woodford asserts *Die Waffen nieder!* "empower[ed] the individual readers to think of themselves as part of a community of like-minded companions" (2012, 206). Although Woodford analyzes Suttner's effective use of a sentimental narrative style, which relies on the reader's emotional response, to critique militarism and protest gender inequality in nineteenth-century society, she only mentions briefly that *Die Waffen nieder!* "was read widely by men and women alike" (211). Drawing on a comparison first made by Russian novelist Leo Tolstoy, Braker compares the popularity of *Die Waffen nieder!* and Suttner's use of sentimentality to Harriet Beecher Stowe's *Uncle Tom's Cabin* in her 1992 article "Bertha von Suttner: The Harriet Beecher Stowe of the Peace Movement." Braker describes Stowe's sentimental narrative: "She wrote with the intention of persuading readers to her point of view" (78). Suttner, Braker argues later, "attempted to bridge the gap between entertainment and the serious consideration of a problem" (82). This effort resulted in what historian Roger Chickering termed "melodramatic sentimentality"

---

4 According to Penelope Eckert and Sally McConnell-Ginet's sociolinguistic framework, "[A] community of practice is an aggregate of people who come together around mutual engagement in an endeavor. Ways of doing things, ways of talking, beliefs, values and power relations – in short, practices – emerge in the course of this mutual endeavor" (1992, 464).

(1975, 89) and the dismissal of the work by Suttner's critics as ineffective at best, or, at worst, harmful to organized pacifism in Germany.

While Chickering's analysis centers on the novel's impact on the history of the peace movement in Germany, literary scholars Woodford and Ian Foster focus on the novel itself. They highlight Suttner's innovative use of her female protagonist Martha von Tilling, of *raisonneurs*,[5] and of battlefield descriptions as literary techniques that convey the experience of war for her readers (Foster 1991, 208; Woodford 2012, 211). Concentrating on Suttner's protagonist, Martha, Foster evaluates the use of an aristocratic voice as an effective tool for Suttner's social critiques of Austro-Hungarian society (202–203). In addition, Foster echoes the criticism of Suttner's pacifist contemporaries and successors, arguing that the female protagonist's sentimentality distracts from the novel's political message. According to Foster, "the threat that *Die Waffen nieder!* posed to military interests was roundly dismissed, yet in the same breath reluctantly acknowledged" (207). Woodford demonstrates that Suttner's sentimental narrative style captivated readers and spoke specifically to women through the use of the female protagonist (206, 220). Both scholars portray the feminized, emotional role of Martha von Tilling as a key element in *Die Waffen nieder!*. Martha's importance as the first-person narrator of the novel cannot be disputed, yet a gender analysis of the novel reveals Suttner's choice of characters and their respective genders was not simply a function of a self-styled autobiography. Suttner deliberately crafted her characters to speak with authority about class, gender, and political issues in nineteenth-century Europe.

As a female author, Suttner constantly worried about the reception of her work in academic and political circles, going so far as to publish previous novels under gender-neutral pseudonyms to prevent any audience preconceptions. By 1885, Suttner had published sixteen literary pieces under the pseudonym B. Oulot (Cohen 2005, 281). As an established popular fiction writer, Suttner feared her political books would "remain unread by the intended audience" (Suttner 1909, 170). Suttner's fears were not unfounded. She chronicles an incident in her memoirs that attests to the widespread belief that women should not be active in politics or political writing. While attending a dinner party, Suttner overheard a conversation about her book *Das Maschinenzeitalter* (The machine age, 1889), which was published under the gender-neutral pseudonym "Jemand" or "Someone." When Suttner remarked that she might read the book she was immediately rebuffed by the men discussing her work – "It is not a book for la-

---

5 The *Oxford Dictionary of Literary Terms* defines "raisonneur" as "A character in a play who appears to act as a mouthpiece for the opinions of the play's author [...]" (Baldick 2008).

dies!" (1909, 179). Suttner felt vindicated because this incident confirmed her conviction that, contrary to widespread belief, women could indeed write serious studies of political and social issues (Hamann 1996, 265–267). It also demonstrated that she was correct to assume that her work might not be taken seriously by intellectuals and political leaders if the fact of her female authorship was well-known. As the story reveals, most of her Austrian and German contemporaries felt that politics was not a socially acceptable occupation for women. This was a stereotype that Suttner, who imagined herself as a legitimate contributor to political debates regardless of her sex, adamantly rejected.

In 1889, Suttner published *Die Waffen nieder!* under her own name, painstakingly staging the story in an effort to ensure that her message was not easily dismissed simply because she was a female author. She complicates the heroine's voice with the claim that Martha published her autobiography at the request of her second husband, Friedrich von Tilling. Friedrich insisted that she continue his pacifist work after his death. Suttner's messages, therefore, acquired certain legitimacy through the fictional legacy of a man who had learned from his experiences at war. Moreover, Suttner uses *Die Waffen nieder!* to demonstrate the range of individuals affected by the experience of war, all the way down to children who perished from a cholera epidemic sparked by soldiers quartered in Martha's village (Suttner 315–326). Indeed, as Sylvester argues, "people can be inside the [war] matrix in a variety of experiential ways" (2013, 5).

Die Waffen nieder! is a study in gender relationships cloaked in an open critique of militarism as a masculine concept. Even though Suttner felt that "there is no difference between the male and female sex in regard to their position on the peace issue" and criticized women who presented peace as an explicitly feminine cause, she tailored her narrative to the realities of nineteenth-century Europe (Hamann 1996, 267). This echoes Sylvester's argument that everyone is impacted by the "war matrix" (2013, 5), as Suttner describes the protagonist, Martha, flanked on all sides by militarism as "a general's daughter, wife of a first lieutenant and [...] mother of a corporal" (15). Martha's first husband Arno makes this statement as a joke, referring to their son as a corporal because society dictates that he will grow up to be a soldier based solely on his sex. Through Martha's voice, Suttner questions the necessity of war, only to have her repeatedly silenced and dismissed by her father and other strong male characters, reflecting Suttner's own experiences in nineteenth-century Europe.

Foster recognizes the power of Martha's husband Friedrich's voice in his evaluation of Suttner's use of *raisonneurs*, or characters that speak with the author's voice, as an effective persuasive strategy (1991, 208–212). However, he does not adequately problematize the fact that two of the three *raisonneurs* he identifies – Friedrich and Dr. Bresser – are male voices. Closer analysis reveals that even Foster's third *raisonneur*, Martha herself, speaks with an element of Friedrich's authority through his desire for her to continue their activism. Suttner deliberately threw off the authorial guise of anonymity with *Die Waffen nieder!*, and yet acknowledged the advantages of employing a male voice to support her most important pacifist messages. Friedrich, for example, issues critical prescriptions for world peace. "Peace is the greatest blessing, or rather the absence of the greatest curse," he asserts, challenging the views of Martha's militaristic father when the female protagonist cannot effectively do so herself (97).

While the female *raisonneur* comments on the state of gender relations, Suttner cunningly places the strongest political messages in the mouths of male characters. In one of Friedrich's most explicit statements in the novel he asserts, "I hate war. If only every man who feels the same would dare to proclaim it aloud, what a threatening protest would be shouted out to heaven!" (155). His observations while serving in the army are crucial to Suttner's message and break social taboos. Friedrich frequently writes home about the horrors of war and he wonders why other men "bring fresh... joyful images" home (239). He concludes that his comrades remain silent and indifferent about the most horrible aspects of conflict and tailor their stories to heroic models, which they learned in school rather than reality. In Suttner's eyes, this social "silence" about nineteenth-century battlefield atrocities, in this case the Second Schleswig War in 1864, only perpetuated the myths that war was an honorable affair and encouraged men like Martha's first husband Arno to strive for a place fighting on the frontlines.

Suttner's use of graphic, or thick, description in her battlefield scenes is a key element in both the novel's literary success and its appeal as an introductory text for the organized peace movements in Germany and Austria. Historian Irwin Abrams argues that Suttner was drawn into the peace movement largely through writing about it. Her experience of writing about war – that Sylvester would understand as one of many ways to experience war – transformed her into a pacifist (Abrams 1996, xiv). These war scenes were integral to the success and purpose of the novel. Sylvester affirms "[T]he body can experience war physically – through wounds and attending to wounds, through running, firing, falling, having buildings fall on it, *writing about war*, filming moments of war, photographing war, feeling hungry or sick during war and so on" (2013, 5, my emphasis). I contend that Suttner not only intensified her commitment to pacifism through "writing about war," but also the act of reading her vivid battle descriptions represents another experience of war, which must be considered through Sylvester's framework. The war scenes in Suttner's novel initiated or reacquainted readers with the gruesome battlefield scenes; yet the author accompanied the reader through Martha as her narrator, filtering the experience for the audience and attempting to guide readers to the end goal of peace activism.

Both men and women have historically become pacifists as a result of brutal experiences in armed conflicts. For instance, Swiss businessman Henri Dunant, who was a co-recipient (with French pacifist Frédéric Passy) of the first Nobel Peace Prize in 1901 and established the International Committee of the Red Cross, was shaped by his experiences as an inadvertent witness of the bloody battlefield at Solferino in the Italian War of 1859. Dunant shared his observations in the 1862 book *A Memory of Solferino*, in order to "awaken the abhorrence of war in his readers" (Brinker-Gabler 1986, 213). In a similar effort, Suttner shepherds her readers through the necessary experience of war as a rite of passage on the way to becoming defenders of peace.

Suttner and other pacifists of her time, such as Alfred Fried, were convinced that the peace movement had to become a mass movement, and she viewed her book as a rallying cry for that cause.[6] Germanist Gisela Brinker-Gabler argues that, *Die Waffen nieder!* was the "most important antiwar novel written before Erich Maria Remarque's *Im Westen nichts Neues (All Quiet on the Western Front,* 1929)" (27). As evidence, Brinker-Gabler cites a 1905 article in the *Frankfurter Zeitung* (Frankfurt newspaper) which proclaims that when *"[F]riedensfreunde"* (friends of peace) were questioned about their motives for joining the peace movement, they "almost always" answered that *Die Waffen nieder!* convinced them (Brinker-Gabler 26). It is no wonder that by the time World War I began over 200,000 copies of her novel had already been purchased and a new German edition was released in November 1914. Suttner offered a frame for interpreting and understanding the militaristic spirit surrounding war and the traumatic experiences of the conflict on the front and at home (Bock and Bock 2006, 406). In addition, Foster notes that her chronological chapter headings, which end with 1889, the year *Die Waffen nieder!* was published, reinforced the urgency of her critique of militarism (1991, 204).

Sylvester interrogates the connections between war as a physical experience and war as an emotional experience, demonstrating that the two types of experiences "interlock" in important ways (2013, 6). Suttner's use of clear descriptions of battles and their aftermath to create, and in some cases recreate, the experience of war for her audience reflects this complexity. As narrator, Martha describes how painful it is to relate stories of war and battlefield anguish and, as quoted earlier, she hopes that it will also be a painful experience for the read-

---

6 For background information on Suttner and the rise of organized pacifism in Europe, see Cooper (1991), Chapter 3.

er (427). Suttner explicitly connects the emotional experiences of reading *Die Waffen nieder!* with the readers' corporeal responses to battlefield scenes. As political scientist Neta Crawford contends, "[f]eelings are internally experienced, but the meaning attached to those feelings, the behaviors associated with them, and the recognition of emotions in others are cognitively and culturally construed and constructed" (2000, 125). Martha's stories and opinions are quickly dismissed by her militaristic father and other belligerent characters in the novel, yet Suttner's readers emotionally identify with her plight. Readers may sympathize with Martha's feelings of frustration, drawing connections to their own experiences with militaristic critics. It is only after Martha physically visits the battlefields in Bohemia to look for her husband that her stories begin to receive an audience. With this Suttner suggests those who experience war firsthand are most equipped to speak out against nineteenth-century European militarism. She thus constructs Martha's rite of passage through war (288), cementing her status, as Foster argues, as a *raisonneur* (1991, 208–212). Suttner's readers also experience this rite of passage as they read the battlefield scenes and feel many of the same emotions as Martha.

Women who remained uncritical of militarism did not escape Suttner's critique. The character of Martha's friend Lori Griesbach, who happily accepts her position as an upper-class patriotic woman and officer's wife, receives harsh treatment from the author for being complicit in the militaristic system. For example, Lori laments the fact that her husband did not participate in the Second Schleswig War, but she takes comfort "in the next campaign" (181) as an opportunity for him to prove himself on the battlefield, thus attaining higher status in Austrian society. Martha immediately chastises her: "What are you thinking of? [...] What should a war be waged about now?" (181). Lori apathetically responds, "[r]eally I have nothing to do with that. Wars come – and there they are. Every five or six years something breaks out. That is the regular course of history" (181). Suttner's careful gender framing, however, is often overlooked by scholars and activists who either take an essentialist perspective on her position as a female author, such as Chickering and Foster, or showcase the entire novel as a foundational work for the organized peace movement, like Braker.

Historian Anne Dzamba argues that scholars cannot understand Suttner's "program for peace" without first acknowledging her interpretation of past and future gender relations (1989, 62). Indeed, Dzamba describes Suttner's critique of gender relations as the most controversial topic in *Die Waffen nieder!* and one reason why Suttner's publishers were reluctant to publish it in the first place (66). Though contemporaries and scholars have been intrigued by the novel's literary success, Suttner's keen observations of central European culture and gender conflicts also provide historians with a lens into everyday aristocratic life at the end of the nineteenth century in addition to her own pacifist position. As a pacifist, Suttner believed in the goal of ending the "war" between the sexes as well as the struggles between nations and classes. Despite this belief, she prioritized her pacifism over feminist activism. Though she was often invited to join women's societies or participate in their events, Suttner maintained a distance from feminist and women's activism. She saw it as a possible distraction from her larger purpose of establishing peace and disarmament (Hamann 1996, 257, 267–271). *Die Waffen nieder!* is a testament to this goal, combining a gendered critique of society with Suttner's platform for peace.

Complicating the legacy of pacifism as a woman's issue, biographer Brigitte Hamann shows that Suttner was equally critical of the women who touted peace as an explicitly feminine cause. She countered arguments that women were naturally inclined to oppose war and violence by virtue of their sex with examples of women who enthusiastically supported war.[7] Suttner took a radical position on equality, stating "[T]here is no difference between the male and female sex in regard to their position on the peace issue" (Hamann 1996, 267). For Suttner, the issue of peace was universal. This did not prevent her from engaging critically with class and gender inequalities in her activism and novels, however. By refusing to acknowledge the traditional roles of men as fighters or defenders and women as mothers and supporters of the nationalist effort, Suttner made a powerful statement. *Die Waffen nieder!* serves as a key example. Here, Suttner fights the militaristic traditions of European society, as well as the class and gender constructions, which both perpetuated and glorified conceptions of war.

Nineteenth-century German militarism, including the exclusion of women from conscription and suffrage, created a gendered dichotomy between war and peace. This dichotomy is reinforced, as historian Gail Bederman claims, by the fact that "electoral politics dramatized and reinforced men's connection, as men, to the very real power of government" (1995, 13). Suttner herself acknowledged the pervasive perception of this dichotomy in 1903 and linked the trend to the fact that "women also support the peace movement, namely, *Frau Bertha*" (Hamann 1996, 268). Over the course of the twentieth century, politicians, activists, and historians lamented the lasting effects of the gendered characterization of peace as a feminine concept. For example, Chickering dismisses Suttner's work as a liability to the early German peace movement without problematizing, however, her central role in creating the pacifist community at the

---

7 See also Julie Shoults's essay in this volume regarding the intersection of gender and pacifism in the works of Hermynia Zur Mühlen (1883–1951), who drew inspiration from and reffered to Suttner's famous novel in her own texts. Like Suttner, Zur Mühlen questions women's purportedly "natural" opposition to war and violence.

center of his study (1975, 93). This characterization of pacifism as feminine complicated the use of peace as a viable platform in twentieth-century party politics, a space traditionally occupied by men.

Ever since the publication of *Die Waffen nieder!*, Suttner's pacifist position has been relegated to the political margins. Positioned opposite dominant narratives of masculine militarism in nineteenth-century Germany, Suttner's moral pacifist position contributed to the implicit gendering of peace as feminine by many activists and politicians. A critical examination of Suttner's historical context and a closer reading of her novel illustrate the impact of her status as a woman on the novel's reception. Despite Suttner's original intentions, her sex combined with her position as a co-founder of organized German pacifism fostered a lingering feminine stereotype of peace in German politics. Historian Kathleen Canning argues that gender histories "follow their own temporalities," meaning that they do not fit comfortably into "established chronologies and categories" (2006, 60–61). The history of peace and pacifism as a gendered concept reinforces Canning's claim. Suttner's perceived role in strengthening the stereotype of peace as feminine is evident in the various German and English language editions of *Die Waffen nieder!*, where forewords and prefaces, such as Brandt's cited at the beginning of this essay, reveal the tensions surrounding Suttner's identity as female pacifist and commentator on politics and gender relationships.

Historians trace the origins of organized peace movements in Germany to 1892 when Suttner and Alfred Fried founded the German Peace Society (Chickering 1975, 4–8). At this time, Suttner clearly understood her own position in nineteenth-century European society where "politics was an absolute taboo-theme for young ladies," who were marginal to the masculine strongholds of militarism and party politics (Brinker-Gabler 1986, 12). Indeed, she sought to avoid stereotypes of her pacifist work as essentially feminine and actively engaged with debates on sexual equality in her work and public talks. Suttner envisioned a modern world with "[m]an and woman side by side, born equal, with equal rights – woman strengthened, man made milder, both ennobled to the evolving genre of humanity" (qtd. in Hamann 1996, 258). The second preface to the 1914 English edition of *Lay Down Your Arms* addresses Suttner's concerns about gender stereotypes directly. On the eve of World War I, translator T. Holmes urges readers not to pursue "sentimental emotions and vague protests," characteristics typically considered as feminine, after reading the book and to have a "business-like discussion of the means by which the resort to war may be at any rate rendered more and more infrequent," instead (ix). Holmes sought to avoid the stigma associated with Suttner's emotional critique of militarism by advocating a rational, implicitly masculine, approach to peace activism.

Suttner's moral view of peace shaped the general tone of the pre-World War I peace society. Like Holmes, DFG co-founder Fried critiqued her brand of ethical pacifism, favoring his own concept of scientific pacifism, grounded partially in Marxist theory, as a more politically viable concept. Fried did not directly challenge Suttner's position as a female pacifist. His reconceptualization of the pacifist position based on scientific logic and political theories, however, confirms Chickering's claim that Fried and other male pacifists questioned the "efficacy" of Suttner's moral ideology (1975, 94). Fried based his pacifist theory on two realms traditionally dominated by men: Marxist theory, which informed Social Democratic political strategies at this time, and scientific arguments based on logic. A member of the German Social Democratic Party (*Sozialistische Partei Deutschlands*, SPD), then often described as a "peace party," Fried believed that those who possessed the political and economic power to prevent war would not be persuaded by morals. His scientific pacifism provided a rational counter to Suttner's moral view. Drawing on the ideas of Karl Marx, Russian sociologist Jacob Novikow, German pacifist Ludwig Quidde, German lawyer Eugen Schlief, and Polish banker Ivan Bloch, Fried hoped to influence politicians and sought ways to exert a pacifist influence on those who held political power (Chickering 94–108). Fried's choice of scientists and politicians as role models for his own ideology can be seen as an effort to situate his pacifism in a more masculine framework. In the context of nineteenth- and early twentieth-century Germany, Brinker-Gabler notes that the DFG was not conceived as a political organization, but a non-partisan one (1986, 12). This structural limitation affected the organization's appeal to new members as much, or more than, its grounding in Suttner's *Die Waffen nieder!* or Fried's scientific pacifist ideologies.

Thirty-five years after the initial publication of *Die Waffen nieder!* and five years after the outbreak of World War I, Bertha von Suttner's legacy remained a point of contention among activists. Weimar-era journalist and antimilitarist Carl von Ossietzky, for example, described Suttner as "a gentle perfume of absurdity" (qtd. in Chickering 1975, 92). Drawing explicit connections between *Die Waffen nieder!* and pacifist impotency in Weimar political culture, Ossietzky was one of the most prominent pacifist critics of Suttner's pacifist ideology. He believed that the German peace movement was founded in Suttner's "feminine sentimentality" and prevented pacifist participation in the male-dominated realm of party politics. Historian Jennifer Anne Davy shows that the "militaristic rhetoric" of pacifists like Ossietzky was grounded in their own gendered understandings of politics as masculine and of the stigma of the peace movement as feminine (2005, 155). At a moment of intense frustration in a society dominated by militarism, Ossietzky looked abroad to other national pacifist organizations led by prominent male figures. He imagined that pacifist impotency in Weimar-era politics was a distinctly German occurrence linked to Suttner's legacy (1994, 373).

Ironically, Ossietzky focused his *Sonderweg*-like[8] criticism on Suttner's novel although her work continued to be popular among pacifists beyond German borders and influenced some of the foreign pacifists he admired. French diplomat Paul d'Estournelles de Constant, for example, wrote that Suttner "lived for the idea [of peace] – now she will live on through this idea" (qtd. in Brändle-Zeile 1983, 157).[9] Nonetheless, Ossietzky sharply criticized German pacifists, revealing more tangled threads of gender stereotypes in Weimar political culture. Pointing abroad to British pacifist Ramsay MacDonald and French pacifist Edouard Herriot, Ossietzky drew a stark contrast between their political successes and the lack of political achievements by the German peace movement whose "origins lay in the sentimental novel of a very delicate and sheltered woman" (Ossietzky 1994, 373–374). As opposed to the "political" pacifism of the two foreign male statesmen, Ossietzky accused the German peace movement of being "illusionary" and "distrustful" of politics as well as of any pacifist leaders who tried to embrace actual political strategies (373–374). German pacifists, according to the journalist, ignored the realm of politics, which he characterized as masculine, at their own peril.

Ossietzky maintained that the pacifist movement was gendered as "feminine." He targeted Suttner, and the concept of *"weiblichen Pazifismus"* (feminine pacifism) advocated also by activists like Lida Gustava Heymann (1980, 65–66), as a key source of pacifist weaknesses. According to Ossietzky's tirade, Suttner was primarily responsible for pacifists' willful collective ignorance of politics. He painted "Peace Bertha" as a woman who purposefully expressed her doctrine through "whining self-pity" (*Wehleidigkeit*) (Ossietzky 1994, 374). As demonstrated earlier in this chapter, Ossietzky's assertions of Suttner's political "ignorance" could not be farther from the truth. Suttner carefully chose the vehicles for her pacifist messages with a clear understanding of nineteenth-century militarism and politics.

Though as a journalist Ossietzky possessed a certain transnational awareness and clearly looked beyond German borders himself, he neglected to acknowledge the fact that Suttner's novel circulated outside German and even European borders. The English translation, among others, was already into its second edition by 1914. Interestingly, the translator's preface to this edition re-

---

8 *Sonderweg* is the argument that Germany was on "a different or special historical path" (Jefferies 2008, 10).

9 "Sie hat für unsere Idee gelebt – nun wird sie durch die Idee lebendig erhalten werden."

veals a certain effort to guide readers away from types of peace activism characterized by "sentimental emotions and vague protest" (Holmes ix). The wide, transnational, and continued circulation of *Die Waffen nieder!* challenges Ossietzky's 1924 claims of a German pacifist *Sonderweg* linked to Suttner's role as female co-founder of the DFG.

Female pacifists from the Weimar Republic to the Federal Republic of Germany, by comparison, carefully leveraged Suttner's legacy as a female pacifist in their arguments for political change. In the 1920s, Women's International League of Peace and Freedom (WILPF) activist Lida Gustava Heymann, and in the 1970s, *Aktionsgemeinschaft Unabhängiger Deutscher* (Action Group of Nonpartisan Germans, AUD) and Green activist Elly Bommersheim attempted in very different historical and political contexts to mobilize Suttner's image as a female author, pacifist, and Nobel Prize winner in their political arguments: Heymann by appropriating Suttner's specific identity as a woman and Bommersheim by mobilizing Suttner as a symbol of the peace movement.

WILPF represented a contemporary foil to Ossietzky's brand of masculine belligerent pacifism (*kriegerischer Pazifismus*) during the Weimar period. Instead of efforts to gender pacifism as more masculine, and therefore supposedly more politically viable, radical pacifists and founding editors of the WILPF publication *Die Frau im Staat* (The woman in the state), Heymann and Anita Augspurg, advocated an explicitly feminist pacifism. No less political than Ossietzky's efforts to masculinize pacifism, these women challenged gender norms by calling for the equal standing of men and women. Heymann cited the "masculine, destructive principle" of violence as the opposite of the feminine principles of "mutual aid, goodness, understanding, and cooperation" (1980, 65); she even went so far as to declare that "feminine essence, feminine instinct is identical to pacifism" (66).[10] German WILPF leaders viewed an increase in female participation in politics and governing coalitions as a potential political strategy and solution to the problem of war.

Augspurg and Heymann grounded their feminist pacifism in the belief that the increased presence of women in the masculine realm of politics through universal suffrage would bring peace. Drawing positively on Suttner's legacy, they called for mild, peaceful men and women to participate in top-level politics and to mediate impulses to solve international conflicts with violence (Davy 2005, 158–164; Braker 1995, 106). Ironically, they embraced the stereotypes about Suttner for their own agenda and used her image as a woman to push for female representatives in party politics. While this image of Suttner aligns

---

10 "Denn weibliches Wesen, weiblicher Instinkt sind identisch mit Pazifismus."

with Augspurg's and Heymann's feminist goals, Suttner herself, as Hamann shows, "resolutely resisted all temptation to present the peace movement as a typically feminine movement against the masculine principle of war" (1996, 267). Here, Heymann and Augspurg took Suttner's ideas to an extreme, deliberately drawing on a common language of motherhood and femininity to unite female peace activists and using an image of a feminine pacifism which, however, polarized general peace activists in the Weimar Republic.[11]

The continuity of Suttner's influence as a female pacifist is best illustrated in 1979 when the NATO *Doppelbeschluss* (Double-Track) decision reignited the German peace movement.[12] Men and women alike called on Suttner's image as a founding leader of organized pacifism in Germany. The case of WILPF member Elly Bommersheim (1894–1986) demonstrates one activist who carried Suttner's influence with her. From 1977 to 1986, Bommersheim corresponded with early German Green Party activist and founder Petra Kelly (1947–1992). The relationship between Bommersheim and the much younger Kelly exemplifies the mechanics of the transgenerational pacifist community of practice forged partly by Suttner's ideas in *Die Waffen nieder!*. As Bommersheim describes in her 1977 letter, "I am 83 years old and have been a pacifist since 1914 when I lost the man whom I wanted to marry" (Letter [1 Apr. 1977]).[13] A contemporary of Suttner, Bommersheim's World War I experiences, particularly of loss, shaped her pacifist identity, underscoring the significance of the framework Sylvester later developed. She became a WILPF member in 1916 and worked with many German and international peace organizations (Letter [1 Apr. 1977]). Indeed, Bommersheim strove to connect Petra Kelly with her network of colleagues, such as American Gary Davis in May 1977, throughout their correspondence (Letter [22 and 25 June 1977]).

Bommersheim references Suttner frequently in her advice to Kelly. She closes her first letter in April 1977 with the quote "Die Waffen nieder" alongside her own quote from 1974, "Those who arm have no right to speak of peace" (Letter [1 Apr. 1977]).[14] In May 1979, Bommersheim, who was a music teacher and pia-

---

11 See Allen (1991, 3–12) for a detailed discussion of this phenomenon among feminists in Germany.

12 On 12 December 1979, NATO (North Atlantic Treaty Organization) leaders planned to station nuclear weapons in Western Europe in response to Soviet deployment of similar range missiles. This decision sparked an unprecedented series of protest events in West Germany. See Geiger "Der NATO-Doppelbeschluss" (2012) for further reading.

13 "Ich bin 83 Jahre alt und seit 1914, wo ich den Mann verlor, den ich gern geheiratet hätte, Pazifistin."

14 "Wer rüstet hat kein Recht vom Frieden zu sprechen."

nist, integrated Suttner's legacy even further into the present pacifist community of practice, including music she composed to the "Wechselgesang" (responsive song) from Suttner's third book in *Die Waffen nieder!* (Suttner 2006, 192). Bommersheim set the verses from Suttner's book to music and dedicated it to Kelly and the Green Party. Perhaps she was prompted by the 1979 NATO debates about positioning nuclear missiles in West Germany (NATO *Doppelbeschluss*).

The "Wechselgesang" is Suttner's critique of the deterrence policies. Holmes' translation of the lyrics, intended for two voices, reads: "My preparations are defensive. Your preparations are offensive. I must prepare because you are preparing. I am preparing because you prepare. Then let us prepare, Yes, let us go on preparing" (1914, 207). Suttner's "Wechselgesang" demonstrates the absurdity of militarism in the Austrian Empire and Prussia by setting events during the prelude of the 1866 Austro-Prussian War to song, accompanied by the "orchestra" of newspapers to stoke the nationalist fires. Bommersheim explicitly links Suttner's deterrence critique to the absurdity of the Cold War arms race, declaring "my version of B[ertha] von Suttner's '*Wechselgesang*', whereby she already made armament laughable 110 years ago, I dedicate to you [Petra Kelly]" (Letter [5 May 1979]).[15] In 1979, as in 1866, the majority of political leaders and guardians of national interests and armaments were men. Indeed, Social Democratic Chancellor Helmut Schmidt, a war veteran, not only represented the West German government during the NATO *Doppelbeschluss* debates, he led a faction of the SPD who had come to believe that deterrence worked (Nehring 2013, 182). Bommersheim drew on *Die Waffen nieder!* to illustrate the parallels between nineteenth-century militarism and what many Germans perceived as a masculine arms race during the Cold War (Davis 2009).

Male pacifists in the late twentieth-century community of practice also drew connections between their own marginal and often extra-parliamentary political positions and Bertha von Suttner's marginalized female voice in the nineteenth century. A 1981 letter from Mannheim activist Dr. Walter Baumhauer to Green Party leader Roland Vogt includes a speech that aligns Suttner's legacy in the peace movement with the movement's political impotence in the face of global conflicts and the cycle of war in the early twentieth century. Baumhauer acknowledges Suttner's role as a founder of the German peace movement. He writes, "[Suttner] fought courageously against scorn, jeers and personal attacks. All her efforts had no influence whatsoever, the First World War came with its

---

15 "Meine Vertonung von B.v. Suttners 'Wechselgesang', womit sie die Rüstung schon vor 110 Jahren lächerlich machte, widme ich Euch!"

senseless destructive battles" (Letter [14 Sept. 1981]).[16] He continues on to cite the inability of Ossietsky's No-More-War movement and other Weimar groups to stop World War II. In all, Baumhauer's speech echoes Ossietzky's frustration with the peace movement's long-term failure to exact social change. Baumhauer's use of Suttner in this speech is, however, indicative of a broader shift in political perceptions of the gender of peace in the latter twentieth century. By the time of the NATO *Doppelbeschluss*, the pacifist community of practice and the realm of party politics in Germany had changed significantly. Whereas party politics in the Weimar Republic and early Federal Republic were dominated by men, this formal political realm saw an increase in female participation in the 1970s and 1980s, particularly due to the electoral success of the nascent Green Party in the early 1980s.[17]

Politician and activist Elisabeth Brändle-Zeile documents changing attitudes about the gender of peace in her book *Seit 90 Jahren: Frauen für den Frieden* (90 years: Women for peace, 1983) and directly links Suttner's image as a spokeswoman for organized pacifism to her gender. The front cover features photos of Suttner and Kelly, and inside there are quotes from the two women. Brändle-Zeile compares Kelly's pacifist and political achievements to Suttner's, implicitly positioning Kelly as the more successful figure. Suttner, Brändle-Zeile argues, only succeeded in creating peace societies, whereas Kelly "stands in the middle of a worldwide peace movement" (134). Brändle-Zeile recognizes the strength of the Greens as an international movement and party empowered by shifting perceptions of peace as "feminine." Similar to Ossietzky, Brändle-Zeile measures success through political power. The key difference in 1983, however, was the tangible success of female pacifists in the realm of party politics as the Green Party cleared the five-percent hurdle required to have representation in the German Bundestag.

As Chancellor Willy Brandt noted "every reader must decide for him or herself" which Suttner legacy to privilege (1977, vi). Writing at the cusp of the largest non-partisan peace demonstrations in German history – 150,000 activists descended on the West German capital in Bonn in 1981 – Brandt's emphasis on individual political agency is indicative of an increasing depolarization of "feminine" pacifism and "masculine" party politics fostered by the pacifist community of practice. Importantly, the fascination with Bertha von Suttner's

---

16 "Sie hat tapfer gegen Hohn, Spott und persönliche Angriffe angekampft. Alle ihr Bemuhen hatte keinerlei Einfluß, der erste Weltkrieg mit seinen sinnlosen Vernichtungschlachten kam."
17 The percentage of female Bundestag representatives in the 9th legislative period (1980–1983) was 20.1% versus 13.9% in the 8th legislative period (1976–1980) (Feldkamp and Sommer 2003, 6).

identity endures as well, not least in the many digitized editions of *Die Waffen nieder!* and the 2014 Austrian film made for television *Eine Liebe für den Frieden* (A love for peace), which features her relationship with Alfred Nobel (Egger). Suttner's lasting influence as a female founder of organized pacifism and the continued resonance of the literary experience of war through *Die Waffen nieder!* among advocates for peace remains an integral part of politics and popular culture in the German-speaking countries. As this study demonstrates, a gender analysis of *Die Waffen nieder!* provides a new perspective on the endurance of the novel as a symbol of organized German pacifism and contextualizes the controversies gender assumptions about peace prompted in German politics from the time of the book's initial publication to the present day.

Works Cited

Abrams, Irwin. Introduction. *Bertha von Suttner: A Life for Peace*, by Brigitte Hamann, translated by Ann Dubsky (Syracuse UP, 1996), pp. xiii–xx.

Allen, Ann Taylor. *Feminism and Motherhood in Germany, 1800–1914* (Rutgers UP, 1991).

Baldick, Chris. "Raisonneur." *The Oxford Dictionary of Literary Terms* (Oxford UP, 2008). https://proxy.ulib.csuohio.edu:2212/view/10.1093/acref/9780199208272.001.0001/acref-9780199208272-e-951>. Accessed 21 Mar. 2017.

Baumhauer, Walter. Letter to Roland Vogt (14. Sept. 1981). Akte 1720. Petra Kelly Archiv/ Archiv Grünes Gedächtnis, Berlin.

Bederman, Gail. *Manliness & Civilization: A Cultural History of Gender and Race in the United States, 1880–1917* (U of Chicago P, 1995).

Bock, Sigrid, and Helmut Bock. "Bertha von Suttner: Arbeiten für den Frieden." Nachwort. *Die Waffen nieder!*, edited by Bock and Bock (Verlag der Nation, 2006), pp. 405–457.

Bommersheim, Elly. Letter to Petra Kelly (1 Apr. 1977). Akte 1720. Petra Kelly Archiv/ Archiv Grünes Gedächtnis, Berlin.

Bommersheim, Elly. Letter to Petra Kelly (22 June 1977). Akte 1720. Petra Kelly Archiv/ Archiv Grünes Gedächtnis, Berlin.

Bommersheim, Elly. Letter to Petra Kelly (25 June 1977). Akte 1720. Petra Kelly Archiv/ Archiv Grünes Gedächtnis, Berlin.

Bommersheim, Elly. Letter to Petra Kelly (5 May 1979). Akte 1720. Petra Kelly Archiv/ Archiv Grünes Gedächtnis, Berlin.

Brändle-Zeile, Elisabeth. *Seit 90 Jahren: Frauen für den Frieden* (Windhueter Druck- und Verlagskollektiv, 1983).

Braker, Regina. "Bertha von Suttner as Author: The Harriet Beecher Stowe of the Peace Movement." *Peace & Change*, vol. 16, no. 1 (Jan. 1991), pp. 74–96.

Braker, Regina. "Bertha von Suttner's Spiritual Daughters: The Feminist Pacifism of Anita Augspurg, Lida Gustava Heymann, and Helene Stoecker at the International Congress of Women at the Hague." *Women's Studies International Forum*, vol. 18, no. 2 (Mar. 1995), pp. 103–111.

Brandt, Willy. Geleitwort. 1977. *Die Waffen nieder!*, by Bertha von Suttner (Gerstenberg, 1982), pp. v–vi.

Brinker-Gabler, Gisela, editor. *Kämpferin für Frieden: Bertha von Suttner: Lebenserinnerungen, Reden und Schriften* (Fischer Taschenbuch Verlag, 1986).

Canning, Kathleen. *Gender History in Practice: Historical Perspectives on Bodies, Class & Citizenship* (Cornell UP, 2006).

Chickering, Roger. *Imperial Germany and a World Without War: The Peace Movement and German Society, 1892–1914* (Princeton UP, 1975).

Cohen, Laurie. "Looking in from the Outside: Bertha and Arthur von Suttner in the Caucasus, 1876–1885." *Ab Imperio*, vol. 3 (2005), pp. 257–284.

Cooper, Sandi E. *Patriotic Pacifism: Waging War on War in Europe, 1815–1914* (Oxford UP, 1991).

Crawford, Neta C. "The Passion of World Politics: Propositions on Emotion and Emotional Relationships." *International Security*, vol. 24, no. 4 (2000), pp. 116–156.

Davis, Belinda. "Europe Is a Peaceful Woman, America Is a War-Mongering Man? The 1980s Peace Movement in NATO-Allied Europe." "European History – Gender History," *Themenportal Europäische Geschichte* (2009), www.europa.clio-online.de/essay/id/artikel-3554. Accessed 25 Sept. 2017.

Davy, Jennifer A. "'Manly' and 'Feminine' Antimilitarism: Perceptions of Gender in the Antimilitarist Wing of the Weimar Peace Movement." *Frieden – Gewalt – Geschlecht*, edited by Davy and Karen Hagemann (Klartext, 2005), pp. 144–165.

Dunant, Henri. *A Memory of Solferino*. 1862. Translated by the volunteers of the District of Columbia chapter [of the Red Cross] (Cassell, 1947).

Dzamba, Anne O. "Bertha von Suttner, Gender, and the Representation of War." *Essays in European History: Selected from the Annual Meetings of the Southern Historical Association, 1986–1987*, edited by June K. Burton (UP of America, 1989), pp. 61–72.

Eckert, Penelope, and Sally McConnell-Ginet. "Think Practically and Look Locally: Language and Gender as Community-Based Practice." *Annual Review of Anthropology*, vol. 21 (1992), pp. 461–490.

Egger, Urs, director. *Eine Liebe für den Frieden: Bertha von Suttner und Alfred Nobel*. Mona Film Produktion (2014).

Feldkamp, Michael F., and Christa Sommer. *Parlaments- und Wahlstatistik des Deutschen Bundestages 1949–2002/03* (SDV Saarbruecker Druckerei & Verlag GmbH, 2003).

Foster, Ian. *The Image of the Habsburg Army in Austrian Prose Fiction 1888–1914* (Peter Lang, 1991).

Geiger, Tim. "Der NATO-Doppelbeschluss: Vorgeschichte und Implementierung." *"Entrüstet Euch!" Nuklearkrise, NATO-Doppelbeschluss und Friedensbewegung*, edited by Christoph Becker-Schaum, et al. (Ferdinand Schöningh, 2012), pp. 54–69.

Hamann, Brigitte. *Bertha von Suttner: A Life for Peace*. Translated by Ann Dubsky (Syracuse UP, 1996).

Heymann, Lida Gustava. "Weiblicher Pazifismus." *Frauen gegen den Krieg*, edited by Gisela Brinker-Gabler (Fischer Taschenbuch Verlag, 1980), pp. 65–70.

Holmes, T. "Preface to the Second Edition." *Lay Down Your Arms: The Autobiography of Martha von Tilling*, translated by Holmes (Longmans, Green, and Co., 1914), pp. ix–x.

Jefferies, Matthew. *Contesting the German Empire, 1871–1918* (Blackwell Publishing, 2008).

Nehring, Holger. *The Politics of Security: British and West German Protest Movements and the Early Cold War, 1945–1970* (Oxford UP, 2013).

Ossietzky, Carl von. "Die Pazifisten." *Carl von Ossietzky Sämtliche Schriften*, edited by Baerbel Boldt, et al., vol. 2 (Rowohlt, 1994), pp. 371–375.

Reisenberger, Dieter. *Geschichte der Friedensbewegung in Deutschland von den Anfängen bis 1933* (Vandenhoeck & Ruprecht, 1985).

Remarque, Erich Maria. *Im Westen nichts Neues* (Propyläen-Verlag, 1929).

Suttner, Bertha von. *Lay Down Your Arms: The Autobiography of Martha von Tilling.* Translated by T. Holmes (Longmans, Green, and Co., 1914).

Suttner, Bertha von [Jemand]. *Das Maschinenzeitalter: Zukunftsvorlesungen über unsere Zeit* (Verlags-Magazin, 1889).

Suttner, Bertha von. *Memoiren von Bertha von Suttner* (Deutsche Verlags-Anstalt, 1909).

Suttner, Bertha von. *Die Waffen nieder! Eine Lebensgeschichte.* 1889. Edited by Sigrid and Helmut Bock (Verlag der Nation, 2006).

Sylvester, Christine. *War as Experience: Contributions from International Relations and Feminist Analysis* (Routledge, 2013).

Woodford, Charlotte. "Bertha von Suttner's *Die Waffen nieder!* and Gabriele Reuter's *Aus guter Familie:* Sentimentality and Social Criticism." *The German Bestseller in the Late Nineteenth Century*, edited by Woodford and Benedict Schofield (Camden House, 2012), pp. 206–223.

James M. Skidmore
Ricarda Huch's First World War

In his bestselling book *The Sleepwalkers: How Europe Went to War in 1914* (2013), historian Christopher Clark uses the word "sleepwalkers" only once, in the final sentence of the book, to sum up what he has written about the politicians, generals, and others who led Europe into the Great War: "the protagonists of 1914 were sleepwalkers, watchful but unseeing, haunted by dreams, yet blind to the reality of the horror they were about to bring into the world." Pithy and punchy, this statement is also ambiguous. The momentum towards war was not inevitable or unstoppable, but rather the result of an inability, or an unwillingness, of the hundreds of lead actors involved to pull Europe back from the brink. But can "sleepwalkers" be held accountable for their actions? Are sleepwalkers really responsible, or are they partially victims themselves, caught in an in-between state that prevents them from understanding the ramifications of their thoughts and actions?

If nothing else, World War I woke Europeans up to the reality of what they had been sleepwalking into, a modern world in which a conflict of the type Europe had seen many times before could result in destruction that had never been seen before: the deaths of some 8.5 million combatants and perhaps as many as 13 million civilians (Royde-Smith 2017), massive property damage, and the loss of cultural artefacts and heritage. In its aftermath the war has been understood as an awakening, a caesura between the premodern and the modern, between the nineteenth and twentieth centuries. The war ushered in the era of modern technological warfare, and some would go so far as to say the era of technology itself. After the war, mass – mass media, mass entertainment, mass political movements – would become the norm. In the realm of thought, modernism became the watchword. Much more than a literary style, modernism came to stand for a sensibility that dominated much of the cultural production in the Western world. At the same time, the war generated a more irrational *Weltanschauung* that can be interpreted as a reaction against technology and modernism. Historian Modris Eksteins points out in *Rites of Spring: The Great War and the Birth of the Modern Age* that, for the veterans of the war, the "burden of having been in the eye of the storm and yet, in the end, of having resolved nothing, was excruciating" (2000, 294). The horror of the war was bad enough for those directly involved in it; the futility of the conflagration was oppressive.

German writer, poet, and historian Ricarda Huch (1864–1947) was one of the intellectual sleepwalkers. She was caught off guard by the outbreak of war but, like so many writers, artists, and opinion-makers, quickly became engrossed by

https://doi.org/10.1515/9783110572001-008

the fever that marked the first few months of the conflict; as the war dragged on, she returned to her usual preoccupations and concerns. In one sense, she actually had very little to do with the war and its discourses, and even spent about half of it in neutral territory (Switzerland). She wrote no history of the war nor of the years leading up to it. Nevertheless, even though Huch's explicit commentary on World War I was confined to its initial stages, it would be a mistake to think that she did not engage with the war. Like other sleepwalkers, she was "haunted by dreams," but hers were dreams of a Germany she thought long lost. Before World War I, Huch's attention had been drawn to the cultural malaise that she and others believed afflicted her generation and her country. Her assessment of the issues and problems was not sociological in nature, but idealistic, that is, largely confined to the realm of ideas. Huch's conception of a bygone ideal was her sleepwalking dream, allowing her to greet the outbreak of the war with rhetorical flights of fancy, hoping that Europe was finally waking up to the existential crisis it had long ignored in favor of industrialization, imperialism, and nation-state building.

Did the war wake Huch from her dreams? This chapter examines her engagement with World War I and considers its impact on her intellectual productivity. It looks at a variety of works written just prior to and during the war: *Der große Krieg in Deutschland* (The great war in Germany, 1912–1914), later renamed *Der Dreißigjährige Krieg*, her history of the Thirty Years' War; the essays "Wir Barbaren und die Kathedralen" (We barbarians and the cathedrals, 1914) and "Krieg und Kunst" (War and art, 1914); the biographical sketch *Wallenstein: Eine Charakterstudie* (Wallenstein: A character study, 1915); the poems "Einem Helden" (To a hero, 1915), "Das Kriegsjahr" (The war year, 1920) and "Wilson" (1920). What will become clear is that Huch saw the age as one ripe for heroes – not the nationalistic kind that surface during times of war, but more idealistic figures who embodied for her truer, deeper values that could find a home in Germany. The national unity proclaimed by Kaiser Wilhelm II and others in 1914 proved illusory by the time the war ended four years later, and in any event it did not correspond to Huch's ideal of unity, shaped by her earlier preoccupation with Romanticism and idealized in her notion of the harmonious personality that she had developed in her two-volume study *Die Romantik* (Romanticism, 1899–1902). The notion of a purifying war, the war that would liberate Germany from its maladies and put it on the path to renewal, held some attraction for Huch. But how naïve was that belief, considering her deep familiarity with the destruction of the Thirty Years' War, Germany's other great war?

Today Huch is a largely forgotten writer, though in her time she was an important figure on the German cultural landscape. She has not been well served by assessments of her life and work by friends and well wishers that have bordered on the hagiographical, or that used Huch as a repository of the conservative nostalgia for a Germany that existed in the minds of many intellectuals prior to World War II but was rarely evident in reality. Huch's work nevertheless deserves to be addressed on its own terms. At its best, literary history situates the writings of authors within the social discourses and intellectual culture of a particular time and place, and doing so here will afford us a new perspective on one woman's involvement with a war that had enormous consequences for German society.

Anyone acquainted with Ricarda Huch's work knows that she usually defies categorization, be it as an historian, a novelist, or even as a woman writer. Historian Silke Fehlemann's useful investigation of the war experience of German women writers does not treat Huch for two reasons: she was one of the few women who had been accepted into the ranks of the intelligentsia (2014, 72) and she did not write any World War I novels (2014, 89). What is intriguing about Huch is that even though she was a pioneer for certain German women at the time, having made a name for herself in literary circles, she did not construct herself as a woman writer. She had little contact with the bourgeois and proletarian women's movements, and wrote even less about them. In fact, she wrote sparingly about World War I, and what little she did write was largely impersonal. Fehlemann's study ignores Huch because she does not belong to that category of women whose writing and public voices emerged thanks to the war, or who responded to the horrors of war with memoirs or fiction. But our picture of women writing war is incomplete if we do not reflect on how the few women regarded as intellectuals at the time of World War I responded to it, or how their work from that period is to be understood within the context of this world-changing event.

In the small garden patch of scholarship that is Huch studies, Huch's relationship to World War I is a corner that has seen very little tilling. Examinations of Huch tend to look inward, focusing on Huch's remarkable and eventful life: twice married and twice divorced, her second husband being both her cousin and brother-in-law, whose daughter – her niece – had a dalliance with her first husband, thereby causing that marriage to break down; one of the first German women to earn a doctorate (in Switzerland in 1891, in history); a working single mother who made her living as an independent writer; one of the few intellectuals to take an early and consequential stand against Nazism. In short, she is known more for her life than her actual intellectual work, and for many years the reception of her work was dominated by the effusive semi-professional scholarship of a coterie of devoted friends and followers, whose lasting impact was the tendency to read Huch more in relationship to her own life than to the intellectual or social contexts in which she lived and circulated.

The activities and opinions of German intellectuals during World War I have been studied exhaustively, but it is still helpful to review some key positions in order to contextualize Huch's position in contemporary discourses. In *The Spirit of 1914: Militarism, Myth and Mobilization in Germany* from 2000, historian Jeffrey Verhey questions the notion that there was a unity of purpose and enthusiasm at the beginning of the war; he successfully demonstrates that the spirit of 1914 was more propaganda than fact, a manufactured unity that was used to manipulate support for a war that had its fair share of critics and dissenters. Nevertheless, Verhey admits that Germany's public intellectuals demonstrated a high degree of uniform support for the war. It was seen as an opportunity to address Germany's spiritual void, an affliction diagnosed years earlier by Friedrich Nietzsche. For leftist critic and feuilletonist Siegfried Kracauer it had become clear that the *Vaterlandsgefühl* (patriotism) that dominated public discourse at the beginning of the war was an expression of relief by those who had lamented the absence of ideals in the German empire; for some of them this expression was the letting loose of inner feeling, for others it was an opportunity to commit themselves to something greater, something deeper than themselves (Kracauer 1990, 20–22). The "ideological crusade" (Kramer 2007, 162) of writers who elevated the war into an idealistic *Kulturkampf* (struggle between cultures) manifested itself for example in socialist economist Werner Sombart's claim that the war had awakened the heroic German spirit (1915, 117) and in literary giant Thomas Mann's assertion that the war brought purification, liberation, and hope (1914).

Intellectuals like Mann, Sombart, and others were so engrossed in the realm of ideas, and so far removed from the realities of modern technological warfare and military planning, that they had no idea what would befall their country, its soldiers and their families. Given their emotional endorsement of Germany's righteous cause, it is not surprising that intellectuals would mount campaigns to justify the war and defend Germany's honor, though it is remarkable that many of these campaigns upheld the system that Kracauer thought so many had found reprehensible. A good example of this is the famous appeal "To the Civilized World" ("An die Kulturwelt"), also known as the Manifesto of the 93 (for the 93 professors, writers, and artists, all male, who signed their names to the declaration). Issued in early October 1914, in response to the wide-scale foreign condemnation of Germany's conduct of the war in Belgium and France, in particular the brutal treatment of civilians and the destruction of heritage sites, most notably the university library in Louvain and the Cathedral of Notre-Dame at Reims, the manifesto asserts German unity – "The German Army and the German people are one" ("To the Civilized World" 1919, 285) – and rejects any notion that Germany acted as the aggressor. But the manifesto also defends German militarism in no uncertain terms and, in so doing, reiterates the claims that Germany must defend itself for fear of being destroyed. To state that German culture could not exist without the protection of the German military is consistent with the trend of defensive patriotism that marked the early days of the war. The chauvinistic tone of these manifestoes was a far cry from internationalism and fraternity that marked the "Gelehrtenrepublik" (republic of scholars) before the outbreak of the war (vom Bruch 2005, 392). The alleged unity of people and army would be sorely tested during the war; the mutiny of sailors in 1918 and the military's contempt for the citizenry that was so famously expressed after the war by the *Dolchstoßlegende* (stab-in-the-back legend) demonstrated that this unity was more imaginary than real.

Ricarda Huch signed at least two such manifestoes. The "Aufruf zur Würde" (Appeal to dignity) reiterated the idea that Germany had been forced into war in order to defend its place in the world and its own particular culture. Another, "Aufruf an die Frauen des Auslandes" (Appeal to women in foreign countries), was signed in September 1914 by 35 prominent artists, writers, and intellectuals such as Clara Viebig, Isolde Kurz, and Käthe Kollwitz. Claudia Siebrecht calls the appeal "one of the most overt examples of women's political activism in the early weeks of the war" (2013, 23). The text states that women are proud of Germany's cultural heritage and goes on to defend Germany against charges of barbarism: "We mothers, wives and sisters would feel responsible, too, if German men had actually violated the commandments of *Kultur* and humanity. But we know that when our husbands and sons, our brothers and friends risk their lives to defend the fatherland, they do not cease to be representatives of the German culture that we – men and women – have created together" (qtd. in Siebrecht 2013, 23).

Whether or not the signatories were willfully ignoring the excesses of the German invasion of Belgium and France is not known. But as Siebrecht points out, "loyalty, support, and in some cases enthusiasm for the national cause quite accurately characterize the response of female artists and female intellectuals in 1914" (2013, 25), and Huch's work from this period supports this observation. Her more substantial contributions to the discourses surrounding the "spirit of 1914" came in the form of two essays, "Wir Barbaren und die Kathedralen" which appeared in the *Frankfurter Zeitung* on 16 October 1914, and "Krieg und Kunst" which was included in the November 1914 edition of the *Süddeutsche Monatshefte* devoted to the theme of "Das neue Deutschland" (The new Germany). "Wir Barbaren und die Kathedralen" was clearly written in response to the foreign criticisms of the German army's disregard for heritage sites in its conduct of the war. Huch begins her essay with the bold assertion that it is unrealistic, if not absurd, to expect war to be peaceful. During times of peace, people should expect peaceful behavior; during times of war, people should expect warlike behavior: "war is based on violence and destruction" (1966–1974k, 843).[1] She admits that excesses will occur, but that is the nature of the beast. Defending Germany against the charge of being uncultured, she criticizes the notion that art and heritage should be protected at the cost of life or military advantage: "one thing is certain: only a people that instinctively values life and human beings above art is capable of creating art" (1966–1974k, 844). Her ironic adoption of the term barbarian, which came into widespread use in France after events like the bombardment of the Reims cathedral, signals her understanding that the French will use the destruction of their cultural heritage to poke the flames of its fury. She nevertheless refuses to admit to any misbehavior on the German side: "we Germans should not feel obliged to rationalize [our actions]. Indeed, we should rather say that we destroy works of art when it's necessary for victory, since victory and keeping the war far from our borders is the goal that we are pursuing with all our strength" (1966–1974k, 845). Her argumentation here is quite similar to one of the statements made in "To the Civilized World": "Every German would, of course, greatly regret if in the course of this terrible war any works of art should already have been destroyed or be destroyed at some future time, but inasmuch as in our great love for art we cannot be surpassed by any other nation, in the same degree we must decidedly refuse to buy a German defeat at the cost of saving a work of art" (1919, 285). Huch and the other intellectuals claim that Germans are lovers and protectors of art, except when they must destroy it in the name of the greater good, namely the preservation of Germany and German culture itself.

Huch's essay is also quite forceful in its endorsement of the war as a purifying measure. In her view, massive wars such as the one just started are evidence of their own necessity. They occur because the time is right for them to occur: "Great wars take place when something old is ready for destruction and something new is ready to arise" (1966–1974k, 844). Huch sharply criticizes those who would cling to the old instead of looking forward to the new, and it is because this war promises to be a war of renewal that Europe need not worry if it loses the odd cathedral: "Europe is wealthy enough to spare more than one cathedral if out of their ruins a purified and rejuvenated humanity rises up" (1966–1974k, 845).

I have explained elsewhere that World War I caught Huch by surprise (Skidmore 2005, 24–25). Even so, that did not prevent her from supporting the war. In a memoir about her first husband written in the 1930s and first published after her death in 1947, Huch remarks that in 1914, she was paying little attention to

1 All translations of Huch's texts into English are my own.

politics; discussions about the Balkans and the responses of Russia and England interested her not in the least. When war does break out she is convinced it will end quickly with a German victory, much as had been the case with the Franco-Prussian War (1870 – 1871), her first conscious memory (1966 – 1974h, 321 – 322). In a letter to her friend Marie Baum in early September 1914, Huch inveighs against "the ugly popular instincts" disguised "beneath the mask of patriotic fervor"; but she is not worried about the war lasting very long, convinced as she is of the "the superiority of German strength and culture" (1986, 59). The ambivalent manner with which she greets the war stands in stark contrast to the blunt statements she makes in "Wir Barbaren und die Kathedralen." In another letter to Baum dated 24 October 1914, she admits that the destruction of old cities does indeed cause her pain. What seems to upset her most, however, are the ignorant, chauvinistic reactions and drumbeating at home: "I find it all depressing what the war has so far brought, for example, at home. Everything is so petty, loud-mouthed, and much of it is really quite barbaric" (qtd. in Bendt and Schmidgall 1994, 203).

Huch's concern about the atmosphere at home in the early months of the conflict leads her to make her voice heard in the public discussion surrounding the war. In a letter dated one week prior to the aforementioned letter to Baum, Huch writes to the editor of the *Süddeutsche Monatshefte*, Paul Nikolaus Cossmann, because he had yet to publish some poems of hers, and Huch wants to prevent their appearance: "I hope you aren't thinking of publishing these poems, for I would certainly be lynched if people thought that in these times I am occupied with such frivolities" (qtd. in Bendt and Schmidgall 1994, 204). Instead she offers him, free of charge, the essay "Krieg und Kunst," but she needs to know right away if he could publish it; if not, she would offer it to a daily newspaper so that it could see the light of day before becoming out of date.

The *Süddeutsche Monatshefte* was fully supportive of the war, and "Krieg und Kunst" appeared in the second special issue devoted to "Das neue Deutschland." The essay is not a renunciation of her previous "Wir Barbaren und die Kathedralen"; she reminds her readers that it is impossible to fight a war without hating and wanting to inflict damage on one's enemies. Ostensibly she wrote the essay to reject the suggestion made by foreign writers and artists, namely the Italian Gabriele d'Annunzio, the Belgian Maurice Maeterlinck, the Frenchman Romain Rolland, and Ferdinand Hodler of Switzerland, that Germany would destroy art and cultural heritage deliberately and maliciously. But at the same time Huch uses the essay to criticize a fast-rising patriotic parochialism in Germany that would shun non-German art and writing: "art is international and should not be touched by the passions of war, or at least not soiled by them" (1966 – 1974e, 743). In trying to hold Germans back from this excessive nationalism, she argues that the cause of the thoughtless patriotic surge is the civilian population's ignorance about how to handle war. She relates the anecdote of a Russian soldier who carried a wounded Austrian soldier back to the Austrian regiment. The Russian explains that he acted as a human being; when he returns to battle, he will also return to acting like a soldier and will be prepared to kill his enemy. Huch takes this as a sign that soldiers, unlike civilians, have figured out how to confront their enemies. Huch stresses that she is not against hating one's enemy; at most she only urges restraint, arguing that this genuine hatred is undermined if one tries too hard to diminish the standing of the foe (746). In a way, Huch is trying to separate honorable warfare from blatant nationalism; she admires the noble heroism that the former can foster while disdaining the jingoistic chauvinism that sullies the conduct of soldiers.

Huch's explanation for the exaggerated reactions of Germans on the home front – they feel guilty about their inaction, so they try to make up for it with words – recalls her own frustration at not being able to contribute directly to the war effort. In her view, the exuberance of citizens behind the front lines is their way of compensating for not being able to be on the front itself. Personally, Huch thought that being in the thick of it would be thrilling and life-affirming. In correspondence with various friends and acquaintances in the early months of the war, Huch laments that being a woman prevents her from going off to war (Skidmore 2005, 25–26). She envies her publisher Anton Kippenberg's activity in the training of soldiers and writes to him in February 1915: "If I could go into battle, I'd be there heart and soul, but as it's not possible, I continue my normal life" (1986, 63). Huch's reasons for wanting to march to war are less nationalistic than personal, however. By early 1915 she had come to understand that the war is a power game, and it is for that reason that she rejected the criticism of some of her friends and acquaintances that she was not displaying enough patriotism. Rather, her interest in joining the fight was spiritual, in a sense. As she relates to Baum, falling in battle would be a beautiful and fulfilling end to her life (Skidmore 2005, 26). Huch's correspondence strongly suggests that she did not want to die for the glory of her country; she was simply taken with the ideal of dying a hero's death.

This interest in heroism and the heroic influenced some of Huch's activity during the war. In 1916 she and her daughter moved to Switzerland and would not return to Munich until October 1918. As material conditions worsened in Germany, she had been advised to go there in order to treat a chronic digestive ailment and to be able to better provide for her daughter. She also wished to distance herself from the art historian Heinrich Wölfflin, with whom she had become infatuated. Acquaintances and friends were less than sympathetic with Huch for leaving Germany at this critical hour (Skidmore 2005, 28). In December 1916, she gave two public lectures, in St. Gallen and Zurich, entitled "Über den Begriff des Helden" (On the concept of the hero). No known copy of the lecture exists, but it is clear from a review in the social democratic Swiss newspaper *Volksrecht* that Huch's fascination for heroism forged in the great conflicts of European history did not resonate with the Swiss audiences. The nameless reviewer makes her or his skepticism about Huch's concept of heroism plain by reporting her beliefs objectively, though not without a hint of sarcasm: "War is required to produce heroes, and eternal peace would therefore be regrettable, because heroes would become extinct as a result" (qtd. in Bendt and Schmidgall 1994, 209).

Huch also addressed the heroic ideal in her poetry from this period. It seems that she wrote very little poetry during the war; the volume of poetry *Alte und neue Gedichte* (Old and new poems) that appeared in 1920, contained mostly poems from before the conflict (Hoppe 1951, 123), somewhat unusual when collections of poetry commemorating – or even celebrating – the war were popular. One poem by Huch that was likely written during the war, "Einem Helden" (To a hero), appeared in *Poesie des Krieges* (Poetry of war), a 1915 collection edited by literary historian Alfred Biese, one of the many anthologies appearing during the war that, as Nicolas Detering has pointed out, served to canonize enthusiasm for the war (2013, 122). This poem is largely unremarkable, but it evokes in lyrical form Huch's heroism motif:

> You who have fought to the end,
> Be wakened by the trumpet's blast,
> Strap on your sword and turn
> Your face proudly to the dawn. (1966–1974a, 276)

Of note here is the absence of overt nationalism or patriotism as seen in the essay "Krieg und Kunst." Huch sings the praises of heroism, not of German heroes. Another poem written during the war, "Das Kriegsjahr," is similar in tone and subject matter, with a column of soldiers, wreaths in their hair, marching towards "sacrifice [...] flushed they press on to battle and death" (1966–1974f, 275). The poem "Wilson" is clearly written after the war when it became apparent to Huch and other Germans that U.S. President Woodrow Wilson's "Fourteen Points," his proposal for the basis of a peace to end the war, were just empty talk. The poem's opening lines – "You shall not be destroyed by noble flame / You belong to the cold of hell" (1966–1974j, 284) – are extremely explicit in their anger and disgust. By denying Wilson the "noble flame," Huch characterizes him as anti-heroic, and in this way asserts the distinction between noble and base, between heroic and despicable. To read the poem from a nationalist perspective is possible, but doing so would undermine the poem's more universal message of the type of personality that can, or rather cannot, be called a hero.

In 1914 the last volume of Ricarda Huch's three-volume history of the Thirty Years' War had just appeared. Even though Huch's *magnum opus* was already in bookstores by the time the artillery started shelling enemy targets in August 1914, it is worthwhile considering this work in relationship to Huch's writing during and about World War I; literature can resonate beyond the time and context of its creation. The first two volumes of *Der große Krieg in Deutschland* had appeared in 1912, and the trilogy proved to be successful during the war as well as afterwards, being renamed *Der Dreißigjährige Krieg* (The Thirty Years' War) in the late 1920s in order to distinguish it from that other Great War that had recently concluded. Whenever this work is the subject of scholarly inquiry, the discussion usually turns to whether or not it is history or a novel; in the collected edition of Huch's works (1966–1974) it is included with the novels and not the histories. Huch does not chronicle the period in straightforward fashion, the approach (more or less) she would later take with her *Deutsche Geschichte* (German history), the first volume of which appeared in 1934. Instead, she presents a series of scenes and vignettes, over 200 in all, that the reviewer Thea Gerstein would call a "history as mosaic" (1912–1913, 352). These scenes rotate: members of the ruling class, figures from science and culture, religious leaders, and simple folk whose lives are affected by the decisions of the more powerful all get their time in Huch's spotlight.

Germanist Susan Anderson has noted that "Huch constructs a narrative that revives the German Baroque period in all its horror and wildness. Her chronicle [of the Thirty Years' War], with its confusion of episodes, chronology, and characters, offers a chilling testimony to a world gone awry" (1994, 153). This approach, this "confusion," was thought of as original, and historian Angelika Schaser contends there is evidence to suggest that Huch had always intended to write history in a new, more literary manner (2012, 58). Academic historians, who at this time were almost all male, ignored the work since it did not correspond to their idea of the genre. Women embraced the book and wrote many reviews of it, whereas men tended to be more irritated by it (Schaser 2012, 75–76). Huch's achievement also signaled to other women their entry into historians' circles (Schaser 2012, 80). There is no doubt that the originality of Huch's history of the Thirty Years' War made a mark; many histories of the war appeared leading up to the quincentenary in 1918 of the war's beginning, but Huch's remained popular thanks to its composition, accessibility, and thoroughness.

Although both Anderson and Germanist Waltraud Maierhofer stress that Huch's history is a panorama of the effects of the Thirty Years' War on all those unable to control events around them, they note a special interest in women, as they are often presented as the most visibly powerless (Maierhofer 2005, 327). Even Huch's portrayal of Friedrich Spee, a Jesuit known for opposing the witch hunts of the 1600s, is one example of the attention Huch paid to the lot of women during the conflict. While Anderson argues that Huch's "text on the Thirty Years' War reveals her sympathy for the disenfranchised" (1994, 143), and Schaser sees it as a history of the German people under the yoke of its rulers (2012, 72), it would be too simplistic to think that Huch's principal goal was to be a voice for the poor and downtrodden. The broad strokes of Huch's historical brush show how everyone and everything was affected by this war; there was no aspect of life left untouched, and thus her vignettes portray rulers and intellectuals, priests and farmers, women and children as they come to terms with the all-consuming conflict.

Much has been made of the closing scene of *Der große Krieg in Deutschland*. Set in 1650, two years after the Peace of Westphalia concluded the Thirty Years' War, a Lutheran minister's daughter is murdered by a Catholic soldier. Just as the pastor is about to kill the soldier in an act of revenge, the soldier's commander arrives on the scene and offers to execute the soldier in retribution, and to set an example for the other soldiers that such wanton violence will no longer be tolerated. But Huch's pastor instead comes to his senses; it is the first peaceful Easter in thirty years, and even if it has been tarnished by the death of his daughter, the pastor demands that no more blood be shed. The Catholic soldiers join the Protestants in holy communion, and harmony – between Catholics and Protestants, between noble and peasant – appears to be restored as the pastor buries his daughter and takes in her child as his own. The standard scholarly interpretation is to view the book's finale as a subdued signal for hope and optimism. Anderson disputes, however, that harmony has been restored; the "garden of Germanic paradise" that "informs and grounds [Huch's] calls for social and spiritual reform" (Anderson 1994, 153) has not been realized at the end of Huch's telling of the war's tale. Indeed, the pastor is an "antidote to modern decadence, but this power is still weak" (Anderson 1994, 153), too weak to bring about a new and better era to replace the thirty years (and more) of strife and disunity.

It is odd that Huch's work on the Thirty Years' War, with its vivid descriptions of the hardships and heartache caused by war, would not have led her to write in a similar vein about the war she actually experienced. Instead, throughout the fall and winter of 1914–1915 she worked on a spin-off of sorts, *Wallenstein: Eine Charakterstudie*, which appeared in 1915, but failed to gain much recognition. All the same, Germanist Steffan Davies, in his thorough study of the figure of Albrecht von Wallenstein in German literature, has demonstrated that Huch's *Wallenstein* has more to say about Huch's frame of mind during World War I than previously thought. Most significantly, Davies shows that Huch was working within two contexts – one literary, one contemporary: "Huch's study should by no means be seen as 'an adaptation of' or 'based on' [Friedrich] Schiller's character. Its impetus was concern with her times, not any form of homage to Schiller; yet it was in Schiller's thematic language that she found the means to express her own ideas" (2009, 183). Davies emphasizes the Schiller angle to Wallenstein throughout his monograph, and although Huch, as an admirer of Schiller, would surely have been familiar with the great poet's play, the fact is that her Wallenstein is based on her study of the history of the Thirty Years' War; Schiller is not even mentioned in Huch's *Wallenstein*. Nevertheless, the difficulty with the historical figure Wallenstein, as Davies points out, is that the general did not really possess the qualities to make him a national icon; his popularity rested on his ambiguity, which made him ripe for interpretation and dramatization, but not for mythmaking. Quoting Aleida Assmann, Davies asserts that "'national memory [...] is receptive to historical moments of triumph and trauma', but only 'provided they can be integrated into the semantics of a heroic narrative,' a condition Wallenstein could not meet" (2009, 204). This might explain why scholarship on Huch has largely detoured around her take on Wallenstein; it is more of a negative than positive example of Huch's interest in the heroic nature, even if he embodied much of what Huch had advocated elsewhere, namely "his supposed opposition to particularism, religious politics, and outmoded bureaucracy" (Davies 2009, 205). Unlike *Der große Krieg in Deutschland*, written in a high literary style and structured as a pastiche of emotions, characters, and ideas, *Wallenstein* did not cause any great stir in the middle of World War I nor does it provide very much insight into Huch's thinking that is not available elsewhere.

The ending of *Wallenstein* illustrates just how idiosyncratic a writer Huch could be. Throughout the book Huch describes Wallenstein as troubled, a man of great talents who is nevertheless waylaid by a weakness of character. When she comes to the scene of Wallenstein's assassination, which she believes he met with the dignity for which he strove his entire life (1966 – 1974i, 654), she introduces an entirely new character from a different era, Charles Albert, King of Sardinia who died in 1849. In her estimation, both figures shared a desire to rise above the parties vying for power in their respective eras, yet both also lacked the strength of character to maintain such independent positions. They were aware of their weaknesses, and sought to compensate for them by appealing to higher powers – Charles Albert to God, Wallenstein to the stars in the heavens. "Both men felt called to do great things, but both avoided attempting them because they knew they were too weak to succeed" (657). "Both perished," Huch writes, "when they were obliged to break free from the shelter [of fantasy] and *act* [...] The dignified comportment with which they met their fate casts a refined [veredelten] shine on their disharmonious lives" (657, emphasis mine). As I mentioned above, Huch's study at the turn of the century of German Romanticism, coupled with her understanding of some of Johann Wolfgang von Goethe's work, had impressed upon her the importance of the harmonious personality. By contrast, Wallenstein is a failed hero because he cannot balance the two drives of fantasy and action, of dream and deed. Unlike the heroes in her First World War poems, Wallenstein may be a person for whom Huch has great sympathy, but his life is unable to live up to the needs of the moment, and thus he is portrayed in a negative light. Like the pastor at the end of Huch's history of the Thirty Years' War, Wallenstein may be nobly inclined, but he is still too weak to act, to strap on his sword and turn his face proudly to the red glow of the morning sky (see "Einem Helden" quoted above). This inability to act might remind one of Clark's sleepwalkers, though in this instance the passivity is a failing to meet the challenges of war, not to prevent war from happening in the first place.

Anderson argues that Huch's treatment of the Thirty Years' War expresses "fear of increasing disharmony, and her critique of rationality and technology" (143), motifs that surfaced throughout Huch's career and writings. Can one go further, as Schaser does, to argue that the concerns Huch addressed in her study of the seventeenth-century war resonated strongly with a public consumed by World War I? "The Germans, who saw themselves caught up in a war for which they didn't feel responsible, concentrated on the pain that this war brought them. In this context a book that depicted the collapse of the state, mass death and unspeakable pain in a war that was not prevented by incompetent princes was seen as the inevitable German destiny" (Schaser 2012, 77–78). Taken together, Anderson's and Schaser's readings of *Der große Krieg in Deutschland* consider the book a critique of two types of modernization: the general modernization (or rationalization) of Western society, best seen in the increased role of technology in human life, and a more specific German problem, the social and political disharmony precipitated by the gradual rise of a state form alien to the German "way." It would not be difficult to imagine that Germans, caught in the midst of a terrible war, the propaganda for which claimed that Germany was in a fight for its very existence, might read Huch's story of the Thirty Years' War with special interest.

Wallenstein shows us, however, that Huch's response to modernity was to dwell in a nostalgia for a noble ideal of heroism, a notion fortified by the poems Huch wrote in direct response to World War I. Readings such as Anderson's and Schaser's incorporate Huch's postwar writings in their contextualization of Huch's treatment of the war and its importance to her overall worldview, but the contemporary reader, not knowing how World War I would end and unable to imagine the difficulties the country would face in defeat, might not have been able to gain such insights. Just how many would have responded positively to Huch's romantic idealism is unclear, but it seems that even Huch soon realized that the war had changed things. With the collapse of the imperial system and the introduction of universal suffrage, Huch took a more active interest in the day-to-day political life of her country than she had before 1914. She even attempted to win a nomination for a seat in the federal parliament with the new bourgeois Deutsche Demokratische Partei. The histories she wrote in the 1920s and 1930s, for example her history of the 1848 revolution (1930) and especially her three-volume general history of Germany (1934–1949) became more focused on questions of politics and state formation that preoccupied her as Germany struggled with Weimar democracy and Third Reich dictatorship. Most scholars, and Anderson and Schaser can be counted among them, read Huch's history of the Thirty Years' War within the continuity of Huch's writing before and after World War I.

Anderson advocates a gendered reading of the Huch oeuvre that bridges the divide caused by World War I: "We can see how she finds a continuity in Wilhelmine and Weimar German decadence through her persistent criticisms of post-medieval German culture. Huch's many accounts of femicide in the narrative reveal her critique of a modern world order that has cast off its feminine, community-oriented, creative, intuitive side, thereby throwing itself into disequilibrium" (1994, 152). I would argue that this is a slight misinterpretation of Huch's original idea that she first expounded in her turn-of-the-century study of German Romanticism. One of Huch's key arguments in *Die Romantik* was that the human being had two polarities. *Bewußtsein* (consciousness) was the more rational or Appollinian polarity, also referred to as *Geist* or woman/female/feminine; *Unbewußtsein* or *Unbewußten* (subconciousness) was the other, Dionysian polarity, also referred to as *Natur* or man/male/masculine. According to Huch, these polarities reached a brief moment of harmonization during Romanticism, namely in the author of Novalis who was able to poeticize ("poetisieren") all of existence (1966–1974g, 79). In the years following Nietzsche's analyses of cultural malaise, such concepts were not necessarily that novel (cf. Thomas Mann's essay "Gedanken im Kriege," mentioned above), though Huch's integration of them into Romanticism was enlightening to many (including Thomas Mann).

I read Huch's emphasis on the noble warrior-hero in her First World War poems, and even its negative counterpart in *Wallenstein*, as an attempt to put her romantic dream at the service of the crisis of her time. At first glance her slightly chauvinistic 1914 essays do not seem to fit into this framework; their language is more gruesome, as seen in this excerpt from "Wir Barbaren und die Kathedralen": "out of a sea of blood climbed that wondrous beauty, [Johann Sebastian] Bach's music. Great wars don't come into being unless something old is decaying and something new is ready to rise" (1966–1974k, 844). The argument can be made, however, that the new greatness is the idea of the harmonious, noble hero. Of course, one wonders how writers like Huch could not see that the belief in war as a necessary step on the path to cultural renewal privileged ideas over lives and ideals over people. As a woman, Huch could not realize her desire to participate in the heroic struggle that was taking place on the battlefields of France and Belgium; had she been able to, she would have been disabused of the notion that that struggle was anything but bloody and awful. Even her three-poem cycle "Frauen" (Women), published in the *Bismarck-Jahrbuch für Frauen* (Bismarck yearbook for women) in 1917, while acknowledging the quiet and forgotten suffering of women on the homefront, fails to criticize or call into question the war in the first place. These intellectual sleepwalkers of the Great War, both those who embraced Germany's war aims and those who, like Huch, were more reserved in their nationalism, could not comprehend the disaster they were advocating; they were, to use Clark's words once again, "watchful but unseeing, haunted by dreams." Huch's conception of the heroic ideal was her dream, and it may well have prevented her from understanding that what she hoped would be born out of war would not be achievable. Her postwar historical writing paid more attention to the "facts on the ground" as a result, though Huch would never fully let go of her idealism.

Works Cited

Anderson, Susan C. "Against Modernity and Historicism: Ricarda Huch's Representation of the Thirty Years' War." *Colloquia Germanica*, vol. 27, no. 2 (1994), pp. 141–157.

Bendt, Jutta, and Karin Schmidgall. *Ricarda Huch: 1864–1947: Eine Ausstellung des Deutschen Literaturarchivs im Schiller-Nationalmuseum Marbach Am Neckar, 7. Mai– 31. Oktober 1994* (Deutsche Schillergesellschaft, 1994).

Biese, Alfred, editor. *Poesie des Krieges* (G. Grote, 1915).

Clark, Christopher M. *The Sleepwalkers: How Europe Went to War in 1914*. EPUB (HarperCollins, 2013).

Davies, Steffan. *The Wallenstein Figure in German Literature and Historiography 1790–1920* (Maney Publishing for the Modern Humanities Research Association, 2009).

Detering, Nicolas. "Sammelen und Verbreiten." *Populäre Kriegslyrik im Ersten Weltkrieg*, edited by Detering, et al. (Waxman Verlag, 2013), pp. 121–154.

Eksteins, Modris. *Rites of Spring: The Great War and the Birth of the Modern Age* (Houghton Mifflin, 2000).

Fehlemann, Silke. "Building Home: The War Experience of German Woman Writers 1914–1918." *Krieg und Literatur/War and Literature: Internationales Jahrbuch zur Kriegs- und Antikriegsliteraturforschung/International Yearbook on War and Anti-War Literature*, vol. 20 (2014), pp. 69–95.

Gerstein, Thea. "Historie in Mosaik." *Die Frau*, vol. 20, no. 6 (1912–1913), p. 352.

Hoppe, Else. *Ricarda Huch: Weg – Persönlichkeit – Werk* (Dr. Riederer-Verlag), 1951.

Huch, Ricarda. *Alte und neue Gedichte* (Insel, 1920).

Huch, Ricarda. *Briefe an die Freunde* (Manesse, 1986). Manesse Bibliothek der Weltliteratur.

Huch, Ricarda. *Deutsche Geschichte: Gesammelte Werke*. Edited by Wilhelm Emrich, vol. 10 (Kiepenheuer & Witsch, 1966–1974a). 11 vols.

Huch, Ricarda. "Einem Helden." *Gesammelte Werke*, edited by Wilhelm Emrich, vol. 5 (Kiepenheuer & Witsch, 1966–1974b), p. 276. 11 vols.

Huch, Ricarda. "Frauen." *Gesammelte Werke*, edited by Wilhelm Emrich, vol. 5 (Kiepenheuer & Witsch, 1966–1974c), p. 279–281. 11 vols.

Huch, Ricarda. *Der Große Krieg in Deutschland: Gesammelte Werke*. Edited by Wilhelm Emrich, vol. 3 (Kiepenheuer & Witsch, 1966–1974d). 11 vols.

Huch, Ricarda. "Krieg und Kunst." *Gesammelte Werke*, edited by Wilhelm Emrich, vol. 5 (Kiepenheuer & Witsch, 1966–1974e), pp. 743–747. 11 vols.

Huch, Ricarda. "Das Kriegsjahr." *Gesammelte Werke*, edited by Wilhelm Emrich, vol. 5 (Kiepenheuer & Witsch, 1966–1974f), p. 275. 11 vols.

Huch, Ricarda. "Die Romantik." *Gesammelte Werke*, edited by Wilhelm Emrich, vol. 5 (Kiepenheuer & Witsch, 1966–1974g), pp. 17–646. 11 vols.

Huch, Ricarda. "Unser Mannochen." *Gesammelte Werke*, edited by Wilhelm Emrich, vol. 9 (Kiepenheuer & Witsch, 1966–1974h), pp. 245–365. 11 vols.

Huch, Ricarda. *Wallenstein: Gesammelte Werke*. Edited by Wilhelm Emrich, vol. 9 (Kiepenheuer & Witsch, 1966–1974i), pp. 521–627. 11 vols.

Huch, Ricarda. "Wilson." *Gesammelte Werke*, edited by Wilhelm Emrich, vol. 5 (Kiepenheuer & Witsch, 1966–1974j), p. 284. 11 vols.

Huch, Ricarda. "Wir Barbaren und die Kathedralen." *Gesammelte Werke*, edited by Wilhelm Emrich, vol. 5 (Kiepenheuer & Witsch, 1966–1974k), pp. 843–845. 11 vols.

Kracauer, Siegfried. "Vom Erleben des Kriegs." *Schriften*, edited by Inka Mülder-Bach, vol. 5.1 (Suhrkamp, 1990), pp. 11–22. 8 vols.

Kramer, Alan. *Dynamic of Destruction Culture and Mass Killing in the First World War* (Oxford UP, 2007).

Maierhofer, Waltraud. *Hexen – Huren – Heldenweiber: Bilder des Weiblichen in Erzähltexten über den Dreißigjährigen Krieg* (Böhlau, 2005).

Mann, Thomas. "Gedanken im Kriege." *Die neue Rundschau* (25 Nov. 1914: n. pag). EPUB.

Royde-Smith, John Graham. "World War I." *Encyclopedia Britannica*, www.britannica.com/event/World-War-I/Killed-wounded-and-missing. Accessed 15 Feb. 2017.

Schaser, Angelika. "Der große Krieg in Deutschland: literarische Geschichtsschreibung als weibliche Geschichtswissenschaft?" *Denk- und Schreibweisen einer Intellektuellen im 20. Jahrhundert: über Ricarda Huch*, edited by Gesa Dane and Barbara Hahn (Wallstein, 2012), pp. 56–80.

Siebrecht, Claudia. *The Aesthetics of Loss: German Women's Art of the First World War* (Oxford UP, 2013).

Skidmore, James M. *The Trauma of Defeat: Ricarda Huch's Historiography during the Weimar Republic* (Lang, 2005).

Sombart, Werner. *Händler und Helden: Patriotrische Besinnungen* (Duncker und Humblot, 1915).

"To the Civilized World." *The North American Review*, vol. 210, no. 765 (1919), pp. 284–287.

Verhey, Jeffrey. *The Spirit of 1914: Militarism, Myth and Mobilzation in Germany* (Cambridge UP, 2000).

Vom Bruch, Rüdiger. "Geistige Kriegspropaganda: Der Aufruf von Wissenschaftlern und Künstlern an Die Kulturwelt." *Europa und die Europäer: Quellen und Essays zur Modernen Europäischen Geschichte*, edited by Rüdiger Hohls, et al. (Franz Steiner Verlag, 2005), pp. 392–394.

Julie Shoults
Hermynia Zur Mühlen

Writing a Socialist-Feminist Pacifism in the Aftermath of WWI

"And then came the war" (53).[1] This sentence alone comprises all of chapter eight in Hermynia Zur Mühlen's novella "Lina: Erzählung aus dem Leben eines Dienstmädchens" (Lina: Tale of a housemaid's life, 1924/26),[2] signifying a distinct rupture in the protagonist's world. The chapters that follow trace the impact of World War I on Lina's life, from decreased wages for increasingly strenuous labor, to her brother's death on the front and eventually the protagonist's suicide. While her life as a housemaid is always difficult, it is not until her brother is killed in action that she loses all hope of a better future: "Then she became quiet, completely indifferent, as if everything inside her had died" (56).[3] It is a somber tale that Zur Mühlen produces to show that Lina's misery would have been ameliorated if she had joined the socialist movement. The transformative power of international socialism at both personal and societal levels is a theme that permeates Zur Mühlen's writings. While her exile works after 1933 have received attention for boldly challenging nationalist ideologies that contribute to war and conflict, similar internationalist approaches in her earlier texts remain largely overlooked by scholarship. In fact, Zur Mühlen constructs and disseminates a unique form of socialist-feminist pacifism through her writing in the aftermath of World War I, combining socialist perspectives with a feminist consciousness in hopes of engaging women politically to preclude future wars.

Austrian aristocrat-turned-socialist Zur Mühlen (1883–1951) devoted her literary career to promoting socialist perspectives, as poor health throughout her life limited her ability to engage in the movement in other ways. Although she fondly recalls riding her bicycle through town as a child shouting, "Down with the government! Down with the nobility!" (2010, 23), secretly hoping to be arrested, her writing eventually replaced this type of agitation. Contextualizing Zur Mühlen's work in relation to the socialist, feminist and pacifist move-

---

1 While several of Zur Mühlen's works have been translated into English, most have not. I use translated texts when available, but all translations of original German texts are my own. In the latter cases, the original German quotes are included in footnotes only where the precise language or terminology helps to illustrate my arguments and interpretation.
2 According to Ailsa Wallace, this text was originally serialized in the journal *Arbeiterstimme* (Worker's voice) in 1924 before appearing in novella format in 1926 (2009, 111).
3 "Dann wurde sie ruhig, völlig abgestumpft, als wäre in ihr alles erstorben."

https://doi.org/10.1515/9783110572001-009

ments of the early 1900s, I analyze how these "isms" converge in a variety of her texts and inform her depiction of World War I. As a literary scholar, I read Zur Mühlen's texts alongside the historical context and discourses that informed her work and draw on current scholarship from multiple disciplines, including Germanistik and Gender Studies, in order to explicate the socialist-feminist pacifism she constructs via her didactic popular literature.

Zur Mühlen's literature is didactic in that she often employs the genre of the *Bildungsroman*, or novel of education,[4] which serves a social function. Discussing this genre, Rita Felski notes that such novels represent "an ideological site, an active process of meaning production" (1989, 126), and she asserts, "The education of the protagonist is simultaneously that of the reader" (137). Not only do Zur Mühlen's characters undergo a process of socialization or education, but readers are also encouraged to learn the same lessons and empathize with these figures. Zur Mühlen incorporates a similar style in her shorter texts, simply condensing the development process of the protagonist and shaping a narrative focused on imparting a particular message. This message generally relates to Zur Mühlen's own evolving beliefs on socialism, feminism, nationalism and pacifism, which personal experiences of her social and political context influenced.

Zur Mühlen was very much engaged with the developments of her time, and she incorporated historical figures and events in her fictional texts. These often serve as catalysts for her characters to alter their views and/or spring into action, whereas they were previously politically ambivalent. Zur Mühlen experienced such transformations in her own life; for instance, when she heard news of the Russian Revolution in 1917, she decided to make a decisive break with her privileged aristocratic life and join the revolutionary cause: "I broke with my old world and dared to leap into the new. [...] I was no longer a single individual struggling senselessly against overpowering opponents, but a tiny part of a great whole which I could serve, in however modest measure, to the best of my ability" (2010, 156). In the discussion that follows, I examine the interplay of the fictional worlds Zur Mühlen created and the social and political realities that she lived. What specific lessons related to war and nationalism are imparted via the fictional characters and scenarios Zur Mühlen creates? How are these lessons informed by the evolving socialist, feminist and pacifist discourses of her time, and how does her work highlight points of both convergence and divergence amongst these movements? What role does gender play in her characters' abil-

---

4 Jennifer Redmann also discusses the genre of the *Bildungsroman* and its employment by female authors to provide wartime role models for girls in her essay in this collection.

ities and opportunities to engage in political agitation? Finally, how might she believe critiquing World War I in her postwar writing will have an impact on (the prevention of) future conflicts? Zur Mühlen was clearly ambitious in her authorial goals and believed deeply in the causes she espoused.

Situating Zur Mühlen within the "isms" that influenced her work

As Zur Mühlen witnessed social and political inequalities around her while growing up and in relation to World War I, socialism eventually became a strong force in her life. The underpinnings of socialist beliefs can be traced back to egalitarian societies over many centuries, and socialism is often used as an umbrella term to rein in various branches of thought, including Marxism, social democracy and communism. Rather than disentangle these diverging theoretical frameworks here, I examine Zur Mühlen's portrayal of socialism as a broad social and political movement. She felt restricted by party platforms and found greater freedom to express her own understanding of socialism outside of formal political parties. She also believed that divisions between socialist parties contributed to the eventual rise of National Socialism, so she conveyed socialist ideology in broad terms, particularly from the late 1920s onward, in order to appeal to as many people as possible. While her perspectives shifted over time, her conception of socialism as the attempt to form an egalitarian society characterized by a spirit of cooperation and solidarity across boundaries of social class, gender and nation remained firm. She also emphasized the importance of equality of opportunities in the public realm regardless of an individual's status in a particular society. Finally, she viewed socialism as a future-oriented system that places a high value on youth while incorporating people of all ages. Ultimately, Zur Mühlen wished to see a society in which gender and social class did not marginalize its members.

Many of Zur Mühlen's contemporary female socialists, like Rosa Luxemburg (1871–1919), regarded the women's movement as unnecessary and even redundant, since socialism is premised on the equality of all people. Other fellow socialists and political activists, including Lily Braun (1865–1916) and Clara Zetkin (1857–1933), who did not think that women's specific concerns would simply be resolved in realizing a socialist society, rallied around the "woman question." The notion of feminism was particularly contentious within much of the socialist movement because it was commonly equated with the bourgeois women's movement. Attempts to bridge these two movements were viewed negatively by many socialists who felt that it diverted attention from the proletarian struggle. In turn, many members of the more moderate women's movement regarded the socialist movement as too radical.[5] Drawing on the words of August Bebel to describe this division, historian Ute Frevert writes that despite "common ground between women in the bourgeois and Social Democratic movements [...] they perceived each other as 'enemy sisters'" (1997, 146). In spite of this animosity, some socialists and members of bourgeois women's movements shared a belief in pacifism and a desire for international peace, although they brought different theoretical approaches to the topic.

While theories and discussions of pacifism influenced members of both the international socialist and feminist movements at the turn of the century, with the onset of World War I many quickly shifted their views. In her discussion of international feminist pacifists, social scientist Lela Costin observes, "The outbreak of war triggered a surge of patriotism and penalties for pacifist attitudes" (1982, 304). Historian Amira Gelblum similarly notes that in the nations involved, "most feminists – like the socialists – chose nationalism over internationalism and rushed to support their belligerent governments" (1998, 308). Branded as unpatriotic and subsequently persecuted, pacifists from both the feminist and socialist movements were generally silenced, censored and even punished for the duration of the war. Yet in the 1920s these pacifist voices found more receptive postwar audiences as many people, including Zur Mühlen, wished to prevent future conflicts after experiencing the devastation of World War I. In the introduction to their international and interdisciplinary collection *The Women's Movement in Wartime* (2007), Alison Fell and Ingrid Sharp state, "once the conflict was over, women were criticized for the same jingoistic response that had hitherto been praised, while the pacifist voices that had been largely silenced and dismissed came to the fore" (14). Germany was no exception, and the postwar literary market experienced a new openness to antiwar literature.

---

5 See historian Richard J. Evans's chapter "The Impossible Alliance" in *Comrades and Sisters* (1987) for a detailed discussion of the tensions between the socialist and feminist movements in Europe during the late 1800s and early 1900s, which he asserts hindered progress in both movements. Jean Quataert's chapter on "Class versus Sex Identity: Clara Zetkin and Lily Braun" in *Reluctant Feminists in German Social Democracy, 1885–1917* (1979) also illustrates the historical conflicts between the two movements while elaborating on the rivalry between these two key figures in the socialist women's movement. Fellow historian Barbara Beuys traces the development of various women's movements in Germany in *Die neuen Frauen: Revolution im Kaiserreich 1900–1914* (The new women: Revolution in the *Kaiserreich*, 2014), demonstrating a trajectory of progress while also highlighting the connections and rifts between individuals and organizations; Beuys addresses the tensions between socialists and members of bourgeois women's organizations throughout her text.

Zur Mühlen capitalized on this opportunity to promote her pacifist ideals. While she was not entirely antiviolence, as she often endorsed violence in support of revolutionary objectives, she was distinctly against wars perpetuated for nationalistic goals. In her autobiography *Ende und Anfang* (*The End and the Beginning*, 1929), Zur Mühlen writes, "When the war broke out, I was still in Davos. It was not difficult for me to be unpatriotic" (2010, 151), adding that she had friends and family from many nations and would not choose sides. Some of her first translations in 1917 and 1918 were of antiwar books,[6] but she did not face the strict censorship as authors before her because she began her literary career at the end of the war.

Although World War I is seldom the exclusive focus of Zur Mühlen's texts, she illustrated its devastating, lasting impact and included antiwar sentiments in many of her fictional works published during the Weimar Republic. Her literary career took off upon her move to Frankfurt am Main in 1919, after she spent the war years in Davos, Switzerland, recovering from illness. Not only was she a prolific translator, but she also authored her own works across multiple genres, including fairytales, crime fiction, short stories, feuilletons, novellas, novels and an autobiography, all of which incorporated socialist themes and proved popular in her time.[7] Much of her work appeared in newspapers and literary journals before being published in book form, which further increased her readership. Literary scholar Andrea Hammel confirms, "Hermynia Zur Mühlen's work was certainly published, widely read and positively reviewed during the 1920s and early 1930s" (2008, 45). Zur Mühlen's literary output is nothing short of immense, yet critical literature on her oeuvre is largely lacking. Because she used popular genres to appeal to broad audiences, Zur Mühlen's works for the most part have been relegated to the category of *Trivialliteratur*, except for her exile writings, which

---

6 Zur Mühlen states that her "first substantial piece of work was a translation of the Russian antiwar novel, *The Yoke of War*, by Leonid Andreyev" (2010, 158), and other socially critical texts by British author Douglas Goldring, American writer Floyd Dell, and French politician Henri Guilbeaux, among others, followed. She also translated many of American socialist "muckraker" Upton Sinclair's novels into German during the 1920s and is largely responsible for sparking interest in his works amongst German-speaking audiences.

7 From her first publication in 1917/18 until her death in 1951, Zur Mühlen translated over 100 books, and she published more than 35 books, six collections of fairytales, and hundreds of short stories and articles, as well as numerous radio plays (Wallace 2009, 1). At times she published under pseudonyms, including Lawrence H. Desberry, Traugott Lehmann and Fransiska Maria Hartenberg, and her texts have been translated into thirteen languages. The most complete bibliographies available of Zur Mühlen's literary output can be found in the appendices of Ailsa Wallace's *Hermynia Zur Mühlen: The Guises of Socialist Fiction* (2009) and Manfred Altner's *Hermynia zur Mühlen: Eine Biographie* (1997).

are deemed to be more serious than her earlier texts and consequently have been granted more academic attention.[8] Thus, as Hammel notes, Zur Mühlen's biography and career are often separated into two phases (2008, 42).

A member of the German Communist Party (*Kommunistische Partei Deutschlands*, KPD) from 1919 to about 1929, Zur Mühlen refers to this period as her propagandistic phase (1937, 185). The works she produced during this period are generally dismissed by critics as "potboilers" or simply as propaganda unworthy of scholarly analysis. The second phase of her career, then, is defined by her break with the KPD and her experience of exile, as the rising threat of National Socialism led her to flee to Austria in 1933, and later to Slovakia and England. Yet this dichotomous approach to the author's life and work omits her many contributions to women's literature on nationalism and war throughout her career. In the only existing monograph on the author, *Hermynia Zur Mühlen: The Guises of Socialist Fiction* (2009), literary scholar Ailsa Wallace examines a broad range of Zur Mühlen's writings and positions her as an expert navigator of literary markets, adapting her socialist message to a variety of popular literary forms. Wallace interprets the author's choice of genres as reflective of her didactic political goal of spreading socialist ideals to broad audiences. Despite changing attitudes towards notions of *Trivialliteratur* or *Gebrauchsliteratur* (trivial or functional writing), Zur Mühlen's early works continue to remain under-investigated, yet here they form the basis for my study of her depiction of World War I. Similar to Wallace, I maintain Zur Mühlen used popular literary genres to reach wide audiences with an antiwar message she deemed urgent. Her political intentions make these texts far from trivial.

In fact, German authorities in the Weimar Republic took Zur Mühlen's texts very seriously, and she quickly accumulated a police file for "subversive activities" while living in Frankfurt. Not only did she draw attention for her affiliation with the KPD, but also for living "in wilder Ehe" (out of wedlock) with her partner Stefan Klein. Charges of high treason were levied against her for publishing the story "Schupomann Karl Müller" (Policeman Karl Müller, 1924), in which the title character, a World War I veteran, has reservations about his work for the police force. Zur Mühlen traces the character's moral transformation in the text. The policeman, Karl, believes that his sole purpose is to maintain order, though

---

8 See, for example, the works of Andrea Hammel (2008) and Eva-Maria Siegel (1993), and two collections edited by Deborah Vietor-Engländer, Eckart Früh and Ursula Seeber (2002). In "Hermynia Zur Mühlen's Fight Against the 'Enemy Within'" (1998), Deborah Vietor-Engländer dismisses many of Zur Mühlen's earlier works as "potboilers" (76) and labels her 1934/47 novel *Eine Flasche Parfüm* (A bottle of perfume) "a mere triviality" (78). In the article, Vietor-Engländer focuses on three of Zur Mühlen's exile novels that she states "can be considered serious" (76).

his mother implores him to reconsider his role: "For whom are you preserving order? [...] [O]nly for the lazy, the exploiters. You protect them so that they can rob the poor without interruption" (1924b, 15).[9] Eventually Karl's conscience leads him to question his actions while on the job against oppressed groups, including disabled war veterans. For example, while arresting a blind veteran for begging on a cold winter day, Karl recognizes that he could have been in the same position as this man had he fared differently in the war. Karl asks a young boy to pass along money to the beggar before he arrests him, and then he rationalizes to himself that the man will have food and shelter in prison, yet he still feels guilty. Later in the story, Karl marches with the socialist demonstrators that he should be arresting, even giving them his gun. Authorities viewed this story as dangerous "because its author so effectively used literary weapons to motivate readers to direct political action" (King 1988, 131). The high treason charges against Zur Mühlen for "Schupomann Karl Müller" were eventually dropped, yet this incident vouches for the political power of Zur Mühlen's written word even before her "more serious" exile writings, such as the novel *Unsere Töchter, die Nazinen* (Our daughters, the Nazis, 1934), appeared. The novel was banned shortly after its publication, and all copies were ordered to be destroyed due to its explicit antiwar, anti-Nazi stance.

Zur Mühlen's commitment to the broader goals of socialism remained even though she aligned herself with the KPD in the immediate aftermath of World War I, dismayed that the German Social Democratic Party (*Sozialdemokratische Partei Deutschlands*, SPD) had supported Germany's war efforts in 1914. She depicts this split within the left wing in Germany in various fictional texts, drawing attention to its political impact in relation to war, violence and peace. In her novel *Der Tempel* (The temple, 1922), numerous characters are engaged in the socialist movement in Berlin, and their meetings illustrate the historical divide between the reformists willing to support the war and those with more radical, revolutionary goals, leading some to leave the group. Unlike the apathetic title figure of the novella "Lina: Erzählung aus dem Leben eines Dienstmädchens," another working-class character, Kati, finds her resolve in the socialist movement, yet she opts for the KPD over the SPD because her husband fell in the war, and she feels betrayed by the majority SPD. In time, Zur Mühlen herself grew disillusioned by the KPD, and although she eventually left the party, she remained firm in her socialist beliefs, especially her belief that international socialism offered the greatest chance of achieving peace. In *Unsere Töchter, die Na-*

---

9 "Für wen erhältst du die Ordnung aufrecht? [...] [N]ur für die Faulenzer, die Ausbeuter. Du schützest sie, damit sie ungestört die Armen ausrauben können."

zinen, she continues to thematize this political split and implies that the lasting division between socialists and communists contributed to the rise of the right-wing National Socialists. For example, lamenting that the workers have split into separate parties amidst the postwar political turmoil, working-class Kati states, "Especially now they must all stick together and build a new socialist country" (1934, 10). Disappointed by the socialist parties, Kati's daughter, Toni, eventually joins the Nazi party, as she has lost her job and finds their unified stance and their platform to be promising for workers. Through the figures in this novel, Zur Mühlen demonstrates that regardless of actual party affiliation, all social-ist-minded individuals must work together to defeat the Nazis and to further the goals of international socialism and maintain peace. She evokes World War I to warn of possible consequences of such a political division, blending his-torical facts with fictional characters to impart her ideas.

Zur Mühlen's socialist stances on World War I

The depictions and discussions of World War I in Zur Mühlen's literary texts re-flect socialist and communist discourses, in particular the words of fellow fe-male socialists Rosa Luxemburg and Clara Zetkin. Zur Mühlen agreed with both their emphasis on the class struggle (*Klassenkampf*) as it related to the war, echoing in her works Luxemburg's pronouncement that, "'Defending one's fatherland' cannot mean playing the role of cannon fodder under the com-mand of an imperialistic bourgeoisie" (1919, 91). Zur Mühlen also took to heart Zetkin's call in the early months of the war that women, although limited in their political rights, should utilize their social power to support socialist broth-erhood over war: "Let us use our words and actions in order to influence the nar-row circle of our family and friends as well as the broad public" (2015, 115). As historian Susan Grayzel notes in *Women and the First World War* (2002), some radical socialist and Marxist women across Europe used antiwar sentiments to push for revolution rather than just reform, believing that voting rights were not enough to achieve necessary change; instead they wanted to replace the sys-tem with a new social(ist) order (92). Luxemburg and Zetkin were both impris-oned for their outspoken opposition to the war, and Luxemburg was eventually murdered in 1919 for her political work, a death that Zur Mühlen alludes to in some of her fictional texts, including *Der Tempel* (1922). While Luxemburg and Zetkin often spread their ideas via speeches, pamphlets and political journals, Zur Mühlen used literature to promote the need for the revolutionary changes sought by the socialist movement, with the benefit of hindsight since the war had ended. Here I want to explicate how Zur Mühlen, in her staunch antiwar stance, draws on socialist ideas regarding the role of the proletariat in the war, critiques the war as a source of capitalist exploitation rather than patriotic honor, and emphasizes that women should instill socialist values in their children.

Even before World War I began, many socialists maintained the position that the proletariat could hinder a war by refusing to work, though Zur Mühlen illustrates in her fictional texts that this did not come to fruition. Anatol, a radical figure in her 1922 novel *Der Tempel*, encourages workers at a train station to strike, telling them that they can impede the war effort by preventing the trains from carrying soldiers and supplies to the front. Zur Mühlen has him passionately proclaim, "Do you know what your work means? It means murder, the murder of your brothers. Without your work these trains won't depart" (1922, 119). His provocation is unsuccessful, and the workers continue laboring as he is arrested and subsequently sentenced to six years in prison (119 – 120). This belief that the working class would protest the war is also challenged by the housemaid Lina, whose daily chores leave her too tired to even think about the war. It is not until her brother is drafted that she truly comprehends its significance and horror: "Now Lina also cursed the enemies, the war. Trembled at every ring of the doorbell, jolted out of bad dreams with a scream, saw the boy wounded, captured, dead. In her anguish she neglected the household," for which she is subsequently reprimanded (1926, 54).[10] Later, while she mourns her brother's death, her employer spouts nationalist drivel that offers her no comfort: "Herr Oberlehrer [Kuttner] spoke moralistically of heroic death, which was unfortunately denied to him because of his lame leg. Lina, who was peeling potatoes, felt the uncontrollable desire to jab the knife into his body" (55).[11] Yet Lina suppresses this "desire" and continues working; even after losing her brother, she is too overwhelmed by financial need to take a stand against the war. These literary examples highlight Zur Mühlen's conviction that socialists needed to do more to politically engage workers in pacifist activity, as their spontaneous resistance, that socialists hoped for, was not actually forthcoming during World War I.

Despite Lina's disengagement with direct political action, Zur Mühlen's character still recognizes the exploitative nature of the war. While watching troops on their way to the train station one day, Lina suddenly recalls a painting in which

---

10 "Da verfluchte auch Lina die Feinde, den Krieg. Zitterte bei jedem Läuten an der Tür, fuhr mit einem Schrei aus bösen Träumen auf, sah den Buben verwundet, gefangen, tot. In ihrer Qual vernachlässigte sie den Haushalt."

11 "Herr Oberlehrer sprach salbungsvoll vom Heldentod, der ihm leider, seines lahmen Beines wegen, versagt sei. Lina, die eben Kartoffeln schälte, fühlte den wahnsinnigen Wunsch, ihm das Messer in den Leib zu stoßen."

an ox similarly draped in flowers is led to the slaughter (1926, 54). Although many socialists historically supported World War I, others denounced the war as a form of capitalist exploitation, in which the members of the proletariat became cannon fodder in an imperialistic war to benefit the powerful. Luxemburg and Zetkin put forth this argument in various speeches and publications,[12] and Zur Mühlen espoused the same in her postwar literature. Strong denunciations come from her figures who experience the war firsthand. As in the story "Schupomann Karl Müller," "Der Deutschvölkische" (The German nationalist, 1924) also features a World War I veteran, Wilhelm Meier. In contrast to Karl Müller, whose mother was a pacifist and who felt a greater connection with enemy soldiers than with his jingoist compatriots during World War I, Wilhelm Meier was raised in a patriotic household and maintains his nationalistic loyalties after the war, proudly wearing a swastika. Yet after he experiences harsh treatment from fellow nationalists, who enlist him to infiltrate and spy on the KPD, he finds true friends in the KPD and comes to see communism as a way to create stronger bonds than nationalism. Wilhelm eventually reevaluates the war as class exploitation, not a source of national honor, feeling that capitalist cowards sent members of the lower classes, like himself, to fight for their bourgeois interests and way of life. He now believes: "Patriots are those who want to see their country free and just" (1924a, 36).[13] Zur Mühlen creates both protagonists – Wilhelm and Karl – as working-class men who come to develop a sense of solidarity with other members of their class and to recognize their exploitation through their postwar experiences and interactions. World War I, then, serves as a catalyst for their socialist transformations in these texts. Wilhelm even dies at the hands of German nationalists when he tries to warn KPD members that the nationalists plan to attack their meeting; ironically, he survived a war against "enemy" soldiers only to be killed in a political struggle at home. Through the construction of such stories, Zur Mühlen stresses the inequalities and harm perpetuated not just by war but also by nationalistic ideologies that fuel divisions and conflict.

A final socialist trope regarding the war that Zur Mühlen consistently introduces is the necessity of raising children to be socialists who reject nationalistic

---

12 See, for example, Rosa Luxemburg's "Die Sozialistische Internationale" (The Socialist International, 1915) in *Frauen gegen den Krieg* (Women against war, 1980) and *The Crisis in the German Social Democracy: The "Junius" Pamplet*, which she wrote while in prison in 1915 but was not published until 1916. Clara Zetkin also addresses the topic of class exploitation in World War I in "To the Socialist Women of All Countries" (1914) and "Women of the Working People" (1915), both anthologized in *Clara Zetkin: Selected Writings* (2015).
13 "Patrioten sind jene, die ihr Land frei und gerecht sehen wollen."

wars. In her view, it is the responsibility of mothers. As the leader of the socialist women's movement, Zetkin also emphasized women's maternal role even before the war, when she asserted in 1912, "If we mothers impart in our children from earliest youth a deep disgust for war, if we plant the seeds of an awareness of socialist brotherliness in their souls, so will come a time in which even in the gravest danger, no power in the world will be capable of ripping this ideal from their hearts" (1980, 141). This point is also consistently underscored in the resolutions that emerged from conferences of international organizations of socialist women in 1910, 1923 and 1928, excerpted in Gisela Brinker-Gabler's collection *Frauen gegen den Krieg* (Women against war, 1980, 137–138, 260–261, 267–276).

In Zur Mühlen's novel *Der Tempel* (1922), the pastor laments even before the outbreak of World War I that youth are concerned with militarism rather than peace, and the character of young Lene Selder tells him about the work she is doing in the socialist movement, which gives her hope for a better future (93). Later at the bourgeois Selder family's Christmas celebration, several of the men in the family discuss their desire for war to awaken their nation while one of the children stands up to sing a song calling for harmony. Here Zur Mühlen constructs a stark contrast between these belligerent and peaceful voices from different generations. In the story "Kleine Leute" (Little people, 1925), Martha, the wife of a shopkeeper, and her mother are moved to action when they attend a public lecture in which a Russian, communist woman claims that it is women's duty to nurture children so that the next generation creates a better world. Motherhood also sparks aristocratic Erika's feelings of pacifism in the novel *Reise durch ein Leben* (*A Life's Journey*, 1933), in which she eventually comes to socialism and the hope that women will educate children to be antiwar. Finally, in the novel *Unsere Töchter, die Nazinen* (1934), working-class Kati refers to children as "the hope of the future" (103), and aristocratic Agnes worries about the youth who are brought up under National Socialism, pondering, "What should, what can become of these children?" (104). These writings spanning more than a decade illustrate Zur Mühlen's unwavering belief that women, regardless of social class, can raise the next generation in a way that will prevent future wars, namely by incorporating socialist ideology. And though historically socialists and feminists often clashed, Zur Mühlen shows that socialist and feminist pacifists actually shared the belief that motherhood held a key to a peaceful future.

Zur Mühlen's feminist consciousness and war

While Zur Mühlen emphasized her socialist politics in her literature, she did not claim a feminist perspective, even though she consistently illuminated gender inequalities in her texts. In fact, she denied any feminist affiliation throughout her career. In a short piece from 1934 entitled, "Radiosendungen für Frauen" (Radio programs for women),[14] she leads with, "Although I am by no means a feminist [...]" (103),[15] before articulating a critique of the superficial content of male-narrated radio programs directed specifically at women. Her aversion to the label of "feminist" may have resulted from the predominant conceptions of feminism as a bourgeois women's movement in the early 1900s and through her prior membership in the KPD, which prioritized the class struggle over gender. Still, I argue that she conveys a feminist consciousness through her texts, as issues of gender play a critical role in many of her works, and she addresses aspects of a gendered experience of war and desire for peace. In doing so, she combines elements of feminist pacifism with the socialist perspectives previously discussed, thus constructing a form of what I call socialist-feminist pacifism for her readers.

Following World War I, Zur Mühlen recognized the need to provide powerful literary models for readers and for young women in particular. In her 1919 essay "Junge-Mädchen-Literatur" (Young girls' literature), she condemns the contemporary literature for girls and young women, which in her view sets limited horizons for females by encouraging them to follow traditional, bourgeois gender roles, with marriage as their ultimate goal.[16] She specifically critiques texts that promote German nationalist ideologies and marriage to a military officer, a "professional murderer" in Zur Mühlen's eyes, as a reward for a German girl's virtuous nature (473). She explains:

> The most virtuous heroine, blond, blue-eyed and meek, receives a lieutenant as her reward for her virtue; the less-virtuous brunette, brown-eyed and lively, must make do with a civil servant. Hero mothers "happily" sacrifice their sons, hero brides their husband, for Kaiser

14 Reprinted in *Nebenglück: Ausgewählte Erzählungen und Feuilletons aus dem Exil von Hermynia Zur Mühlen* (Happiness on the side: Selected stories and feuilletons from Hermynia Zur Mühlen's exile, 2002), edited by Deborah Vietor-Engländer, Eckart Früh and Ursula Seeber (103–104).
15 "Denn trotzdem ich keineswegs eine Feministin bin [...]."
16 See Maureen Gallagher's discussion of this "Mädchenliteratur" in her essay in this volume. Zur Mühlen critiques the exact form of "Backfischbuch" that Gallagher analyzes in her essay.

and fatherland. The glory of the German character is emphasized and re-emphasized; the non-German is at best a laughable figure [...]. (473)[17]

Noting that young readers of these books are particularly impressionable, she cautions, "On this amoral filth they unconsciously form their views, their principles" (474).[18] Employing a plant metaphor, Zur Mühlen calls for these "weeds" to be pulled out and replaced with a literature that will nourish young women to grow into strong individuals. She insists that this is an important task because female readers are future mothers who can raise their sons and daughters to be "independent, strong people, builders of a free, brotherly world,"[19] and to promote cooperation with other nations over war (474). While this stance reflects aspects of Zur Mühlen's socialist pacifism, her discussion of and emphasis on motherhood in this essay and in many of her fictional texts also engage important elements of feminist pacifism. In fact, her writings ultimately convey many ideas that aligned with feminist pacifist thought of the early 1900s. Regarding World War I, Grayzel writes:

> Feminist pacifist arguments against war appeared even before its outbreak and most centred on three aspects of feminism: the international solidarity that existed among women and feminism's commitment to internationalism, its appeal to women as mothers and caregivers who were therefore inherently opposed to war, and the existence of women's oppression and their lack of basic political and social rights. (2002, 80)

All these points are supported in Zur Mühlen's works, though in this section I explicate how she brings in aspects of her socialist ideology to build on feminist pacifist arguments.

While Zur Mühlen's view of international solidarity incorporated both genders, she illustrated the idea that women in particular could connect across borders based on common experiences as women despite the war at hand. Many female characters in her texts come together and support each other as women regardless of nationality or class status. In *Unsere Töchter, die Nazinen*, Gräfin Agnes resents other members of the nobility for protecting their power and priv-

---

17 "Die tugendhafteste Heldin, blond, blauäugig und sanft, bekommt zur Belohnung ihrer Tugend einen Leutnant, die weniger Tugendhafte, brünett, braunäugig und lebhaft, muß mit einem Assessor vorlieb nehmen. Heldenmütter opfern 'freudig' ihre Söhne, Heldenbräute den Bräutigam für Kaiser und Vaterland. Der Herrlichkeit des deutschen Wesens wird betont und wiederbetont, der Nichtdeutsche ist im besten Fall eine lächerliche Figur [...]."
18 "An diesem amoralischen Dreck bilden sie sich ganz unbewußt ihre Anschauungen, ihre Prinzipien."
19 "[...] freie, starke Menschen, Erbauer einer freien, brüderlichen Welt."

ilege and does all she can to support the lower-class women who work on her estate during World War I as they face shortages of food and other goods. When one of these women, Kati, who cleans houses to support her family, watches her husband board a train to the front, she thinks of all the women in other towns and countries saying good-bye to the men in their lives. Zur Mühlen stresses empathy across national borders and solidarity even with "enemy" women. International feelings trump national feelings for many female characters in *Der Tempel*, as well, with women from Germany, Italy and England cooperating in the socialist antiwar movement. The supporting character Frau von Reuter insists on the importance of internationalism and of helping others across borders because she considers everyone a human being. As an English-woman living in Berlin during World War I, Frau von Reuter expresses a sense of guilt and responsibility for the suffering she witnesses around her, tearfully telling Lene, "I'm ashamed to look the people in the eye" (1922, 137). Feeling that her country's participation in the war has contributed to this misery, she slowly sells everything she owns to help feed the hungry children she sees on the streets. When Lene asks why she is not wearing her diamond ring, Frau von Reuter replies, "An old woman does not need rings [...] but small children need milk" (137). Even though many actual women of the belligerent nations during World War I were guided by nationalism, Zur Mühlen's fictional charac-ters resonated with historical expressions of internationalism and unity. As Gray-zel observes, "Across national boundaries, groups of women mobilised other women for peace by using similar appeals. They called upon women as mothers, as the victims of war, as persons denied fundamental political rights like voting, and as exploited workers to rally them to oppose the war" (2002, 83). Like these pacifists, Zur Mühlen draws on common experiences of women and depicts fe-male characters in these various roles to build – via literature – support for last-ing peace.

For some German women across social classes coping with the impact of World War I during and after the war – in both the historical reality and in Zur Mühlen's fiction – , feelings of solidarity and support for pacifism were tied to shared experiences in nurturing roles, not limited to motherhood. De-scribing Germany at the turn of the century, historian Ann Taylor Allen explains, "In women's political discourse, 'motherhood' became a metaphorical term for a distinctively female claim to rights based on women's service to society" (1991, 11). This meant that women's contributions to society through nurturing roles were acknowledged even if they were not mothers or if their actions were not di-rected at their own children. Throughout Zur Mühlen's texts we see female char-acters resisting nationalist views and refusing to support the war because of their loved ones, whether husbands, fathers, brothers or sons. When Herr Kuttner in "Lina" preaches to his housemaid, "It is an honor to give sons, brothers and husbands to the fatherland. Every German woman should be proud of that," Lina wonders, "And what has the fatherland done for us that we should give him our most beloved?" (1926, 54). Lina, who supports her younger brother Franzel as if he were her own child, has no desire to sacrifice him for her country, and characters from other texts similarly reject the notion that such sacrifice is honorable. Aristocratic Steffi in Zur Mühlen's 1932 novel *Das Riesenrad* (*The Wheel of Life*) is traumatized by her 21-year-old son's death in World War I. A decade later she continues to mourn this loss and preaches antiwar sentiments to her young niece Marie as she grows up. And in Zur Mühlen's 1933 novel *Reise durch ein Leben*, Erika, the daughter of an aristocratic family but now the housewife of a bourgeois lawyer, reads Bertha von Suttner's prominent pacifist novel *Die Waffen nieder!* (*Lay Down Your Arms*),[20] which influences her desire to raise her son Wilhelm without a nationalistic or militaristic ideology. Her husband and his family, however, encourage Wilhelm to be a soldier one day, to honorably serve his country and improve his social status. When they present seven-year-old Wilhelm with a military uniform as a gift, an enraged Erika protests, "I don't want my son to become a murderer!" (1933, 253). Eventually Erika leaves when her husband announces that he will raise his son as he sees fit and her son announces that he hates her. Even though Wilhelm is only ten and too young to serve in the war, she imagines him in uniform shooting other children and feels helpless to protect him. Estranged from her own son, Erika seeks other means besides motherhood to positively influence the world around her. She branches out into the socialist movement in search of peace – for herself and for her society. Rather than perpetuate nationalist rhetoric related to war, Zur Mühlen has female characters in these texts assert, whether as sisters, aunts or mothers, that sacrificing the nation's youth to military aims is not an honorable goal.

Motherhood was seen as a defining feature of women at the turn of the century and was framed according to various positions on the war.[21] Germanist Ingrid Sharp clarifies that both pacifists and antipacifists in Germany focused on motherhood and employed maternalist discourses in order to reinforce their positions (2014, 199). Allen similarly claims, "by 1914, the discourse on motherhood was so prevalent and powerful in the feminist movement that it encompassed

---

20 For a deeper analysis of Suttner's novel and its impact on German discourses of pacifism throughout the twentieth century, see Shelley Rose's essay in this collection.
21 See also Cindy Walter-Gensler's essay in this volume for perspectives on motherhood in women's WWI literature. She addresses both the support of nationalist discourses and challenges to it in this literature.

the widest possible spectrum of positions, from strident nationalism to pacifism" (1991, 233). As a result, the war deeply divided both the socialist movement and the women's movement in Germany. Although the majority of German feminists, including Gertrud Bäumer (1873–1954), supported the war, for others such as Anita Augspurg (1857–1943), Lida Gustava Heymann (1868–1943) and Helene Stöcker (1869–1943), "maternal ideology [...] provided the most powerful rationale for the opposition to the war" (Allen 1991, 232). While nationalist discourses encouraged women to sacrifice their sons to the nation, feminist pacifists challenged such approaches, purporting rather that mothers are inherently peaceful. As literary scholar Sharon Ouditt explains, "The argument that women know the cost of human life as they are responsible for bearing it forms the root of many of the writings on woman-centred pacifism" (1994, 141). In her analysis of pacifist journals edited by women, comparative and cultural studies scholar Bruna Bianchi argues that this link between maternal feelings and pacifism was used to develop a new pacifism during the war which carried into the postwar years and crossed national borders. She terms this "absolute pacifism," explaining: "Antithetical to militarism, it was based on the concept of strong womanhood and motherhood," and was therefore tied to the "'female' disposition of nurturing" (2014, 177). In the forms of feminist pacifism described by these scholars, the focus was placed on motherhood and childhood as reasons to eradicate war and promote internationalism, and essentialist discourses deemed women's pacifism to be "natural."[22]

Although many of Zur Mühlen's characters express their pacifism as mothers, this does not mean that they are inherently pacifists. Rather, they are "educated" during the course of the text, in line with the genre of the *Bildungsroman*. While antiwar sentiments in characters from diverse class backgrounds, such as Martha, Steffi and Erika, are prompted by maternal feelings and a desire to protect their own children, as well as the youth of the world, these women come to their pacifist positions through the encouragement of others. For instance, Martha in "Kleine Leute" attends a public lecture that educates and inspires her, and Erika of *Reise durch ein Leben* is strongly influenced by Suttner's novel and her discussions with a female relative. Furthermore, Zur Mühlen does not limit women's pacifism to mothers or even to women in her texts. Describing the peace literature of World War I, Ouditt writes, "These [mythical] properties [of motherhood] are seen, spontaneously and universally, to align women with pacifism

---

22 See Shelley Rose's essay in this volume for a further discussion of how notions of gender had a lasting impact on pacifist discourses and conceptions of pacifism in Germany in the twentieth century.

on the grounds that mothers have a special concern for the creation and preservation of human life. A binary opposition thus emerges: men are life-takers, women life-makers" (1994, 131). Yet Zur Mühlen challenges this "binary opposition" often put forth by feminist pacifists, presenting an alternative perspective on gender and (non)violence which allows for greater ambiguity and diversity.

Zur Mühlen's short story "Wolfi" (1936) clearly defies this "binary opposition." Seven-year-old Wolfi is playing with his ten-year-old sister and her nine-year-old female friend. The two girls want to play "beheading," and they assign Wolfi the role of executioner, but he refuses, even though his victim is just a doll. He states, "A person should never hurt another person. Otherwise he feels this pain somewhere inside himself. But you [his playmates] are evil" (376),[23] noting that the girls like to cause others harm, such as the time his sister hit a dog. When Wolfi refuses to play along, the girls continue the game, laughing while one of them steps into the executioner role. Meanwhile, Wolfi opts for a constructive role and rebuilds the "city" that was destroyed when they played "earthquake." When they are older, Wolfi is forced to go to war, lamenting that he has always believed that people are good, yet now he is supposed to kill people. One girl recalls the games of their youth, remembering that Wolfi preferred to play doctor and cure dolls; he was always a kind soul who wanted to help and heal others rather than cause pain (376–377). The ending informs readers of his fate: "Wolfi fell in the second year of the war. But he certainly died before that, during the first attack on the enemy, who were humans to him, whom he was [, by his conviction, JS] not allowed to cause harm" (377).[24] The young girls in this story find pleasure in causing others pain and enact violence in play while Wolfi refuses to enact violence and demonstrates compassion. Here Zur Mühlen interrupts essentialist rhetoric regarding gender and (non)violence: her male characters are not naturally prone to war or violence, as Wolfi would rather die than hurt others, and her female characters are not inherently peaceful.

Other male characters in Zur Mühlen's earlier texts also challenge essentialist notions of gender. Similar to Wolfi, the title character of "Schupomann Karl Müller" does not enjoy going to war: "The war aroused no patriotic enthusiasm in Karl Müller whatsoever. He balked at the thought of killing people who had done him no harm, people he did not even know" (1924b, 8). Instead, Karl sees the war merely as senseless destruction of order and life, and when he en-

---

23 "Man darf niemand wehtun. Sonst spürt man es selbst, irgendwo ganz drin. Aber ihr seid böse."

24 "Wolfi fiel im zweiten Kriegsjahr. Aber gestorben ist er bestimmt schon früher, beim ersten Angriff auf die Feinde, die für ihn Menschen waren, denen man nicht wehtun durfte."

counters dead enemy soldiers up close, he feels the same sense of solidarity with them that he used to feel with his fellow factory workers (8). In Zur Mühlen's construction, Karl does not want to enact violence on other human beings or be a "life-taker," to use Ouditt's phrase. In *Der Tempel*, the bourgeois character Gustav is a young scientist studying in Berlin while his older brother, Heinrich, earns an Iron Cross for his military service. Gustav notes the contradiction in that murder was always considered wrong but now was rewarded with an Iron Cross, and he expresses no desire to participate in warfare (1922, 120–121). When Gustav witnesses Karl Liebknecht's antiwar demonstration and arrest on Potsdamer Platz in 1916, a factual event portrayed in this fictional text, he states that Liebknecht was arrested for speaking the truth and begins to see the war itself as the actual crime. Gustav subsequently refuses to turn over a formula he develops for poison gas to the German government. Zur Mühlen demonstrates that science is not an apolitical endeavor, as Gustav's discovery could be employed as a weapon of war. When two men appear at Gustav's door requesting his formula, he tells them, "Who gives you the right to my brain and the work it produces? I engaged with the subject because it interested me, but not in order to turn countless innocent people into murderers" (133)[25] and asserts, "I don't care about your damned government!" (134).[26] Despite threats and later imprisonment, he will not allow his nation to use his discovery to harm other people. Although these officials tell Gustav it is his patriotic duty to help his country win the war, he maintains, "I am not a patriot" (133), and he will not be responsible for the violent suffering of "enemy" soldiers he no longer sees as the enemy. While Zur Mühlen also depicts many male characters who espouse violent, nationalist rhetoric, these male figures allow her to subvert the notion that men are naturally prone to war and violence and to demonstrate that men can also support pacifist ideals.

Not only does Zur Mühlen challenge notions of masculinity as intrinsically violent, but she also questions women's inherent nonviolence by portraying female characters ready to engage in violent contexts. These women wage their own political "wars" for the end goal of peace. For instance, in *Der Tempel*, Lene's male comrades in the socialist movement do not allow her to take part in protests deemed too dangerous for her as a woman and mother. At the end of the novel, though, she joins in the November Revolution on the streets of Berlin, regardless of potential violence, as she believes a socialist revolution will ul-

---

25 "Wer gibt euch ein Recht auf mein Gehirn und dessen Erzeugnisse? Ich habe mich mit der Sache befaßt, weil sie mich interessierte, aber nicht, um an unzähligen Unschuldigen zum Mörder zu werden."
26 "Ich pfeife auf eure verdammte Regierung!"

timately bring peace to Germany. Mothers Kati and Agnes and daughters Toni and Claudia in *Unsere Töchter, die Nazinen* all place themselves in danger at different points in the novel in order to defend their leftist beliefs and to challenge the Nazis. They suffered through World War I on the homefront and fear similar conflicts if the Nazis gain power. Confronted by young male Nazis while defacing swastika graffiti, Kati speaks negatively of Hitler, and two socialist men intervene before the Nazis cause her harm. Agnes hides townspeople escaping Nazi persecution and allows her motorboat to be used to transport them across Lake Constance into Switzerland. Agnes's daughter Claudia dies defending an old man being assaulted by Nazis on the street, and when Toni leaves the Nazi Party to work alongside her mother for the socialists, Kati reflects on her awareness that Toni could suffer a similar fate: "But she does not belong only to me, my Toni, she belongs to something bigger, and I have no right to hinder her work" (140).[27] Zur Mühlen's portrayals here question women as naturally peaceful and protective of their children's lives and recognize women's readiness to engage in violence. Grayzel notes that women's use of violence or violent tactics related to the war and wartime conditions challenged notions of women's inherently nonviolent nature (2002, 97), yet many feminist pacifists maintained this essentialist notion during and after World War I. Other scholars have pointed out that many women did not necessarily enact violence themselves but endorsed violence by supporting their nation's war efforts, thereby also challenging essentialist gendered assumptions.

In both fictional and nonfictional writings, Zur Mühlen critiques women who defend the war and uphold nationalistic beliefs. In her 1919 essay "Junge-Mädchen-Literatur," she criticizes bourgeois women who support the war and celebrate reports of high numbers of fallen enemy soldiers, writing that these women only worry about their own children and the nation's soldiers while ignoring starving children on the streets and others in need. She blames not just the women themselves but also outside factors and influences, and provides a literary depiction of such a mother in *Der Tempel*. Frau Selder sends a letter to her son Gustav, and he shares it with his sister Lene. Gustav laughs in disbelief at a passage regarding fallen enemy soldiers, commenting, "Our good, gentle mother, a joyful message that 20,000 people have been killed!" (1922, 122). Furthermore, Gustav is shocked to learn that he has disappointed and embarrassed

---

27 In some ways, this statement echoes the nationalist rhetoric in which mothers proudly sacrifice their sons for the fatherland, as here a mother is prepared to sacrifice her daughter for the socialist cause. While this may seem contradictory to Zur Mühlen's pacifist ideals, in her works she supports the notion of sacrifice for revolutionary goals that she deems admirable, but not sacrifice for nationalistic aims.

his parents; despite his academic successes, they wish he would enlist in the military alongside his older brother so that they can offer both of their sons in the fight for the fatherland. Here Zur Mühlen reproduces the nationalist rhetoric of sacrifice and simultaneously questions this rhetoric when Gustav ponders his mother's desires: "I would have thought a woman would scream: 'Give me my son back, what right do you have to put his life on the line? What concern do I have for your damned fatherland? I want my child!'" (122–123). In response, Lene explains that in her experience many women actually think this, yet they are too cowardly to speak up, and she believes that once women's suffering and doubt over the war grows to be too much they will finally find the courage to express their true feelings (123).

Lene is disgusted by her mother's letter and refuses to read it to the end, yet the explanation that she offers Gustav is telling in terms of Zur Mühlen's message about women and war here. While it is clear that Lene abhors the idea that sacrificing one's child for the nation is honorable, she subtly blames propaganda and social influences for women's feelings rather than the women themselves. Lene implies that women want to protect their children, yet they may not know how to resist the propaganda and social pressures surrounding them. In some ways Lene's statement supports the feminist pacifist argument that women inherently wish to protect their children, even though they showed outward support and even enthusiasm for World War I.

The fact that so many women backed their nations' war efforts contradicted feminist pacifists who endorsed the essentialist belief in women's inherent peacefulness. Sharp observes in "Blaming the Women" (2007), "Heymann and Augspurg's conviction that women in their natural state had an innate love of peace that made it impossible for them to support killing remained intact throughout the war despite all evidence to the contrary" (76), further noting that female supporters of the war greatly outnumbered pacifists (77). Writing after the war, Zur Mühlen takes up this contradiction in her literature, implying that women supported the war because of outside factors. Furthermore, she asserts through her characters that women could find the courage to speak up against these social pressures if they were to actively engage in the socialist movement.

The strongest aspect of Zur Mühlen's socialist-feminist pacifism is that the socialist movement provides women with opportunities to advance their political agency, which empowers them to work towards peace. Feminist pacifists of the early 1900s recognized women's lack of social and political rights, though Zur Mühlen's solution depicted in her literature is not to engage with women's movements, but rather to become socialists. Many of her female characters join socialist movements in order to ameliorate their struggles related to the war, and this gives them confidence in themselves and hope for a peaceful future. One stark exception is the housemaid Lina, who ignores her working-class friend Kati's request to join the KPD. Despite losing her husband in the war and raising their four children alone, Kati's political involvement sustains her through these challenges, whereas Lina's suicide at the end of the novella reflects her feelings of hopelessness regarding her lot in life, as she did not manage to identify with an empowering cause. Zur Mühlen's positive female figures, particularly wives and mothers, are drawn to the socialist movement for various reasons but ultimately all seek a more harmonious and just world.

Although she did not claim to be a feminist, Zur Mühlen shared in the feminist stance that women's roles as wives and mothers are not grounds for relegating them to the private sphere. Rather, she illustrates that precisely these positions as wives and mothers could be politically empowering when they draw women into the public sphere in times of war and peace. For instance, in "Kleine Leute" Martha's whole family struggles in the aftermath of World War I, and she directly blames the war for their financial hardships. Because her brother fell in the war, Martha is left to support her aging parents, but her husband's shop does not bring in much money due to the hyperinflation of the early 1920s. She also experiences a difficult birth because of her poor health linked to her poverty. Martha and her mother find themselves drawn to communism because they see that Russia takes care of mothers and children. In defiance of her father, who states that women should focus on caring for their families and leave politics to men, Martha and her mother prove that family concerns are political as they engage with the KPD. Their entry into politics is through their concerns as mothers, and their political work provides them with a sense of accomplishment. Zur Mühlen's text thus recognizes women's influence on politics in general and against war in particular and encourages political engagement for all, including "little people."

Zur Mühlen's female figures largely gain agency through roles as wives and mothers, and become politically engaged through women's issues, rather than foreign policy or military strategy, which reflects the historical reality of the time.[28] Discussing *Unsere Töchter, die Nazinen* as a scholar of German literature, Eva-Maria Siegel observes that despite the images of strong women in the novel,

---

28 Throughout Zur Mühlen's life, women involved in politics, even if they were not wives and mothers, were generally relegated to social welfare projects, such as housing, public health, education and the protection of mothers, which have historically been viewed as the "proper" domain of women since they link to females' traditional and biological roles as caretakers. For more on the allocation of projects within the socialist parties of the early 1900s in particular, see Adelheid von Saldern (1998) and Christl Wickert (1986).

their power is ultimately tied back to their motherhood rather than offering them new roles, and she notes that this is similar to Zur Mühlen's earlier texts (1993, 46). In this aspect, then, Zur Mühlen's perspective is more in line with moderate feminists than revolutionary socialists. Writing about the influence on postwar peace negotiations of the Women's International League for Peace and Freedom (WILPF), which historian Erika Kuhlman refers to as "one of the most active female political organizations of the Great War era" (2007, 229), Kuhlman states, "They positioned the power women held as mothers in competition with men's power in the political realm" (240). This had unintended effects, as Kuhlman concludes: "[...] it simply reinforced the notion of separate spheres that kept women marginalized from politics" (240). While Zur Mühlen's texts reproduce this discourse to a certain extent, she simultaneously pushes for the expansion of women's political engagement, preferably through socialism, even if gendered roles are slower to transform.

Finally, similar to feminist pacifists of the early and mid-1900s, Zur Mühlen puts forth the idea that women's participation in the political realm would prevent future war and conflict. Feminist pacifists tied this presumption to essentialist notions of gender, but Zur Mühlen counters with a socialist perspective, as her female figures find their way into politics via the socialist, not feminist, movement. In her discussion of antiwar women in belligerent nations during World War I, Grayzel notes that some saw the potential to use the war as an opportunity to illustrate the necessity of including women in the political realm, stating, "They insisted that a world that listened to their voices would not, and never in future, be a world at war" (2002, 79). Sharp similarly argues, "The pacifists, however, did not accept the necessity or inevitability of this or any war, seeing it instead as a man-made disaster, a further instance of the failure of male government and demonstration of the necessity of women's involvement in the state" (2014, 198). For Zur Mühlen, though, women's participation in politics would not be enough to transform society and achieve peace if they did not also follow socialist tenets.

Conclusion

Reflecting on her impressions of World War I in her 1929 autobiography, Zur Mühlen states, "All I could see was poor devils being driven pointlessly and uselessly to death; I also saw the one thing that is capable of putting an end to imperialist wars" (2010, 151). While this "one thing" is international socialism here, when we examine her oeuvre, it appears that she actually recommends the combination of two – socialism and feminism. Feminism, socialism and pacifism intersect in Zur Mühlen's writings, and it is through this construction and dissemination of her socialist-feminist pacifism in her popular literature that she interrupts nationalist discourses that contribute to war and conflict and offers her perspectives on achieving a lasting peace. Zur Mühlen's bold challenges to nationalist rhetoric and ideologies are not limited to her exile literature of the 1930s and beyond, but rather permeate her entire literary and essayistic oeuvre, including her earlier texts depicting World War I and its aftermath. Their overt and underlying messages consistently appeal for international solidarity and peace.

Works Cited

Allen, Ann Taylor. *Feminism and Motherhood in Germany, 1800–1914* (Rutgers UP, 1991).

Altner, Manfred. *Hermynia zur Mühlen: Eine Biographie* (Peter Lang, 1997).

Beuys, Barbara. *Die neuen Frauen: Revolution im Kaiserreich 1900–1914* (Carl Hanser, 2014).

Bianchi, Bruna. "Towards a New Internationalism: Pacifist Journals Edited by Women, 1914–1919." *Gender and the First World War*, edited by Christa Hämmerle, et al. (Palgrave Macmillan, 2014), pp. 176–194.

Brinker-Gabler, Gisela, editor. *Frauen gegen den Krieg* (Fischer Taschenbuch Verlag, 1980).

Costin, Lela B. "Feminism, Pacifism, Internationalism and the 1915 International Congress of Women." *Women's Studies International Forum*, vol. 5, no. 3/4 (1982), pp. 301–315.

Evans, Richard J. *Comrades and Sisters: Feminism, Socialism and Pacifism in Europe 1870–1945* (St. Martin's, 1987).

Fell, Alison S., and Ingrid Sharp. "The Women's Movement and the First World War." Introduction. *The Women's Movement in Wartime: International Perspectives, 1914–19*, edited by Fell and Sharp (Palgrave Macmillan, 2007), pp. 1–17.

Felski, Rita. *Beyond Feminist Aesthetics: Feminist Literature and Social Change* (Harvard UP, 1989).

Frevert, Ute. *Women in German History: From Bourgeois Emancipation to Sexual Liberation*. Translated by Stuart McKinnon-Evans (Berg, 1997).

Gelblum, Amira. "Ideological Crossroads: Feminism, Pacifism, and Socialism." *Borderlines: Genders and Identities in War and Peace 1870–1930*, edited by Billie Melman (Routledge, 1998), pp. 307–327.

Grayzel, Susan R. *Women and the First World War* (Routledge, 2002).

Hammel, Andrea. *Everyday Life as Alternative Space in Exile Writing* (Peter Lang, 2008).

King, Lynda J. "From the Crown to the Hammer and Sickle: The Life and Works of Austrian Interwar Writer Hermynia zur Mühlen." *Women in German Yearbook*, vol. 4 (1988), pp. 125–154.

Kuhlman, Erika. "The 'Women's International League for Peace and Freedom' and Reconciliation after the Great War." *The Women's Movement in Wartime: International Perspectives, 1914–19*, edited by Alison S. Fell and Ingrid Sharp (Palgrave Macmillan, 2007), pp. 227–243.

Luxemburg, Rosa. *The Crisis in the German Social-Democracy: The "Junius" Pamphlet*. 1916 (Socialist Publication Society, 1919).

Luxemburg, Rosa. "Die Sozialistische Internationale." *Frauen gegen den Krieg*, edited by Gisela Brinker-Gabler (Fischer, 1980), pp. 95–99.

Ouditt, Sharon. *Fighting Forces, Writing Women: Identity and Ideology in the First World War* (Routledge, 1994).

Quataert, Jean H. *Reluctant Feminists in German Social Democracy, 1885–1917* (Princeton UP, 1979).

Saldern, Adelheid von. "Modernization as Challenge: Perceptions and Reactions of German Social Democratic Women." *Women and Socialism / Socialism and Women: Europe Between the Two World Wars*, edited by Helmut Gruber and Pamela Graves (Berghahn, 1998), pp. 95–134.

Sharp, Ingrid. "Blaming the Women: Women's 'Responsibility' for the First World War." *The Women's Movement in Wartime: International Perspectives, 1914–19*, edited by Alison S. Fell and Ingrid Sharp (Palgrave Macmillan, 2007), pp. 67–87.

Sharp, Ingrid. "'A Foolish Dream of Sisterhood': Anti-Pacifist Debates in the German Women's Movement, 1914–1919." *Gender and the First World War*, edited by Christa Hämmerle, et al. (Palgrave Macmillan, 2014), pp. 195–213.

Siegel, Eva-Maria. *Jugend, Frauen, Drittes Reich: Autorinnen im Exil 1933–1945* (Centaurus, 1993).

Vietor-Engländer, Deborah. "Hermynia Zur Mühlen's Fight Against the 'Enemy Within: Prejudice, Injustice, Cowardice and Intolerance.'" *Keine Klage über England?: Deutsche und österreichische Exilerfahrungen in Großbritannien 1933–1945*, edited by Charmian Brinson, et al. (Iudicium, 1998), pp. 74–87.

Vietor-Engländer, Deborah J., et al., editors. *Nebenglück: Ausgewählte Erzählungen und Feuilletons aus dem Exil von Hermynia Zur Mühlen* (Peter Lang, 2002).

Vietor-Engländer, Deborah J., et al., editors. *Vierzehn Nothelfer und andere Romane aus dem Exil von Hermynia Zur Mühlen* (Peter Lang, 2002).

Wallace, Ailsa. *Hermynia Zur Mühlen: The Guises of Socialist Fiction* (Oxford UP, 2009).

Wickert, Christl. *Unsere Erwählten: Sozialdemokratische Frauen im Deutschen Reichstag und im Preußischen Landtag 1919 bis 1933* (Sovec, 1986). 2 vols.

Zetkin, Clara. "Frauen gegen den imperialistischen Krieg!" *Frauen gegen den Krieg*, edited by Gisela Brinker-Gabler (Fischer, 1980), pp. 139–143.

Zetkin, Clara. "To the Socialist Women of All Countries." *Clara Zetkin: Selected Writings*, edited by Philip S. Foner (Haymarket Books, 2015), pp. 114–116.

Zetkin, Clara. "Women of the Working People." *Clara Zetkin: Selected Writings*, edited by Philip S. Foner (Haymarket Books, 2015), pp. 130–132.

Zur Mühlen, Hermynia. "Der Deutschvölkische" (Vereinigung Internationaler Verlags-Anstalten, 1924a).

Zur Mühlen, Hermynia. *Eine Flasche Parfüm*. 1934 (Schönbrunn, 1947).

Zur Mühlen, Hermynia. *The End and the Beginning: The Book of My Life*. Translated by Lionel Gossman (Open Book, 2010).

Zur Mühlen, Hermynia. *Ende und Anfang: Ein Lebensbuch* (S. Fischer, 1929).

Zur Mühlen, Hermynia. "Junge-Mädchen-Literatur." *Die Erde*, vol. 14/15 (1919), pp. 473–474.

Zur Mühlen, Hermynia. "Kleine Leute" (Vereinigung Internationaler Verlags-Anstalten, 1925).

Zur Mühlen, Hermynia. *A Life's Journey*. Translated by Phyllis and Trevor Blewitt (Cape, 1935).

Zur Mühlen, Hermynia. "Lina: Erzählung aus dem Leben eines Dienstmädchens." 1924 (Vereinigung Internationaler Verlags-Anstalten, 1926).

Zur Mühlen, Hermynia. "Radiosendungen für Frauen." *Nebenglück: Ausgewählte Erzählungen und Feuilletons aus dem Exil von Hermynia Zur Mühlen*, edited by Deborah J. Vietor-Engländer, et al. (Peter Lang, 2002), pp. 103–104.

Zur Mühlen, Hermynia. *Reise durch ein Leben* (Gotthelf, 1933).

Zur Mühlen, Hermynia. *Das Riesenrad* (Engelhorn, 1932).

Zur Mühlen, Hermynia. "Schupomann Karl Müller: Eine Erzählung" (Vereinigung Internationaler Verlags-Anstalten, 1924b).

Zur Mühlen, Hermynia. "Selbstbiographie." *Das Wort*, vol. 2, no. 4/5 (1937), pp. 184–185.

Zur Mühlen, Hermynia. *Der Tempel* (Vereinigung Internationaler Verlags-Anstalten, 1922).

Zur Mühlen, Hermynia. *Unsere Töchter, die Nazinen*. 1934 (Aufbau, 1983).

Zur Mühlen, Hermynia. *The Wheel of Life*. Translated by Margaret Goldsmith (Barker, 1933).

Zur Mühlen, Hermynia. "Wolfi." *Fahrt ins Licht: Sechsundsechzig Stationen*. 1936 (Sisyphus, 1999), pp. 374–377.

Constructing the Labor of War:
Girls, Mothers and Nurses

Jennifer Redmann
Girls Reading the Great War

German and Anglo-American Literature for Young Women,
1914–1920

Introduction

World War I ushered in a new form of industrialized warfare, one that erased distinctions between military and civilian spheres and transformed the homefront into a secondary battleground. As a result, World War I has been described as a "total war" in that it, as historian Roger Chickering writes, "encompassed the lives of every man, woman, and child in the belligerent states" (2007, 1). Even popular novels for teenaged girls in Germany, Great Britain, and the United States integrated wartime events into previously apolitical plots. By presenting young female readers with positive examples of fictional wartime girls ready to "do their bit" on behalf of their respective nations, this literature served as an instrument in the "mobilization of morale" (Chickering 2004, 46). In these books, for example, German girls "eagerly take up their knitting needles as weapons like never before" (Albert 1915, 69),[1] while British girls, "[l]ike the other soldiers of the Empire" (Marchant 1919, 101), step forward to work in munition factories or on the front lines as nurses. One American girls' novel, Edna Brooks' *The Khaki Girls of the Motor Corps* (1918), opens with a scene in which the protagonist plays the following song for her father in an effort to gain his permission to go abroad as an ambulance driver:

> My heart is with our Allies
> Fighting Huns in far off France,
> And I'd surely join the Sammies
> If I only had a chance;
> Though I'm just one little home girl
> Count me loyal to the core;
> And watch me do my biggest bit
> To help win the war. (9)

Beginning in 1914, this focus on war in the lives of fictional young women marked a shift in the well-established genre of popular novels for girls. The "girl" – both as reader and fictional character – is a figure on the threshold:

---

1 All translations from German into English are my own unless otherwise stated.

https://doi.org/10.1515/9783110572001-010

no longer a child but not yet an adult woman, she might be at home, at school, or even working outside the home, but as long as she is unmarried (and young enough to still be marriageable), she is considered a girl.[2] A typical girls' novel of the late nineteenth and early twentieth centuries centers around the joys and sorrows of a young, female protagonist between the ages of fourteen and twenty as she makes the transition to adult womanhood. Although this plot arc is realized in a variety of ways, a unifying characteristic of the genre lies in its function as a kind of teenaged girls' *Bildungsroman*, or novel of education. The girls' novel as *Bildungsroman* traces the protagonist's maturation process through experiences within the home, at school, among friends, and, by the early twentieth century, in the worlds of travel and work. The girl's self-centered immaturity frequently leads to entertaining misadventures, but with the help, advice, and forgiveness of sympathetic mothers and teachers, the girl learns to put the needs of others before herself and her own desires. These lessons effectively prepare her for adult womanhood, which is synonymous with the roles of wife and mother.

With the outbreak of World War I in 1914, the boundaries of the girls' *Bildungsroman* opened up to encompass political and military concerns. Just how fictional girls respond to wartime challenges and expectations, however, differs significantly in books published in Germany, Britain, and the United States during the war. Whereas British and American protagonists are mobile heroines, contributing to the war effort not just in the home, but in factories and even on the front lines, most German heroines remain closely tied to the domestic sphere, a sphere that has been recast as a metaphor for the entire nation. British and American wartime books for girls depict female characters who serve their country in ways that overturn standard associations of femininity with domesticity, even if the plots ultimately reaffirm a woman's primary role as wife and mother. While British and American female protagonists are frequently lauded as extraordinary individuals for their heroic efforts, German girls demonstrate their worth by disappearing into the ever-expanding ranks of patriotic German women.[3]

Through a comparative analysis of popular, war-themed novels for girls and young women published between 1914 and 1920 by fourteen German, British,

---

2 In German, the terms *junge Mädchen* (young girls) and *erwachsene Mädchen* (grown girls) were sometimes used to distinguish between girls at either end of the approximately decade-long period of girlhood.

3 Maureen Gallagher comes to similar conclusions regarding German WWI novels for girls and young women in her essay in this volume, though she compares these texts with German novels about the colonial wars while my focus is on providing a transnational analysis.

and American authors, this essay offers insights into an under-studied aspect of these cultures during World War I. An examination of the wartime genres of German and Anglo-American girls' literature sheds light on the ways in which literary representations of war intersect with questions of gender, age, and national identity in a transnational context. Recent studies of World War I, such as the three-volume *Cambridge History of the First World War* (2014), edited by Jay Winter, have taken a transnational perspective on the war as a point of departure. In advocating for such an approach, historian Michael Neiberg has called on fellow scholars

> to turn your gaze away from the national narratives that have dominated our understandings of [World War I] and instead see the wider European world where men and women shared much in common. Social class, regional loyalties, generational differences, gender, political affiliation, and religion (to name just a few) were identifications that transcended national borders, even if they impacted different parts of the European world in different ways. (2008, 32)

A study of the wartime girls' *Bildungsroman* is particularly well-suited to a comparative, transnational approach because, in spite of linguistic and cultural differences, German, British, and American novels of the war years have much in common: a focus on one or more young female characters, depictions of wartime events, and a representation of war as a moment of positive transformation for girls transitioning to adulthood.[4] At the same time, an analysis of generic differences between the novels published in Germany and those that appeared in Britain and the U.S. between 1914 and 1920 sheds light on differing cultural attitudes and ideologies regarding girls and their relationship to the nation that emerged in response to the unique challenges faced by women during the war years.

In this essay, I begin with a discussion of genre as a dynamic social and textual construct that facilitates communication between individuals and within groups, and across time. When applied to the wartime girls' *Bildungsroman*, as I do in the main body of the essay, genre theory serves as a compelling tool of historical analysis, helping us to understand how authors of popular literature in three combatant nations responded immediately to changing conceptions of gender roles. This approach brings together my own scholarly interests in German literary texts and cultural and historical studies. The transnational framework also allows me to engage with intercultural issues that form the center of my work as a teacher of German in an American university setting, but rarely

---

4 We can attribute these commonalities to a parallel history of literature for girls as it emerged in all three countries in the mid-nineteenth century. I outline this history briefly in my essay.

find their way into scholarly endeavors that generally focus only on the German context.

As the title of this essay indicates, it addresses girls *reading* war rather than women *writing* war. I have chosen to emphasize the question of genre, that is, an analysis of the fictional genres that were popular with girls, over that of authorship, in spite of the fact that this girls' literature was written almost exclusively by women. Because I draw examples from a fairly large number of texts, space restrictions do not allow me to address the details of the authors' biographies, and in most cases, little is known about them. Few of these authors are read today; two exceptions are Else Ury (1877–1943) in Germany, whose ten-volume *Nesthäkchen* (1913–1925) series remains in print, and Angela Brazil (1868–1947), the most famous author of British "school stories" for girls, such as *A Patriotic Schoolgirl* (1918). In the case of the American wartime girls' books, the question of authorship grows murky. The American market in the early twentieth century was dominated by the mass-market series book pioneered by the Stratemeyer Syndicate and subsequently adopted by other publishers (see Hamilton-Honey).[5] Series aimed at girls, such as the four-volume *Khaki Girls* series (1918–1920) by Edna Brooks, have women's names on the covers, but the actual authors may or may not have been women.

Setting authorship aside, an analysis of popular literature for girls through the lens of genre focuses our attention on the text itself within a social context. I draw on two aspects of genre theory – genre as social action and genre as world – to investigate connections between the thematic content of girls' novels and shifting understandings of gender, age, and national identity in German, British and American cultures during World War I.

In "Genre as Social Action" (1984), Carolyn Miller, a scholar of rhetoric and communication, lays out an understanding of genre as a social category, defining genres as "typified rhetorical actions based in recurrent situations" (159). As such, genre acquires meaning "from situation and from the social context in which that situation arose" (163). From this perspective, textual production is, as linguist Gunther Kress explains, "no longer an individual, expressive act, but a social, conventional act performed by an individual, any individual" (1999, 463). An understanding of genre as social act offers insight into the contexts in which instantiations of a genre were produced. By tracing changes with-

---

5 Edward Stratemeyer (1862–1930), creator of the syndicate that bears his name, devised a new way of mass-producing literature for youth. He developed character portraits and plot outlines for the volumes in a given series, then hired ghostwriters to write the books, paying them a modest fee for their work. In this way, multiple volumes of a single series could be brought to the market at once.

in a genre field, we can also trace corresponding changes in the social life from which the texts of a particular genre emerged. As Tzvetan Todorov notes in a book on the work of Mikhail Bakhtin: "Genre is a sociohistorical as well as a formal entity. Transformations in genre must be considered in relation to social changes" (1984, 80).

Because World War I brought sweeping changes to both the public and private spheres in Germany and Great Britain (and, to a lesser extent, the United States following its entry into the war in 1917), the genre of the girls' *Bildungsroman* came to be dominated by the war, reflecting its unprecedented impact on the lives of young women. Furthermore, the wartime setting and events featured in this literature affected the way young female readers viewed their place in society, since, in the words of literary critic John Frow, "the generic organisation of language, images, gestures, and sound makes things happen by actively shaping the way we understand the world" (2015, 2). In other words, sociohistorical and textual, genre-based worlds interact and inform one another in and through the actions and responses of a community of writers and readers.

In addition to the idea of genre as social action, Bakhtin's concept of genre as world, or, more specifically, as "a model of the world put forward by the text" (Todorov 1984, 83), provides a useful way of understanding the intersection of literature and society at a given historical moment. Todorov defines such a world as "a relatively bounded and schematic domain of meanings, values, and affects, accompanied by a set of instructions for handling them" (93). In my view, this understanding of genre offers a particularly apt framework for reading girls' literature, a collection of genres that emerged in the late nineteenth century in concert with a unique girls' culture (or world) that positioned the young female reader not merely as a daughter subject to her parents' wishes, but as a consumer with her own tastes and interests. An analysis of genre as world focuses on a text's thematic structure and content: how the text creates a coherent and plausible world, the kinds of actions and actors one finds in that world, and the significance that accrues to them. A comparative study of German, British, and American texts from this time period reveals key differences in the nature of girls' wartime textual worlds – specifically, how young female protagonists are able to act and where they are able to move – that can tell us much about how war reshaped cultural concepts of gender, national identity, and girlhood and adulthood in these three countries.

The worlds of wartime girls' literature

Central to my analysis of girls' literature is a discussion of the spaces to which female protagonists have access and the activities they are able to perform within those spaces. Although space, mobility, and action take on new importance in books for girls written during World War I, one could describe the history of girls' literature beginning in the mid-nineteenth century in terms of the successive emergence of new genres defined primarily through the young female protagonists' independent access to new spaces outside the domestic sphere: city streets, schools and universities, workplaces, the wider world. I would argue that the representation of these spaces and the heroine's ability to navigate them successfully symbolize her journey from girlhood to womanhood (her *Bildung*), and that this transition stands as a unifying theme of girls' literature as a whole.

The earliest genres of girls' literature on both sides of the Atlantic were domestic novels that focused on a girl's role within the family. Starting in the 1870s and 1880s, the new genre of the school novel depicted a girl leaving home to complete her transition to womanhood at a boarding school, a seemingly utopian world populated exclusively by girls and women. By the end of the century, books for girls took characters out of schools and into the world. Late nineteenth-century British adventure novels for boys, such as those by G.T. Henty (1832–1902), were frequently set in far-flung and exotic corners of the British empire, such as India, the Middle East, and Africa,[6] and by the first decade of the twentieth century, authors such as Bessie Marchant (who was known as "the girl's Henty") began writing adventure tales aimed at girls. In such stories, the empire offers a realm in which gender roles, out of necessity, can and must be redefined, while at the same time a girl's presence exercises a domesticating influence over the wilderness and its "uncivilized" inhabitants. German adventure stories for girls do not exist in this vein, although by the turn of the century, the settings of many girls' books do shift from home and school to the wider world of travel (to England and Asia, for example), study, and work. In books for American girls, on the other hand, mobile heroines seek out adventure in their own backyards. In writing about the series *The Motor Girls* (1910–1917), literary critic Nancy Tillman Romalov contrasts domestic heroines of the nineteenth century with these twentieth-century New Women. The Motor Girls are on the move, demonstrating through their various adventures "courage, stamina, physical

---

6 Henty wrote over 100 historical adventure novels, such as *To Herat and Cabul: A Story of the First Afghan War* (1902).

strength, independence, and leadership qualities" (2005, 232). Romalov does note, however, that romance finds its way into these plots, indicating that the girls' adventures are a passing phase in their maturation process before they marry. This is a recurring theme across the travel/adventure books in all three countries: girls' pre-marital freedom and mobility is possible only because it exists as a temporary phase of life, one that will end with a return to the home.

The successive emergence of the domestic, school, and travel/adventure genres for girls reflected new rights and new educational and employment opportunities for women that were achieved through the ongoing work of the women's movements on both sides of the Atlantic at the turn of the century. Images of the New Woman influenced girls' literature through the rise of the heroine who is able to defy the expectations of domestic femininity. To use literary critic Sally Mitchell's term, the New Girl "is neither a child nor a (sexual) adult. [...] The ascription of immaturity and transition gives her permission to behave in ways that might not be appropriate for a woman" (1995, 25). In this sense, girls' literature served as an outlet for female readers to live out their desires for wider spheres of action and activity.[7] This situation became even more marked during the war years.

The three subsections that follow open up three textual worlds of the girls' *Bildungsroman* that appeared during World War I. The first, "Domestic soldiers," focuses on the home as wartime front, one in which young women fight the enemy indirectly through patriotic sacrifice. This world is populated exclusively by German girls; after gathering a corpus of well over 100 novels, I have yet to identify a British or American novel that limits the wartime girls' sphere of activity so strictly to the home. A very different wartime world is the focus of the second section, "Encountering the enemy on the homefront." Here the British and American heroines move into the public sphere, taking on wartime service duties or jobs in munition factories. While the work the girls do is held up as exemplary, it is the hidden presence of enemy spies that generates suspense and drives the plots forward. Finally, "Mobile heroines on the front lines" presents novels in which the protagonists journey to the front lines of the war and engage the enemy alongside men. The demands of war offer these mobile heroines an opportunity to extend the boundaries of their world, but the radicality of this

---

7 For example, in Berta Clément's *Lebensziele* (Life goals, 1907), the girl protagonist convinces her mother to let her take the streetcar alone with a girlfriend from the suburbs of Berlin to the center of the city to pick up her father's watch. The girls indulge in pastries and silly pranks, but then they lose the claim check and cannot complete the errand. In their shame and distress they learn a lesson: because they put their own impulses ahead of duty, they realize that they were not deserving of such independence.

move is nearly always tempered by narrative assurances that the protagonist retains her femininity, even in a war zone.

Domestic soldiers

By reemphasizing domestic values as a form of patriotism and national service, World War I books for German girls largely reverse the historical trend toward an increasing expansion of the spatial boundaries of a girl's fictional world. In these wartime novels, once private activities become political actions on behalf of the nation, as is evident in the 1916 novel *Morgenrot* (Dawn) by Bertha Clement.[8] In this passage, the main character, Ruth von Buchheim, reflects on her role as a woman at a profound moment in German history:

> In this momentous time, the Fatherland needed everyone, not just its sons but also its daughters: outside persevering in a bloody battle – inside persevering in household work. Only then would England's plan to starve Germany fail.

> Ruth drew up her young body. Her courage and power grew with the increasing difficulties. What did England know of the unsurpassable organization of the German economy? What did it know of German women? Did it think that their will to victory was not as firm and unshakeable as those who committed their lifeblood day and night on the field of battle? Wouldn't women do everything to stretch their reserves and practice the greatest thrift? Wouldn't they commit everything so that the soldiers could endure, so that the bony arms of hunger and distress would not be stretched out to them? (146)

This passage clearly demarcates the boundaries of a woman's world: her efforts do not lie "outside persevering in a bloody battle" but "inside persevering in household work." The heroine Ruth – and by extension all German girls – steels herself to fight enemy England through economy and sacrifice. Historian Ute Daniel has noted that, in the latter half of the war, when nearly all foodstuffs in Germany were rationed and the problem of malnutrition grew, social pressure on women to economize increased (1993, 145). This cited passage sends a clear message to women about their culinary responsibilities to country.

In spite of the author's stirring use of rhetorical devices (in its use of parallelism, hyperbole, and metaphor, the passage bears all the hallmarks of effective

---

8 Bertha Clement (1852–1930), author of *Morgenrot*, is identical with Berta Clément, author of the novel *Lebensziele* (referenced in note 7). Within her huge oeuvre of over 90 books for girls, Clement's first name is usually spelled with an "h" and her last name with an accent over the first "e." It is possible that she chose to drop the accent during World War I in order to distance herself from the French origins of her family name.

propaganda), it is hard to imagine a girl reader finding much excitement in the call to be thrifty. The real driving force behind the plot of *Morgenrot* lies instead in the secret romance between Ruth and a soldier, Helmut von Brachwitz. In an illustration from the novel (fig. 1), Ruth sits with Helmut's grandmother, the only person who knows of her love for him, and laments that she has not heard from him. The escaped ball of yarn and the empty open drawer signal the absent loved one; the overall narrowness of the image lends the domestic environment a sense of confinement. The scene depicted here belies the notion that wartime circumstances could open up new spheres of activity for women. Instead, we find an image of a cozy, prewar world gone awry, threatened by outside forces: the walls seem to be closing in and the painting on the left about to fall off the wall. In this world, readers learn, the highest virtues for women, those that will be rewarded in the end with marriage, are not courage in action, but quiet patience and loyalty.

Not all of the girls in German wartime books contribute to the war effort solely through home-bound activities. Ruth von Buchheim's sister Renate cares for wounded soldiers, as does Magda Toppler in Else Ury's *Das Ratstöchterlein zu Rothenburg* (The Rothenburg councilman's little daughter, 1917). Their work is, however, domestic rather than professional in nature: both girls volunteer in convalescent hospitals and are able to continue living at home with their families. As unpaid Red Cross workers, they spend most of their time cheering up soldiers, reading to them and writing letters for them – activities for which a well-bred, middle-class girl needs no training. Obviously, the work will end when the war ends.

Although German middle-class women did not enter the paid workforce in the same numbers as their British counterparts during World War I (see Grayzel 2002, 31), through the efforts of the National Women's Service, many German women did take on new volunteer roles outside the home. Johanna Klemm's *Die wir mitkämpfen* (We who also fight, 1916) celebrates one of the young female characters, Ruth Giselher, for her wide-ranging accomplishments in service of the nation: "[Ruth] had made herself useful this year in so many different areas! She had written and translated, cooked and scrubbed, played music for a good cause and helped needy warriors' wives find jobs" (229). Ruth Giselher's final job, however, involves caring for two small boys whose mother is dead and whose father serves as an officer at the front. When the father returns on leave, Ruth agrees to marry him, thereby reaffirming the temporary nature of work outside the home and the primacy of women's maternal role.

Like Ruth Giselher, Ilse Schirmeck in Else Hofmann's *Deutsche Mädel in großer Zeit* (German girls in great times, 1916) steps out of her comfortable middle-class life of leisure to work on behalf of the war effort as a Red Cross volun-

Figure 1: Illustration from Bertha Clement, *Morgenrot* (1916). Collection of the author.

teer caring for the wounded. In the final pages of the book, author Hofmann shifts the focus away from the main characters to celebrate in stirring terms all that women have accomplished and provided in the war by taking over jobs vacated by men. The book's conclusion, however, makes clear that, as proud as girls and women might be to work in the place of men, a woman's true calling lies in maintaining the home in anticipation of the soldiers' return:

> And so continue on your path, you loving, fearless, courageous German girls and women! You, the Kaiser's female army in gray! And when our brave men return home from the field, then let them find a peaceful place, the home for which they have suffered! Then step back

from the positions you were allowed to fill in the difficult war years. Give back to the man what once belonged to the man. You will have enough work – work that is suited to women's hearts and women's hands! (182–183)

This narrative reflects cultural anxieties raised by the fact that for the first time during the war, significant numbers of middle-class women were working outside the home (and that working-class women had moved into jobs once reserved for men, although their experience is not represented in this literature). Historian Susan Grayzel writes, "Women were at one and the same time declared to be essential for the war effort yet patronized, feared, and condemned for infringing upon male roles" (2010, 267). Hofmann's text forecloses on the possibility that working women might be condemned for their efforts by asserting the primacy of women's domestic role over all others and by reminding readers that women will eventually have to relinquish jobs "that once belonged to the man."

The final lines of Charlotte Niese's *Barbarentöchter* (Barbarians' daughters, 1915) send a similar message: "May God protect Germany – and every hearth that we are keeping warm for the tired warriors, so that they may one day find what they have been fighting for: home" (240). As this and other German girls' books make clear, in spite of their homefront service, German women do not fight their country's battles, but are instead an essential component of the *Heimat*, the home for which men fight. One could argue that this situation placed German women in an untenable position: they were exhorted to serve the nation by actively upholding and maintaining a nostalgic, prewar ideal of home, even as the social order that fostered that ideal of home was being destroyed by war.

Encountering the enemy on the homefront

In contrast to the German novels discussed above, British and American wartime girls' books unabashedly celebrate opportunities for middle-class heroines to take on exciting new jobs outside the home: as munition factory workers in Brenda Girvin's *Munition Mary* (1918) and Bessie Marchant's *A Girl Munition Worker* (1916), or as farm laborers in Marchant's *A Transport Girl in France* (1919). Within these workplace settings, the protagonists perform additional heroic service by identifying and capturing German spies. As intrepid spy catchers, girl heroines are able to contribute to the war effort by engaging, like their soldier counterparts, with the enemy, but they make use of what are portrayed as some distinctly feminine weapons: curiosity and intuition. At the same time, by hunting down and confronting dangerous spies, the young female protagonists in these books demonstrate a level of bravery not typically associated with femininity at that time. Ironically, these moments of gender-bending are often followed by scenes in which the girls fall into a faint, clearly overcome by the magnitude of what they have done. In Marchant's *A Girl Munition Worker*, protagonist Deborah Lynch stops a German Zeppelin raid on the munition factory by shooting the man who is attempting to guide the airship to its target. Immediately after she successfully gets off her shot, "the shock and terror of it robbed her of her senses, and for the very first time in her life Deborah fainted" (173). Later, Deborah downplays her achievement when she says: "I did my best to shoot straight, but, trembling as I was, I could not have done it if Divine strength had not held my arm steady" (252). In this scene, the homefront appears not as a metaphorical but a real battleground, one in which a girl has the ability to engage – and defeat – her enemy directly. One could easily imagine the next stage in this development: a scene of a woman as an Amazonian warrior, ready to take up arms and fight alongside men. However, Deborah's "feminine" fear and trembling, I would argue, overturns any such association; she hits her target not because she is able to shoot, but because God helps her, and by extension, her country, in an extraordinary moment. Implicit in this moment is the idea that, once the war is over and spies no longer lurk around every corner, temporarily expanded gender roles will return to their prewar state.

Similar scenes appear in other girls' novels of the time. The title character in Girvin's *Munition Mary* uncovers a German spy ring that had infiltrated a munition factory and sabotaged the efforts of female workers to prove themselves equal to the new task of manufacturing shells. Upon securing the spies' capture, however, "[a]ll [Mary's] pluck went. Suddenly she felt she was just a weak girl with no self-control or courage left. She sank down into a chair and burst into a flood of tears" (1918, 275). Modern American heroines are also not immune to Victorian fits of the vapors. The main character of a wartime novel set in Wyoming, Martha Trent's *Helen Carey: Somewhere in America* (1918), learns that a railway bridge has been sabotaged by German spies and manages, quite remarkably, to stop a train full of soldiers from derailing by throwing a lasso across it. Like her fellow British spy catchers, however, this masculine gesture is followed by a quite feminine collapse. After the train comes to a stop, the engineer "jumped to the ground and raced back along the track and almost stumbled over a limp little body in a blue dress that lay huddled in a heap by the side of a big gray automobile" (205).

The activities of these characters, both as working girls and as spy catchers, clearly challenge the notion that a girl's or woman's world must be limited to the domestic sphere. At the same time, the radicality of this message is tempered by frequent reminders of the heroines' femininity, beauty, and physical and emotional fragility. Even though the characters in these books do contribute to a redefinition of gender roles by stepping into factories (or, as discussed in the next section, donning uniforms), nearly every novel ends with the promise of a husband on the horizon. The Anglo-American girl protagonist's exit from this adventure-filled world, a world to which German girls receive no admittance, is marked very clearly by the marriage altar. At a time when discourses of gender were in flux, portraying unmarried young women in new but temporary roles may have served as a means of managing both girls' desire for a wider range of professional opportunities and adult anxieties about the prospect of such changes to women's roles. In a discussion of American girls' literature published between 1860 and 1940, literary critic Peter Stoneley notes that "the girl [...] is instrumental in articulating and assuaging the fear of social change. Her growing up can naturalize change and make it seem more manageable" (2003, 2). In these wartime novels, the girl protagonist's ongoing maturation process lends meaning and import to the otherwise entertaining series of adventures. By allowing the protagonist to prove her character through adversity and struggle, the war itself becomes a form of *Bildung*, turning out women who are ready to serve the postwar nation as wives and mothers.

Mobile heroines on the front lines

While enemy spies figure into British and American girls' novels set on the front lines of the war, even apart from any such intrigue, a girl's life in the world of the battlefield generates its own excitement and tension. A number of girls serve as nurses, a role that combines feminine nurturing with bravery. The sixteen-year-old title character in British author Edith C. Kenyon's *Pickles: A Red Cross Heroine* (1916), described in the opening pages as "lithe, strong, yet somewhat small in figure, with a quantity of red-gold hair, waving and curling in a coil above her head, and trying to escape from the thick plait down her back" (9), embodies the dual nature of the brave war zone nurse. When her father refuses to allow her to join the Red Cross in France, Pickles hitches a ride on a bi-plane with her friend Charley and drops bombs on the Germans along the way. Through a series of adventures, she reveals her skills as a "crack shot" (103) and automobile driver, and she even manages to capture a group of German soldiers by drugging their drinks. Her obligatory maternal side, however, comes out when she finds her missing soldier brother and saves his life, treating him tenderly as he lies wounded on a battlefield: "[Pickles] succeeded at last in making him swallow a little brandy, and warm water from her thermos, and she bathed his face, grown over with a young beard and whiskers, and all the time she spoke little, sweet, loving words, as a mother might over her child" (154).

As mentioned earlier, German novels featuring girls in nursing roles generally place them in convalescent hospitals close to home. An exception is Anna Meißner in Sophie Kloerss's *Im heiligen Kampf* (In the holy battle, 1915), a twenty-five-year-old trained nurse who is immediately sent to Belgium with the invading German troops in the fall of 1914. In a central scene of the novel, Anna bravely defends a caravan of wounded soldiers under her care when it is attacked by Belgian resistance fighters, blocking their access to the ambulance with her body. During the altercation, she is stabbed in the shoulder and captured as a prisoner-of-war. After her rescue, Anna returns home, and even after convalescing, she remains a broken woman unable to work. Furthermore, the ending of the novel makes clear that, unlike her sister who had worked as a nurse on the home front, Anna will never marry. Within this *Bildungsroman*, the trauma of Anna's experience does not promote a positive maturation into womanhood (as defined by the establishment of her own home and family), but instead leaves her sad and alone. In contrast to her heroic British and American counterparts, Anna's story offers a cautionary tale to female readers, a negative example of what can happen if a young woman abandons the safe confines of home and her domestic role in the family.

In addition to nurses, British and American wartime books feature plots involving young women in military auxiliary positions – the American Khaki Girls are ambulance drivers, and Bessie Marchant highlights the work of the British women's Volunteer Auxiliary Detachment in *A V.A.D. in Salonika* (1917). The absence of books about German women serving as military auxiliaries corresponds to the historical invisibility of women in these roles. German women were admitted to auxiliary roles only in the final years of the war, when men were no longer available, and although nearly as many women served as auxiliaries as nurses, they never enjoyed the cultural prestige of nurses (see Schönberger, 2002). Unlike nurses with their white, habit-like garb, German auxiliaries did not wear uniforms and were sometimes mistaken for prostitutes. Because the auxiliaries were also well paid, they contradicted the notion that women's wartime work was a form of sacrifice for the good of the country. "[I]n contrast to the nurses," historian Bianca Schönberger writes, "the [German, J.R.] auxiliaries' service transgressed traditional ideals of gender roles. If women could successfully take up the jobs of soldiers, for whom were the men fighting then?" (2002, 100).

This issue does not seem to have applied to British and American auxiliaries. Joan Mason, the protagonist in the American novel *The Khaki Girls Behind the Lines* (1918), epitomizes the wartime heroine, travelling from the U.S. to Europe on a warship, then working on the front lines in France as an ambulance driver. The qualifications for the driving corps to which Joan belongs mirror those of the historical Smith College Relief Unit, a group of graduates from the women's college who served primarily as aid workers to French civilians. As a member of the fictional Windsor College's "Trusty Twenty" ambulance corps, Joan Mason navigates the war zone and comes directly under fire:

> Setting her teeth, Joan drove the ambulance forward. Thanks to bursting shells, which continued to explode, some of them uncomfortably close to the ambulance, she could see her way quite plainly.
>
> "If I can only get away from this section, I can make the hospital, I know I can," she muttered determinedly. [...]
>
> Putting on all the speed she dared under the circumstances, Joan valiantly gripped the wheel. Her first feeling of panic had vanished the instant she realized that she was under fire. The flash and roar of the opening bombardment had dismayed her but briefly. She was now cool and collected. She would race Death and beat him. (142–143)

An illustration of this scene provides the frontispiece for the book (fig. 2). In uniform and behind the wheel, Joan is scarcely recognizable as a woman. Instead, the ambulance dominates the image and appears as a kind of weapon, with the spray coming off its tires mirroring the star-like exploding shells. Although Joan clearly has the strength of character to negotiate a war zone, her success is also dependent on her ability to operate a machine, a hulking vehicle that counteracts the physical weakness that comes with being a woman. This scene corresponds to a description of the wartime female ambulance driver in a 1916 article from *The Times:* "With her perfected physique, her sharpened brain, her various and potent influence, [she] may indeed be counted in a new sense the *Primum mobile* of the world in the remaking; and in her gracious presence, moulded by the exercises of the playing-fields to a more generous beauty, lies a rich symbolism of promise" (qtd. in Doan 2006, 30). This newspaper article balances its description of the female ambulance driver's physical strength and potency with emphasis on her grace and beauty. Similarly, Joan Mason is presented in the first volume of the "Khaki Girls" series, *The Khaki Girls of the Motor Corps* (1918), as "a veritable picture of girlish grace and loveliness" (31), even after spending the day in blue overalls working on her car. The radical reshaping of gender roles inherent in the image of a girl who can both drive and repair vehicles is overturned, at least in part, by her ability to transform herself, chameleon-like, into a lovely, ultra-feminine young woman whenever the occasion requires it. Grayzel notes that during the war, "[t]he two roles most subversive of gender – female soldiers and male war-resisters – remained anomalous and suspect" (2010, 274). In this context, Joan's effortless transformation from androgynous ambulance driver to pretty girl served to counter any sub-

SETTING HER TEETH, JOAN DROVE THE AMBULANCE
FORWARD.

The Khaki Girls behind the lines   *Page* 142

Figure 2: Frontispiece from Edna Brooks, *The Khaki Girls Behind the Lines* (1918). Collection of the author.

versive subtext in the narrative while also offering the girl reader a figure of identification and a wartime story of her own.

The transformative power of female protagonists' wartime experiences

A key theme that unites the genre of the girls' *Bildungsroman* across national borders is the depiction of a young female protagonist's maturation and growth as she navigates the transitional phase from girlhood to womanhood. Although this theme appears in the wartime literature of all three countries discussed here, the nature of that transformation differs dramatically. British and American fictional girls see the war as a patriotic opportunity for individual growth, action, and achievement. The heroine of Marchant's *A V.A.D. in Salonika*, for example, chastises herself for failing (at her first attempt) to catch a German spy:

> [Joan Haysome] had always wanted to do something really great for her country. She had just yearned to distinguish herself. Here was a chance ready-made for her. She might have caught a spy red-handed and have achieved real renown, but she had failed to seize the opportunity. (1917, 55)

Whereas the desire to "distinguish herself" and "achieve renown" motivates this British heroine's wartime service, fictional German girls experience something very different: war calls them to place country and family before themselves, to subordinate any individual desires to the collective good of the nation. In so doing, they are transformed from self-centered, superficial girls to selfless, patriotic young women.

This transformative process appears in numerous German *Bildungsromane* for girls. In Hofmann's *Deutsche Mädel in großer Zeit*, the main character Ilse has grown up pampered in a wealthy Berlin home. Her brother's friend has loved her for years, but in the months prior to war he grows dismayed by how shallow she has become:

> When Ilse left school, she got caught up in a sea of pleasures, of superficialities. That was not the Ilse he had dreamed of. She knew nothing of duty. She allowed herself to be carried on waves of wealth and lost any depth. She had no idea how that pained him. Sometimes he thought: a storm should come to shake up the youthful soul, to shake it to its very core! (1916, 36)

The storm he longs for is, of course, the war, and not surprisingly, it has the desired effect. But it is not Ilse alone who experiences a transformation, as one of her friends declares: "'War purifies, most definitely, [...] war creates new people, it turns us all over again and again!'" (127). This statement extends to young female readers the idea, asserted early in the conflict in the supposed wave of German enthusiasm known as the "Spirit of 1914," that war would counteract the negative, degenerative effects of modern life by hardening men into fighters (see Verhey, 2000).

An examination of the titles of Anglo-American and German wartime books for girls reveals a contrasting focus on the individual versus the collective. British and American titles often refer to the individual protagonists, the new roles they have assumed during the war, and the places to which they travel: *Munition*

Mary, Pickles: A Red Cross Heroine, A Transport Girl in France, A V.A.D. in Salonika, The Khaki Girls Behind the Lines. The German books, on the other hand, frequently bear abstract titles that express the enormity of war and the expectations for women as a group: *Stille Opfer* (Quiet sacrifice), *Stilles Heldentum* (Quiet heroism), *Daheim in großer Zeit* (At home in great times), *Deutsche Mädel in großer Zeit* (German girls in great times), *Im heiligen Kampf* (In the holy battle). Given that the body of literature written by women and marketed to girls emerged and expanded in concert with the middle-class women's movements in Germany, Britain, and the United States, I would argue that the difference in focus in the Anglo-American and German World War I girls' books could be attributed, at least in part, to differences in the ideological character of those movements. While the American and British women's movements focused on suffrage and other individual rights for women, the German bourgeois women's movement insisted on the positive impact that women's "natural" maternal nature could have on the public sphere and the nation as a whole (see Rowold 2010, 6).

Implicit in the German novels' focus on the national collective is the idea that *modern* girls, in their selfishness and vanity, have contributed to a general crisis in the German nation, one that will only be mitigated through men's sacrifice on the battlefield and women's willingness to embrace once again the values of purity, simplicity, and domesticity. In spite of all the new opportunities for German women that came during World War I, then, in wartime novels for girls, these opportunities are circumscribed by a clear "nationalist-maternalist rhetoric" (Dollard 2006, 213). German women and girls are exhorted to put the needs of their country before themselves, choosing the home over professional advancement and sacrificing any individual ambition for the sake of the nation. To behave otherwise indicates both a lack of femininity and, worse, a lack of patriotism.

These mixed messages regarding women's roles lived on in German society after the war. German women's suffrage, granted in 1918, was born not of a feminist campaign but of revolution, and once in possession of the right to vote, most women cast their ballots for conservative, confessional parties rather than for those that supported women's emancipation (see Sneeringer, 2002). To an extent, the young, single women who experienced the freedoms of New Womanhood during the Weimar era did succeed in refashioning gender identities, but, as historians Renate Bridenthal, Atina Grossmann, and Marion Kaplan write, these New Women were also blamed by conservatives "for everything from the decline of the birth rate and laxity of morals to the unemployment of male workers" (1984, 13). The image of women as selfless mothers serving the nation continued to occupy a central place in political discourse during the Weimar Republic, and, after 1933, it resonated even more strongly in National Socialist ideals of womanhood.

Conclusion

Popular books for girls published during World War I reflect the all-encompassing effects of the war on the populations of the combatant countries. Within the established genre of the girls' *Bildungsroman*, the war led to the creation of new wartime fictional worlds for German, British, and American readers in which girl protagonists contribute to the war effort through various forms of exemplary patriotic service. For British and American heroines, the war expands the boundaries of their worlds, offering them new opportunities to demonstrate a feminine brand of courage and effectiveness. For German protagonists, however, war leads to a contraction of their fictional worlds as the domestic sphere, and the woman within it, are held up as the heart of the nation. These differences between the Anglo-American and German girls' *Bildungsroman* emerge only through a transnational analysis, reminding us that the experience of war – and the way war is written and read – is fundamentally shaped by age, gender, and national identity.

Works Cited

Albert, Emily. *Daheim in großer Zeit* (Verlag von Levy & Müller, 1915).

Brazil, Angela. *A Patriotic Schoolgirl* (Blackie and Son, n.d. [1919]).

Bridenthal, Renate, et al. "Introduction: Women in Weimar and Nazi Germany." *When Biology Became Destiny: Women in Weimar and Nazi Germany*, edited by Bridenthal, et al. (Monthly Review Press, 1984), pp. 1–29.

Brooks, Edna. *The Khaki Girls Behind the Lines* (Cupples & Leon, 1918).

Brooks, Edna. *The Khaki Girls of the Motor Corps* (Cupples & Leon, 1918).

Brooks, Edna. *The Khaki Girls in Victory* (Cupples & Leon, 1920).

Brooks, Edna. *The Khaki Girls at the Windsor Barracks* (Cupples & Leon, 1919).

Chickering, Roger. *The Great War and Urban Life in Germany* (Cambridge UP, 2007).

Chickering, Roger. *Imperial Germany and the Great War, 1914–1918.* 2nd ed. (Cambridge UP, 2004).

Christaller, Helene, et al. *Stille Opfer* (Verlag von Otto Rippel, 1915).

Clément, Berta. *Lebensziele* (Union, n.d. [1907]).

Clement, Bertha. *Morgenrot* (Loewes Verlag Ferdinand Carl, n.d. [1916]).

Daniel, Ute. "Der Krieg der Frauen 1914–18." *"Keiner fühlt sich hier mehr als Mensch...": Erlebnis und Wirkung des Ersten Weltkriegs*, edited by Gerhard Hirschfeld, et al. (Klartext, 1993), pp. 131–150.

Doan, Laura. "Primum Mobile: Women and Auto-mobility in the Era of the Great War." *Women: A Cultural Review*, vol. 17, no. 1 (2006), pp. 26–41.

Dollard, Catherine. "Marital Status and the Rhetoric of the Women's Movement in World War I Germany." *Women in German Yearbook*, vol. 22 (2006), pp. 211–235.

Frow, John. *Genre* (Routledge, 2015).

Gellert, Wanda. *Stilles Heldentum* (Meidinger, n.d. [1916]).

Girvin, Brenda. *Munition Mary* (Humphrey Milford, n.d. [1918]).

Grayzel, Susan R. *Women and the First World War* (Pearson, 2002).

Grayzel, Susan R. "Women and Men." *A Companion to the First World War*, edited by John Horne (Wiley-Blackwell, 2010), pp. 263–278.

Hamilton-Honey, Emily. *Turning the Pages of American Girlhood: The Evolution of Girls' Series Fiction, 1865–1930* (McFarland, 2013).

Henty, G.T. *To Herat and Cabul: A Story of the First Afghan War* (Blackie and Son, 1902).

Hofmann, Else. *Deutsche Mädel in großer Zeit* (Gustav Fock, n.d. [1916]).

Kenyon, Edith C. *Pickles: A Red-Cross Heroine* (Collins Clear-Type Press, n.d. [1916]).

Klemm, Johanna. *Die wir mitkämpfen* (Interim-Verlag, Adriaan M. van den Broecke, 1916).

Kloerss, Sophie. *Im heiligen Kampf* (Union Deutsche Verlagsgesellschaft, 1915).

Kress, Gunther. "Genre and the Changing Contexts for English Language Arts." *Language Arts*, vol. 76, no. 6 (1999), pp. 461–469.

Marchant, Bessie. *A Girl Munition Worker* (Blackie and Son, n.d. [1916]).

Marchant, Bessie. *A Transport Girl in France* (Blackie and Son, n.d. [1919]).

Marchant, Bessie. *A V.A.D. in Salonika* (Blackie and Son, n.d. [1917]).

Miller, Carolyn R. "Genre as Social Action." *Quarterly Journal of Speech*, vol. 70 (1984), pp. 151–167.

Mitchell, Sally. *The New Girl: Girls' Culture in England, 1880–1915* (Columbia UP, 1995).

Neiberg, Michael S. "Toward a Transnational History of World War I." *Canadian Military History*, vol. 17, no. 3 (2008), pp. 31–37.

Niese, Charlotte. *Barbarentöchter* (Verlag von Georg Wigand, n.d. [1915]).

Romalov, Nancy Tillman. "Mobile Heroines: Early Twentieth-Century Girls' Automobile Series." *Journal of Popular Culture*, vol. 28, no. 4 (2005), pp. 231–243.

Rowold, Katharina. *The Educated Woman: Minds, Bodies, and Women's Higher Education in Britain, Germany, and Spain, 1865–1914* (Routledge, 2010).

Schönberger, Bianca. "Motherly Heroines and Adventurous Girls: Red Cross Nurses and Women Army Auxiliaries in the First World War." *Home/Front: The Military, War and Gender in Twentieth-Century Germany*, edited by Karen Hagemann and Stefanie Schüler-Springorum (Berg, 2002), pp. 87–113.

Sneeringer, Julia. *Winning Women's Votes: Propaganda and Politics in Weimar Germany* (U of North Carolina P, 2002).

Stoneley, Peter. *Consumerism and American Girls' Literature, 1860–1940* (Cambridge UP, 2003).

Todorov, Tzvetan. *Mikhail Bakhtin: The Dialogical Principle*. Translated by Wlad Godzich (U of Minnesota P, 1984).

Trent, Martha. *Helen Carey: Somewhere in America* (Goldsmith, 1918).

Ury, Else. *Nesthäkchen*. 10 vols. (Meidinger, 1913–1925).

Ury, Else. *Das Ratstöchterlein zu Rothenburg* (A. Anton & Co., n.d. [1917]).

Verhey, Jeffrey. *The Spirit of 1914: Militarism, Myth and Mobilization in Germany* (Cambridge UP, 2000).

Winter, Jay, editor. *The Cambridge History of the First World War*. 3 vols. (Cambridge UP, 2014).

Cindy Walter-Gensler

Käte Kestien's *Als die Männer im Graben lagen*

WWI Criticism through the Lens of Motherhood

> "They were just all out of their minds, the sons, the teachers, the fathers – all of them. Only the mothers saw how it really was; they sensed how it would turn out. How it did turn out."
> (Clara Viebig, *Töchter der Hekuba*[1])

Literary responses to WWI exist in abundance, and much has been written about the literature of this "war to end all wars." Yet, as has been decried by past scholars, criticism makes little reference to German women's writing on this subject,[2] and if it does, it primarily views the works of bourgeois or aristocratic authors as relevant to the topic (e. g., Catherine O'Brien and Hans-Otto Binder). One example is the more recent research of literary critic Andre Kagelmann on Thea von Harbou (2009; 2014), as well as historian Silke Fehlemann's study that focuses on writers such as Margarethe Böhme (1867–1939) and Ida Boy-Ed (1852–1928), who, in telling stories of their own social and class-bound background, thematize war-related issues of "bourgeois families that have connections and kinship relations all through Europe" (2014, 75). Further reflecting the social status of socioeconomically privileged women, novels about nurses on the front line, positions held predominantly by single, upper-class females,[3] became an extremely popular genre.[4] In contrast, writers rarely focused on the experiences

---

1 All translations from German into English are my own unless otherwise stated. Originals significant for my argument can be found in notes following the translations: "Sie waren eben alle nicht bei Sinnen gewesen, die Söhne nicht, die Lehrer nicht, die Väter nicht – alle nicht. Nur die Mütter sahen, wie es wirklich war; die ahnten wie es kommen würde. Gekommen war" (Viebig 1917, 150).

2 In their introduction to *Intimate Enemies: English and German Literary Reactions to the Great War 1914–1918* (1993), Franz Karl Stanzel and Martin Löschnigg write, "Much remains to be done, however, in an assessment of the share of [German] women writers in Great War literature" (35). Ironically then, only one of their volume's twenty-eight essays features novels by female German authors, namely Walter Hölbing's contribution "'Cultural Paradigms' and the 'Gendered Eye': World War I in the Works of U.S. and German-Language Women Authors," which discusses two novels by Hedwig Courths-Mahler and Ina Seidel.

3 See Schönberger (2002) on the social backgrounds of German nurses in WWI, especially 88–89.

4 Bestselling novels of this category are, for instance, Anny Wothe's *Die den Weg bereiten: Ein Zeitroman* (Those who prepare the way: A novel of its time, 1916), Adrienne Thomas' *Die Katrin*

https://doi.org/10.1515/9783110572001-011

of working-class women in fictional narratives about WWI.[5] Moreover, as literary scholar Binder notes, "although the war is presented almost exclusively as an evil" (1997, 112), realistic depictions of its devastating effects on the home front are often missing in these written accounts. Binder suggests that female authors frequently utilized the war as an adventurous backdrop for romantic plots (114), as, above all, the era's immensely popular books by German novelist Hedwig Courths-Mahler (1867–1950) illustrate,[6] despite her working-class roots (Sarkowicz and Mentzer 2011, 198). And yet, as this essay will demonstrate, novels by women writers of proletarian or working-class origin[7] – I use the terms interchangeably here when referring to a socioeconomic class of wage earners whose living depends largely on manual labor – as well as works by female authors voicing the realistic and often negative wartime experiences of their peers do exist. Moreover, they contribute significantly to a more complex representation of women's experience of WWI and add a new layer to our understanding of German maternal pacifism in the 1930s.

To simultaneously address the largely-overlooked area of female German working-class novelists and women's literary representations that reflect critically on WWI rather than romanticizing it, I provide a historically contextualized close reading of the novel *Als die Männer im Graben lagen* (When our men lay in the trenches, 1935) by the German author Käte Kestien, pseudonym for Maria Margarethe Harder (1898–1936). Unlike many of her bourgeois and upper-class peers, Kestien narrates the story of a nameless married working-class mother who has to balance difficult and dangerous work in an ammunitions factory with tending to her family, while her husband Franz is off fighting

---

wird Soldat (*Katrin Becomes a Soldier*, 1930) or Meta Scheele's *Frauen im Krieg* (Women in war, 1930). For a more detailed discussion of the literary representation of nurses and further examples see Veth 1995, 457, as well as O'Brien 1997, 27 and 45. See also Margaret Higonnet's essay in this volume.

5 According to O'Brien, Clara Viebig marks an exception in this context. She not only portrays, but "treats working-class characters seriously and with sympathy" in her novels (1997, 53). Moreover, Binder mentions the works of Nanny Lambrecht as depicting proletarians (1997, 110). Yet in both cases, these characters appear mostly at the margins, while the main protagonists share Viebig and Lambrecht's bourgeois background.

6 Walter Hölbing comes to the same conclusion as Binder, arguing that the works by Courths-Mahler – and this also applies to Ina Seidel – thus do not adopt "a critical or alternative" view on the war, but rather like their male colleagues "perpetuate conventional concepts of glorious warfare and individual heroism" (1993, 458).

7 In this context, see also Sabine Hake's *The Proletarian Dream: Socialism, Culture, and Emotion in Germany, 1863–1933* (2017), which likewise highlights the existence of a forgotten archive of a wide range of artwork produced by and in the name of the working class.

the war. In doing so, the author "recalls in evocative detail the many aspects of hardship endured by German women," at the home front, as noted in the British anthology *Women's Writing on the First World War* (Cardinal et al. 1999, 114), which features a short, translated excerpt of Kestien's book. Strikingly, critical reviews of war literature by German female authors largely ignore Kestien or devote only a short side note to the fact that her novel portrays the burdens of proletarian mothers in wartime (Veth 1995, 458). In my reading of the novel, however, this content is exactly what sets apart *Als die Männer im Graben lagen* from the great many narratives by middle- and upper-class novelists who thematize women's WWI experiences. As my analysis will show, the novel is significant precisely because it provides a new critical perspective on the experience of working-class mothers during WWI. Additionally, Kestien's representation of the dire effects of war becomes a powerful narrative of remembrance.

A close reading alone might not immediately reveal Kestien's work as an antiwar narrative. But an interdisciplinary approach that takes into consideration the novel's publication date and Kestien's larger cultural work underscores the novel's antiwar missive, especially when compared to Ina Seidel's (1885–1974) tremendously popular novel *Das Wunschkind* (*The Wish Child*, 1930). While Kestien's work is the main focus of my examination, Seidel's novel, which glorifies the sacrifices of mothers in wartime, serves as an important counter point to Kestien, who utilizes the figure of the mother to criticize war. *Als die Männer im Graben lagen* was written after the devastating outcome of WWI and during a time when new conflicts during the Third Reich were surfacing. The novel thus serves as a warning of the hardships and the effects of war on civilians, specifically on proletarian mothers, an emphasis which probably allowed for the work to be published and successfully distributed in 1935, despite its negative portrayal of WWI and its implicit pacifist message. Under the veil of portraying women who appear to fulfill their social and moral duties as self-sacrificing mothers by becoming silent heroines who serve the fatherland – women's ideal social role as promoted by National Socialists and by Seidel in her bestseller – Kestien was able to publish her book and circumvent Nazi censorship, even though Germany was well on its way in preparing for war. Kestien's work not only passed censors by superficially echoing National Socialists' ideals of motherhood, the novel was even praised and marketed as "the German woman's *Iliad*" (Maier 1935, 36), thereby finding its way to a broad reading public. Taking into account the representation of class and considering the historical context of 1935 and its promotion of motherhood, my interdisciplinary analysis of *Als die Männer im Graben lagen* explores Kestien's critique of war through the lens of motherhood in the tradition of Clara Viebig's *Töchter der Hekuba* (*Daughters of Hecuba*, 1917).[8]

Käte Kestien: A working-class critic of WWI

The social and cultural context of the production of Kestien's novel is critical to understanding the author's agenda and the significance of her work as an anti-war manifesto. Therefore, I will briefly provide some biographical information about the author and discuss the sociopolitical and economic circumstances that Kestien responded to in her depiction of motherhood and the Great War before moving to my textual analysis.

Maria Margarethe Harder, who wrote under the pseudonym of Käte Kestien, was born in 1898 in a village in Schleswig-Holstein. As one of six children of a housemaid and a day laborer, she grew up in poverty (Wedel 2010, 406). Unfortunately, little is known about her youth and early adulthood, other than that she did not receive an education beyond grade school. Similarly little is known about Harder's specific experiences of WWI, except that she moved from one occupation to the next as opportunities presented themselves. Whether working as a prison warden or as a journalist for the liberal *Hamburger Fremdenblatt* (Tramitz 1991, 311), she remained committed to advancing the cause of the socioeconomically underprivileged. Her personal experiences of losing several family members in WWI contributed to her becoming a pacifist.

Harder's political engagement culminated in 1929, when she moved to Berlin and became the managing director of the Social Democratic Party's (SPD) in-house film production company, which produced and distributed party-sponsored films. During this time she also wrote articles for the popular women's magazine *Frauenwelt* (Women's world), a weekly publication for proletarian women sponsored by the SPD. Furthermore, Harder published film reviews in Social-Democratic papers, and directed two of the SPD's own productions, the documentary *Der Weg einer Proletarierin* (A proletarian's way, 1929) and the film *Lohnbuchhalter Kremke* (Payroll clerk Kremke, 1930), both centering on the exploitation of workers (Tramitz 1991, 311). Contemporary reviewers such as Siegfried Kracauer praised her work as a filmmaker, particularly for her realistic depictions of class differences and social injustices (Böhme 1981, 184–185).

---

8 Recalling the ignored yet accurate prophecies of Cassandra, daughter of queen Hecuba of Troy, Viebig's antiwar novel centers on the unheeded warnings of mothers, predicting WWI's horrible outcome. Her focus on the hardships of women with children at the home front pioneered the perspective of mothers criticizing WWI, which Kestien's book emulates.

Harder was also part of the federal board of the *Arbeiter-Lichtspiel-Bund*, the Cinema Worker's Union (Wedel 2010, 406). Owing allegedly to financial delinquency she lost both her positions in 1931. It is unknown whether she then decided to take on the pseudonym Käte Kestien in reaction to this scandal or out of fear of being prosecuted by the Nazis as a political opponent.

Regardless of the motive for taking on a pseudonym, Harder published her only novel, *Als die Männer im Graben lagen*, as Käte Kestien with the Societäts Verlag in Frankfurt am Main in 1935. Shortly thereafter, she died under mysterious circumstances in a plane crash in March 1936, near Popocatépetl, Mexico (Wedel 2010, 407). Kestien was soon forgotten, especially as few written records about her exist. As a social critic of her times, the specific challenges of female workers appear as a narrative thread in Harder/Kestien's oeuvre, as can be seen in her numerous articles in *Frauenwelt* and her films. Her novel, therefore, must be read as a continuation of her work and as a reminder of the many casualties of war, gender and class-bound suffering. Under the veneer of glorified representations of self-sacrificing motherhood, lies a nuanced critique of war and the roles women play in wartime that sharply contrasts with the predominantly uncritical war literature featuring mothers.

With the beginning of WWI, when male family members began to serve at the front, their roles within the family were often necessarily supplanted by older daughters, mothers, or wives, who had to become the heads of a household, as historians document.[9] Particularly working-class family incomes drastically decreased because of men's missing incomes. Wartime supplementary payments to soldiers' families fell far short of their needs for survival (Daniel 1989, 29). As a result, women with children who previously had not worked outside the home or the family farm tried to take on gainful employment to supplement the family income (Frevert 1989, 155), instead of performing tasks like sewing or washing for others that they could do at home. In this way, scarcely or totally unremunerated "invisible" female employment on farms and in households relocated working women to "visible" occupations with salaries in jobs often formerly held by men, including factory work (Daniel 1989, 35). Like Kestien, women learned to do jobs for which they had not been previously trained.

Still, due to their limited financial resources in combination with unequal pay and the increasing scarcity of goods, German working-class women and their children experienced growing hardships during WWI (Daniel 1989, 30). They faced ex-

---

9 See for instance Erika Kuhlman's *Of Little Comfort: War Widows, Fallen Soldiers, and the Remaking of the Nation after the First World War* (2012), as well as Frevert 1989, 153–155 and Daniel, 1989, 27. Moreover, Jennifer Redmann's essay in this volume also illustrates the reflection of these shifting gender roles in the novels of the period.

treme shortages of housing,[10] medicine, clothes, and especially food during and after the war, particularly after the allies' economic blockade prevented the import of food and raw materials that Germany depended on (Davis 2000, 22–23). As a result, working-class mothers often suffered from weakened immune systems because of inadequate diets, poor living conditions, and extreme exhaustion due to working long hours under horrible conditions (Daniel 1993, 135). In addition to managing their households and finding food, working-class women were consequently more prone to diseases like tuberculosis and pneumonia (Davis 2000, 184). Like their mothers, many proletarian children suffered from malnourishment often connected to a lack of fat intake,[11] life-threatening diseases, or the lack of a sufficiently warm environment (Davis 2000, 186).

Working-class women and their children experienced the material hardships of the war to a larger extent than their bourgeois and aristocratic counterparts who enjoyed greater financial resources and better overall living conditions throughout the war (Mommsen 2001, 131). Despite the efforts of working-class mothers to survive and take care of their families, conservative media during and after the war frequently blamed these hard-working *Kriegerfrauen*, the wives of soldiers, for neglecting their offspring, cheating on their soldier husbands, having extravagant wishes, and, most of all, being too critical of the war and of the authorities (Daniel 1989, 272). In contrast, magazines and newspapers praised women of the middle and upper classes for suffering silently and bravely. Narratives by bourgeois and aristocratic writers likewise portrayed the wartime struggles of middle- and upper-class females more favorably, as Binder, O'Brien, and Fehlemann discuss. Kestien's narrative, in contrast, presents the unvarnished, grim social and physical realities working-class families with fewer resources experienced during WWI.

Told from the perspective of the oldest daughter of a family of eight children, who, unlike her siblings, is given no name, Kestien's novel illustrates the daily challenges of working-class mothers in a rural area whose children grow up impoverished during wartime. While male family members are called to the front, the nameless mother in the story stays behind to run the small family farm and large household, and to raise her children singlehandedly. Without enough family members left – only her daughters and the youngest son are still with her – the mother is no longer able to maintain the farm. About two years into the war, the family is forced to move to the city to live with relatives. The mother and her

---

10 As Daniel demonstrates, many *Kriegerfamilien* had to move in with relatives, mainly because they could not afford rent anymore (1993, 135).

11 See especially Davis's chapter on the "Battles over Butter" (2000, 76–92).

oldest daughter, who has turned eighteen, accept any opportunity to work. Yet despite working, they still cannot afford to buy enough food for the family. The younger daughter Christel consequently dies of malnutrition. The oldest daughter, who now works in an ammunitions factory, marries and soon welcomes a baby boy. Yet this child will never know his father, who like all but one male family member dies in battle. By the close of the novel, WWI has officially ended, but the surviving characters who return to their former rural home never are able to overcome the suffering and losses caused by the war.

Similar to Erich Maria Remarque's novel *Im Westen nichts Neues* (*All Quiet on the Western Front*, 1929), Kestien's *Als die Männer im Graben lagen* must be understood as a critical take on the romanticization and glorification of war often found in the works of fiction by economically privileged female authors during or shortly after WWI. With her empathic focus on working-class mothers, Kestien provides a counter perspective, for instance, to Seidel's popular book *Das Wunschkind* about an aristocratic widow who raises her son alone in wartime. While Kestien depicts WWI and Seidel the Napoleonic Wars (1803–1815), this difference is unimportant regarding the novels' messages, either criticizing or supporting war.[12] Contrary to Kestien, Seidel's novel intertwines war and motherhood by stressing women's "natural" roles as mothers of future soldiers, who show greatness in accepting the deaths of their sons on the battlefield as a necessary sacrifice for the greater good of the German nation. Seidel saw her book as "a tree, which a German mother has planted in the name of uncountable sisters, to honor and remember fallen German sons" (1934, 190). While Seidel's novel sold fewer than 50,000 copies between 1930 and 1932, it became a bestseller almost instantly after 1933, in no small part due to both her publisher's and the Nazi party's extensive marketing efforts of the novel as an example of "good" *völkisch* (racial-nationalistic) literature.[13] Moreover, the reception of *Das Wunschkind* was very positive from the first day of its publication, with critics calling it a

---

12 The example of Bertha von Suttner's pacifist novel *Die Waffen nieder!* (*Lay Down Your Arms*, 1889), likewise centering on various past wars, but with a profound influence on the era's discussion of war in general, also underscores that it is not important which war the author incorporates in order for the reader to understand the message. See Shelley Rose's chapter in this volume.

13 A brochure distributed by the publisher Deutsche Verlags-Anstalt Stuttgart advertised the printing of the 50th thousand in 1933. By 1944, nine new editions of *Das Wunschkind* had been printed, with 440,000 copies sold. See Bestand Ina Seidel, Grey Folder X: Seidel, Ina: "Verlagsmitteilungen," Deutsches Literatur Archiv Marbach. For more detailed information on the marketing of the book, see Barbian 2011, 65.

"great, timeless woman's novel."[14] By the time Kestien wrote *Als die Männer im Graben lagen*, Seidel had already become a household name and her narrative that glorified battle and the sacrifices women endure during wartime – accepting the death of loved ones without complaint – resounded throughout Nazi Germany.[15]

Given the scope of Seidel's popular reception, it is safe to assume that Kestien was familiar with the content of Seidel's novel as well as its success with National Socialist critics and readers alike. As an experienced writer and reviewer, Kestien must also have been aware that following a similar scheme in producing a book centered on motherhood, war, and sacrifice held the promise of any author to earn acclaim similar to Seidel. Kestien, however, had to deceive censors and critics by passing off a critical antiwar narrative as popular women's literature. While the Nazis had already banned other novels critiquing WWI, including Viebig's *Töchter der Hekuba*,[16] the socialist Kestien successfully published her narrative in 1935 with the same critical stance toward society and political authority that can be found in her earlier films. I will now turn to the novel itself in order to illustrate how Kestien's careful design balances social criticism in ways that set it apart from Seidel's book and those of other upper-class novelists who glorify WWI, and war in general, and the ideal of the *Heldenmutter*, the hero mother who not only gives birth to (war) heroes, but who herself is heroic.

Public identification with proletarian mothers in wartime

Kestien's 1935 novel *Als die Männer im Graben lagen* highlights the difficult situation of proletarian mothers during WWI immediately on its opening page:

> Back then, when the men lay in the trenches, women filled in for them everywhere. Any kind of work that men suddenly had to put down, women learned to carry out [...]. And all their other daily tasks remained as well. They made use of the nights and still did not get it done. During the day, they worried about their children at home or on the streets, and their scant sleep was disrupted by their sorrows about the husbands and the brothers

---

14 See "Zum 65. Geburtstag der Dichterin Ina Seidel." *Die Welt* 14 Sept. 1950, which can be found in Bestand Ina Seidel, Grey Folder X: Seidel, Ina: "Mediendokumentation": Deutsches Literatur Archiv Marbach.
15 For a detailed discussion of Seidel's narrative in relation to its reception see Krusche 2011, 14–18.
16 See O'Brien 1997, 52–53.

and the sons in the field. Then hunger was added, and now for the women every hour became a sometimes superhuman struggle with despair. (5)[17]

Taking over the jobs of the men gone to war, in addition to their own tasks at home, while learning to survive with minimal sleep and food, all mothers in Kestien's book appear to be endowed with an extraordinary resilience to meet the challenges of daily life.

That this working-class mother is no exception, but instead represents the fate of many women who also dealt with the double burden of working mothers in wartime, is underscored by the fact that the maternal protagonist remains nameless – like her oldest daughter who over the course of the novel replaces her role – while all other characters have names. Praised and marketed as "the story of the unknown mother of the Great War" ("Die Geschichte der unbekannten Mutter im Weltkrieg" 1935, 2), Kestien's novel appears on the surface to serve as a literary monument to brave, nameless mothers, who had to fight like the soldiers at the front for survival, but whose stories had not been told. Yet her narrative depicting WWI serves to remind her readers of the devastating effects of war in a time when Nazi Germany was becoming increasingly militarized. The novel must be understood as a warning and a call to reason to prevent further suffering and social injustice, by focusing on the female population.

By depicting the heroic efforts of working-class women to balance their various roles, Kestien's novel sheds light on how class and motherhood influence the experiences of women during a war designed by an imperial government that did not value them. In particular, the author emphasizes that the main protagonists – and all the working-class women they stand for – suffer especially from total war, which is warfare designed to embattle civilians. Unlike their bourgeois counterparts, who, according to one protagonist manage to maintain households "in which people still lived splendidly" (170), these nameless women cannot even rest when they are sick. For instance, a female coworker in the ammunitions factory where Kestien's heroine finds employment after moving to the city, declines going to the hospital, although she is severely injured in a work-related accident. Not only does she fear the loss of the income she de-

---

17 "Damals, als die Männer im Graben lagen, sind Frauen an allen Stellen für sie eingesprungen. Jegliche Arbeit, die die Männer so plötzlich aus den Händen legen mußten, lernten die Frauen verrichten [. . .]. Und all ihr anderes Tagwerk blieb ihnen auch. Sie nahmen die Nächte zuhilfe und wurden doch nicht fertig. Sie bangten am Tage um die Kinder zu Hause oder auf der Straße, und der notdürftige Schlaf wurde ihnen zerrissen durch die Sorge um die Männer und die Brüder und die Söhne im Feld. Dann kam der Hunger noch dazu, und nun war jede Stunde der Frauen ein manchmal übermenschliches Ringen mit der Not."

pends on, but she would have nobody to look after her four children while recovering in a clinic (134). Similarly, when the narrator herself suffers from pneumonia, she continues to work until she collapses. But even then, she begs the doctor who has been called, "Make me healthy again soon, doctor! You know how it is: being sick is a luxury poor people cannot afford, it's the most certain way to fall into dire straits" (258).[18] For Kestien's characters, the motivation to work is thus not ambition, patriotism, or emancipation, as the media often proclaimed during and after WWI, but sheer survival. The novel thus evokes a class-consciousness that is absent in middle- or upper-class accounts of the home front.

Resting when it is most needed is not the only "luxury" proletarian mothers cannot afford. The main protagonist listens in disbelief to a childless friend who explains how busy the hairdresser is, in spite of the war (192). "The loss of beauty," that is, the diminished physical attractiveness resulting from wartime conditions, is, as Elisabeth Domansky argues, another recurring theme in *Als die Männer im Graben lagen* (1997, 440). In Kestien's novel it is almost exclusively young single, albeit working-class women who are able to afford this "luxury" (192). For a working-class mother, like the main character, such an expenditure is unthinkable, as she has to put every penny towards buying food for the numerous mouths she has to feed. Consequently, poor women like herself inevitably appear "spent" and "haggard" (40).

When working-class mothers in Kestien's novel have some free time, usually only on a Sunday afternoon, they are unable to relax or find time for themselves because they must catch up on household chores or attend to their family's needs. Working day and night, they are shown to suffer from extreme exhaustion. Kestien's protagonists preferably take on nightshifts in factories (133) that pay more and allow them to be home in the daytime, so that they, for instance, can take their babies to the park to let them enjoy much-needed fresh air and sunlight (191). Oftentimes unable to stay awake because of a constant lack of sleep, the mother learns of a system of attaching one end of a string to the baby carriage, and the other end to her foot so that she can lie in the grass and sleep (194). Here Kestien again illustrates the kind of exhaustion the war causes particularly for proletarian mothers, something that sets them apart from their single peers as well as from middle- and upper-class mothers.

Not surprisingly, another character who works in the ammunitions factory states that the soldiers at the front actually have better living conditions than working women with children like her on the home front:

---

18 "Machen Sie mich schnell wieder gesund, Herr Doktor! Sie wissen doch: für arme Leute ist Kranksein ein Luxus, durch den sie am sichersten in Not geraten!"

[F]or the soldier things will come to an end eventually! Either he gets killed or not! If he gets killed, he rests in peace! If he doesn't get killed, then he gets to leave the battlefield for some time in between fighting. But who relieves us here at home or here [in the factory] even for only one hour? Who? Who? Nobody! And nobody cooks a thick pea soup with bacon for our children and us [...] as the soldier always can count on! (163)[19]

The outlook for proletarian mothers at the home front is bleak. They never have a "break," and Kestien even suggests that they are worse off than the soldiers at the front. In this passage she casts the dire situation of her protagonists on the home front in very similar ways to Viebig's *Töchter der Hekuba*, where a poor, hungry working-class female confronts an aristocrat: "What do you think, my lady, what is more difficult? To lie in the trenches, or to sit inside here, with absolutely no end in sight? One of those [soldiers] naturally knows: Soon a grenade will come, and then I'm gone [...] But we – ?" (1917, 218).[20] Both narratives equally underscore that there is nothing heroic about poor women suffering from the negative effects of the war at home. Rather, they experience such desperation that they envy the soldiers facing death on the front. Kestien's novel counters representations popular in the press and in the majority of novels by female bourgeois and aristocratic authors that cast working-class *Kriegerfrauen* during and after WWI as supposedly longing for extravagant conditions.

After the war had already taken the lives of three of the protagonist's soldier sons, Kestien describes the heart-wrenching sense of despair when the youngest daughter Christel dies from malnutrition (182), despite her mother's continuous efforts to save her by letting the child have her mother's butter rations. With this plot development, the author illustrates that the brutality and inhumanity of war does not stop at the front line, but also kills innocent civilians at home. The mother anguishes: "I felt a dull pain, now that I could gaze at her sunken face with time and knew that she had died from the war. The butter bowl I promised her, the butter bowl, which should never have been empty, that would have

---

19 "[F]ür den Soldaten hat die Sache doch mal ein Ende! Es erwischt ihn oder nicht! Erwischt es ihn, so hat er Ruhe! Erwischt es ihn nicht, so kommt er mal inzwischen und mal ganz raus aus dem Manöver. Wer aber löst uns hier zu Hause oder hier [in der Fabrik] auch nur für eine Stunde ab? Wer? Wer? Niemand! Und niemand kocht unseren Kindern oder uns mal eine dicke Erbsensuppe mit Speck [. . .] wie sie dem Soldaten immer sicher ist!"
20 "Was glauben Sie wohl, meine Dame, was schwerer ist? Im Schützengraben liegen oder hier so drinne sitzen, daß man überhaupt kein Ende von absieht? So einer weiß doch: Nu kommt gleich 'ne Granate, und dann bin ich weg [. . .] Aber wir – ?"

kept our Christel alive" (183).[21] To highlight the casualties of war who are forgotten or obscured in heroic nationalist rhetoric, Kestien explicitly states that the war and the resulting food shortage are responsible for the girl's death, something that could have been prevented in peacetime when the family lived in the country. In doing so, the author elicits sympathy from the reader, who is compelled to empathize with the mourning mother who has to bury another child. Kestien's maternal heroine, however, cannot accept the death of Christel as a necessary sacrifice of a mother in wartime. This is exactly where Kestien's novel sharply contrasts with Seidel's *Das Wunschkind*, which suggests that all children must be expendable in wartime and that it is "natural" for women to suppress their own feelings for the greater good of the German nation at all costs.

While the opening paragraph of Seidel's 1930 bestseller casts its heroine Cornelie as a nurturing mother, tending to her seriously ill infant (Part 1: 7), the narrative voice informs the reader, when the child dies soon afterward, that the protagonist, "a soul of superhuman strength" (Part 1: 15),[22] suddenly feels "empty of all wishes, except the will to fertility" (Part 1: 20).[23] Several things about this plot twist and the construction of this phrase are noteworthy, beginning with the usage of "wishes" versus "will." The noun *wish* refers to an unarticulated personal desire as opposed to the noun *will* as the formulated and eventually enforced action to fulfill a desire. As we know, the term "will" becomes a critical word for Nazi propaganda and planning. Cornelie is thus presented as active and able to achieve what she wants, yet without ego-driven personal desires. Seidel additionally underscores this notion as she refrains here from communicating through Cornelie's own narrative voice, replacing the personal "I" perspective with the impersonal narrator's point of view. In this respect, connecting fertility to will (and the nation's future) allows Seidel to emphasize individuals' agency when it comes to reproduction, but without phrasing it as a personal desire. Seidel's strategic use of words and narrative voice foreshadow Gertrud Scholtz-Klink's later famous call, "Say to yourselves, 'I am the *Volk*.' The tiny individual self [ich] must submit to the greater you [Du]" (qtd. in Koonz 1987, 178). That is, Seidel suggests women should not act selfishly, but rather assume their "natural" role as mothers of as many children as possible, sacrificing their personal wants for the German nation's needs regarding procreation and producing

---

21 "Ein nagender Schmerz fiel mich an, wie ich jetzt mit Zeit ihr eingefallenes Gesicht betrachten konnte und wußte, daß sie am Krieg gestorben war. Der Butternapf, den ich ihr versprach, der Butternapf, der nie leer werden sollte, der hätte unsere Christel am Leben gehalten."
22 "eine Seele von übermenschlicher Kraft."
23 "leer von allen Wünschen bis auf den einen Willen zur Fruchtbarkeit."

a *Volk*. From its very beginning, then, Seidel's novel, in contrast to Kestien's work, links the image of nurturing and self-sacrificing mothers for the state and a "good" woman's natural duty to bear children for this state.

This perhaps explains why Cornelie seduces her husband the same night her first son dies. Seidel signals to the reader in this passage that a woman's reproductive function and her "will to fertility" are her most important contributions to the society in times of both peace and war. Since Cornelie indeed becomes pregnant again (Part 1: 20), Seidel emphasizes the triumph of the protagonist's "will" in making her "wish" for another son come true. To replace one child with the next also highlights not only subordination of personal feelings for the benefit of the nation, but also how readily the state is willing to replace individuals in the service to a greater cause, a stance very different from Kestien's.

When Cornelie learns that this second son, Christoph, who becomes a soldier like his father and grandfather before him, dies on the battlefield (Part 2: 479), she again displays no emotional reaction and refrains from any criticism of the war. Unlike the officer who was her son's friend and who cannot hold back his tears when informing her about Christoph's death, Cornelie calmly remarks: "you keep on fighting, and we keep on suffering" (Part 2: 482).[24] Yet while she recognizes the pain of women, including herself, losing their family members due to war, she makes clear that this is the supposed circle of life that will only be broken on Judgment Day: "Then the son puts the crown on his mother's head" (Part 2: 483),[25] and she is rewarded for her sacrifices.

By contrast, Kestien's mother figure cannot overcome the emotional wounds caused by the death of her children. Her grief is agonizing and she has no desire to instantly reproduce to replace her dead children with new ones – more children who also would suffer and be killed for the state's ambitions. The author's critical and pacifist stance does not allow her heroine to buy into politics that readily replace individuals needed to fuel an eternal machinery of war. Unlike Seidel, Kestien enlists her character's trauma to criticize the war. Different than constructing women as bearers of soldiers, she underscores that the "maternal bond purportedly being one of the primary causes of female pacifism," is a theme that is recurrent in some women writers' more critical responses to the Great War (O'Brien 1997, 30).[26] In Kestien's view it is not "natural" for a mother to silently accept her children's deaths and their own suffering as a contribu-

---

24 "ihr kämpft weiter, und wir leiden weiter."
25 "Dann setzt der Sohn der Mutter die Krone aufs Haupt."
26 See also Julie Shoults's essay in this volume for a discussion of feminist pacifism in the early 1900s and its influence on the works of Hermynia Zur Mühlen (1883–1951), another socialist author who, like Kestien, wrote antiwar literature in the aftermath of World War I.

tion to the war effort, but instead both serve as catalysts to protest against war. For her, there is no need to wait until Judgment Day to end the suffering of mothers; peace would be enough.

An alternative *Heldenmutter* circumventing censorship: Some conclusions

In her article "Vom stillen Heldentum der deutschen Frau im Weltkrieg: Käte Kestien und ihr autobiographischer Roman" (About the German woman's silent heroism during the World War: Käte Kestien and her autobiographical novel, 1991), which, to my knowledge, is the only article written on *Als die Männer im Graben lagen*, historian Angelika Tramitz attempts to answer the question of how this novel was able to pass the Nazi censors, despite its "subversive and antiwar undertones" (314). Tramitz concludes that because the author writes only about the daily challenges women confronted during WWI, censors misread the novel as a heroic monument to German mothers. Furthermore, Tramitz argues that Kestien, although an outspoken opponent of war and its discourse of heroism, failed to write a compelling antiwar book, as critical undertones alone would not suffice. According to Tramitz, the author did not address the question of who is responsible for the war or show the total destruction of all areas of life, both of which, Tramitz asserts, are needed to articulate a clear antiwar message (316).

While I agree with Tramitz that the censors and reviewers clearly "misread" Kestien's novel, my close reading of her work suggests that the author intended for them to do so. The book probably would not have been published had she either chosen to portray the brutality of WWI on the battlefield instead of its effects on women and children at home or pointed directly at those responsible for wartime suffering, further politicizing the narrative. The same can be assumed had she intended to strengthen the analogy of the home front with battle lines. By concentrating on the representation of the suffering and sacrifice of proletarian mothers during WWI, Kestien could have used Tramitz's exact arguments, claiming she did not write an antiwar narrative because the war on the battlefield never appears in the novel. Moreover, when the socialist author Kestien plays with images of heroic mothers in wartime, her style may appear "without literary merit" (Tramitz 1991, 312), but in the context of National Socialist censorship it can also be read as a carefully designed and well-chosen strategy to appeal to Nazi critics and pass as a novel similar to Seidel's *Das Wunschkind*, while at the same time underscoring the negative implications of any war on civilians, particularly working-class women and their children.

Given the evidence presented in my analysis of her novel and given Kestien's professional background as a successful filmmaker, writer, and reviewer, I propose that the National Socialist "misreading" and subsequent marketing of her novel as a "good book" in 1935 was no coincidence. The pacifist author Kestien wanted her novel to represent the fallacy of war as a solution to national objectives to reach a broad audience, and she knew how to achieve this. By writing and reminding her readers in 1935, about the everyday challenges women experienced during WWI, the author does not actually construct a literary monument for them, as one male reviewer claimed at the time (Maier 1935, 36), but instead reifies her novel's antiwar message during a time Nazi Germany was preparing for the next world war. Through emphasizing the helplessness of mothers to prevent the suffering and death of the most innocent, their children, Kestien demonstrates that these women are not heroes in the sense of displaying exceptional powers. Instead of glorifying these women's supposedly heroic efforts, as suggested in Seidel's novel, the images of desperation that Kestien offers speak particularly to the female readers who lived through WWI. I therefore concur with Tramitz that there are no heroes in *Als die Männer im Graben lagen* (1991, 311).

In my reading of *Als die Männer im Graben lagen*, the unheroic underscores the true nature of war and the author's antiwar stance. Even without scenes from the front, the author reveals the brutality and inhumanity of war as much as, for instance, Remarque's *Im Westen nichts Neues*. Kestien's novel highlights proletarian mothers' share of the national grief and loss; its strict focus on the experience of working-class women with children on the home front represents the "truth" of war, because as Viebig stated nearly two decades earlier towards the end of WWI, mothers "saw how it [war] really was" (1917, 150). Kestien's narrative highlights the agony these women endured, an agony no less overpowering than that suffered by the men in the trenches, but exacerbated by the utter neglect of their needs, as they helped to support the war through their labor. Thus, by presenting realistic depictions of proletarian mothers' experiences on the home front, Kestien effectively criticizes WWI through the lens of motherhood.[27]

In doing so, Kestien simultaneously stresses that working-class women suffered to a greater extent than popular representations of them by their bourgeois or aristocratic counterparts would acknowledge. Working-class women are not only challenged emotionally, but also physically destroyed in Kestien's literary

---

27 For a similar stance expressed in Käthe Kollwitz's artwork on war and motherhood see Martina Kolb's essay in this volume.

representation of WWI. This sets her text apart from works by female authors of the middle- and upper-classes that seemingly ignore this reality. In articulating what her proletarian peers had to live through from 1914–1918, Kestien's narrative opens up a new perspective on the German home front within the genre of war literature by women, further expanding its established canon.

Als die Männer im Graben lagen serves not only as an example of a female working-class author's perspective on WWI, but also, and perhaps equally important, it invites further research on texts that have lapsed into obscurity and deserve reexamination, particularly regarding practices of politically oppositional women writers using popular aesthetics and discourses in order to promote their own, subversive messages. Writing for the censor requires readers to see what is not said as much as what is.

Works Cited

Barbian, Jan-Pieter. "'Ich gehöre auch zu diesen Idioten': Ina Seidel im Dritten Reich." *Ina Seidel: Eine Literatin im Nationalsozialismus*, edited by Anja Hesse (Kadmos, 2011), pp. 31–84.

Binder, Hans-Otto. "Zum Opfern bereit: Kriegsliteratur von Frauen." *Kriegserfahrungen: Studien zur Sozial- und Mentalitätsgeschichte des Ersten Weltkrieges*, edited by Gerhard Hirschfeld (Klartext, 1997), pp. 107–128.

Böhme, Hartmut. "Geschichte und Gesellschaft im bürgerlichen Roman der Weimarer Rebuplik." *Sozialgeschichte der deutschen Literatur von 1918 bis zur Gegenwart*, edited by Jan Berg, et al., (Fischer, 1981), pp. 354–380.

Cardinal, Agnès, et al., editors. *Women's Writing on the First World War* (Oxford UP, 1999).

Daniel, Ute. *Arbeiterfrauen in der Kriegsgesellschaft: Beruf, Familie und Politik im Ersten Weltkrieg* (Vandenhoek & Ruprecht, 1989).

Daniel, Ute. "Der Krieg und die Frauen 1914–1918: Zur Innenansicht des Ersten Weltkrieges in Deutschland." *'Keiner fühlt sich hier mehr als Mensch...': Erlebnis und Wirkung des Ersten Weltkriegs*, edited by Gerhard Hirschfeld, et al. (Klartext, 1993), pp. 131–149.

Davis, Belinda. *Home Fires Burning: Food, Politics, and Everyday Life in World War I Berlin* (U of North Carolina P, 2000).

Domansky, Elisabeth. "Militarization and Reproduction in World War I Germany." *Society, Culture, and the State in Germany, 1870–1930*, edited by Geoff Eley (U of Michigan P, 1997), pp. 427–463.

Fehlemann, Silke. "Building Home: The War Experiences of German Women Writers 1914–1918." *"Then Horror Came Into Her Eyes...": Gender and the Wars*, edited by Claudia Glunz and Thomas F. Schneider (Vandenhoek & Ruprecht, 2014), pp. 69–95.

Frevert, Ute. *Women in German History: From Bourgeois Emancipation to Sexual Liberation*. Translated by Stuart McKinnon-Evans (Berg, 1989).

"Die Geschichte der unbekannten Mutter im Weltkrieg." *Literaturblatt der Frankfurter Zeitung* (2 June 1935), p. 2.

Hake, Sabine. *The Proletarian Dream: Socialism, Culture, and Emotion in Germany, 1863–1933* (De Gruyter, 2017).

Hölbing, Walter. "'Cultural Paradigms' and the 'Gendered Eye': World War I in the Works of U.S. and German-Language Women Authors." *Intimate Enemies: English and German Literary Reactions to the Great War 1914–1918*, edited by Franz Karl Stanzel and Martin Löschnigg (C. Winter, 1993), pp. 447–464.

Kagelmann, Andre. "Frauensache: Der 'Vorkrieg' Thea von Harbous." *Heroisches Elend: Der Erste Weltkrieg im intellektuellen, literarischen und bildnerischen Gedächtnis der europäischen Kulturen*, edited by Gislinde Seybert and Thomas Stauder, vol. 1 (Lang, 2014), pp. 781–799.

Kagelmann, Andre. *Der Krieg und die Frau: Thea von Harbous Erzählwerk zum Ersten Weltkrieg* (Media Net-Edition, 2009).

Kestien, Käte. *Als die Männer im Graben lagen* (Societäts-Verlag, 1935).

Koonz, Claudia. *Mothers in the Fatherland: Women, the Family, and Nazi Politics* (St. Martin's, 1987).

Krusche, Dorit. "Frau und Krieg: Etappen einer Werkgeschichte Ina Seidels." *Ina Seidel: Eine Literatin im Nationalsozialismus*, edited by Anja Hesse (Kadmos, 2011), pp. 11–30.

Kuhlman, Erika. *Of Little Comfort: War Widows, Fallen Soldiers, and the Remaking of the Nation after the First World War* (New York UP, 2012).

Lohnbuchhalter Kremke. Dir. Marie Harder. Perf. Anna Sten, Hermann Vallentin and Inge Landgut (Naturfilm Hubert Schonger, 1930).

Maier, Hansgeorg. Review of *Als die Männer im Graben lagen*, by Käte Kestien. *Die Literatur: Monatsschrift für Literaturfreunde*, vol. 37, no. 11 (1935), p. 36.

Mommsen, Wolfgang J., editor. *Gebhardt Handbuch der deutschen Geschichte: Die Urkatastrophe Deutschlands – Der Erste Weltkrieg 1914–1918*. 10th ed., vol. 17 (Klett-Cotta, 2001).

O'Brien, Catherine. *Women's Fictional Responses to the First World War: A Comparative Study of Selected Texts by French and German Writers* (Peter Lang, 1997).

Remarque, Erich Maria. *Im Westen nichts Neues* (Propyläen-Verlag, 1929).

Sarkowicz, Hans, and Alf Mentzer. *Schriftsteller im Nationalsozialismus: Ein Lexikon* (Insel, 2011).

Scheele, Meta. *Frauen im Krieg* (Leopold Klotz, 1930).

Schönberger, Bianca. "Motherly Heroines and Adventurous Girls: Red Cross Nurses and Women Army Auxiliaries in the First World War." *Home/Front: The Military, War and Gender in Twentieth-Century Germany*, edited by Karen Hagemann and Stefanie Schüler-Springorum (Berg, 2002), pp. 87–114.

Seidel, Ina. "Mediendokumentation." Bestand Ina Seidel. Grey Folder X: Seidel, Ina. Deutsches Literatur Archiv, Marbach.

Seidel, Ina. "Über die Entstehung meines Romans 'Das Wunschkind.'" *Dichter, Volkstum und Sprache: Ausgewählte Aufsätze und Vorträge* (Deutsche Verlags-Anstalt, 1934), pp. 185–197.

Seidel, Ina. "Verlagsmitteilungen." Bestand Ina Seidel. Grey Folder X: Seidel, Ina. Deutsches Literatur Archiv, Marbach.

Seidel, Ina. *Das Wunschkind* (Deutsche Verlags-Anstalt, 1930).

Stanzel, Franz Karl, and Martin Löschnigg. Introduction. *Intimate Enemies: English and German Literary Reactions to the Great War 1914–1918*, edited by Stanzel and Löschnigg (C. Winter, 1993), pp. 13–37.

Suttner, Bertha von. *Die Waffen nieder!* (Pierson, 1889).

Thomas, Adrienne. *Die Katrin wird Soldat* (Propyläen-Verlag, 1930).

Tramitz, Angelika. "Vom stillen Heldentum der deutschen Frau im Weltkrieg: Käte Kestien und ihr autobiographischer Roman." *Krieg und Literatur / War and Literature*, vol. 3, no. 5 (1991), pp. 310–318.

Veth, Hilke. "'Literatur von Frauen': Literatur der Weimarer Republik, 1918–1933." *Hansers Sozialgeschichte der deutschen Literatur vom 16. Jahrhundert bis zur Gegenwart*, edited by Bernhard Weyergraf, vol. 8 (C. Hanser, 1995), pp. 446–482.

Viebig, Clara. *Töchter der Hekuba* (Fleischel, 1917).

Wedel, Gudrun, editor. "Kestien, Käte." *Autobiographien von Frauen: Ein Lexikon* (Böhlau, 2010), pp. 406–407.

Der Weg einer Proletarierin. Dir. Marie Harder. Perf. Vera Baranowskaja (Arbeiter- und Lichtspiel Dienst, 1929).

Wothe, Anny. *Die den Weg bereiten: Ein Zeitroman* (Enoch, 1916).

Margaret R. Higonnet
Three Nurses' Life-Writing
Scrapbook, Portrait, and Construction of a Self

Nurses' autobiographical literature about World War I can be considered an analogue to that by soldiers, but with distinctly gendered features, as a growing body of scholarship suggests. Regina Schulte, for example, has shown that nurses consider themselves to be the "sisters" of soldiers (1996, 121), and Alon Rachamimov cites Red Cross representative Käthe von Mihalotzy's phrase "female generals" for women who wage a "war" against the sufferings inflicted in prisoner of war camps (2006, 33). Because the subject of nursing texts stands at the nexus of three historical fields – women's evolving gender roles in wartime, military medicine, and women's contributions to war literature – it has drawn a variety of kinds of study, most of it by historians. Diaries, memoirs, and sketches by nurses and doctors in English and to a lesser extent French literature have attracted literary critics such as Claire Tylee (1991) and Ruth Amossy (2005), as well as nursing historians such as Christine Hallett (2014), Margaret Darrow (2000), and Yvonne Knibiehler (2004). By contrast, critics have undertaken relatively little literary analysis of such texts in German, whether by German, Austrian, or Swiss women. As this group of writers shared a common language (although they might be separated by ethnicity and regional language), women eager to serve with the Central Powers might volunteer with the Austrian Red Cross, since, as Elisabeth Domansky notes, the Austrian army accepted women physicians and in their need for trained personnel accepted Swiss nurses as well (1996, 437). Nationality could then become a blurred category. Such factors, however, cannot explain the paucity of literary analyses of German nursing accounts.

An important early resource for the history of German nurses during the war is Marie Elisabeth Lüders, "Frauenarbeit in der Etappe und im besetzten Gebiet" (Women's work in the Etappe and in occupied territory, 1918). Later sources include Lüders' 1936 volume *Das unbekannte Heer* (The unknown army); an article by Hugo Kerchnawe, "Die Schwester" (The sister, 1936); and a rich collection of excerpts compiled by Elfriede von Pflugk-Harttung, *Frontschwestern* (Sisters at the front, 1936). For the most part published in the mid-thirties, even later than women's memoirs in England and France, such nursing histories surveyed national enrollment statistics and traced the broad array of women's medical and para-medical "auxiliary" functions and their assignments to the home front or to different war zones at the several fronts where the Central Powers

https://doi.org/10.1515/9783110572001-012

were fighting. Modern medical histories have followed up these different kinds of nursing assignment and textual evidence. Thus, Alon Rachamimov has studied women's assignments to inspect prisoner of war camps in the East. Rachamimov's article about the nurses and other aristocratic women who visited POW camps in Russia reviews the complex goals of these distinguished women, who had the familial connections and social status to inspect camps and insist on reforms, as they distributed warm clothing, tobacco, and money in their efforts to improve the health and morale of the men. Leo van Bergen mined German nurses' accounts when assembling a chronology of different types of wounds as well as diseases, and tracing the international development of medicine over the course of the war. Van Bergen surveys the representations of battle injuries by year, diseases related to trench conditions, mental neuroses (and their outcomes such as suicide), and institutional type. His wide-ranging yet brief citations do not, however, include literary analyses of texts. Institutional functions are laid out in Ursula von Gersdorff's *Frauen im Kriegsdienst 1914 – 1945* (Women in war service, 1969). Bianca Schönberger has focused on different sites of women's medical work corresponding to the particular situation of the Central Powers, who were fighting on many fronts, including Africa as well as Italy and the Middle East (2002, 87). She notes that about 28,000 out of 92,000 German nurses worked in the "Etappe," or occupied zones behind the military front line rather than on the home front.

Monika Kunz's master's thesis on "Das Bild der Krankenschwester in Literarischen Zeugnissen der Kriegskrankenpflege im Ersten Weltkrieg" (The image of the nurse in literary testimonials about nursing in the First World War, 1991) is the sole detailed study of five autobiographical accounts, including one that I discuss here by Helene Mierisch (1896 – 1987).[1] Although her degree was in Germanistik, Kunz primarily screened those texts for their factuality and political attitudes; she is rather skeptical about women's accounts of their motives, assessments of medical institutions, and memories of their patients. More recent cultural scholars such as Annette Kliever and Christa Hämmerle have shifted the focus to nurses' expressions of national identities, psychological relations to patients, and their articulation or repression of pain and trauma. Like Regina Schulte, who gathered themes and metaphors in nursing texts, these critics turn to the psychological dimension of narrative and thereby lead to more strictly narrative issues, focused on the writer's personal development, linguistic ruptures, and dialogic structures of contact. Not only is a significant corpus of nursing texts in German still coming to light, but possible differences in perspective be-

---

1 My thanks to Anna von Hammerstein for securing a copy of Kunz.

tween nurses from the Allied powers and those from the Central Powers therefore remain to be explored.

Introductory questions

My analysis here develops the recent turn toward literary questions by analyzing the structures of three German diaries about nursing or auxiliary work. These life-writings represent two intertwined formal emphases: on the one hand, compilations of vignettes and portraits of soldiers (Hedwig Voss [dates unknown] and Baroness Enrica von Handel-Mazzetti [1871–1955]), and on the other hand, personal growth (Helene Mierisch). These two strands must be contextualized, however, by larger questions about how we understand the cluster of autobiographical genres we call "diary" or "memoir" in the frame of wartime, when a second, historical narrative underpins but may also rupture the personal narratives. Each of my examples presents a different emphasis, suggesting a spectrum of autobiographical writing. Voss focuses on what she hears rather than what she herself does in her work for the Red Cross; her emphatically nationalist voice projects a self, but the text is more descriptive than autobiographical. Handel-Mazzetti self-consciously tells the story of a soldier with whom she worked for several months in a hospital, at the same time recognizing herself in the mirror of their relationship; the result is a double narrative, at once biographical and autobiographical. Mierisch focuses above all on her calling to become a nurse, as she uses the chronological diary format to trace her apprenticeship and growth over four years.

Many questions arise about women's medical diaries and memoirs concerning their conformity to shared narrative patterns and tropes of war, as they trace an individual trajectory in the context of larger historical narratives about the war. Do what Mikhail Bakhtin calls "chronotopes," or the linkages between time and space, shape diary narratives according to the year of the war and changing age of the nurse? Over time, as women are called upon to perform a succession of different tasks in different locations, and slip from one position to another, from canteen worker to work on a ward, do terms such as "nurse" or "auxiliary" blur in their meaning? Do perpetual emergencies at the threshold between life and death fracture the normal 24-hour rhythms of day and night that organize a diary and its continuities, forcing the text to "buckle and stretch" (McLoughlin 2015, 1219)? Does the war itself cut into and bracket the beginning and ending of the autobiographical narrative, and thereby help place the experiences it records? How does the physical location of labor (whether geographically in the combat zone, in a casualty clearing station, or in an isolation ward for risky infectious diseases) generate temporal narrative patterns? Does travel to and from different fronts mix travelogue or adventure story with historical reportage? Do different narrative modes emerge from portraits of an individual patient, of a cluster of men in a ward, or of passers-by briefly encountered at a canteen in a train station? Only a few of these questions can be addressed here, but they point suggestively toward a broader examination of autobiographical narrative form, inflected both by war and by gender.

In her study of antiwar texts, Annette Kliever questions whether women as mothers have a different perspective on war from that of men (2000, 179). In a similar vein, Christa Hämmerle establishes the theme of "social motherhood" that impelled women into wartime nursing (2014, 92). Ruth Amossy suggests some French accounts fall back on stock idealized images of the nurse (2005, 19–40). Certainly, we must ask what may be characteristic gendered traits of a nurse's tale, such as maternal and sororal metaphors, in contrast to what Samuel Hynes calls *The Soldiers' Tale* (1997). These tropes draw on feminized roles, anchored in the nursing sisterhoods of religious orders, in an analogy to the "brotherhood" found in men's war diaries. Hynes claims that we must seek the "meaning" of the war in "personal witness" by the men who performed "the actual killing" at "the center of war's compound story" (1997, xii). He traces "one huge story of men at war," a grand narrative with all its ordinariness, inconsistency, and variety, yet also shaped by master metaphors (xiii). It is inconceivable to him that a woman could be "at the center."

When we turn to nurses' tales, we find a focus on healing, not killing, in a "war" against the mortality statistics to demonstrate women's meaningful work. Across their different circumstances nurses invoke the leitmotif of nursing itself as a form of combat. In addition, women's voices assume multiple perspectives in relation to the men they serve and the institutions within which they work, transforming the monologic first-person into the dialogic structure of daily dramas. Many of these autobiographical works therefore are set into a succession of perspectives and frames. Not only do successive days reframe events, but successive versions of life-writing recast experiences, both during the war and in subsequent decades. Nurses' accounts of their work were hastily recorded in letters and diaries, then sometimes revised and given coherence in memoirs that date to the 1930s, a period that complicated the politics of their publications. To record their experiences meant to spell out a wide range of the institutional and organizational challenges they had to meet. Ironies and contradictions crop up in surprising places. As we shall see in the case of Helene Mierisch, nurses' specific encounters with superior medical officers, with the military command, with prostitutes, and with their patients elicit powerful micro-narratives punctuating the routines that typify the daily diary.

Sometimes these life-narratives string together accounts about others, most often soldiers, who would usually be the primary voice and focus in conventional war stories by men. When nurses ventriloquize the stories that soldiers told, they often create a structure like a portrait gallery, lining up vignettes that gradually form a larger picture of the war – its moments of heroism, its brutal impact, and its costs. Paradoxically, the autobiography becomes a frame like a nurse's blank scrapbook to record the voices of others. At other times the voice of the author draws our attention to her own struggles and personal growth, as she wrestles with the contradictions of military medicine between healing and fostering the return of men to the battlefront. As women assumed new roles, their self-understanding changed. Just as students of war literature have focused on the experience of trauma in the writings of soldiers, we also note evidence of trauma in the struggle of medical staff to bring their experiences to paper (see Higonnet 2002). This evidence protrudes, especially in gaps between episodes recorded, shifts in voice from immediate present tense to retrospective, or shifts from observation to commentary.

The gendered differences between these two types of voice and tale reflect socially constructed roles and familial models and metaphors. Although medicine was perceived as a nurturing role, and military nursing had begun to open up to women, the German army kept women in the "Etappe," or zone behind the battlefront. (Male orderlies first served at the actual battlefront instead of women.) Unlike a soldier at the front, whose participation in combat is usually mandatory, a nurse at the front typically explains her presence as the result of a persistent quest to serve next to men (Higonnet 2014, 128 – 140). Alternatively, she feels called by soldiers' need for maternal nurture. Like the men, nurses seek a tone of immediacy in their journals, diaries, and letters, when they report their ordinary experiences as participants in the war effort. For the most part, however, they distinguish between the primary roles of men and their own secondary roles as metaphorical mothers or sisters. Perspective, when aligned with such metaphorical roles, is a key factor in narrative structures. I distinguish therefore between episodic structures such as vignettes that focus on a succession of individual soldier-patients and those that gradually build a self-portrait of the narrator. Some nurses ventriloquize the voice of a soldier, who speaks apparently of the most "authentic" experiences. Yet others foreground the disruptive, even broken qualities of wartime discourse that expose dysfunctions manifest in propaganda. As Hämmerle argues in her study of Austrian nurses' unpublished manuscripts, nursing trauma may find expression in "elliptical, impressionistic and staccato-like language" (2014, 100). Rhetorical breaks can also emerge from comic contrasts between High German and dialect, or between moments of humor and others of pathos. The nurse's claim to speak authoritatively about her war experiences may be bolstered by photographs of herself in uniform, of what she has seen and where she has been; her scrapbooks may contain letters from patients or colleagues, and other documentation preserved but not published. The diary then becomes a kind of chronotope that maps the diarist's presence near the front, with references to the succession of battles from which the wounded have arrived. Yet proof that she is at the front may paradoxically be obscured by the use of initials rather than place or personal names, in conformity with censorship. For both men and women, central to the experience of war is estrangement: one becomes a stranger to one's past self, emotionally in exile from family and home.

A scrapbook of vignettes

As Hynes and others have noted, personal witness may be poured into different if related forms of letters, diaries, and retrospective memoirs. The loose group or subgenre of war memoirs that are organized as portraits corresponds to certain assumptions about a woman's role as both nurse and author; it is her task to serve, and a stock narrative feature of nursing accounts is her scribal role in hospitals at the rear (Higonnet 2017, 117–119). One of the most widely read nurses' texts of the war was Russian Sofia Fedorchenko's 1917 *Narod na voinie*, excerpted and translated as *Ivan Speaks* in 1919. When it was translated into German as *Der Russe redet* in 1923, Walter Benjamin praised it in a 1926 review as "the true face of war," as pain made visible through fragments of testimony.[2] Fedorchenko's text consists exclusively of brief passages transcribing nameless soldiers' voices, a key factor in Benjamin's assessment, linked to his privileging of orality in his essay "The Storyteller" (1936). More generally, this genre of portraiture combines first-person conversational excerpts with dialogue, description, or commentary, lined up like beads on a string.

An early, unpretentious German example of such episodic transcriptions interspersed with reflection is Hedwig Voss's 1915 *Im Dienste des Roten Kreuzes* (In the service of the Red Cross). Voss's compilation of paragraph-long sketches, reflections, and snatches of conversations, which she subtitles "Erlebnisse und Eindrücke aus dem Weltkrieg 1914" (Experiences and impressions from the 1914 World War), strives to achieve the effect of documentary, as the work of a scribe recording "Augenblicksbilder," or "snapshots," as she puts it (1915, 6). The short, ninety-three-page text offers one kind of chronotope, which moves

---

2 All translations from German into English are my own unless otherwise stated.

from moment to moment and place to place. To achieve immediacy, Voss often uses the present tense and interjects her emotional responses into what she over-hears or observes. In her verbal scrapbook, she mixes first-person accounts with third-person accounts by those whom she claims to observe. At the same time, although undated, her descriptions and her division of the text into three longer segments suggest temporal succession over the first year of the war. Subtitles connect place to time: first canteen work at the "Train Station," then work at a "Lazarett" or military hospital, and finally the experience of orderlies "In the Field." These locations correspond to shifting types of service as well as to the expansive experience of an unfolding war in 1914 to 1915. If the first page honors peace by describing the famous contrast between a splendid golden Au-gust and the threat of war, the following pages record the enthusiasm of young soldiers whose trains and bodies are decorated with flowers and oak branches, representing them as ancient Germanic sacrificial offerings (1915, 12). The station platform witnesses both departures of joking young men and the return of the wounded, both those headed to the West and those arriving from the Eastern Front with Russian prisoners and refugees.

As a symbolic nexus, the platform reminds her readers that Germany is fight-ing multiple enemies. Voss's nationalistic sketches may draw some of their stock images and sentimental narratives from soldiers she served or from newspapers. Many in her own voice, I believe, could not come from her own direct observa-tion but from an observation she copied. Thus, the shorter third section "In the Field" retells an ironic story about a wounded lieutenant, whose faithful dog at-tracts attention from medical staff, only to be a killed by a bomb that also kills the dog and the stretcher-bearer (77). Her less melodramatic but intensely patri-otic descriptions of scenes at the station that she probably did observe describe the German people as united in a "crusade" (9). She sees enemies everywhere: in the period of early spy-mania, she worries about Russian girls who come to study but stay after the declaration of war, and about greedy refugees whom she con-demns as ubiquitous treacherous observers (50–51). She justifies the destruction of fine architecture in order to achieve victory – a reference to international de-bates over the destruction of Louvain in Belgium and of the cathedral of Reims in France (32–33).

The binary structure of many sketches reinforces Voss's tendency to myth-making, which she formulates in her praise of German soldiers for their "Nibe-lungen" fidelity and unyielding courage (92). The final page, or "Closing chord," envisions a midnight visit from a gigantic veiled female figure of War, who carries a sword as a red cross, another allegorical symbol of German right-eousness (92). Voss constructs racist antitheses: she praises the German people as generous, conscientious, thorough, and precise, as opposed to the British;

she repeatedly describes German soldiers as good-humored and handsome, by contrast to pale and small Russian prisoners (12). Although the Red Cross was in principle neutral, each organization was national, and she refuses to feed Russian prisoners; they are then, however, fed by their German guards, who resist her own nationalism (27–28, 37–38, 41). Since she tells the story at her own expense, we may suspend judgment. The true enemies of the Germans, she believes, are the English, whom she describes as "devils" who began the war (5, 34, 72). She describes "devilish" enemies who under cover of night stab sleeping German patients (78). A colorful sketch of a first-aid station set up in a half-ruined church juxtaposes Germans, Zouaves, French and English lying all alike on straw. But Voss emphasizes that a guard must carry a gun to protect the nurses from enemy patients she calls treacherous "beasts" (91). The labor of nurse and guard side by side symbolizes Voss's view that the Red Cross is "a great silent Army" (76). Her heroic image of abstract warfare is modified by her recognition of PTSD avant la lettre: one traumatized patient expresses his pain through disconnected words, "There, there, blood, smoke, oh!" and another laughs irrationally (34, 86). This too is an obligatory trope of war: the breakdown of language and meaning glimpsed in passing.

One of the most surprising passages in Voss's sketches is an impromptu reflection on the gentleness of orderlies with the wounded:

> Often I must smile. From somewhere words came to mind: 'Women are born caregivers, born cooks, and so forth. They should stay in place, and not compete with men in other domains.' And now? The men perform these tasks too, what is left for women? That they must now in infinitely many professions replace their men and really do their jobs, will surely not happen. Yet perhaps it will. Will the war also bring an upheaval in values here? Then thanks to war after all. (35)

Voss's self-aware irony about social clichés and about her own attitude toward the war comes to the surface briefly in response to changes she doubts will happen. The observation of such gender changes often appears in women's autobiographies. Yet the crisp inversion of gender roles sticks out in this text that otherwise promotes conventional propaganda. Published during the war, this collage of observations is structured not so much by historical events as by nationalist fervor and political antitheses. Voss relies on allegory to give meaning to her sketches and to exhort civilians to volunteer. Inadvertently, however, the text opens questions about gender roles that it cannot answer.

A double portrait

A more fully developed example of autobiography as an occasion to portray one or more soldiers is well represented by the Austrian Baroness Enrica von Handel-Mazzetti (1871–1955), who was known for her historical novels about the Counter-Reformation and the Thirty-Years' War. Handel-Mazzetti supported a reserve hospital in Linz set up in a high school or *Gymnasium* across the street from her home, and was twice decorated by the Red Cross. She recorded her official auxiliary Red Cross work and her view of the war first in a scrapbook filled with newspaper clippings, photos, and letters, then in a complexly ironic portrait of a wounded Tyrolean soldier in a semi-autobiographical text entitled *Der Blumenteufel* (The flower devil, 1916). Over two years, she published a set of hospital portraits, *Unter dem österreichischen Roten Kreuz* (Under the Austrian Red Cross, 1917) and a war novel, *Ilko Smutniak, der Ulan* (Ilko Smutniak, the Ulan, 1917), evidence of her commitment to recording the aspects of war she had observed in Linz. While *Der Blumenteufel*, her account of the soldier Josef Schmid, has been mistakenly described as a "nursing novella" by Konstanze Fliedl (1989, 195), surviving scrapbooks include the letter written by Handel-Mazzetti's cousin on Schmid's behalf and other documents about her patient's loss of his hand and her efforts to help him, as well as a photo of his eventual marriage (Dallinger 2009, 88). Through her Tyrolean patient, Handel-Mazzetti offers us a portrayal of the psychological impact of war on the injured. Her voice hesitates and zigzags, as she steers between the Scylla and Charybdis of condemning the daily hecatombs of war and the medical bureaucracy (1916, 45, 47), while celebrating the spirit of sacrifice embodied by a soldier who has lost the use of his hand to shrapnel. As a historical account from a localized Tyrolean standpoint, the text plays with dialect and folk culture to express an aristocrat's affectionate loyalty to the people.

At the opening of the semi-autobiographical text, Handel-Mazzetti tells us she has been emotionally exhausted by the deaths of two soldiers, after watching anxiously at their bedsides in a hospital that has lost only four patients out of hundreds. The Baroness focuses at the hospital on problems of morale: she stops by regularly with a bottle of wine or other small gifts such as postcards for the soldiers, and writes letters home for those too weak or uneducated to write themselves. Sometimes she holds the hand of a dying patient until he falls unconscious. She is the kind of society woman who in many nurses' accounts is the object of satire. The wife of the school porter, Frau Wieser, who now runs practical affairs in the hospital, calls upon Handel-Mazzetti to assist in the care of the dangerously ill Tyrolean, Schmid. His wounded hand has been partly amputated, infected and nearly paralyzed with tetanus, which was widespread in World War I. He cannot be visited until that crisis is past. His longer-term illness, however, is extreme depression. In a military-medical context where wounds and disease take precedence over psychiatric care, the civilian narrator understands the importance of hope and emotional recovery in the struggle for survival, and quickly grasps the longing of Schmid for both his mother and his motherland. "Heimweh," or homesickness, is the key to Schmid's slow recovery. His devotion to Tyrol reflects the Tyrolean cult of the freedom-fighter Andreas Hofer, and the novelist sees the young man's love of the land as an echo of the myth of Antaeus, who regained strength when he touched the earth (1916, 81). The narrator's womanly insight implicitly undercuts the priorities of military agendas and medical treatment.

This simple and forthright patient absorbs all her attention, as depression makes his recovery uncertain. Schmid's hope of Austrian victory enables him to affirm the meaning of his sacrifice. Weeks go by as he waits to recover from tetanus, then waits for a message to reach his mother with an invitation to Linz, and finally waits for a third, renewed request for release from the hospital to be approved. All the waiting is saturated with stoic suffering, which Handel-Mazzetti interprets as typical of Tyrolean courage and humble readiness to sacrifice for Austria, even though she repeatedly condemns the war. As a highly cultivated novelist, she interpolates literary allusions to Antaeus, Cincinnatus, and Gaius Mucius Scaevola, as she traces the stages of his suffering. While the text presents readers with crafted literary effects, Handel-Mazzetti insists that it is not fiction, and indeed it overlaps with the more explicitly documentary hospital sketches of *Unter dem österreichischen Roten Kreuz*. Half-way through the narrative, she has offered to pay for the mother's trip to Linz. She begins Chapter VI by explaining that, "If I had wanted to invent a war novella, here would be my finest chapter, the highpoint" of the mother's arrival (1916, 48). But life composed (dichtete) this story, not Handel-Mazzetti herself.

In this double portrait of herself and the Tyrolean the Baroness playfully mocks her own wealth, by contrast to the poverty of the peasant's family, whose small piece of land lies two hours' walk from the nearest train station. Likewise, when Schmid tells her that an elderly man had placed a coat over him as he lay on a stretcher at the station, she notices that she has bound her Red Cross armband onto a silk velvet embroidered coat. Her elegant prose contrasts in a deft counterpoint with the amusingly clipped Tyrolean dialect spoken both by Frau Wieser and by Schmid. Although the Baroness offers to pay for the mother's visit to the hospital, the farmwoman cannot afford to leave her sick husband and small farm, so the only way to reunite the youth with his family is to compose a letter that convinces the medical authorities to release him. The letter becomes the main event: a healing action, a fiction, and a moment of self-transformation. When the narrator prepares to write a letter on behalf of Schmid's semi-literate mother, the sympathetic regimental surgeon (who has read and admired some of her novels) warns her to focus on substance, not style. As an embedded reader, he brings about change in the author and her text. She must abandon verbal conventions and stylistic embellishments to ventriloquize the peasant's voice and that of his mother. She must translate the mother's oral tongue into written form without losing its savor and strength of feeling.

When the Baroness writes in the name of Schmid's mother, she realizes that she is writing as if she herself were his mother, marking a turning point in her self-understanding in relation to the war, emotionally as well as artistically. Voice itself has transformative agency. Similarly, the housekeeper Klara Wieser, like the unwed and childless Handel-Mazzetti, assumes a maternal role toward all her patients, and the doctor, who recognizes the weight of Schmid's "embodied longing" (1916, 70), is loved by the soldiers whose lives he saves, as if he were their "father" (72). The Baroness is glad not to be an actual mother. "I could not survive the loss of a son in battle" (41). She observes the pathos of a legless soldier who must learn to walk again on prostheses, accompanied by his mother, who had taught him as a toddler twenty years before.

The narrator concludes at the moment of Schmid's departure for his home and mother, with a salute to the soldiers who sacrifice themselves for the fatherland and their Kaiser. Although she will continue to work at the hospital, his tale has reached its conclusion. She has learned to be a national mother rather than a blood mother (1916, 74). At the same time, she insists forcefully that she has neither praise for war nor hatred for the enemy (91). As her patients remind her, the enemy "are men like us" (91). They all belong to the family of mankind.

Over the course of the sketch, Handel-Mazzetti has created a double portrait – of Schmid and of herself. At one level, this metanarrative reflects on how to tell a war story through the narrator's self-mockery, as she uses the soldier as a corrective mirror, to better understand herself. From start to finish she reminds us that she hates war. Hans-Otto Binder notes that she condemns the euphemisms (Schönrederei) about the war (1997, 119). As a writer, she rejects "hollow dithyrambs" in wartime that belie the brutal reality of the bloodbath in which humanity is drowning (1916, 47). "No rhetoric can purify the massacres of the people," she writes (47–48). In the first pages, she condemns the most horrific and inhuman events in the news (7), and at the end, she laments the pitiless war and the sorrows it brings, with bitter pain for mothers of all nationalities. As we can see in this double narrative, the war memoir focused on a single soldier's portrait can inscribe at the same time a portrait of the writer's own transformation through care for her patients. Self-portraiture moves to the foreground in such narratives and war diaries, where it reflects both war-related events and the lived experiences of hospital work.

Autobiography as self-construction

Diaries as a form can be understood as a construction of the self through reflection on experience. Wartime diaries often trace the evolution of a nurse's self-understanding in tandem with her observations about the many facets of the war she encounters. Such patterns of development may remind us of the *Bildungsroman* form, or the novel of education.[3] Yet we must recall Charles Carrington's ironic comment that soldiers pick up their "education in a strange school" (qtd. in Wohl 1979, 225), and Eric Leed's forthright rejection of the cliché that war is a "rite of initiation" or "education" (1979, 73). A diary's construction of time and space can make it an effective vehicle for replicating dominant discourses, as we saw in Voss, as well as for a resistant construction of the self.

The fairly typical wartime diary by Helene Elisabeth Mierisch (née Augustin), follows the path of her own gradual transformation, amid individual acts of recall, memorializing, and witness. Signing her book with her married name, Helene Mierisch, "Sister Elisabeth" framed her published diary, *Kamerad Schwester, 1914–1918* (Comrade sister, 1934), with a foreword of 1934 about her revisions to the text; it explains that she dropped purely personal details, filled out occasional telegram-like jottings, and changed names of colleagues (3). Such changes are in fact common in published diaries. Although this text has been called an "autobiographical fiction" by Sophie Häusner (2015, 299), its complex composition process and documentation can be traced in her notebooks ("Nachlass"),[4] like the documentation kept by Handel-Mazzetti. A characteristic documentary gesture is Mierisch's inclusion of a photograph in her Red Cross uniform as a frontispiece to two of her diaries. At key points Mierisch refers to her process of textual composition and revision, filling in entries after the fact, or noting that she or her friend Heinrich cannot speak about their experiences. In 1934, she stripped away place and personal names; these were restored in the condensed version of *Kamerad Schwester* in the first part of her 1957 memoir *Ärzte, Schwestern und Sol-*

---

3 For a discussion of the genre of the *Bildungsroman* as it relates to patterns of development prescribed to young female readers during wartime, see Jennifer Redmann's essay in this volume.

4 Photographs that accompanied the auction of Mierisch's papers and scrapbooks show a mix of photographs, letters and other documents from which she drew her memoir. The collection now belongs to the Sächsisches Rot-Kreuz-Museum, Beierfeld.

daten (Doctors, sisters, soldiers), which selectively reproduces the first volume, but then includes in a second part her relief work during World War II. ("Ida" had been the pseudonym of Lina, for example, and "Dr. Koch" that of Dr. Back.) Most important for scholar Monika Kunz, Mierisch changed her implicit patriotic views in her two later autobiographical texts – *Ein Griff ins Leben: Aus meiner Schwesternarbeit* (A Plunge into life: From my work as a nurse, 1953), and *Ärzte, Schwestern und Soldaten* (1991, 106). For Kunz these modifications and tacit name-changes constitute falsification ("Fälschung" or "Verfälschung," 99). Alternatively, we could say that as she lived through a second war, the story Elisabeth had to tell evolved, as we learn already from the final section of *Kamerad Schwester*, "Nachklang" (Reminiscence), which looks back from 1934 at reunions with those whom she had known on different medical teams (299–301). Thus the 1934 text, *Kamerad Schwester*, presents a hybrid, a war diary with a retrospective frame that allies it to a memoir. This little-known autobiographical text provides examples of the mobility of nursing work, the rich psychological dimensions of a nursing diary, and insights into the artistry of scarce war writings by women from the medical field.

Kamerad Schwester constructs a life-narrative with several strands. One traces the backdrop of wartime Germany from August 1914 to December 1918, which is thinly sketched at times when Elisabeth is on leave. The structure of the four-part diary cuts across the German war effort without detailed depiction of the impact of combat, as much of Elisabeth's life in hospitals is passed in isolation. The first section traces her quest for a post at a cloister-hospital in Avricourt; the next her continuing work in an epidemic ward during 1915–1916 and increasingly at the operating table; third, she records her transfer to Poniewiecz (Panevėžys) in Lithuania in February 1917 to work as an operating nurse and, finally, she glimpses revolution in White Russia followed by her return to Germany after the Armistice in 1918, when she encounters Spartacists. In 1917 on a trip home she observes the war's impact on the home front: no clothes for sale, queues for food, and misery that leads to the theft of food and linens, as well as children begging on the streets. Her position on the Eastern Front enables her to observe that treaties do not necessarily end wars. Instead, civil war has broken out in Russia. Moreover, when her unit returns to Germany and Berlin in December 1918, an uprising of Spartacists bars the nurses' entry into the city. Thus she traces the temporal arc of the war through glimpses along the trajectory of her own displacements.

We readily fill in the arc of her private narrative. Starting at seventeen, Elisabeth Augustin notes her increasingly serious relationship to a young man her age, Heinrich Mierisch, with whom she exchanges promises of fidelity in 1914 (1934, 9). The rhythm of their relationship is marked by the "wall of people" that separates them at the mobilization on 1 August (10), then his enlistment as a pilot and later sailor, and his hospitalization when his torpedo boat explodes. Each Christmas she sends him gifts and they exchange letters, but for three years they are separated, reuniting only in spring 1917, when their happiness is framed by home front sufferings, amid people who are starving and sick (152–153). Mental telegraphy (in what may be an echo of Charlotte Brontë's *Jane Eyre*) warns her that Heinrich has been in danger, an intuition which he confirms in a letter (193). But she does not see him again until June 1918, after he has influenza and has been terribly burned and scarred. The afterword briefly confirms that, once he had completed his postwar studies, she left hospital work and married Heinrich in 1921 (301).

The linear structure of a nursing diary displaces the romance plot that so often marks a young woman's war story, thereby opening up an alternative plot for the protagonist. Elisabeth traces her own wartime career over five years, as she seeks a nursing post, acquires skills on the job, and develops confidence in her own medical judgments, until she finally finds a job after the war running a regional hospital. The individual significance of the diary is marked by her purchase of the notebook as a birthday gift for herself in 1913, to confide her inner ambition to become a nurse (1934, 5). Already at sixteen, she was inspired by propaganda films about the Balkan wars to volunteer with the Red Cross, whose rules prevented her enlistment. Her ambition was shaped by the militarized discourse of the period that prepared young European women as well as men to volunteer when war broke out in 1914. When she observes the young men of her town volunteering in August 1914, she asks, "Why am I not a boy, and must sit here inactive?" (11). She will overcome the problem of her age by registering for a month's training as a Samaritan, gaining a certificate in September 1914. "Now I am finally 'someone,' with a stamped paper in my hand on which I can build" (12). Entering the profession signifies personal growth and social status here. Still a year too young, she falsifies the date of her birth on her nursing certificate (13), buys her nursing uniform, and simply leaves home in October by train for Saarburg, where the chief medical officer declares he does not need her. Undaunted, she tracks down a small military hospital (Lazarett) at Avricourt that has called for help, where she is welcomed.

This hospital becomes Elisabeth's new home and site of apprenticeship. In the next weeks Doctor "Koch" asks her to take over a ward for highly infectious diseases. Her urgent desire to serve is rewarded by a sense of vitality in the crush of work; serving alone on an isolation ward in November 1914 she jots down, "I had never felt so alive" (1934, 29). She takes over a ward for those sick with typhus and pneumonia, which lies behind a barbed wire fence, itself a striking metaphor for the parallels between nursing and fighting (57). Over the course of the war her willingness to take on difficult tasks leads her to treat epidemics of pneumonia, dysentery, tuberculosis, meningitis, diphtheria, and scarlet fever. Through experience and observation of another nurse, she develops diagnostic skills. By December 1914, when she is still new at the hospital, she rescues a patient from a thrombosis, defying a mistaken order by a medical student, while the doctor is momentarily out of the room (44 – 45). At several points Sister Elisabeth notes that conflict marks relationships in the hospital as well as on the battlefield. She finds herself taking on responsibilities for typhus patients that were refused by older nurses (40), or replacing a religious sister who prays rather than serve her patients (41). She resists a psychiatrist who is a stickler for tidy drawers, a martinet who falsely accuses her of theft, and a third doctor, her patient, who self-medicates with alcohol and sleeping pills and starts to shoot his pistol before she wrests it out of his hand. Was it attempted suicide or murder, she wonders (211). Ultimately, she is supported by her supervisors and recommended for two medals.

On her first wartime birthday on Christmas Day in 1914, Elisabeth is recognized by a fellow nurse as a "comrade." Sister Ida says, "My child, let us use 'Du' as soldiers do. You are a true war volunteer, a good comrade sister" (1934, 53). At the end of January 1915 she observes that she clings with every fiber to her work and to the people on her team (62). Like Handel-Mazzetti, Mierisch perceives her work as psychological as well as medical. She buys a lute in August 1915, with which she soothes the patients and unites the wards in group singing (120). She amuses the tuberculosis ward of twelve patients by telling them stories about her travels while on leave, embedding a travelogue within her diary. The text follows the rhythm of her hospital work, alternating between sustained work in the operating room for over twenty-four hours and comic moments of relief, when she and the men escape from the confinement of hospital life. Elisabeth selectively details her shifts but she also gives ample space to the hijinks of her patients, who play games to celebrate the Kaiser's birthday, bake potatoes in secret late at night, or climb the hospital walls in order to buy a beer (68). Such humor is presented as therapeutic both for the patients and for herself, as she must maintain distance from the painful losses she experiences.

On her first leave in March 1915, Elisabeth realizes that she cannot tell people at home about her hospital experiences (1934, 71). Trauma creates a gulf between the experiencing self that jots down abbreviated notes about shocking wounds and wounding conflicts, on the one hand, and the strategies she uses to narrate, on the other. Just as she cannot talk to others at home, she writes sparingly about these experiences in the diary. Instead, when she is granted a brief leave, she seeks new sights and experiences to cleanse her memory. Nonetheless, the "Lazarett" becomes her second home where she works to create social unity. Perhaps as a symptom of that unity, the author inserts letters and stories from her former patients (104, 120, 194–200). Such hybrid incorporation of other forms and voices is, in fact, common in war diaries.

Frustrated by medical bureaucracy and petty chicanery (1934, 133), Elisabeth decides in 1917 to transfer to the Eastern Front. There she undertakes nursing of every kind: not only in wards for infectious diseases but the operating ward where she helps in major operations on skin burns, frozen limbs, damaged knees, and complicated facial and hand wounds. In an emergency, she ties off an artery that is hemorrhaging (178). She takes on the task of narcotics sister, showing that she has learned by observation to deliver anesthesia. She assists the otolaryngologist working with syphilitics (190) and helps the surgeon during a Caesarean and two midnight abortions or "appendicitis" cases for prostitutes (224). In one ward, she treats mental cases with electric shock (188).

Mierisch's diary is of interest because of her attention to types of temporality. A war diary is intrinsically episodic because it follows the round of the calendar, marked by repeating holidays such as the birthday of the Kaiser or Whitsuntide and by personal anniversaries as well as by unpredictable military events. The literal passage of time is punctuated by the arrivals and departures of injured or sick men at a hospital. Constantly interrupted, the diary is paradoxically also a continuous flow in the present. The periodic structure of the year is reinforced by recurrent images and themes that confer unity. Elisabeth, for example, begins her diary, *Kamerad Schwester*, with notes about her seventeenth birthday on Christmas 1913; this motif returns on each of the four following Christmases, triggering thoughts about how she has changed.

At the same time, irregularity and fragmentation characterize Mierisch's diary, as one might expect of a text produced under stress; they sharpen the vividness of her account. Under the pressure of working around the clock in November 1914, she has written nothing. She therefore retrospectively narrates in a block her struggle in the isolation ward to deal with typhus and the stench of dysentery, training orderlies in basic hygiene. Elsewhere she also notes that she simply has no time to write, and must catch up occasionally by jotting notes about a span of unrecorded days. She assures us on Christmas Eve, 1914, that she does not want to write an "official war report," since she knows that her dates are not always exact. "When I have a moment then quickly I dash down something, and in the end, it doesn't matter whether the events are nailed down with chronological precision" (1934, 48). Later she asks why she should continue to keep a diary, since the form is so repetitious, with perpetually repeated operations (167). Next to great actions she finds excessive trivia ("Kleinkram," 167). When she is travelling by train, in fits and starts, she "scribbles" in the cold with stiff fingers. As she describes her parting from old friends,

Elisabeth observes that a diary recording her feelings runs the risk of becoming sentimental: "diaries have a shadow side" (132).

Sister Elisabeth naturally observes changes in women's lives, including her own. Particularly in this respect, her story connects her life to a larger historical transformation. Soldiers want to know what her marital status is; she resists those inquiries, since she is committed to her work as well as to Heinrich. Her own changes are striking: on one return home in January 1916, she longs to be back "home" at the front, to her father's dismay; she feels "rootless and foreign" and longs to rejoin the working group with whom she has daily shared "joy and sorrow" (1934, 96). In this passage, her diary entry records her psychological state, as an autobiography would. At the same time, she takes stock of the historical changes Germany underwent while she has been working in frontline hospitals. She observes that at home women wear uniforms as tram-conductors and have assumed new jobs; she hears from a friend about a Russian women's battalion, probably that of Maria Botchkareva (189). Two women in a train accuse her of being a prostitute (a common suspicion of nurses who worked on men's bodies) and spit on her (269). Her friend Lilly commits suicide when accused of promiscuity (226). In transit from her cloister hospital on the Western Front to the Eastern Front in January 1917, Elisabeth visits an old friend, Erich Bürger, at his home in Strassburg. His mother comes upon them in laughing banter, and is amazed by their comradeship. In her own youth, women had to choose between being engaged or behaving like strangers. "The times have changed," Mrs. Bürger observes (129). Elisabeth responds that physical boundaries remain in place, but shared work, sorrow and joy bind men and women in a "beautiful community" (129). Mierisch acknowledges that war has changed social conventions between women and men.

Elisabeth's diary weaves together the threads of romance with Heinrich Mierisch, her professional success (her two medals), and the German experience of war from mobilization to defeat and withdrawal on the Eastern Front. These strands meet in the conclusion of the diary, in contrast to the generally open-ended nature of the diary form. Here, the Armistice in November 1918, followed by the withdrawal of German forces and medical staff over the next weeks, colors the diary's darkened mood and observations as it draws to a close. The final pages trace the breakup of the medical unit, as some doctors abandon the nurses and patients to take an express train, or *Durchgangszug* (*D-Zug*), while the nurses, orderlies, and returning soldiers split off to reach different mandatory points of demobilization. Germany's defeat underscores the weight of these conflicts and ruptures. By November 1918, rumors and news about anarchy breaking out in Germany cast doubt on the meaning of service. Orderlies go on strike, and in the chaos soldiers think only of alcohol and women. In the midst of this social decomposition, Elisabeth recognizes that it will be hard to leave her friends, since they have been fused "like a great family" (1934, 271). At the same time, the prospect of a return home, which Elisabeth shares with the soldiers for whom she cares, promises the reestablishment of her relationship to Heinrich and to the community they shared. Even as her medical unit is dissolving, she looks forward to reunions with her colleagues.

In 1934 Mierisch, the author of the 1914–1918 diary, challenges her readers in her last pages to think about whether the next fifteen years have brought closure. The diary concludes with an afterword about her reunions with her medical comrades. While the text's narrator Elisabeth does not track historical events – she witnesses most of the war second hand, from inside the hospital and even inside a barbed-wire isolation ward – by the end of the war, she is directly affected by the chaos of the Russian revolutionary period and German demobilization in a country whose government was in chaos. Thus her own uncertainties about her future run parallel to uncertainties about what lies ahead for the German nation. In fact, Mierisch's two further memoirs about her life after the war and her later nursing service during World War II challenge us to reread her experiences, as she rereads and rewrites her original diary.

Directly connected to this problem of rewriting is a question about audience. While for Voss, the readers she directly addressed were civilians whom she urged to volunteer, for Mierisch, the audience is more complicated. First, the diary is a mirror in which she observes her own growth. In turn, the record she keeps becomes a tribute to some of the soldiers for whom she has cared, many of whom have died. Ultimately, the medical community that takes shape over the war years becomes both her family and her audience. She foresees that her book of 1934 will find readers (it was reprinted in several editions) and inspire young women of the next generation to become nurses. That the primary audience was her colleagues reinforces the centrality of her career to this life-narrative, whose originality is located in the vision of a young woman's potential.

Conclusion

These three examples of nursing war diaries, despite their different voices and narrative strategies, represent an autobiographical mode of immediacy, as they record encounters with soldiers and other war experiences in a zone of the present, even if not literally in the present tense. More than other forms of life-writing, the diary, even when it strings together vignettes about patients, can project a self taking shape along a linear trajectory. That chronological movement need not lead to simplification. As Handel-Mazzetti's text shows, portraiture and self-portrayal can coincide and interact. Thus, the process of shaping the narrative may lead to discovery and self-discovery. Shifting tasks produce changing perspectives. The war diary, in particular, can fuse the autobiographical and the historical. Professional apprenticeship may, however, outweigh historical testimony. We have observed the hybridity of form in diaries that incorporate letters or travelogues into the frame of a largely professional record of work. Nurses, unable to jot down notes as events take place, often take time at the end of a few days to recollect intervening experiences, sliding toward the retrospective form of a memoir. They may insert texts, just as they quote stories told by others. Modern work on autobiography has also recognized the artistic dimension of such writing. When nurses' notes consist of fragments or scattered words, they extrapolate a narrative from those clues. Such reconstruction frequently lies behind published war diaries. Conversely, the diarist may select from hundreds of pages the most striking passages that capture the intensity of her years of service and the powerful attraction of sisterhood. Paradoxically, the linear nature of a diary does not prevent experimentation with different types of temporality, corresponding to the crush of work, interruptions and flashbacks, vacation leisure, or the menace of military or political events. The vitality of these war diaries reflects their authors' orchestration of war and work rhythms.

Works Cited

Amossy, Ruth. "Ecriture littéraire et parole testimoniale: Les récits des infirmières de 1914–1918." *Esthétique du témoignage*, edited by Carole Dornier and Renaud Dulong (Maison des Sciences de l'Homme, 2005), pp. 19–40.

Bakhtin, M. "Forms of Time and of the Chronotope in the Novel: Notes Toward a Historical Poetics." *The Dialogic Imaginations: Four Essays*, edited by Michael Holquist, translated by Caryl Emerson and Holquist (U of Texas P, 1981), pp. 89–258.

Benjamin, Walter. Review of *Sofja Fedortschenko: Der Russe redet.* 1926. *Gesammelte Schriften Band III: Kritiken und Rezensionen*, edited by Hella Tiedemann-Bartels (Suhrkamp Taschenbuch, 1991). www.textlog.de/benjamin-kritik-fedortschenko-russe-redet-aufzeichnungen-stenogramm.html. Accessed 7 Apr. 2017.

Benjamin, Walter. "The Storyteller: Reflections on the Works of Nikolai Leskov." *Illuminations*, edited by Hannah Arendt, translated by Harry Zohn (Schocken, 1968), pp. 83–109.

Binder, Hans-Otto. "Zum Opfern bereit: Kriegsliteratur von Frauen." *Kriegserfahrungen: Studien zur Sozial- und Mentalitätsgeschichte des Ersten Weltkriegs*, edited by Gerhard Hirschfeld, et al. (Klartext, 1997), pp. 107–128. www.erster-weltkrieg.clio-online.de/_ Rainbow/documents/Kriegserfahrungen/binder.pdf. Accessed 7 Dec. 2017.

Dallinger, Petra-Maria. "Einblicke: Die Kriegstagebücher der Enrica von Handel-Mazzetti 1914–1917." *Tagebücher: Aufzeichnungen aus bewegten Zeiten*, edited by Petra-Maria Dallinger (StifterHaus, 2009), pp. 81–92.

Darrow, Margaret H. *French Women and the First World War: War Stories of the Home Front* (Berg, 2000).

Domansky, Elisabeth. "Militarization and Reproduction in World War I Germany." *Society, Culture and the State in Germany, 1870–1930*, edited by Geoff Eley (U Michigan P, 1996), pp. 427–463.

Fedorchenko, Sofia. *Der Russe redet: Aufzeichnungen nach dem Stenogramm von Sofja Fedortschenko.* Translated by Alexander Eliasberg (Drei Masken Verlag, 1923).

Fliedl, Konstanze. "Etwas ganz Grosses und auch etwas Schweres: Der erste Weltkrieg im trivialen Frauenroman." *Österreich und der Grosse Krieg, 1914–1918: die andere Seite der Geschichte*, edited by Klaus Amann and Hubert Lengauer (Verlag Christian Brandstäter, 1989), pp. 192–200.

Gersdorff, Ursula von, editor. *Frauen im Kriegsdienst 1914–1945* (Deutsche Verlags-Anstalt, 1969).

Hämmerle, Christa. "'Mentally broken, physically a wreck…': Violence in War Accounts of Nurses in Austro-Hungarian Service." *Gender and the First World War*, edited by Hämmerle, et al. (Palgrave, 2014), pp. 89–107.

Häusner, Sophie. "Traditional Costume, Nurse's Dress, Uniform: The Clothing of Red Cross Nurses in the First World War, as Presented in the Autobiographical Texts of Adrienne Thomas and Helene Mierisch (1930/34)." *Fashioning the Self in Transcultural Settings: The Uses and Significance of Dress in Self-Narratives*, edited by Claudia Ulbrich and Richard Wittmann (Ergon, 2015), pp. 299–320.

Hallett, Christine E. *Veiled Warriors: Allied Nurses of the First World War* (Oxford UP, 2014).

Handel-Mazzetti, Baroness Enrica von. *Der Blumenteufel: Bilder aus dem Reservespital Staatsgymnasium in Linz* (Volksvereins-Verlag, 1916).

Handel-Mazzetti, Baroness Enrica von. *Ilko Smutniak, der Ulan: Der Roman eines Ruthenen* (Kempten, 1917).

Handel-Mazzetti, Baroness Enrica von. *Unter dem österreichischen Roten Kreuz* (Pustet, 1917).

Higonnet, Margaret R. "At the Front." *The Cambridge History of the First World War*, edited by Jay Winter, vol. 3: Civil Society (Cambridge UP, 2014), pp. 121–152.

Higonnet, Margaret R. "Authenticity in Art and Trauma Narratives of World War I." *Modernism/ Modernity*, vol. 9, no. 1 (2002), pp. 91–107.

Higonnet, Margaret R. "Ventriloquizing Voices in World War I: Scribe, Poetess, Philosopher." *Landscapes and Voices of the Great War*, edited by Angela K. Smith and Krista Cowman (Routledge, 2017), pp. 115–130.

Hynes, Samuel. *The Soldiers' Tale: Bearing Witness to Modern War* (Penguin/Allen Lane, 1997).

Kerchnawe, Hugo. "Die Schwester." *Ärzte und ihre Helfer im Weltkrieg 1914–1918: Helden im weissen Kittel: Apotheker im Weltkriege*, edited by Burghard Breitner and Rudolf Rauch (Göth, 1936), pp. 17–25.

Kliever, Annette. "'Der Tag wird kommen …': Zur Analyse der Anti-Kriegstexte von Frauen seit dem Ersten Weltkrieg." *Frauen in Kultur und Gesellschaft: ausgewählte Beiträge der 2. Fachtagung Frauen-/Gender-Forschung in Rheinland-Pfalz*, edited by Renate von Bardeleben (Stauffenburg, 2000), pp. 175–187.

Knibiehler, Yvonne. "Les anges blancs: naissance difficile d'une profession féminine." *1914–1918, combats de femmes: Les femmes, pilier de l'effort de guerre*, edited by Evelyne Morin-Rotureau (Autrement, 2004), pp. 47–63.

Kunz, Monika. "Das Bild der Krankenschwester in literarischen Zeugnissen der Kriegskrankenpflege im Ersten Weltkrieg." Magister-Hausarbeit am Fachbereich Germanistik (Freie Universität Berlin, 1990/91).

Leed, Eric. *No Man's Land: Combat and Identity in World War I* (Cambridge UP, 1979).

Lüders, Marie Elisabeth. "Frauenarbeit in der Etappe und im besetzten Gebiet." *Deutscher Tagesanzeiger*, (28 Aug. 1918).

Lüders, Marie Elisabeth. *Das unbekannte Heer: Frauen kämpfen für Deutschland, 1914–1918* (E.S. Mittler, 1936).

McLoughlin, Kate, et al. "Writing War, Writing Lives." *Textual Practice*, vol. 29, no. 7 (2015), pp. 1219–1223.

Mierisch, Helene. *Ärzte, Schwestern und Soldaten: Erlebtes aus zwei Weltkriegen* (Koehler, 1957).

Mierisch, Helene. *Kamerad Schwester* (Hase & Koehler, 1934).

Mierisch, Helene. Nachlass. Sächsisches Rot-Kreuz-Museum, Beierfeld.

Mierisch, Helene. "Nachlass der Krankenschwester Helene Mierisch." Photographs, Lot 383, Bene-Merenti auction, 1 Oct. 2016. www.the-saleroom.com/de-de/auction-catalogues/bene-merenti-auktionen/catalogue-id-benemerenti10009/lot-2974f337-5eda-4d27-9fe0-a68300ef046c. Accessed 3 Apr. 2017.

Mierisch, Helene Elisabeth Augustin. *Ein Griff ins Leben: Aus meiner Schwesternarbeit* (Koehler, 1953).

Pflugk-Harttung, Elfriede von, editor. *Frontschwestern: Ein deutsches Ehrenbuch* (Bernard & Graefe, 1936).

Rachamimov, Alon. "'Female Generals' and 'Siberian Angels': Aristocratic Nurses and the Austro-Hungarian POW Relief." *Gender and War in Twentieth Century Eastern Europe*, edited by Nancy M. Wingfield and Maria Bucur (Indiana UP, 2006), pp. 23–46.

Schönberger, Bianca. "Motherly Heroines and Adventurous Girls: Red Cross Nurses and Women Army Auxiliaries in the First World War." *Home/Front: The Military, War, and Gender in Twentieth-Century Germany*, edited by Karen Hagemann and Stefanie Schüler-Springorum (Berg, 2002), pp. 87–114.

Schulte, Regina. "The Sick Warrior's Sister: Nursing during the First World War." *Gender Relations in German History: Power, Agency and Experience from the Sixteenth to the Twentieth Century*, edited by Lynn Abrams and Elizabeth Harvey (U College London P, 1996), pp. 121–141.

Steiner, Petra. "Selbstdeutungen und Missdeutungen von Frauen an der Front: Literatur von und über Krankenschwestern im Ersten Weltkrieg." *Kritische Ausgabe*, vol. 9 (2003), pp. 24–25. www.kritische-ausgabe.de/hefte/krieg/steiner.pdf. Accessed 2 Sept. 2017.

Tylee, Claire. *The Great War and Women's Consciousness: Images of Militarism and Womanhood* (U of Iowa P, 1991).

van Bergen, Leo. *Before my Helpless Sight: Suffering, Dying and Military Medicine on the Western Front 1914–1918*. Translated by Liz Waters (Ashgate, 2009).

Voss, Hedwig. *Im Dienste des Roten Kreuzes: Erlebnisse und Eindrücke aus dem Weltkrieg 1914* (Walter Seifert, 1915).

Wohl, Robert. *The Generation of 1914* (Harvard UP, 1979).

Narratives of Loss and Grief in Art and Literature

Erika Quinn
Writing and Reading Death
German Women's Novels of World War I

Writing in 1915 about how World War I confronted society with pressing new psychological challenges, psychoanalyst Sigmund Freud (1856–1939) described the "altered attitude toward death" the war had created:

> The individual who is not himself a combatant – and so a wheel in the gigantic machinery of war – feels conscious of disorientation, and of an inhibition in his powers and activities. I believe that he will welcome any indication, however slight, which may enable him to find out what is wrong with himself at least. (1957c, 275)[1]

There were many reasons for the disorientation and depression that Freud observed among the populace on the home front. The war, which its leadership had promised would be a short one, lasted well beyond anyone's imagination at its initial outbreak. The optimism of the first months, when casualty lists were published in newspapers and posted at police stations, gave way to more private communications about the countless deaths. Uncertainty about the course of the war and the fate of loved ones increased anxiety among those at home; half of the soldiers killed in the conflict were not identifiable (Chickering 1998, 101). By the end of the war, not a single family was untouched by battlefield death; all women became mourners, embarking on the process of reckoning with death (Kauffman 2001, 311–314). While women may not have publicly discussed their losses, they were not alone: they knew millions of others shared a similar experience.

In addition to mass death, another experience that linked German women together during the war experientially and imaginatively was reading. The late nineteenth century had seen a reading revolution, with literacy rates in Germany reaching 90% in 1900 and a concomitant increase in the number of publications (Reuveni 2006, 152). Reading flourished as an activity during the war despite a dramatic reduction in the numbers of books published (Reuveni 2006, 19, 76). Women of all classes read for entertainment during a time when sociability was altered by men's absence, but also to meet emotional and psychological

---

1 While Freud and his translator use the third person masculine neutral pronoun, I suggest that women too suffered from the effects Freud described. Further on in the essay "Thoughts for the Times on War and Death," Freud specifies that he was describing the population he was most familiar with, the domestic one (291–292).

https://doi.org/10.1515/9783110572001-013

needs. Reading fiction was an important part of coping with the upheaval and uncertainty of the wartime years. As Freud had noted, readers wanted both emotional and cognitive orientation (Reuveni 2006, 80; Barndt 2010, 105; Schulze 1989, 246), which they sought out in literature. In addition to gaining an emotional release or solace, social theorist Michel de Certeau observes that readers can also engage with texts in meaning-making processes as they bring their own experiences to their reading – they "poach" texts and make them their own (1984, xxi). Readers exercise agency rather than being passive consumers of literature who read in an unengaged or uncritical fashion.

Given the bewildering and wrenching experience of grief millions of women experienced, did any "indications" (1957c, 275) of how to cope with such grief that Freud called for emerge? Did popular culture, thriving in the early twentieth century, provide any models of or venues for mourning? Historians have often focused their attention on social policy in regard to women affected by war, as well as labor policies, in part because states, charitable organizations, and reformers all produced a wealth of documents. Most of these essays, manifestos and tracts are prescriptive in tone, seeking to shape women's behavior in the realms of work, sexuality, family life, and consumption.[2] Women's own responses to the war and to death in particular, however, are relatively scarce for World War I. Popular culture offers the historian rich material through which to explore the experience of grief on the ground. In addition to the physical pain incurred by long working hours and hunger addressed in policy tracts, fiction writers deemed the emotional suffering of grief worthy of attention as well. Women's fiction in particular reveals plausible practices and beliefs around mass death and illuminates the discursive possibilities of mourning, so often privatized and mostly out of our view (Audoin-Rouzeau and Becker 2002, 219; Daniel 1997, 148). When sources are scarce, as in this case, historians turn to theory to help make sense of the meaning of the extant texts as well as to interpret the absence of texts one would expect to be written but were not. This essay employs theoretical stances from Sociology, Anthropology, and Cultural Studies in order to do so. It will present the historical context regarding literature and death and then move to examining the literature itself. The novels and stories I examine in this essay were published between 1915 and 1920 and are products of female writers who enjoyed prolific, bestselling careers, including Dora Duncker (1855–1916), Helene von Mühlau (1874–1923), Clara Viebig (1860–1952) and Anny Wothe (1858–1919).

---

2 See, for example, Gertrud Bäumer, Agnes von Harnack, Lily Braun, and Thea von Harbou.

Popular literature in wartime

Fiction about women's wartime experiences was a bestselling literary genre in Germany during and after World War I. Written mostly by women, these novels (*Unterhaltungsromane*) and short stories featured plot-driven narratives and were aimed at a mass female audience. Akin to romance novels, they were written in a straightforward, realistic style. Such patriotic novels became popular during the Franco-Prussian War (1870–1871), but literature at that time did not explore war's effects on the home front, nor did it engage with mass death in the way that World War I literature did (Brandes 1991, 270). Unlike the earlier literary texts, these *Unterhaltungsromane* depicted home front life during the war, focusing on women's relationships with men and their struggles with new responsibilities and roles, in particular, with mass death, grief and bereavement.

Female authors' search for a "subject position," as well as formal conventions of novel writing, led them to focus on the private, intimate lives of their characters (O'Brien 1997, 6). They sought not only to depict women's wartime experiences, but also embraced a didactic function for literature. For writers like Duncker, von Mühlau, Viebig, and Wothe, the work they produced, "both highbrow and popular, was [...] a crucial mechanism of educating emotions"; authors sought to evoke "appropriate feelings" in their readers in response to wartime suffering (Frevert 2011, 123). While they depicted characters confronted with wartime death, middle-class writers adhered to ideas about bourgeois respectability and patriotism for the most part; characters in these novels who transgress social mores and express grief publicly often hail from humbler class backgrounds. Like the majority of popular fiction, most of these "hold on" (*Durchhalten*) novels encouraged ongoing support for the war in their prescriptive stances toward grief. Women were to "hold on" and hold together, both personally by being "strong" and collectively as a nation until a final victory was achieved. Women's novels were more ambiguous than those written by men, however, as they shared a focus on heroic death in the trenches but also addressed the war's painful effects on the home front.

These popular novels provided new venues and practices of mourning that were both public in that all could access them and private in that they were usually read in solitude. Historian Benedict Anderson has focused on the importance of the rise of literacy and reading rates in creating a sense of connection between people. While he focuses on this process as one that contributed to the growth of a sense of national identity in the early nineteenth century, his concept of an abstract and "imagined community" could also be applied to bereaved women readers. Even though readers did not know each other personally, they could imagine other women in similar plights and empathize with them. With the disruption of kinship and social networks, these new "imagined communities" of mourners allowed women to share their pain not only with characters but also with other readers, serving as an adoptive and informal bond fostered by emotional, empathetic connections (Winter 1995, 29). Historian Erika Kuhlman suggests that this readership of mourners could even transcend national boundaries (2012, 92–95). Women's reading lent them a broader perspective: "Literary [...] productions [...] may operate to draw together shared or common experiences into a wider narrative" (Ashplant et al. 2004, 29). Reading fiction presented a new form of dealing with death, and served as a form of "indication" (1957c, 275) to women about their emotional states that Freud called for.

Fictional portrayals of uncertainty, grief, fear and anger heightened readers' emotional identification with the characters, fostered a sense of shared experience, and brought home the war's violent impact. In doing so, women authors brought to light actions or feelings that otherwise may not have been written or spoken about. Whether as diversion, shared experience, emotional outlet, or anesthetic, war fiction "served as a means by which people negotiated war deaths" (Acton 2007, 41). Because the deaths in this home front literature (Quinn 2014) were not witnessed by the protagonists nor the narrators, the act of dying or dead bodies themselves were rarely portrayed. Rather, death was at times personified, or even more often, figured as the palpable absence and simultaneous presence of the deceased. The presence of a loved one was preserved through the possession of talismanic objects and the curation of sacred spaces. These private acts of remembrance, depicted in a public form, suggested a new kind of engagement with death.

Mass death and mourning

It is not all that surprising that those who were left behind (*Hinterbliebene*) by their fallen loved ones were disoriented as Freud had described, given that mass slaughter in the trenches was new for Europeans. Women in the early twentieth century were generally unaccustomed to the violent death of young people. Other than colonial battles in East Africa and South-West Africa, Germans had not experienced real battlefield conflict since the wars of German unification of the 1860s and 1870s, whose death count numbered less than 30,000 (Showalter 2004, 342). Death rates in the civilian population, too, were declining because of better nutrition. Especially for the middle classes, death had become an occurrence in an older person's life, rather than an everyday event that could affect anyone (Lee 2009).

The new technological nature of the war made it difficult for women to imagine conditions at the front, just as it was for young men until they actually experienced it.[3] While some combatants did write home about conditions at the front, the military censor did its utmost to prevent frank honesty. Death was alien to most of these women, writers and readers alike; authors of these popular novels rarely depicted death or battle scenes. As Freud noted, death was an unwelcome stranger.

The war brought ignorance about death into sharp focus and intensified prior critiques of mourning practices. Freud characterized his contemporaries' attitude toward death as one of denial, as an attempt to "eliminate it from life" (1957c, 289). In the modern era, people sought to "modify the significance of death from a necessity to an accident," treating it as an unusual fate rather than a universal, inevitable outcome (1957c, 290). Rather than squarely face the reality and permanence of death, modern people believed, according to Freud, that "our hopes, our pride, our happiness, lie in the grave with [the deceased]" (1957c, 290). Freud would have argued that the nationalist imperatives of valorizing battlefield death, being loyal to fallen soldiers and avoiding public displays of grief were in themselves forms of neurotic denial. It was this persistence of denial, coupled with the unprecedented number and manner of wartime deaths, that led Freud to call for a new form of mourning and engagement in the bereavement process. Not only were women unaccustomed to death, the means with which they negotiated it also became less effective. Battlefield deaths made traditional mourning rituals impractical if not obsolete. Corpses were either buried *in situ* or were not buried at all, and mourners could not travel to the sites of death until after the war ended, when the *Volksbund Deutsche Kriegsgräberfürsorge* (German War Graves Commission), a voluntary society, gained permission from the state to care for military graves and to organize cemetery tours. Nor could women wear traditional mourning costume because of fabric rationing and admonitions that such clothing could be harmful to morale (Siebrecht 2014, 144; "Keine 'Trauerkostüme'" [No 'mourning costumes'] 1914, 378). In a rare example, author Margarethe Böhme (1867–1939) weighed in on this issue of mourning behavior in her 1915 novel *Kriegsbriefe der Familie Wimmel* (War letters of the Wimmel family).[4] Her heroine Sanna writes to a relative about overhearing a group of women saying that they wanted all mourning clothes to be outlawed because they damaged morale and encouraged selfish wallowing.

---

3 Some examples illustrating this ignorance include Paul Fussell, *The Great War and Modern Memory* (1975, 23) and Kuhlman (2012, 29).

4 See Quinn. Translation of Böhme and subsequent translations of Hurwitz-Stranz, Duncker, Wothe and Viebig are my own.

Sanna retorted in the letter that the "artificial heroism that one wishes upon German women is useless. Mothers and wives who love their sons and husbands and who are happy to have their men under fire do not really exist in Germany, nor in France, Russia, Japan, or England" (105–106). In her view, women are united in grief across national lines and alliances. Sanna insists, "what is involved in mourning a loved one should be left to each person, however she comes to terms with it" (106). The scene's angry denunciation of those who judge mourners suggests that the bereaved can find their own forms of solace, and also reminds readers that they are not alone in their grief; indeed, mourning women are united in their pain across Europe.

Some historians have argued that because the war experience made mourning rituals ineffective, grief was unexpressed due to a lack of vocabulary to address it (Audoin-Rouzeau and Becker 2002, 176). Indeed, two widows, later recounting their wartime experiences in a 1931 collection of memoirs, *Kriegerwitwen gestalten ihr Schicksal* (War widows shape their futures), wrote that when they received notification of their husbands' deaths, "the terrible moment was indescribable" and "it's impossible to describe" (qtd. in Hurwitz-Stranz 82, 90).[5] Women's grief was not often directly expressed in their private writing, such as correspondence or diaries; mourning women, particularly artists, often turned to non-verbal modes of expression (Siebrecht 2015, 78, 90). Nonetheless, the fiction I discuss in my essay does address death in war, albeit through the bereaved's point of view rather than depicting the act of dying itself. In illustrating a variety of acts of grieving, authors attempted to shape their readers' emotions and responses.

There were also particular historical grounds for the silence regarding women's bereavement. During World War I the state and society encouraged women to conduct themselves in a stoic fashion and to be proud of the sacrifices they and their loved ones made for the nation. Prescriptive texts called on women to practice "quiet grief"; this normative concept appeared in novels, consolation books and other discursive sources so that it became a given (Fehlemann 2009, 333–334). The short story collection *Stille Opfer* (Quiet sacrifice, 1915) valorizes this idea of silent suffering. In the volume's four stories by Helene Christaller (1872–1953), Agnes Harder (1864–1939), Sophie Charlotte von Sell (1864–1941), and Auguste Supper (1867–1951), death is depicted solely as its arrival via death announcements, and the women who receive them quickly recover from the shock and grief to become active contributors to society through nursing or volunteer work. Taking into account this strong pressure on women to

---

5 For another analysis of this text, see Erika Kuhlman's chapter in this volume.

mourn silently, it is even less surprising that death does not make a dramatic appearance in prescriptive texts or women's ego documents from the era.

Given the neurotic modern relationship to the reality of death exacerbated by the war, Freud suggested that the arts, in particular literature and theater, could help with the acceptance of death (1957c, 291). Literary scholar Sandra Gilbert muses, "Perhaps we require the ambiguous consolations of fantasy because those who seem so near, whose country has become so incontrovertibly real to the mourner, are yet so far" (2006, 16). War only made that "country" of death even stranger; deaths did not occur at home in bed, but rather in bewildering conditions of mud, bombing and rot. Gilbert's observation about the paradoxical experience of bereavement quoted above illustrates the task of mourning: to negotiate through imaginative work the deceased's new presence-absence (Kauffman 2001, 311–312). As mourners must reevaluate their relationship to the deceased, their own identities shift accordingly.

As the death of a loved one disrupts the bereaved's identity, mourning and remembering that loved one creates new meaning and identity. In the face of mass death, memory became a major idiom in the construction of identity at individual and collective levels (Antze and Lambek 1996, vii). Memories are never simply records of the past, but rather are interpretive reconstructions that show traces of narrative tropes, cultural assumptions and social contexts. Memory becomes a means of refashioning ourselves both individually and collectively (Antze and Lambek xviii). As one remembers, different meaning is attributed to the past, now that the beloved is no longer there to share in a future.

Because of the widespread silence of grieving women during World War I, their private, individual memories can be notoriously tricky to investigate. Beginning with sociologist Maurice Halbwachs, theorists have focused on collective memory, which is public, and therefore often gendered masculine (1980, 52, 58, 78–79). They have examined war monuments, newspaper debates, national holidays, and largely state-sponsored memorial events and structures as ways of interpreting the past and articulating meaning about it.[6] Individual and private memory, however, has not garnered such robust scholarly attention. Building on Halbwachs' work, historian Pierre Nora observed that individual memory, often familial, often female, is "rooted in the concrete: in space, gesture, image, and object" (1996, 3).[7] It bears traces that are unique to the remembering subject or mourner (Becker 2002, 90). Given its non-textuality, individual memory is

6 For details, see Volker Ackermann, Sabine Behrenbeck, Susanne Brandt, Karin Hausen, and Reinhart Koselleck.
7 See also Paletschek and Schraut (2008, 273).

"in permanent evolution, subject to the dialectic of remembering and forgetting, unconscious of the distortions to which it is subject" (Nora 1996, 3). Rather than seeing this malleability of memory as part of the process of reevaluation necessary for mourning, and a characteristic of collective memory as well (Gillis 1994, 3), Nora bemoaned the fact that memory in the modern age had become a "private affair" (11).

With its focus on individual characters' everyday, personal lives and realistic style, popular literature may portray women's private acts of mourning during and after World War I. As part of the larger culture, fiction may depict historical practices in unwitting ways. It also served as a form of collective memory for women affected by the war: combat stories and celebrations of male heroism ignored women's own set of traumatic experiences. By bringing those experiences to life through popular literature, which reached masses of readers, authors and readers contributed to a kind of imagined community or a "fictive kinship" of bereavement (Winter 1995, 47).

Death in literature

Despite strong strictures on displaying grief, mourners surely engaged in a variety of bereavement practices, private and public, scripted and spontaneous. Historian Annette Becker claims, "Where these [fallen] men worked, loved, studied, prayed, and lived, marks of memory proliferate" (2002, 91). In fictional works, private expressions of grief often "happen" to the bereaved, in contrast to carefully scripted official commemorative events, such as the dedication of monuments or national holidays. Like Nora's observations about the creation of individual or private memory, mourning is conducted alone, and often without words: it is en-*act*-ed through contact with familiar objects and spaces. Affect theory as articulated by Sara Ahmed suggests that humans come into contact with objects and through that physical connection and its accompanying sensual pleasure, imbue them with affect: objects accrue emotional meaning with use. The history of contact between the user(s) and the object creates "stickiness" (2004, 169), that is, an emotional affect that can be transmitted to others through contact with the object (89–91).[8] The public silence about women's wartime losses and women's lack of participation in commemorative events "give [...]

---

8 See also Ute Frevert, "Rethinking the Corporeality and Materiality of German Emotions" (2015).

the objects associated with 'private memory' a particular poignancy" (Ashplant et al. 2004, 20).

Returning to Freud's work can help make sense of some mourning practices depicted in wartime fiction. Freud wrote several essays on the topic, including "Thoughts for the Times on War and Death" with which my essay begins. Two better-known essays addressed the process of mourning itself: "On Transience" (1915) and "Mourning and Melancholia" (1917) argued that the loss of a loved one also was a blow to one's sense of self. That selfhood needed to heal through letting go of the loved one, in other words, accepting the death as final, and finding a new love object to take its place. It is possible that these essays were written in reaction to the cult of the fallen soldier that called for a kind of fixity of memory, which Freud viewed as a form of pathological attachment. Yet Freud later amended this rather bleak view in *The Ego and the Id* (1927), in which he recognized that individuals frequently identify with the deceased. Indeed, this "taking in" of the dead beloved in which the mourner's "ego assumes the features of the [lost] object" may be the only way, Freud surmised, to ultimately accept the death (1962, 37).

Contemporary death scholars have adopted this last idea of Freud's. Some of the importance of preserving a physical connection to the dead beloved is because part of mourning entails the "internalized *being* of the dead," meaning mourners continue to enact their connection and identity with the deceased, or internalize it, long after their actual presence is gone (Gilbert 2006, 16). We carry impressions of others; when we come into physical contact, our own body surface is defined, and those impressions can become memories or a form of identification – we "pick up bits and pieces of each other as the effect of nearness or proximity" (Ahmed 2004, 169). The fact that the bereaved often had been living apart from the dead for weeks if not months or years made mourning the deaths of soldiers in World War I even more difficult: the men's absence had become normal if painful. Once they were dead, there was no external difference in women's experience, save for the fact that now mourners no longer anticipated the return of their loved ones.

While most fiction did not directly illustrate the act of dying, some works did draw upon widely shared cultural attitudes about supernatural connections between the living and the dead. These connections served as a way of internalizing the dead in the mourning process. During and after the war many women called upon mediums to connect them with their beloved dead for comfort (Winter 1995, 57–59). Yet in some women's recollections and in fiction, such connections were not always comforting. One war widow recounted in the collection *Kriegerwitwen gestalten ihr Schicksal* that when her husband was drafted, they promised each other a postmortem contact after either one's death. She described a dream she had after falling asleep one afternoon: "[M]y husband was bending over me. I stretched out my arms to him and saw his handsome face, warm with life, smiling at me [...] but as he drew closer, I woke with a cry of fear: I saw a skull across from me" (qtd. in Hurwitz-Stranz 1931, 24). This was not the kind of communication from the beyond that she had hoped for.

The recollection of such powerful dreams, or similar scenes in fiction, demonstrates that the process of mourning is not completely under conscious control. Awakening in the middle of the night, dreamers find themselves at their most psychologically vulnerable, when they are least governed by their rational will. German writers were particularly interested in these psychological processes in the early 1900s and the war provided them an opportunity to explore them further (Langenbucher 1974, 39). Anny Wothe's 1916 novel *Die den Weg bereiten* (Those who prepare the way) bolsters the idea that deep love can create a supernatural and even postmortem connection.[9] The narrator describes how a young, frail woman, forbidden from being with her soldier lover because of his father's pride and her lower social status, takes to her bed shortly before his death. She recounts to a friend, "Last night poor Peter was with me [...] he held my hand and looked sympathetically at me, saying 'You have to be very brave now, little Golde [...] I went before you, to prepare the way to heaven for you.' And then he bent over me, kissed me, and holding his hand I walked up to heaven through clouds and light" (123). The young people's deep love for each other, and Golde's subsequent death, convinces their fathers to allow Peter and Golde to be buried side by side. This "happy ending" seems to reassure readers that physical death is not the end of love, and thus seeks to soften the pain of bereavement.

Another form of preserving a connection with the dead beloved was mediated by a physical rather than supernatural connection. In both fiction and historical practice, everyday objects that provoked floods of remembrance could become talismans to connect women with their dead. Social scientists Elizabeth Hallam and Jenny Hockey observe, "Objects, images and practices, as well as places and spaces, call to mind or are made to remind us of the deaths of others" (2001, 2).[10] These items could serve as an emotional replacement for the actual body or presence of the deceased and become symbolic representations of the ongoing relationship between the living and the dead. Retaining objects to preserve memory allowed mourners to "re-*view* [...] key moments [...] from individ-

---

9 The notion of "those who prepare the way" is articulated frequently in both the Old and New Testaments, e. g., Malachi 3:1, Luke 7:27, Mark 1:2, and Matthew 11:10, to denote angels or prophets sent by God. Wothe's conflation of the Judeo-Christian tradition with German nationalism was common during World War I.

10 See also Carine Trévisan and Elise Julien.

ual lives, [as] they reenact[ed] [...] the very process of mourning itself" (Gilbert 2006, 281). The objects, and the mourner's possession of them, bore witness to a life that has ended. During World War I, mourners kept memorial albums to this end (Acton 2007, 23).

In war fiction, mourning finds spontaneous expression very often through tactile sensations, with the body serving as a repository of imprinted memories, particularly intimate memories of touch. In Clara Viebig's novel *Töchter der Hekuba* (*Daughters of Hecuba*, 1920), the aristocratic young protagonist Lili Rossi experiences a rush of memories, physical sensations, and emotions as she pulls a "delicate white dress, which her [fallen] husband had particularly liked on her" out of a trunk (50). "A raging pain filled her: never, never again would he wrap his arms around her in this dress. Here – here his hand often rested, had stroked gently up and down the pleats. In this dress! He was never more enraptured by her beauty" (50). Viebig's heroine remembers all the "happy hours" that she had spent with him in the dress, and how she had believed her happiness would be permanent. The dress has accumulated meaning through repetitive use and its mediation of the relationship between husband and wife. It has become "sticky" with emotion (Ahmed 2004, 89). Yet its meaning has now been disrupted by the husband's death: no longer will they use it to inspire a romantic moment. During this reminiscence, Lili berates herself: "why did she have to think about death so often now, about his death?" (50). Her last exclamatory thought emphasizes her absent husband's altered presence in the experience she relives, and is saturated with the irony of his final absence. Their shared physical intimacy has been inscribed on her body. Because these memories are so painful, Lili decides to give the dress away. Her body will no longer come into contact with the dress, allowing its imprint to subside from her memory, she hopes.

While Lili's memory in Viebig's novel *Töchter der Hekuba* is presented as a particular one sited on her body, anthropologists have developed a concept of another body beyond the physical one we all possess, the "social body" (Hockey 2001, 57–58). Since death is not only a physical occurrence, but also a social one, many forms of bereavement and commemoration are intended to address the social death – the ending of relationships and perhaps of the deceased's reputation. Sometimes, representations of the individual as he was in ordinary life can help preserve him in collective memory or preserve his influence or inheritance. Like war monuments, relics or objects can also commemorate someone's social body. For women in much of this home front fiction, the deceased is remembered in his familial role as husband, son or father via the spaces inhabited by him in that role.

Often, the bereaved attempt to stop domestic life in order to enshrine the daily lives of the dead. Some scholars have suggested that such "shrines" or sacred spaces are in fact substitute graves (Siebrecht 2013, 3). For example, one fictional widow in Viebig's *Töchter der Hekuba* cannot stand for anyone to use her dead husband's bed. It harbors memories of their last goodbye, when he had "extended his strong soldier's hand to her" (87). This was a habitual place, a shared space of marital intimacy that was used solely by her and her husband over the decades of their marriage. To allow others to use that space of sexual and emotional intimacy would be an act of desecration, or could possibly inscribe a new presence over that of the absent husband. This can be viewed as the bereaved's attempt to contain and manage jarring, intrusive memories (Hallam and Hockey 2001, 118); it could also serve as a means to retain the loved one's presence for as long as possible, to stop the inexorable flow of time that carries the living farther and farther away from the dead.

The mourner's effort to fix time and preserve a long-absent presence can also imprison. The protagonist of Helene von Mühlau's *Der Kriegsfreiwillige* (The war volunteer, 1915), Maria, was widowed fifteen years before the events of the novel take place. In her mother-in-law's guest room, a portrait of Maria's late husband hangs on the wall, glowing in a "ghostly" fashion. Mühlau describes the room: "in the small room the air was close and heavy" (23). Mühlau's character Maria thinks to herself how horrible it all is – "stale air and the large, bright portrait of her husband! That was too much for her" (23). She experiences the portrait as an oppressive force. This can be interpreted as Maria distancing herself from her marriage and reevaluating it as part of her bereavement. She has shed the identity she possessed when married to the man in the picture; she is no longer that woman and does not want to be shackled to her past. "With those pictures on the wall she could not close her eyes" (27). At last she seeks something to hang over the portrait so she can rest. But as she attempts to cover it with a heavy blanket, the portrait falls off the wall. Maria's mother-in-law interprets this as an ill omen, which illustrates the social pressure on Maria and other war widows to remain "faithful." Memory, in the form of mental images, tactile sensations, and aural recollection of their dead is depicted as a burden to these female characters: it reminds them of death and pain, and, in Maria's case, of a past they have left behind. The author relates how Maria feels smothered by the expectation that she remain attached to her husband. The Freud of "On Transience" or "Mourning and Melancholia" would share Mühlau's critique of this form of bereavement as a neurotic form of denial that would leave the bereaved stuck in a pathological pattern. These fictional texts illustrate the difficulty of facing death that Freud identified, but in so doing, contribute to the confrontation with death nonetheless and at times give readers suggestions of behaviors to avoid.

The mourner's difficulty of reconciling fidelity to a dead husband with a need to create a new life is also raised in Viebig's *Töchter der Hekuba*. The protagonist Lili finds the presence of her fallen husband in a portrait less than soothing. Rossi's portrait hangs across from their marriage bed and his melancholy eyes appear not only "sad," but also "full of reproach or even a threat," the longer she gazes at him (168). The portrait asks her, "Have you already forgotten me? So soon?" (168). The cult of the fallen soldier, articulated by state and society, dictated fidelity to the dead. The state was to honor fallen soldiers through a victorious war effort and commemoration; mourners were to remember the dead with reverence and steadfastness (Mosse 1990, 6). This way of thinking about the war dead was the kind of refusal to confront death that Freud had recognized, and one that authors often problematized in their fiction. In Viebig's novel, Lili stretches out her hands to the portrait, imploring, "My poor husband, I will never forget you" (1920b, 168). This vow confronted characters with a political and social burden. The novel suggests that to forget her husband would not only reflect poorly on Lili as a wife, but also as a patriot. Viebig continued the story of *Töchter der Hekuba* in *Das Rote Meer* (The Red Sea, 1920). At the beginning of the second novel, Lili begins to fall in love with another man. This new start is complicated by the haunting presence of her fallen husband: "Lieutenant Rossi climbed out of his evergreen-bedecked grave on Monte Piano in which he had quietly slept, and found his widow at home. At night he went to her bed, speaking words of love and threats" (1920a, 42). The fact that Lili is entering into a romantic relationship with another male character indicates in Freudian terms that her mourning is over: she has found a new love object. Freud hoped society at large could also achieve this reconciliation with loss: "When once the mourning is over, it will be found that our high opinion of the riches of civilization has lost nothing from our discovery of the fragility. We shall build up again all that war has destroyed, and perhaps on firmer ground and more lastingly than before" (1957b, 307).

Just as Maria's mother-in-law in Mühlau's novel believes that keeping her dead son ever-present is a duty, Lili also relates to her husband's portrait from a sense of love mixed with guilt and duty. The parallels between death and sleep, graves and beds is striking: all of these literary instances of preserving the presence of the deceased occur in bedrooms. Preserving the social body of these men as soldiers no longer consoles their widows; rather, it morbidly traps them into fidelity to a corpse. This fidelity, expected in particular by the state, sets up public, commemorative memory in conflict with the private memory and its malleability that Nora identified. The authors memorialize male characters' familial roles as husbands and sexual partners, yet the presentation of these men in military garb, their public uniform, blurs the sharp distinction between the public and private spheres, much as total war did. However, other spaces also could be imbued with an identity, or a social body, especially places of work for men.

In early twentieth-century Germany, physical spaces were strongly gendered and contributed to the "separate spheres" bourgeois gender regime. This means that public spaces – especially workplaces – were gendered male, and private spaces – the home – were gendered female. These strong distinctions were disrupted by the war as women adopted men's jobs in war production or became advocates for their families vis-à-vis civil servants. This "masculinization" of women concerned many cultural conservatives and was an important topic of debate during and after the war (Thébaud 1994, 34–37). One woman's correspondence cited by historian Ute Daniel illustrates the importance of gendered space and everyday habits in grief and memory. The woman was employed at a munitions factory, having taken up her husband's work after he was drafted. She wrote that she was proud to do his work and represent him there. The job was "sacrosanct" to her: in a way, she was *being* her husband, enacting her connection and identity to him. When he died, she abruptly quit the job. In a letter to a friend she explained that the job's sacredness was the reason she could not "do it any more, but [she did not] want to work somewhere else" (qtd. in Daniel 1997, 55). Emulating her husband was no longer possible; the conflict she experienced between honoring him by "being" him, and the reality of his death which made that "being" a fiction, was too much for the widow to handle.

Women entering male spaces to replace or connect with their absent men were portrayed as acting against their feminine natures. Working at a factory was lauded but also seen as a threat to women's femininity. Other male spaces, like offices or studies, were also imbued with this potential danger. A 1915 short story by Dora Duncker, "Prinzeßchen" (The little princess), captures the promise of connection and the danger that entry into male spaces presented to female mourners. In the story, sixteen-year-old Jutta von Helstenberg, the "little princess" of the title, gazes at her beloved father's portrait with a "sudden, hesitant fear" (176). She will not leave the portrait because she is waiting for news from him at the front. A servant convinces her to go outside, but she does not feel at home in Berlin; she is ill at ease without the protection of her father in the metropolis and wonders about people who carry on what appear to be normal lives. She sees two "simple" women garbed in mourning clothes sitting on a park bench and sits with them. One complains that she lost three sons in the war, two in Russia, and one in France. The other replies with scorn that she is lucky: her own husband had both legs shot off and he died a month later in agony after experiencing medical treatments akin to torture (183). Jutta flees from their competition over who has suffered most, disgusted and fearful. Here, Duncker underlines that such unseemly public display is characteristic of the lower classes, not the aristocracy. Jutta decides not to go out any longer, but to remain with her adored father's portrait. She takes the key to her father's study and enters, sitting in his writing chair to read the letter that arrived from him. Then she paces the room, looking at the bookcase. She opens it and looks at the books, which her father promised to read with her in the future. She runs her hand along them, thinking, "Papa had already held all of them" (187). She also looks at his weapons case, smoking table, and, in particular, the small silver cigarette case, which was "almost dear to her, since he had used it every day" (188). This gendered space, the office, is full of her father's masculine possessions: books of philosophy, history and German classical authors; weapons, and smoking accouterments. He regularly used all these objects, which were objects forbidden to her, in particular, the books that she might read and understand "someday" (187). When the news comes that he has been killed, his study no longer is a comforting space to her. The character opens his weapons case and shoots herself, a self-extinguishing and ultimate expression of grief. Her grief, youth and gender made her vulnerable to rash acts, and she could not imagine life without her father. Not only does Duncker's story capture possible modes and practices of grief, but it also offers a message about women's vulnerability and need for male protection.

Fictional depictions of grief often served as prescriptive messages to female readers. Per these authors, mourning was a necessary process for the bereaved to experience, but it need not paralyze or diminish them. Nor should it cause them to transgress class-based codes of self-expression. Despite their desire to restrict expressions of grief, authors' depictions of the private realm of memory and mourning brought such issues into the public sphere through the imagined community of readers who participated in bringing their own meaning and losses to such texts. Women's private losses of husbands and sons were not recognized in the large, public, formal commemorations sponsored by the state in the name of the German nation. Rather, women individually mourned their husbands as rents in the fabric of everyday life. Literature provided one important imagined arena through which women could explore and address their experiences and feelings of grief. Popular fiction often illustrates these non-verbal, non-textual possibilities of enacting grief, which Freud identified. Manipulation of familiar objects like clothing or books, or preservation of shared spaces allowed women to retain a connection with their loved ones. Knowing that fictional characters "shared" a reader's feelings of anxiety and anticipatory grief, as well as the awareness that other readers were engaged with the same texts, contributed to a sense of female community anchored in suffering and a shared possibility of emotional expression.

Works Cited

Ackermann, Volker. *National Totenfeiern in Deutschland: Von Wilhelm I. bis Franz Josef Strauß* (Klett-Cotta, 1990).
Acton, Carol. *Grief in Wartime: Private Pain, Public Discourse* (Palgrave Macmillan, 2007).
Ahmed, Sara. *The Cultural Politics of Emotion* (Routledge, 2004).
Anderson, Benedict. *Imagined Communities: Reflections on the Origins and Spread of Nationalism* (Verso, 1998).
Antze, Paul, and Michael Lambek. "Forecasting Memory." Introduction. *Tense Past: Cultural Essays in Trauma and Memory*, edited by Antze and Lambek (Routledge, 1996), pp. vii–xxxviii.
Ashplant, Timothy G., et al. "The Politics of War Memory and Commemoration: Context, Structures and Dynamics." *Commemorating War: The Politics of Memory*, edited by Ashplant, et al. (Transactions Publishers, 2004), pp. 3–86.
Audoin-Rouzeau, Stéphane, and Annette Becker. *14–18: Understanding the Great War.* Translated by Catherine Temerson (Hill and Wang, 2002).
Bäumer, Gertrud. *Der Krieg und die Frau* (Deutsche Verlags-Anstalt, 1914).
Barndt, Kerstin. "Mothers, Citizens, and Consumers: Female Readers in Weimar Germany." *Weimar Politics/Weimar Subjects: Rethinking the Political Culture of Germany in the 1920s*, edited by Kathleen Canning, et al. (Berghahn Books, 2010), pp. 91–115.
Becker, Annette. "Remembering and Forgetting in the First World War in Western Europe." *Ideas of Europe Since 1914: The Legacy of the First World War*, edited by Menno Spiering and Michael Wintle (Palgrave Macmillan, 2002), pp. 89–104.
Behrenbeck, Sabine. "Heldenkult oder Friedensmahnung?: Kriegerdenkmäle nach beiden Weltkriegen." *Lernen aus dem Krieg?: Deutschen Nachkriegszeiten 1918 und 1945*, edited by Gottfried Niedhart and Dieter Riesenberger (C.H. Beck, 1992), pp. 344–364.
Böhme, Margarethe. *Kriegsbriefe der Familie Wimmel* (Carl Reißner, 1915).
Brandes, Helga. "Das Mädchenbuch der Gründerzeit: Zur Herausbildung einer patriotischen Literatur für Mädchen." *Nationale Mythen und Symbole in der zweiten Hälfte des 19. Jahrhunderts: Strukturen und Funktionen von Konzepten nationaler Identität*, edited by Jürgen Link und Wulf Wülfling (Klett-Cotta, 1991), pp. 256–274.
Brandt, Susanne. "Kriegssammlungen im Ersten Weltkrieg: Denkmäler oder Laboratoires d'histoire?" *"Keiner fühlt sich hier mehr als Mensch …": Erlebnis und Wirkung des Ersten Weltkriegs*, edited by Gerhard Hirschfeld, et al. (Klartext, 1993), pp. 241–255.
Braun, Lily. *Die Frauen und der Krieg* (S. Hirzel, 1915).
Certeau, Michel de. *The Practices of Everyday Life.* Translated by Steven Rendall (U of California P, 1984).
Chickering, Roger. *Imperial Germany and the Great War, 1914–1918* (Cambridge UP, 1998).
Christaller, Helene, et al. *Stille Opfer: Den deutschen Frauen und Jungfrauen in großer Zeit* (Verlag von Otto Rippel, 1915).
Daniel, Ute. *The War From Within: German Working-Class Women in the First World War.* Translated by Margaret Ries (Berg, 1997).

Duncker, Dora. "Prinzeßchen." *Berlin im Kriege: Großstadtskizzen aus dem Kriegsjahr 1914/15* (Globus Verlag, 1915), pp. 173–192.

Fehlemann, Silke. "'Stille Trauer': Deutsche Soldatenmütter in der Zwischenkriegszeit." *Historical Social Research*, vol. 34, no. 130 (2009), pp. 331–342.

Freud, Sigmund. *The Ego and the Id.* Translated by Joan Riviere (The Hogarth Press, 1962).

Freud, Sigmund. "Mourning and Melancholia." *The Standard Edition of the Complete Psychological Works of Sigmund Freud*, edited by James Strachey, vol. XIV (1914–1916) (The Hogarth Press, 1957a), pp. 243–258.

Freud, Sigmund. "On Transience." *The Standard Edition of the Complete Psychological Works of Sigmund Freud*, edited by James Strachey, vol. XIV (1914–1916) (The Hogarth Press, 1957b), pp. 303–308.

Freud, Sigmund. "Thoughts for the Times on War and Death." *The Standard Edition of the Complete Psychological Works of Sigmund Freud*, edited by James Strachey, vol. XIV (1914–1916) (The Hogarth Press, 1957c), pp. 275–300.

Frevert, Ute. *Emotions in History: Lost and Found* (Central European UP, 2011).

Frevert, Ute. "Rethinking the Corporeality and Materiality of German Emotions." German Studies Association Conference (2 October 2015), Washington, D.C. Roundtable presentation.

Fussell, Paul. *The Great War and Modern Memory* (Oxford UP, 1975).

Gilbert, Sandra M. *Death's Door: Modern Dying and the Ways We Grieve* (W.W. Norton and Company, 2006).

Gillis, John R. "Memory and Identity: The History of a Relationship." *Commemorations: The Politics of National Identity*, edited by Gillis (Princeton UP, 1994), pp. 3–26.

Halbwachs, Maurice. *The Collective Identity.* Translated by Francis J. and Vida Yazki Ditter (Harper and Row, 1980).

Hallam, Elizabeth, and Jenny Hockey. *Death, Memory, and Material Culture* (Berg, 2001).

Harbou, Thea von. *Die deutsche Frau im Weltkrieg: Einblicke und Ausblicke.* 2nd ed. (Hesse & Becker Verlag, 1916).

Harnack, Agnes von. *Der Krieg und die Frauen* (Julius Spring, 1914).

Hausen, Karin. "The 'Day of National Mourning' in Germany." *Between History and Histories: The Making of Silences and Commemorations*, edited by Gerald Sider and Gavin Smith (U of Toronto P, 1997), pp. 127–148.

Hockey, Jenny. "Body, Two Bodies Theory." *Encyclopedia of Death and Dying*, edited by Glennys Howarth and Oliver Leaman (Routledge, 2001), pp. 57–58.

Hurwitz-Stranz, Helene, editor. *Kriegerwitwen gestalten ihr Schicksal: Lebenskämpfe deutscher Kriegerwitwen nach eigenen Darstellungen* (Carl Heymanns Verlag, 1931).

Kauffman, Jeffrey. "Mourning." *Encyclopedia of Death and Dying*, edited by Glennys Howarth and Oliver Leaman (Routledge, 2001), pp. 311–314.

"Keine 'Trauerkostüme.'" *Kunstwart und Kulturwart*, vol. 27, no. 24 (1914), p. 378.

Koselleck, Reinhart, editor. *Die politische Totenkult: Kriegerdenkmäler in der Moderne* (Wilhelm Fink Verlag, 1994).

Kuhlman, Erika. *Of Little Comfort: War Widows, Fallen Soldiers, and the Remaking of the Nation After the Great War* (New York UP, 2012).

Langenbucher, Wolfgang. *Der aktuelle Unterhaltungsroman: Beiträge zur Geschichte und Theorie der massenhaft verbreiteten Literatur* (Bouvier Verlag, 1974).

Lee, Robert. "Early Death and Long Life in History: Establishing the Scale of Premature Death in Europe and Its Cultural, Economic and Social Significance." *Historical Social Research*, vol. 34, no. 130 (2009), pp. 23–60.

Mosse, George. *Fallen Soldiers: Reshaping the Memory of the World Wars* (Oxford UP, 1990).

Mühlau, Helene von. *Der Kriegsfreiwillige* (Egon Fleischl & Co., 1915).

Nora, Pierre. *Realms of Memory: The Construction of the French Past*. Translated by Arthur Goldhammer (Columbia UP, 1996).

O'Brien, Catherine. *Women's Fictional Responses to the First World War: A Comparative Study of Selected Texts by French and German Writers* (Peter Lang, 1997).

Paletschek, Sylvia, and Sylvia Schraut. "Remembrance and Gender: Making Gender Visible and Inscribing Women into Memory Culture." *The Gender of Memory: Cultures of Remembrance in Nineteenth- and Twentieth-Century Europe*, edited by Paletschek and Schraut (Campus Verlag, 2008), pp. 267–287.

Quinn, Erika. "Love and Loss, Marriage and Mourning: World War One in German Home Front Novels." *First World War Studies*, vol. 5, no. 2 (2014), pp. 223–250.

Reuveni, Gideon. *Reading Germany: Literature and Consumer Culture in Germany before 1933*. Translated by Ruth Morris (Berghahn Books, 2006).

Schulze, Jutta. "'Berlin im Kriege': Romane und Erzählungen von Frauen zum Krieg (1914–1918)." *August 1914: Ein Volk zieht in den Krieg*, edited by Berliner Geschichtswerkstatt (Verlag Dirk Nishen, 1989), pp. 242–250.

Showalter, Dennis. *The Wars of German Unification* (Hoder Arnold, 2004).

Siebrecht, Claudia. *The Aesthetics of Loss: German Women's Art of the First World War* (Oxford UP, 2013).

Siebrecht, Claudia. "The Female Mourner: Gender and the Moral Economy of Grief During the First World War." *Gender and the First World War*, edited by Christa Hämmerle, et al. (Palgrave, 2014), pp. 144–162.

Thébaud, Françoise. "The Great War and the Triumph of Sexual Division." Translated by Arthur Goldhammer. *Toward a Cultural Identity in the Twentieth Century*, edited by Thébaud, vol. V, *A History of Women in the West* (Harvard UP, 1994), pp. 21–75.

Trévisan, Carine, and Elise Julien. "Cemeteries." *Capital Cities at War, A Cultural History: Paris, London, Berlin 1914–1919*, edited by Jay Winter and Jean-Louis Robert, vol. 2 (Cambridge UP, 2012), pp. 428–467.

Viebig, Clara. *Das Rote Meer* (Egon Fleischl & Co., 1920a).

Viebig, Clara. *Töchter der Hekuba* (Egon Fleischl & Co., 1920b).

Winter, Jay. *Sites of Memory, Sites of Mourning: The Great War in European Cultural History* (Cambridge UP, 1995).

Wothe, Amy. *Die den Weg bereiten* (Paul Franke Verlag, 1916).

Erika Kuhlman
War Widows' Dilemma

Emotion, the Myths of War and the Search for *Selbständigkeit*

The history of World War I widowhood in Germany begins and ends with the post office. Historicizing war widowhood upends conventional WWI history by shifting the focus from the nation-state that fought the war to the individuals who, willingly or not, entered fields of battle, leaving families and communities behind to manage on their own. No sooner had the soldier departed, when the enormous postal correspondence between the battlefield and the household began. According to one estimate, Germans sent and received twenty-eight *billion* cards, letters, and packages through the mail to and from military men between 1914 and 1918 (Ulrich and Ziemann 2010, 15). Thus, mail carriers, too, contributed in their own way to the nation's war effort. Written communication shaped the war experience not only of civilians but of soldiers as well and knitted the presumed divided fronts together. Letters from the field, or *Feldpostbriefe*, were highly sought-after envelopes handed to anxious wives by their mail carriers. Dreaded, however, were the black-bordered telegrams also delivered by the German *Post*.

Sometimes, wives received contradictory telegrams telling them either that their husbands had "died upon the field of honor!" or merely been wounded and lay in a hospital bed, or taken prisoner and sent to an unknown P.O.W. camp. Elisabeth Macke, the wife of the Expressionist artist August Macke, received all three of those messages about her husband (Kuhlman 2012, 33), who died on the battlefield in Champagne, France in 1914. Given the amount of letters written, wives who remained at home often befriended their mail carriers, making it very difficult for the carrier to deliver heart-stopping news; one widow remembered that it took her postman two days to work up the courage to ring her doorbell with the notice of her husband's death (Hurwitz-Stranz 1931, 82).[1] Other sorrows involving the mail include the oft-repeated phenomenon, in which widows learned of their husbands' deaths and then received mail from him days or even weeks later. Given the high volume of mail, it might take a long time for letters to arrive at their destinations. Occasionally, such delayed correspondences would lead the widow to question the previous report of her husband's death (Hurwitz-Stranz 1931, 31). Johanna Boldt received word from the German military in summer 1915, that her husband had died in a Siberian P.O.W. camp in April of

---

1 All translations from German to English are my own, unless otherwise noted.

https://doi.org/10.1515/9783110572001-014

that year; she opened three more telegrams in January, July, and August of 1916, each sent from the Red Cross, all reporting the same news (Hagener 1986, 96–99). Finally, war widows seeking compensation for the loss of their husbands and breadwinners sent their requests to the German War Ministry (later the Ministry of Labor), typically via their local post office.

German Great War widows left a rich legacy of their experiences in print. Widows such as Elisabeth Erdmann-Macke collected her war correspondence with her husband and in 1962 reproduced the letters in a book. Johanna Boldt, another war widow, saved the letters she wrote to her soldier-husband Julius. Their daughter Edith collected and published the missives in 1986 (Hagener 1986) after her mother's death. Finally, Helene Hurwitz-Stranz solicited the remembrances of other German war widows, who sent them to her anonymously. Hurwitz-Stranz published the collection of war memoirs in 1932. These texts will be used to compare the official German government's response to the war and its aftermath to the widows' own thoughts on their war and postwar experiences. The comparison demonstrates that while widows felt and performed the grief brought about by their husbands' deaths, the nation also expected it of them. However, they also sought and found ways to live independent – achieve *Selbständigkeit* – of the (often inadequate) social welfare system that the German nation put in place to help them take care of themselves and their families.

Analyzing the narratives of these war widows' experiences changes the temporality of the war by focusing on the aftermath of the conflict, since widows were forced to deal with the consequences of their husbands' deaths long after the official cease-fire that ended the fighting in 1918. The Great War occurred at the dawning of a modern European society, in which romance more often than not marked the relationship of couples, and widows were expected to demonstrate their emotional attachment to their fallen husbands in ways other than wearing the traditional mourning garb (Kuhlman 2012, 54–56). Modernity also signaled a new era of female economic self-sufficiency. War widows thus had to navigate between mourning the death of their heroic soldier-husbands as symbols of service to the nation, on the one hand, and seeking self-reliance and independence for themselves and their children, on the other hand. Economic independence often meant fighting with the German government to obtain a war widows' pension, and/or seeking training, and a job that could ultimately take a mother away from her children. This, of course, was particularly true of working-class widows.

While conventional histories force the conflict into the beginning and ending dates of 1914 to 1918, war widowhood demonstrates the inability of nations to confine the war to such temporal parameters, and the need to recognize that the so-called "long war" lasted well into 1925 (Mulligan 2014, 9). Widows from all of the combatant nations fought with their governments for compensation long after the presumed end of the military conflict in November 1918 – as long as five decades after the Armistice in one British case (Smith 2013, 117–131). U.S. widows' obligations to embody the expected individual sacrifice for the nation continued into the 1930s, when they honored their husbands' deaths on the battlefields during U.S. government-sponsored trips to France, where most WWI deaths occurred (Budreau 2011, 8). German war widows enjoyed no such tribute. Indeed, Maria Geiger's letter of 12 May 1918, to the German Kaiser pleaded with him to help her bring her husband's dead body home, "for we would love to bury our unforgettable husband and father in the Heimat. I am penniless and can't possibly afford the transfer [...]." There is no record of a response from the Kaiser (Ulrich and Ziemann 2010, 184).

Writing the history of war widowhood also calls for writing a history of emotions often neglected in earlier accounts of the Great War. Although it is impossible to pinpoint the exact number of casualties, most historians agree that nearly two million German soldiers died in the war, leaving some 600,000 widowed wives (Hausen 1987, 128). Black-clad mourners were a common sight in Germany's urban centers. German women, unlike widows in the United States, held fast to prewar mourning fashions that marked them as the symbol of the human emotions of sorrow and despair. The term mourning implies sadness, but the social context also prescribed how women who had lost their husbands were expected to look and act in public spaces and do the "work of mourning" (Hausen 1997, 131); war widowhood, in particular, brought this social dimension out in bold relief. Even though one mourned, war widows were also expected to demonstrate mourning by wearing black mourning garb and a veil, and keeping their faces down-cast during war remembrance ceremonies. The added dimension of a life lost to a national cause such as war exacted a heavy toll on the bereaved who carried with her not only her personal loss, but the loss of a man who had sacrificed his life for the sake of the national cause. In other words, war widowhood became a public, rather than solely private, identity assumed by wives upon their soldier-husbands' deaths. In Germany after 1918, war widows faced the added emotional burden of the nation's humiliating military defeat.

War widows performed their widowhood in a highly politicized context. Germany stood at a precipice in 1918, largely of its own making. Its leaders had sent young men to war with exhilarating expectations of heroism and the promise of a quick victory in 1914, only to watch them succumb to a brutal war that yielded few heroes and no victory. Mourning war widows, as the living embodiment of their dead soldier-husbands, were expected to help heal the nation during the Weimar Republic by raising their children to be patriotic Germans. Widows lacking financial resources could not even provide for their children's basic needs without entering the labor force, necessarily taking them away from what was argued to be their primary concern. The contradiction inherent in this ideological formula put them in an emotional quandary that upper-class widows such as Elisabeth Erdmann-Macke were spared.

Emotions carry with them specific gendered expectations. Carolyn Strange, Christopher Forth, and Robert Cribb have explored the connections between emotion, honor, and ritualized violence primarily among fighting men in their book *Honour, Violence and Emotions in History* (2014). Writing the history of war widowhood in Germany shifts the focus to women's emotional responses to the loss of their soldier-husbands in the context of emotionally-charged moments in national life: the 1914 declaration of war, the call for flag-waving patriotism and unity among a diverse German population, and the feeling of defeat and betrayal in November 1918, that left German society deeply divided during the Weimar Republic.

While many men may have been reluctant to share their wartime emotions, as historian Jason Crouthamel and psychologist Stephanie Shields contend (Crouthamel 2014, 3–4; Shields 2000, 11), women were expected to express their emotions freely. Of all the war widows' writings analyzed in this study, Johanna Boldt's letters exemplify the emotional intensity of fear and uncertainty she experienced in her husband's absence (Hagener 1986). When Boldt looked out her window over the Hoheluft district of Hamburg, she saw recruits marching up and down the streets, and wondered bitterly why other women could enjoy their soldier-husbands' company at home, while hers had been whisked away. When she did not hear from Julius for long periods of time, she worried obsessively that he had grown to enjoy the soldier's life and would no longer come home to her (Hagener 1986, 69). In fact, Julius kept his real war experiences from his wife, but revealed them to his brother, August Boldt on 30 August 1914: "The war is abominable" (qtd. in Hagener 53).[2] The social worker Hermann Geib, who subscribed to the conventional wisdom of women as emotional "beings," argued in 1931 that women brought "heart" – by which he meant feelings – into the business of securing social services for war survivors (Hurwitz-Stranz 1931, 5). However, as members of the assumed "private sphere," women left fewer records of their emotional lives for historians to analyze.

Helene Hurwitz-Stranz understood the plight of widows firsthand, since she worked as an observer on the National Pension Court. Court observers helped court-appointed judges decide how much money widows and other survivors re-

---

2 "Der Krieg ist etwas sehr, sehr schreckliches."

ceived as compensation for their dead soldiers' wartime service from the German government. Hurwitz-Stranz may have asked the widows in court to contribute their stories, and she may also have solicited widows' biographies through the war widows' periodical, *Die Kriegerwitwe* (1920 – 1921). Hurwitz-Stranz's 1931 publication *Kriegerwitwen gestalten ihr Schicksal: Lebenskämpfe deutscher Kriegerwitwen nach eigenen Darstellungen* (War widows shape their futures: The life struggles of German war widows in their own words), set in old-fashioned *Fraktur* type, features the brief but poignant biographies of fifteen war widows, some only two pages long and others several pages in length. All the biographies were published anonymously. Added to their stories are paragraphs written either by Hurwitz-Stranz, or her co-editor, Hermann Geib, about other widows whose stories they had heard. Several people in the 1920s social services community in Berlin also wrote introductions to the book. The contributors include Helene Simon, Geib, Hurwitz-Stranz, Sidonie Wronsky, Käthe Grelle and the formidable women's rights advocate Gertrud Bäumer. The book ends with an essay written by social activist Martha Harnoß.

Hermann Geib and Gertrud Bäumer's essays are the most representative. Geib noted the lamentable absence of widows' voices in social welfare conversations among postwar Germans, and reminded readers that the main goal of war widows was to raise healthy, educated children for Germany's future. Bäumer agreed with Geib's assessment, adding that widows had sacrificed much and suffered along with their heroic husbands. Widows played a major role in helping to rebuild the nation, according to Bäumer. Martha Harnoß's closing essay calls upon war widows to demand justice in the form of social welfare for their husbands' deaths. Her essay prods widows to take an active, public role in reconstructing postwar Germany during the Weimar Republic. Taken together, Hurwitz-Stranz's collection offers widows' individual stories, sandwiched in between the thoughts of social service representatives on the significant experiences and contributions of war widows to German postwar society.

Preserving the anonymity of the widows served to protect the unofficial, private experience of war widowhood from the official, government-sanctioned notion of war widowhood; official widowhood served to uphold traditional myths about the war, while the reality of war widowhood – in which women also sought and struggled with *Selbständigkeit* (self-reliance) – undercut those myths. Gendered myths of war featuring mournful but stoic war widowhoods, too, were disrupted by war widows dreaming about independence, or self-determined futures, since women's futures in reality were typically tied to their husbands – even dead husbands. Underlying all the widows' memoirs in *Kriegerwitwen gestalten Ihr Schicksal*, and even some of the book's editorial commentaries, is that telling the story of war widows forced Germans to face the myths of war, of the heroic soldier, and the ways in which the nation refused to admit defeat that the nation-state sought to uphold during the Weimar Republic. Widows stood at the crossroads of this contradiction: they were enlisted to represent their husbands' supreme sacrifice (uphold society's traditional war myths), but in doing so they reminded the public that the war robbed them of their bread-winners (dead heroes could not put food on the table). It was the emotional expressions in *Kriegerwitwen gestalten Ihr Schicksal* that communicated the discrepancy between the desire for an "orderly family life" (Hausen 1987, 129) that women were expected to create and sustain in war-torn and postwar Germany and the immense disorder and dysfunction in families that resulted from soldiers' deaths in the war that revealed the consequences of war for Germans and German society.

Before historians Robert Weldon Whalen and Karin Hausen began exploring war widows' lives, their perspectives on the war had seldom been included in histories of WWI. Hausen summed up society's treatment of war survivors this way: "The silence surrounding the hard, gray, everyday realities of wartime and postwar life is part of the pathos of hero worship. The innumerable war monuments in the city squares block our view of the realities of war for these women. Instead, women are portrayed as pietas, suffering for the glory of their heroic sons" (1987, 140). Hausen then quotes the president of the German Reichstag, who noted that while the war widows grieve and citizens were to "honor their pain," Germans should instead feel "proud of so many heroic sons who have spilt their blood and laid down their lives in the World War we are fighting for our own existence" (140). Hurwitz-Stranz's volume, in contrast, looks beyond the heroic soldier to the war widows' dismal realities resulting from one of the most horrific wars of the twentieth century.

Studying human emotions in history provides us with the ability to discern more clearly motivation in a social context (Frevert 2010, 68). Widows are expected to act sorrowful, and most of the memoirs in Hurwitz-Stranz's collection indicate that widows interpreted their emotional responses to the news of their husbands' deaths as intense grief; but war widows also acted to secure and protect their economic and social independence, moves that seem self-serving and thus incompatible with – or at least different from – the image of incapacitating sorrow. How did widows make sense of this conflict between the expected outpouring of grief with a desire for *Selbständigkeit* or independence? Historians have been interested in looking at collective versus individual emotion (Roper, in Frevert 2010, 70). The humiliation of defeat seems to have been a collective emotion many Germans experienced after November 1918; how did individual widows rectify their sorrow with this collective emotional response of shame?

The context of Great War widowhood includes the shift in German society from nineteenth century tradition to modernity. In prewar Germany, married women were confined to a subordinate position by virtue of *Züchtigungsrecht* (the right of a husband to beat his wife) and independence in any woman, according to one member of the Reichstag, was a trait to be discouraged (Quataert 1979, 22–23). The position of widows in prewar German society, according to legal scholar Paul Schüler, was so deplorable that the widow would have been better off had she died, rather than losing her husband (Kuhlman 2012, 22). A small but vocal bourgeois women's rights organization existed in Germany before the war, but its propaganda usually couched demands for equality in women's proper role within the home, rather than in public (Quataert 1979, 9–10).

After the war, women were positioned at the forefront of the shift from a premodern to a modern society, which elicited fear and anxiety since men stood to lose power relative to women. The success of businesswomen, such as Johanna Boldt, for example, who improved her husband's *Kolonialwaren* (colonial goods) shop in Hamburg during the war (see below), posed a possible threat to soldiers in the field and their masculinity, as it appeared that women were taking over the public sphere – traditionally the realm of men – in their absence (Hagener 1986, 66–67; Nelson 2014, 80). Historian Elisabeth Domansky argues that German society did not "return to patriarchy" after the war. Added to the deaths of two million soldiers were the physical and mental casualties that left many veterans unable to resume their status as heads of households. Approximately 4,216,058 German soldiers (out of over 13 million mobilized) survived but sustained wounds as a result of the conflict (Domansky 1996, 433–434; Winter 2010, 249). Injured veterans were therefore significant in number. A better explanation for patriarchy's decline, according to Domansky, lay in the authority retained by the German government after the war. Women did not replace men as heads of households (except when they did as widows who obtained economic and social independence) but rather, as Domansky notes (1996, 428), the government coopted the role of patriarchal provider, in large part through its social welfare programs. The government also encouraged public, versus private, mourning and commemorative activities (see below).

But Domansky obscures the degree to which the so-called "New Woman" functioned as a political and economic being during and after the war (Kuhlman 2012, 42). War widows were frequently driven into the labor market and into welfare offices to protest the meager pensions they received in compensation for their soldier-husband's death; both phenomena educated and politicized women, and led to the development of the consciousness of widows as a unified social entity (Harnoß, in Hurwitz-Stranz 1931, 116–117). The context of modernity during the Weimar Republic, coupled with the deplorable status of women in prewar Germany, then, explains war widows' search for and insistence on *Selbständigkeit*. As Robert Weldon Whalen wrote, "the war radicalized German women and drove them into public protest" (1983, 108).

Widows achieving *Selbständigkeit* did so primarily through paid labor. In 1915, according to Katharine Anthony, there were about 10 million married women in Germany. Of those, 2.8 million, or just over twenty percent, worked for wages (Anthony 1915, 196). Although Germany added about 800,000 women and girls to its workforce during the war, the percentage of women who worked remained relatively stable at about 30 percent (Daniel 1997, 276). Karl Nau's study of war widows in the Hessian city of Darmstadt revealed that about 30 percent of war widows worked for wages in 1928–1929. In other places, the figure is higher, including 41 percent in Mönchen-Gladbach, 46 percent in Hagen, and as high as 88 percent in Berlin-Schöneberg. The vast majority of widows had also worked before their marriages (Hausen 1987, 138). Whether they labored outside the home or not, widows in Darmstadt earned between 10 and 20 percent less than their husbands would have, had they lived, according to Nau (1931, 70). Work and how to obtain it constituted an endless worry for war widows, especially those with children.

Statistics such as these, of course, do not reveal widows' emotional responses to their situations. One forty-six-year-old widow's story is typical for those found in *Kriegerwitwen gestalten Ihr Schicksal*. After five happy years of marriage and three children under the age of three, this widow's husband was called up for duty in August 1914. He was wounded in fall 1916, sent back to service three months later, then died of his wounds in March 1917. His widow was pregnant with their last child; a child, as she tells readers, that never knew its father (85). When her husband died, she stopped receiving her "family allowance" from the military. Six months after his death, she still waited to receive her widows' pension while the military investigated her husband's death. She and her family survived on welfare in the meantime, until after the birth of her fourth child, when she received a letter informing her that her request for a pension had been approved. Relieved, she still realized that she had to work outside the home in order to make ends meet. After six years, she suffered from exhaustion to the extent that she required hospitalization. Other working widows in Hurwitz-Stranz's anthology reported that the value of their pensions and earnings plummeted during the years of inflation in Germany (Hurwitz-Stranz 1931, 85–88). Most of the stories recorded in *Kriegerwitwen gestalten Ihr Schicksal* betray a tone of bitterness, balanced with a sense of pride in achieving independence and finding meaningful work.

In addition to economic concerns, Hurwitz-Stranz's widows reported feeling pressure to continue to look after their households and children in the manner that they had been used to when their husbands were still home and in the manner dictated by traditional German norms. This pressure, ironically, came in part from the very people advocating for widows' rights: the social services workers who wrote in *Kriegerwitwen gestalten Ihr Schicksal*. Hermann Geib, for example, insisted that despite widows' financial situation, they should always put their household and children first: "Those involved in helping war widows achieve self-reliance nevertheless always keep the same goal foremost: that children who lost their fathers to the war should always have their mother's care. If the children's upbringing would be endangered by their mother's working, welfare for the family must intervene" (qtd. in Hurwitz-Stranz 1931, 6–7). While the government stood ready to help war widows achieve independence, those with children (97 % of war widows, according to Whalen 1983, 70) were warned that any desire for independence on their part would be overshadowed by society's concern for their children. Helene Simon, too, reminded readers that German soldiers were promised that if they were to perish on battlefields, their survivors would be cared for (Simon in Hurwitz-Stranz 1931, 11). In addition to this circumscribed independence, commentators were careful to couch their praise for the resiliency of war widows alongside their laudatory remarks about their heroic soldier-husbands. Like other prewar German feminists, Gertrud Bäumer viewed German women's primary contribution to German society to raise patriotic children and uphold their husband's heroism (Bäumer in Hurwitz-Stranz 1931, 9).

This message – that Germany as a nation thought less of widows than fallen war heroes – can be seen in how German society dealt with commemoration. German war widowhood in some ways was a less publicly-performed aspect of German society than was the case in other nations, such as the United States and Britain; perhaps not surprising, given German feminists' focus on domesticity. While virtually all nations involved in WWI dealt with injured soldiers and compensation for survivors who had lost their breadwinners in the war, Germany had no official program for war widows as did the United States. In contrast, the U.S. military offered war widows and mothers the opportunity to lay wreaths at their soldiers' graves during an all-expense paid trip to cemeteries in France (Potter 1999). There were no such offers of free trips made to German war widows. Generally, given the multinational scope of the Great War, commemoration activities in many countries became national and international public events that went beyond a quiet ceremony in the village cemetery. "All nations that participated in the war were convinced that the work of mourning ought not to remain the private responsibility of particular families" (Hausen 1997, 128). The public commemorative activities that did take place involving war widows were necessarily more somber affairs in defeated nations (Hausen 128). Also in defeated nations family members could not always bury a body; this of course was true of all nations participating in the Great War, since explosives often rendered soldiers' bodies so badly mangled that they were unidentifiable. But unlike other nations, Germans were prevented from traveling to France to find their loved one's bodies (Depkat 2009, 187–188). This took away the wife's traditional role of caring for her husband's body upon his death and added to a war widow's bitterness. One widow writing in *Kriegerwitwen gestalten Ihr Schicksal* described her feelings of indignation when she concluded that her husband had died in vain, due to Germany losing the war. This particular widow tells readers that she joined an organization of war survivors to help her deal with her intense feelings of resentment (Hurwitz-Stranz 1931, 41). Along the same lines, another widow tells readers that the war "robbed wives of husbands, and children of their fathers," and she concludes by asking, "why?" – a question that undoubtedly evokes the senselessness of war and its losses (Hurwitz-Stranz 64, 66).

Moving commemoration ceremonies from the hands of private individuals to the state resulted in widows' stories being silenced. Mourning the nation's dead soldiers became increasingly the duty of all citizens, not just the widow who was left behind. The *Volksbund Deutsche Kriegsgräberfürsorge* (Association for the Care of German War Graves), together with several veterans' groups, began lobbying for a National Day of Mourning (Hausen 1997, 134). The intent in establishing a special day of mourning in Germany was to reinvigorate the discourse on the heroism of the fallen soldier in German society (Hausen 1997, 128). While none of the contributors to *Kriegerwitwen gestalten Ihr Schicksal* negated the perceived need to honor fallen soldiers, each of them noted the need to bring the sacrifices of widows to the national forefront as part of Germans' remembrance of the Great War. Not surprisingly, given her role as the primary impetus behind the book, Hurwitz-Stranz herself expressed it most compellingly: "Great is the number of books that describe the war experiences and sufferings of the warriors, but up until now, no one has heard the voices of the war widows whose voices others have failed to hear" (13).

Hurwitz-Stranz's book not only offered widows the opportunity to make their experiences known, it had the added benefit of acting as a war myth-buster. One of the most cherished war myths upheld by World War I historians was the notion that women and girls gave their German soldiers a cheerful, enthusiastic send-off in August 1914. Jeffrey Verhey dispells that myth by looking beyond newspaper and film accounts that chronicled the so-called "spirit of 1914" to personal responses to the declaration of war (2000, 47, 63, 92). Hurwitz-Stranz's widows offer even more evidence to contradict this particular myth. One widow's story seems to question the audacity of the suggestion that people were happy to be going to war. "Who could blame me for not being enthusiastic [about the war], he was my love, my everything!" (22). Another widow refers to a sense of unease in August 1914: "I personally had the foreboding feeling that I would never again see my husband and so it was: he was shot through the head on February 17, 1915" (40). One widow describes her feelings as: "Dark clouds fell over Germany when war was declared" (81). Another remembers the August 1914 war declaration as sounding like "a scream from heaven" (90). The title of another widow's story, "How often I worried that our life together might be torn apart," suggests that this particular writer interpreted the war as an unwanted intruder on marital happiness (Hurwitz-Stranz 21). These examples question the pervasive image of the flag-waving, flower-throwing parades documented in earlier histories.

Another myth of war upheld in post-World War I Germany was the celebrated notion of heroism and the so-called "cult of the fallen soldier." George L. Mosse explains the deeply-ingrained nature of this myth in German society (1990, 70–106), and Robert Weldon Whalen recounts the number of ways that the word "hero" appeared in the German language (1983, 24). One of Hurwitz-Stranz's widows did support the "fallen soldier" myth, commenting that she considered her husband to have died heroically for the sake of the Fatherland (1931, 26). But she remains the sole example of a widow repeating the "heroic soldier" trope, and even she does not spend much time explaining his heroism. The other contributors to the volume describe how their husbands' deaths, no matter how they occurred, upended their emotional and economic lives.

Hurwitz-Stranz's widows did support the notion communicated by the social services commentators in *Kriegerwitwen gestalten Ihr Schicksal* that widows' first priority lay in tending to their offspring, and that through their children the widows would feel that they contributed to the betterment of German society. Like war widows generally, most contributors to Hurwitz-Stranz's volume were mothers of young children. One widow commented that she was forced to work outside the home because her pension could not provide enough for her and her child. Daily she had to separate herself from her little one, which disturbed her very much; her child, she writes, was the only thing after the death of her husband that made her life worth living (1931, 27). The wife of a judge who was killed in the war also acted as an observer on the National Pension Court, like Hurwitz-Stranz did. She commented that she mostly did not have sufficient time for her children, even though they were her first priority (32). Another widow described how a friend of hers, also widowed by the war, felt guilty because she could not care for her children properly. She felt driven to do so in part because of the memory of her husband. She was hospitalized after she attempted to commit suicide (58–59). Another commented that in her sorrow over the loss of "my love, my support, my life partner" she nearly forgot her children (82). Johanna Boldt also seemed to forget her children, at least temporarily, as she mourned so deeply that she remained in bed for days on end; her mother warned her grandchildren that their mother was not to be disturbed (Hagener 1986, 101–107). Another widow worked for about a year at an office job, but she finally decided to surrender her position because she could not bear to leave her children at a day-care. The widow's siblings were able to help her with her expenses; she ends her autobiographical account by claiming that she did not know any war widows who would not immediately stop working in order to return to their primary prerogative of mother to their children (Hurwitz-Stranz 1931, 63–64). Child rearing thus was seen as women's most important occupation and foremost means for German women to contribute to a prewar social order in Germany. While few would have widows – or parents generally – neglect their children, the pressure that some widows felt must have interfered with their ability to achieve the independence that most claimed they sought.

One widow in Hurwitz-Stranz's compilation of interviews commented directly on the relationship between her concerns over her children's upbringing and her own *Selbständigkeit*. This widow, the wife of a government official in German East Africa, returned to Germany after her husband's death in the war. She explained to readers that she considered remarrying, which she understood would enable her children to have a father as they grew up. However, in the end she remained a widow, because she worried that her children might not accept a stranger as their father, and, she acknowledged that her children remained her first priority (Hurwitz-Stranz 1931, 54). Another widow addressing the question of remarriage also explained her decision to remain unmarried in light of her children: "It's not our pensions that we're worried [about losing], it's the fact that we've lived so long alone and have learned so much about life, that we lack the courage to meld our lives again with another. Solitude looks better to us [...] we simply want our children happy and fulfilled and to not have to carry any burdens" (Hurwitz-Stranz 1931, 88). About forty percent of war widows remarried by 1924, according to statistics; those who did take new vows lost their pensions as a result, and undoubtedly, the economic freedom – meager though it was – that their pensions represented (Whalen 1983, 109).

Despite the focus on children and family, the notion of *Selbständigkeit* remained an important factor in nearly all the widows' memoirs that Hurwitz-Stranz collected. For those who sought employment – again, nearly all the contributors – they did so out of necessity and to better their family's economic circumstances. But working also led to a great deal of expressed satisfaction, much of which derived from the economic independence that earning a wage represented. One widow wrote, "I realized suddenly, that it would be useless to hang my head. I had the courage to take my fate into my own hands" (57); she joined the war survivors' movement, eventually becoming a city councilwoman (57–58). Another expressed her gratitude to her parents for not being a crutch for her, as she, too, "earned her own bread" (61–62). Another widow found several social services and political positions until she also was elected to the city council as a representative of war survivors, a job she found most rewarding: "My life should not be without substance," she reflected, "or without ideals" (91–92). Work also led some widows to forget their sorrows. One widow worked initially in a furniture factory, but later was hired to work in social services, where, she commented, she could forget her sorrows and help others (27). Another widow who worked with war orphans commented that when she thought about the war and how her life had been afterward, it pleased her that her life had finally become useful (25).

According to Johanna Boldt's memoir, she, too, juggled family life and her obligations to her children. Her struggle to work and care for her family was similar to when her soldier-husband was still alive. She explained to Julius that she was able to maintain his business and provide for her children in his absence. Her brother-in-law, Julius's brother August, however, insisted that she hire a manager after the birth of the couple's second child. She refused, explaining that she was quite capable of running the *Kolonialwaren* (colonial goods) shop. Indeed, she viewed her *Tüchtigkeit* (competency) as her patriotic duty and argued with August that her customers viewed her ability to work in the shop as fortunate, given her husband's absence. When she explained her spat with August to Julius in a letter, however, she couched her words carefully, noting self-effacingly that she had no ambition to improve the shop (though she clearly did) and confirmed women's place in society as inferior to men's. Finally, she confessed to Julius that working in the shop calmed her nerves in such tumultuous times (Hagener 1986, 40–41).

After Julius's death, Boldt became a "New Woman," finding work, arguing with her boss for more pay (he refused, saying that he did not care that she was a war widow with two children to support), then got a better paying job elsewhere. She cut her hair, wore modern clothes, pedaled her bicycle to work every day and learned how to swim. Her oldest daughter found her behavior appalling, but Johanna clearly wanted and obtained *Selbständigkeit* (Hagener 1986, 66–67, 107–110).

All in all, widows trod the path of supreme sacrifice the moment they watched their soldier-husbands' figures recede into the landscape when they left their homes to join their military units. This was a sacrifice that German society expected of women (O'Brien 2007, 247). At the same time, widows were expected to forfeit their own lives for the sake of their orphaned children by raising them in a manner that would make proud their heroic husbands and the nation. At all costs, widows were to ensure that their soldier-husbands had not died in vain. In the meantime, the entity that had caused the soldier's death in battle, the nation that had declared war, made it nearly impossible for widows to rear their children without working, an activity that necessarily took them from their children. Furthermore, war widows could not even expect acknowledgment from the government, since public officials focused on their husbands' presumed heroism and their contributions to the war effort, rather than the sacrifices that women had made.

German war widows' letters and recollections reveal the dual nature of their lives as war widows. German society expected them to remain subservient to the legacies of their dead soldier-husbands and mourn them with downcast eyes. Additionally, they were to perpetuate the narrative of the sacrifice their men had made in the name of the German nation, and raise their orphaned children to be upstanding German citizens. Because the nation did not adequately support war widows, in part because it refused to acknowledge the toll that the war took on widows' lives and their own personal sacrifices alongside their husbands', they were forced to seek work outside of the home that took them away from their children. Through the experience of striving for economic self-sufficiency, however, widows came to relish that new-found independence. *Selbständigkeit* offered widows at least a partial way out of their dilemma, since the sense of achievement that independence brought may have contributed to no longer feeling the need to be acknowledged for their sacrifice. Judging from Hurwitz-Stranz's anthology of women writing war, for those who derived satisfaction from meaningful work, their feelings of fulfillment sufficed.

Works Cited

Anthony, Katharine. *Feminism in Germany and Scandinavia* (Henry Holt, 1915).

Budreau, Lisa M. *Bodies of War: World War I and the Politics of Commemoration in America, 1919–1933* (New York UP, 2011).

Crouthamel, Jason. *An Intimate History of the Front* (Palgrave Macmillan, 2014).

Daniel, Ute. *The War From Within: German Working-Class Women in the First World War.* Translated by Margaret Ries (Berg, 1997).

Depkat, Volker. "Remembering the War the Transnational Way: The U.S.-American Memory of World War I." *Transnational American Memories,* edited by Udo J. Hebel (Walter de Gruyter, 2009), pp. 185–213.

Domansky, Elisabeth. "Militarization and Reproduction in World War I Germany." *Society, Culture, and the State in Germany, 1870–1930,* edited by Geoff Eley (U of Michigan P, 1996), pp. 427–463.

Erdmann-Macke, Elisabeth. *Erinnerung an August Macke* (W. Kohlhammer, 1962).

Frevert, Ute. "Forum: History of Emotions." *German History*, vol. 28, no. 1 (2010), pp. 67–80.

Hagener, Edith. *"Es lief so sicher an deinem Arm": Briefe einer Soldatenfrau, 1914* (Beltz, 1986).

Hausen, Karin. "The 'Day of National Mourning' in Germany." *Between History and Histories: The Making of Silences and Commemorations*, edited by Gerald Sider and Gavin Smith (U of Toronto P, 1997), pp. 127–146.

Hausen, Karin. "The German Nation's Obligation to the Heroes' Widows of World War I." *Behind the Lines: Gender and the Two World Wars*, edited by Margaret Randolph Higonnet, et al. (Yale UP, 1987), pp. 126–140.

Hurwitz-Stranz, Helene, editor. *Kriegerwitwen gestalten ihr Schicksal: Lebenskämpfe deutscher Kriegerwitwen nach eigenen Darstellungen* (Heymann, 1931).

Kuhlman, Erika. *Of Little Comfort: War Widows, Fallen Soldiers, and the Remaking of the Nation after the First World War* (New York UP, 2012).

Mosse, George L. *Fallen Soldiers: Reshaping the Memory of the World Wars* (Oxford UP, 1990).

Mulligan, William. *The Great War for Peace* (Yale UP, 2014).

Nau, Karl. *Die wirtschaftliche und soziale Lage von Kriegshinterbliebenen: Eine Studie auf Grund von Erhebungen über die Auswirkung der Versorgung von Kriegshinterbliebenen in Darmstadt* (Lühe and Company, 1930).

Nelson, Robert L. *German Soldier Newspapers of the First World War* (Cambridge UP, 2014).

O'Brien, Catherine. "Sacrificial Rituals and Wounded Hearts: The Uses of Christian Symbolism in French and German Women's Reponses to the First World War." *The Women's Movement in Wartime: International Perspectives, 1914–19*, edited by Ingrid Sharp and Alison S. Fell (Palgrave Macmillan, 2007), pp. 244–259.

Potter, Constance. "World War I Gold Star Mothers Pilgrimages, Part I." *Prologue Magazine*, vol. 31, no. 2 (1999). www.archives.gov/publications/prologue/1999/summer/gold-star-mothers-1.html. Accessed 6 July 2016.

Quataert, Jean H. *Reluctant Feminists in German Social Democracy, 1885–1917* (Princeton UP, 1979).

Shields, Stephanie A. "Thinking about Gender, Thinking about Theory: Gender and Emotional Experience." *Gender and Emotion: Social Psychological Perspectives*, edited by Agneta H. Fischer (Cambridge UP, 2000), pp. 3–23.

Smith, Angela. *Discourses Surrounding British Widows of the First World War* (Bloomsbury, 2013).

Strange, Carolyn, et al., editors. *Honour, Violence and Emotions in History* (Bloomsbury, 2014).

Ulrich, Bernd, and Benjamin Ziemann, editors. *German Soldiers in the Great War: Letters and Eyewitness Accounts*. Translated by Christine Brocks (Pen and Sword Books, 2010).

Verhey, Jeffrey. *The Spirit of 1914: Militarism, Myth and Mobilization in Germany* (Cambridge UP, 2000).

Whalen, Robert Weldon. *Bitter Wounds: German Victims of the Great War, 1914–1939* (Cornell UP, 1983).

Winter, Jay. "Demography." *A Companion to World War I*, edited by John Horne (Wiley-Blackwell, 2010), pp. 248–262.

Martina Kolb
Intimations of Mortality from Recollections of Atrocity

Käthe Kollwitz and the Art of Mourning

> War tears, rends. War rips open, eviscerates. War scorches. War dismembers. War ruins.
> (Susan Sontag)
>
> [T]he object of war is to kill people. [...] The main purpose and outcome of war is injuring.
> (Elaine Scarry)
>
> [C]atastrophic events seem to repeat themselves for those who have passed through them.
> (Cathy Caruth)[1]

Rather than concentrating on what in the context of World War I has been called *psychopathia martialis* (shell shock and related variants of war trauma), or on accounts of either veteran or civilian patients who have been suffering from traumata as partially ongoing and partially postponed symptoms of violent action and injury directly undergone or witnessed in arenas of combat, this chapter offers an outlook on the survivor's pain of bereavement viscerally experienced beyond theaters of war.[2] The investigation is located at the crossroads of art and psychoanalysis. It tracks the artist's aesthetic imagination as an ethically inclined empathic imagination, while exploring voiced and visually represented expressions of loss and pain (in her diaries and in her art) by a woman civilian in mourning at the home front: Käthe Kollwitz (1867–1945).

Based on interpretations of five medially diverse, but thematically and compositionally closely related works that Kollwitz completed between 1903 and 1932 – two etchings preceding World War I, and a woodcut, a lithograph, and a set of two sculptures following it – my analysis demonstrates how Kollwitz's art of mourning offers an eloquent and haunting account of the human condition as it is tragically intensified by the experience of war and war trauma in general,

---

1 Sontag (2003, 7); Scarry (1985, 61–63); Caruth (1996, 1).
2 The term *trauma* in this chapter refers to the complex of extremely painful, disorienting and often paralyzing violent events, and to the psychic effects caused by their physical and mental ruptures to a person's fragile identity and integrity (e.g., dissociations). See Irene Kacandes (2001, 90), who cites Judith Herman (1992, 33): "Traumatic events [...] involve threats to life or bodily integrity, or a close personal encounter with violence and death." Trauma in this chapter is understood as a mourner's crisis and used in Caruth's understanding of the term: as a crisis located between life and death. See Cathy Caruth (1996, 4, 7).

https://doi.org/10.1515/9783110572001-015

and, in her case more specifically, by the experience of World War I. Anchored in theories of trauma, witnessing and mourning (mainly Freud's and Caruth's), this reading of select images by Kollwitz is historically contextualized through the war theme (World War I in particular) and a comparative discussion of other artists representing war in their work (e.g., Francisco de Goya, Edvard Munch, and Otto Dix).

Kollwitz's graphic scenes of death include personifications of Death as a character, as well as the visual presence of skulls, corpses, and, most poignantly, surviving witnesses who suffer in empathic communion the wounds inflicted on the fallen. Kollwitz's survivors, more often than not, are mothers who mourn the deaths of their children as direct consequences of war – whether by starvation or death in action. While the dead body as a site of crisis is an object that no longer subjectively feels what a grieving survivor compassionately longs to share with it, *empathy* (a translation of the German *Einfühlung*), psycho-aesthetically understood as "the power of projecting one's personality into and [...] comprehending the object of contemplation" (OED), captures the mourner's sentience or affective identification with the dead that this chapter traces.[3]

Whether wandering through the Käthe Kollwitz Museums in Berlin or Cologne, or browsing through exhibition catalogs of Kollwitz's work, the viewer is confronted with an artist's searing portrayal of poverty and illness, ailing and suffering, sick beds and death beds, crime and war, desolation and despair, loss and bereavement, death and dying, grieving and mourning, remembering and memorializing. This striking ubiquity of hardship and violence, calamity and misery, and of recollection and memory in Kollwitz's visual art tends to be accompanied by a strong haptic sense of tender care, between mother figures and children.

Deaths are anything but abstract in Kollwitz's work. Rather, Death frequently makes an appearance concretely, whether as a canonical reminder of mortality (*memento mori*), a more modern skull figure reminiscent of Edvard Munch's lithograph *Kiss of Death* (1899), or, in personified form, as an allegorical visitor reminiscent of Fritz Lang's *Der müde Tod* (The weary death, 1921; original English translation: *Destiny*), a Weimar silent film released during Kollwitz's prolific interwar years. In Lang's film, Death is embodied by an uncanny elderly male fig-

---

3 Alfred Margulies places emphasis on the "fundamental projective nature of empathy," on the "intertwining of subject-object reflections" (1989, xii), on empathy as an "inscape," and on "the imaginative and creative aspects of empathy" (17). His understanding of empathy underscores the empathic dimension of Kollwitz's work as a creative, intersubjective, and ultimately communal process that transcends compassion and commiseration.

ure, a character pictured as a "secretly familiar" physical presence.[4] While worn and weary of summoning the living, knowing full well the immense grief and angst that he has caused in their survivors, Lang's Death, like Kollwitz's numerous embodiments of Death, remains unconquered.

All of Kollwitz's portrayals of Death[5] – whether in the actual presence of a personified visitor (as in Lang's film), or in its absent haunting presence expressed by mourning survivors, cut to the bone, and cut to the quick, that is, to the living. Cathy Caruth emphasizes the "inextricability of the story of one's life from the story of a death" in the traumatic scenario (1996, 8). Within the traumatic paradigm of atemporality, of painfully erroneous sequences, the striking irony of mothers and grandmothers surviving their children and grandchildren becomes particularly paramount, in that theirs is a tale that at once constitutes bearing children and bearing their death. Kollwitz not only experienced such a scene when her son Peter was killed in action early in World War I, but she had imagined and visualized it in the strangest of ways in *Woman with Dead Child* (*Frau mit totem Kind*, 1903, figure 1) – an intimation of mortality that reflects, perhaps, the wound that was anticipated and experienced vatically eleven years before her son's actual passing. It is chilling that the title of Kollwitz's work calls the child dead, as the model for this soi-disant dead child was her living son Peter in 1903.

Woman with Dead Child is a proto-sculptural work that simultaneously conjures Michelangelesque traits of the muscular *Cumaean Sybil* (1508–1512), the filial constellation of the Roman *Pietà* (1498–1499), and the physical posture of Heinrich Füssli's *The Silence* (*Das Schweigen*, c. 1799–1801). In Kollwitz's line etching, mother and child are naked; the woman is alive, the boy is said to be dead. The story of this work's composition is profoundly intriguing. Kollwitz explains in a letter how she prepared the etching: "When Peter was seven years old and I was in the process of making this etching [...] I was drawing myself while holding him in my arms in front of the mirror. That was rather exhausting, and I ended up groaning. Then his little boy's voice said consolingly: oh mother, do

---

4 See Sigmund Freud's "The Uncanny" (1957c, 245), which he defines as the "secretly familiar," that is to say, a form of repetition that ensures the ongoing resurfacing of that which was supposed to remain silent and repressed.
5 Death appears as an embodied figure in Kollwitz's *Death and Woman* (*Tod und Frau*, etching, 1910), *Death Takes a Woman* (*Der Tod nimmt eine Frau zu sich*, black chalk, 1921–1922), *Death and Woman* (*Tod und Frau*, coal, 1922–1923), *Death Seizes a Woman* (*Tod packt eine Frau*, lithograph, 1934), *Death Holds Girl on His Lap* (*Tod hält Mädchen im Schoß*, lithograph, 1934), and *Call of Death* (*Ruf des Todes*, lithograph, 1934–1935) – to name a few.

not worry, it will all turn out very beautifully" (Kollwitz to Beate Bonus-Jeep, qtd. in Bonus-Jeep 1948, 225).[6]

Figure 1: Käthe Kollwitz: *Woman with Dead Child (Frau mit totem Kind)*, line etching 1903, © Käthe Kollwitz Museum Cologne, Germany

The affective identification of the artist autobiographically depicting herself as a mother holding her dead child is repeated in the beholder's interactive relationship with this expressive and empathic work. In her artwork, Kollwitz at

---

6 "Als er [Peter] sieben Jahre alt war und ich die Radierung machte [...] zeichnete ich mich selbst, ihn im Arm haltend, im Spiegel. Das war sehr anstrengend und ich musste stöhnen. Da sagte sein Kinderstimmchen tröstend: Sei man still, Mutter, es wird auch alles sehr schön!" As there is, to date, no English translation of Kollwitz's collected letters or entire diary (only selections from it, translated by Richard and Clara Winston, 1955), all English translations of German text in this chapter, unless indicated otherwise, are my own.

times positions herself as a communicator of foreboding events and witness of impending death. The beholder who views works that depict the traumatic moment of witnessing death perpetuates the artist's acts of an empathic, interactive human imagination that inspired her work in the first place. Caruth's understanding of trauma as expressed in her introduction to *Listening to Trauma* can be applied to Kollwitz, who "create[d] from a locus of vulnerability, a place that is never fully outside, if it is also not fully inside, the traumatic experiences to which [she] respond[s]," thus "creat[ing] a bridge from trauma to testimony and from denial to a future possibility of witness" (Caruth 2014, xviii).

When Beate Bonus-Jeep, Kollwitz's intimate friend, first saw *Woman with Dead Child* on exhibit in 1903, she thought that something horrendous had to have happened to Peter, but soon discovered that he was unharmed. Rather, Kollwitz, whose art betrays an extreme awareness of vulnerability and precarity, had indeed personified pathos, anticipated future loss, and prophetically foreshadowed the later catastrophe. This early rendering of mourning is not commemorative, but based in an intimation of mortality, an acute awareness of the frailty of life. The fact, however, that Kollwitz first drew herself with her living son, but then titled the image *Woman with Dead Child*, is certainly intriguing. The work seems to have been inspired by her sense of loss (in the sense of a mother's postpartum and at the same time prepartum pain of separation) and her deep awareness of bereavement, for instance, through her knowledge and portrayals of the history of previous wars, battles, crimes, and revolts, as well as her familiarity with artistic expressions and literary accounts of human atrocities.[7]

Kollwitz's etching *Battlefield* (1907; see figure 2) is set in the Peasants' War of the early sixteenth century. It shows a foggy nocturnal field of limbs and corpses after what must have been a horrendous confrontation between revolting farmers and their violent oppressors. In it, a mother figure appears to be searching for her dead son. Her lantern sheds light on the veins of her calloused hand as it touches the tender, fair skin of a young face (a hand that resembles that of the woman in Kollwitz's 1903 etching, and a boy's face with his head thrown back, which is thoroughly reminiscent of the portrayal of Peter and his positioning in that same earlier etching). The raddled woman's partial verticality determines the only interruption of the horizontal omnipresence of death – her posture draws attention to the realm of the fallen, to which she extends her tender sympathy. If more subtly, more reticently, and perhaps from a more resigned place than in the overtly passionate *Woman with Dead Child*, this etching also

---

7 For example, Kollwitz addresses war atrocities against women in the etching *Raped* (*Vergewaltigt*, 1907/08) in her cycle *Peasants' War* (*Bauernkrieg*, 1902/1903 – 1908).

Figure 2: Käthe Kollwitz: *Battlefield* (*Schlachtfeld*) – Sheet 6 of the series *Peasants' War* (*Bauernkrieg*), line etching 1907, © Käthe Kollwitz Museum Cologne, Germany

communicates a strong sense of the haptic, as if an emaciated mourning woman's hand sought to touch one last time her dead boy's face. The artist emphasizes this face, thus asserting the memory of the dead boy. It was the historical example of the Peasants' War that inspired Kollwitz to produce further works of mourning nearly a decade before the outbreak of World War I.

In Kollwitz's art, war is represented synecdochically. She refers to war by presenting a part – not by depicting panoramic battles she did not see, but by challenging the viewer with those defining details and iconic images of war (trauma, death, grief, and mourning) that she herself experienced and witnessed. As flesh and blood are synecdoches for the human body (and as essential parts of the body stand for it as a whole), so pain and ruin, dying and death, bereavement and mourning become the integral components of war that Kollwitz emphasizes – in the precise sense of Susan Sontag and Elaine Scarry (see epigraphs one and two). Kollwitz, Sontag and Scarry concentrate on the very aspects of the war story that tend to play a minor role, if that, in male military historiography or in the work of soldier-artists or soldier-writers such as Otto Dix and Ernst Jünger. Like many young men of their generation, including Kollwitz's son Peter, Dix and Jünger both volunteered for combat at the outset of World War I. In contrast to Peter, Dix and Jünger survived. As a highly decorated German soldier, Jünger went on to author the war memoir *Storm of Steel* (*In Stahlgewittern*, 1920), a first-person account of trench warfare, while Dix focused on self-portraiture (the painterly counterpart of first-person narrative) and included gas masks reminiscent of skulls in his work. His famous print cycle *War* (*Der Krieg*, 1924) is modeled on Francisco de Goya's *Disasters of War* (1810–1820) and (re)produces a series of nightmarish, hallucinatory traumatic experiences.[8]

As is well known, Käthe Kollwitz initially welcomed the war with patriotic enthusiasm, supported her son's decision to volunteer, and shared her son's belief in sacrifice, but she radically changed her position on the topic during the war and became an antiwar activist for the rest of her life.[9] She primarily inscribed and depicted war in its premeditative strategies and deliberate consequences – by the trauma and suffering it wittingly imposes when brutally arranging for maiming and dying, for pain and loss. Sontag's formulation can again serve well as a description for Kollwitz and her process: "War tears [...] rends [...] rips open, eviscerates [...] scorches [...] dismembers [...and] ruins." Kollwitz graphically inscribes war as the fatal agent that it is: war purposely and consistently "kill[s and] injure[s]," to mobilize Scarry's pairing. Furthermore, the traumatic catastrophe of war is repetitive (see Caruth, epigraph three).

To recall the title of this volume, Kollwitz has "written war" in a number of challenging ways: as a civilian witness at the home front, rather than a soldier at the front; as a middle-aged woman, rather than a young man; and, crucially, as an artist who expressed herself in visual and written media, analyzed lives and deaths that occurred both well before and during her lifetime, and profoundly examined them. Kollwitz is, in Muriel Rukeyser's poetic words, "the witness" and the "voice" that "moves across time" and the voice that "[s]peaks for the life and death as witness voice" (2005, 459).[10] Kollwitz "bear[s] witness, or tes-

---

8 Ingrid Sharp (2011) comparatively reads Kollwitz's and Dix's works that deal with World War I, challenging the gendered cliché of Dix's detachment versus Kollwitz's emotionality, and thus coming to a refined understanding of both the war and its representations.
9 See Claudia Siebrecht (2008, 265–269) and Katharina von Hammerstein (2015) for Kollwitz's paradoxical stance toward the war, Peter's volunteering, her support, at least initially, of the idea of sacrifice, and her bitter realization of its futility and the human catastrophe later on.
10 In her poem "The Witness," Muriel Rukeyser, who also authored the poem "Käthe Kollwitz," which enters my essay at a later point, phrases it as a rhetorical question rather than a state-

tif[ies]" in Shoshana Felman's sense, in that "as readers and spectators [we] are also witnesses in the second degree to what we are reading" (qtd. in Caruth 2014, 321). Kollwitz testifies to a "historical event" (World War I) and "to an injustice or to a catastrophe [...she] feel[s] needs to be addressed" (Felman qtd. in Caruth 2014, 322). We can apply to Kollwitz what Felman views as an important capacity to "appeal to another, to other human beings, and more generally, [...] to community. To testify is [...] to take the witness stand" (qtd. in Caruth 2014, 322).[11] Kollwitz's artwork attests to the dialog she sought with her immediate and general community.

Kollwitz was a fine reader of world literature and attended many lectures on the subject. Her artwork was heavily inspired by her readings, for instance of Johann Wolfgang von Goethe, Angelus Silesius, Émile Zola, and Rainer Maria Rilke. She was also enthusiastic about the educational impact of the theater. A Berlin performance of Gerhart Hauptmann's *The Weavers* (*Die Weber*, 1892) famously triggered her graphic series titled *Weavers' Revolt* (*Weberaufstand*, 1893–1897). Furthermore, although primarily renowned as a visual artist, Kollwitz was a prolific diarist as well, having bequeathed a substantial collection of diary entries that span more than three decades, including, at their core, her emphatic statements and touching deliberations over the course of World War I. Her entries not only comment on the socio-political events of her day, but also frequently reveal self-reflective passages concerning her work and her life as an artist and a mother in mourning. She also drew and sketched in the diary. During the war, she memorably recorded her son Peter's death in action in Flanders on 22 October 1914 – a loss with immense repercussions on her subsequent life and work as an artist.

Precisely three years after seeing Peter alive for the last time, Kollwitz described herself as "being old," "wandering toward the grave," and "pointing downward" (1989, 334).[12] Claudia Siebrecht summarizes thus: "Kollwitz's diary entries

---

ment: "Who is the witness? What voice moves across time, / Speaks for the life and death as witness voice?" (2005, 459).

11 Felman's stress falls on the narrative, verbal quality of testimony as "perfomative utterance" and "the counterpart of a silence" (Caruth 2014, 321, 326). I apply Felman's points about witnessing to Kollwitz's visual narratives. Kollwitz tended to collect her work in cycles, such as the *Peasants' War* and *War*. A sequence of historically contextualized and iconically related images certainly has the capacity to counter silence and become a story, albeit, with the exception of Kollwitz's diaries, not a story in words. Kollwitz is one of few women artists witnessing in this sense. Women artists recording World War I in words and/or images, such as graphic artist Kollwitz at the home front or photographer Margaret Hall on location (e.g., with her *Grave in No-Man's Land* of 1918–1919), are few and far between.

12 "[D]as Altsein. Das dem Grabzugehn. [...] daß ich von nun an nach unten zeige."

were [...] primarily concerned with [...] the deprivation his [Peter's] death meant for her" (2008, 283), and Sara Friedrichsmeyer states that "[Kollwitz's] diary offered an outlet she required and depended on between 1914 and 1918 [...]. The greatest struggle in her life, according to the evidence of the diary, took place between 1914 and 1918. [...] Critics agree that Kollwitz's graphic works and sculptures demonstrate a lifelong compassion for suffering humanity, and her diary can only substantiate that claim" – a claim largely based in the context of her experience of World War I (1989, 212–214).

After World War I, Kollwitz experimented with a variety of materials, media, and genres, particularly in her printmaking. Her work is expressive, outspoken, and located right at the intersection of the verbal and visual realms. The wounds of the living and the dead that Kollwitz depicted cry out graphically in more than one sense. Wounds demonstrate the body's broken surface and show its injury, precarity, and vulnerability. Similarly, Kollwitz's art pierces, etches, as it were, even if it happens not to be an etching; it draws, tears open, rends, scribes, marks, scarifies – it scorches and eviscerates, exposing bones, skeletons, muscles, and sinews.

If one thinks of the entire spectrum of artistic media, it is the print medium that places writing (which is literally graphic) and graphic art (such as Kollwitz's interwar drawings, woodcuts, lithographs, and etchings) in close proximity to one another. Writing and graphic art rely on printing's reprographic potential; both tend to operate in black and white; both use lines as their primary units of expression; and both proceed two-dimensionally, with calligraphy maximally approaching the visual aesthetics of the act of *graphein*, the Greek verb for "writing."[13] Granted, Kollwitz's eloquent visual text(ure)s of mourning the losses and pains of war are graphic in that they are vivid, explicit, precise, and oftentimes iconic (they quote iconography, ranging from the crucifixion to the *compianto* to the *pietà* to the entombment of Christ). Her art, however, is graphic also because it is autobiographic and psychographic (i.e., descriptive of her external/socio-

---

13 In an etymological reading of the term *graphic* in support of the current argument about the relationship or proximity of graphic art and writing, I suggest that "graphic" not only pertains to writing and drawing, but also to breaking, injuring, and hurting the surface. In the context of "writing war," *graphein* may relate to writing but also to drawing and etching – scratching the surface, marking. An etymological reading of "graphic" is enlightening here, as graphic works depict graphically (visually or verbally), but also describe and inscribe graphically (verbally or visually). Graphic art cuts gashes, glyphs, or makes incisions into metal or wood, for example, marks their surface, I contend, as wounds, scars and pain mark those who suffer them ("marked by pain," "marked by destiny," and so on). Graphic art is descriptive (as geography is descriptive of the earth's surface) and it portrays (as ancient pornography portrayed obscene images of prostitutes).

political and internal/psychological life) and ultimately mnemonic – as it re-cords, re-collects, and re-members that which threatens to be repressed, scat-tered, and dismembered, all of which are essential components of bellicose, martial action and its traumatic sequelae in particular.

Figure 3: Käthe Kollwitz: *In Memoriam Karl Liebknecht* (*Gedenkblatt für Karl Liebknecht*), woodcut 1920, © Käthe Kollwitz Museum Cologne, Germany

A graphic case in point, Kollwitz's woodcut *Memorial Sheet for Karl Lieb-knecht* (1920; see figure 3), subtitled *The Living to the Dead: In Memory of 15 January 1919* (*Die Lebenden dem Toten: Erinnerung an den 15. Januar 1919*), can serve as exemplary evidence. Set and produced in the political turmoil following World War I and thus during a period of a civil war for political power, this work is reminiscent of her earlier draft titled *In Memory of Ludwig Frank* (*Dem Andenken Ludwig Franks*, 1914), dedicated to the German Social Democrat. When Rosa Luxemburg and Karl Liebknecht were murdered in 1919, Liebknecht's family asked Kollwitz to draw Liebknecht's body in the morgue. She minutely ob-served, thoroughly studied, and repeatedly drew not only Liebknecht's corpse, but other corpses in the morgue as well. She also sketched some of the visiting mourners. The powerful impression of innumerable mourners attending Liebknecht's funeral, of which Kollwitz was one, did its part for the final composition, which became an aesthetically and a psychologically complex enterprise.

What followed was a year-long process through various drafts and media, including her diary entries on Liebknecht's mimic, which culminated in the well-known woodcut of 1920. In this work, the mourning man nearest to Liebknecht's body bends over in a gesture comparable to that of the mother figure on the battlefield. While the beholder looks at the body from a vantage point similar to that of the mourning workers in the picture, the only way into this scene is by way of the almost geometrically stretched-out corpse. The layout and the spectral aura of Kollwitz's work are reminiscent of Edvard Munch's *By the Deathbed* (1896), as well as of his first *Self Portrait* (1895), where the skeletal arm of a painter haunted by death frames the picture in the same way that Liebknecht's covered corpse does in Kollwitz's piece, even if the solitude in Munch's work is different from the community that Kollwitz includes. However, Kollwitz's earlier drawings of Liebknecht's face were softer, more intimate, and less ritualistic than this moment of public commemoration would have demanded.

Whether it is the depiction of an individual mourner in a private setting (such as *Woman with Dead Child*), or of an individual mourner in a public space (such as the mourning woman in *Battlefield*), or of a community of mourners in a communal setting (as in the Liebknecht woodcut), the viewer of the work is faced in all these instances of the artist's testimony with the intersection of life and death, with the last and searingly painful encounter between the dead body and the living body, or bodies, of the mourning survivors depicted in the artwork. Both living and dead bodies are characterized by and connected through the representation of the wound that is trauma – itself a site of crisis and catastrophe.

Delving deeper into the notion of *trauma* at this point supports my argument about this work. *Body* denotes both the living body (*Körper* or *Leib*, as in *Leib Christi* [body of Christ] in the historical and Eucharistic senses) and the dead body (corpse or *Leiche* or *Leib*, as in *Leib Christi* in the historical and Eucharistic senses). This linguistic situation, or semantic overlap, I suggest, underlines the complex and precarious proximity of life and death that is crucial for an understanding of trauma. The Greek noun *trauma* signifies "wound" and ultimately derives from the proto-Indo-European root for "rubbing" or "turning," constituting the pain visualized by the wound.[14] Even though the sense of trauma as a psy-

---

14 While challenging Walter Benjamin's argument about the novel and storytelling in the context of World War I and its aftermath, Kacandes addresses the meaning of trauma in its "sense of psychic wounding" – a meaning that Benjamin intended, albeit without using the actual term *trauma* (Kacandes 2001, 89). For the connection of trauma and textual art, see also "Words and Wounds: An Interview with Geoffrey Hartman" (Caruth 2014, 213–235), where Hartman ex-

chic wound is relatively new, trauma's association with the physical wound is much older, so that a radical distinction, in the interdisciplinary context of trauma culturally approached, between physical and mental wounds, seems to be a moot point. Rather than the wound itself (as the etymology of *trauma* suggests), trauma is a "physiological inscription" (Caruth 2014, xv), as well as the story of an expressive wound:

> Trauma seems to be much more than a pathology: it is always the story of a wound that cries out, that addresses us in the attempt to tell us of a reality or truth that is not otherwise available. This truth, in its delayed appearance and its belated address, cannot be linked only to what is known, but also to what remains unknown in our very actions and our language. [...] Is the trauma the encounter with death, or the ongoing experience of having survived it? At the core [...] is thus a kind of double telling, the oscillation between a *crisis of death* and the correlative *crisis of life*: between the story of the unbearable nature of an event and the story of the unbearable nature of its survival. (Caruth 1996, 4, 7)[15]

Caruth anchors her Freudian interpretation of trauma in literary and filmic case studies that lend themselves well to a fresh reading of Kollwitz's mnemonic art of mourning.

Kollwitz's empathic representation and memorialization of Liebknecht and the war dead and their mourners is autobiographical and individual, cathartic and therapeutic. Her son Peter and her grandson Peter were both killed in action (the latter in 1942 in Russia), and Kollwitz survived them as their mother and grandmother (she did not live to see the end of World War II). Her art, however personal, also remains collective, existential, committed to dialog and testimony, and ethically engaged. It is an "appeal to community" (to repeat Felman's phrase quoted earlier). Kollwitz explained on more than one occasion that by way of synecdoche, her dead son and grandson represented all sons and grandsons killed in action – and not in the two World Wars exclusively, but in any war preceding or following them. On the one hand, the unequivocally historical anchoring

---

plains the literary tradition of apostrophe which enables an encounter between the living and the dead. For my usage of the term *trauma*, see footnote 2.

15 Mourning as a variant of mental pain is simultaneously considered a sensation and an emotion akin to the healing of a wound. Although a scar may remain, as language has it, the pain and the time of mourning may, indeed, imply healing. Language has made abundant metaphorical use of this potential, including the many critical places in which the word *trauma* has resurfaced, primarily in the field of trauma studies, but also more colloquially. It is enlightening to recall that Freud early on surmised that a distinction between physical and mental pain was analytically and practically a dubious endeavor and a moot point (1957a, "Appendix C," 171). Recent neuroscientific pain research provides evidence for Freud's intuition of psychic and physical pain as comparable rather than essentially different.

of Kollwitz's committed art grants her the secure position of a highly reliable witness of her time, while on the other hand, her commitment to a timeless human condition beyond one specific historical period opens up an interpretive panorama for an artist who has bequeathed to those born after a visceral and expressive "humanitarian intervention" and "humanitarian testimony" (von Hammerstein 2013, 215, 238).

Scarry has famously written on pain's resistance to expression, its voicelessness, whereas Caruth, Felman and Hartman, among others, have confirmed the "voice" of the wound, while focusing on trauma's resistance – not to expression, but to comprehension. The anachronism of the truth or the reality – be it anticipatory and prophetic, or postponed and posthumous – communicated through the wound's voice as it resurfaces in imagined and reenacted patterns of suffering and repetitions of catastrophe is crucial for an understanding of Kollwitz's expressions of war trauma and her aesthetic ways of mourning the dead. Caruth writes of wounds "experienced too soon" (1996, 4) and of "belated address" (7), thus connecting trauma's complex experiential chronologies and late assimilations to the fact that "the experience of trauma repeats itself" (2), to trauma's "endless impact on life" (7), and to the "itinerary of insistently recurring words or figures" (5). One such figure within Caruth's paradigm is that of *falling*.[16] In German, one might add, this term refers also to those killed in action: *Gefallene*. Kollwitz created a lithograph titled *Killed in Action* (*Gefallen*, 1920) focusing on the pain a widow – and her children – experience when she receives the message that her husband is "gefallen." Visually, Kollwitz manifests the woman's pain in her physical posture.

Pain is a canonical theme in art. Expressions of physical suffering range from the Rhodean Laocoön group and the Crucifix, to Michelangelo's *Pietà* (1498–1499) and Frida Kahlo's *Broken Column* (1944). Depictions of pain resulting specifically from war range from Francisco de Goya's *Disasters of War* (1810–1820), which Sontag uses in her argument about "regarding the pain of others" (2003), to Pablo Picasso's *Guernica* (1937) and others. Representations of mental pain hold a comparable status in the canon, ranging from Albrecht Dürer's *Melencolia I* (1514) to Edvard Munch's *Scream* (1893) – among myriad others. While Kollwitz's art of mourning continues this tradition, she also presents us in uniquely graphic ways with pain and passion, patience and perseverance, and with pathos as that which befalls a subject, as that which is not only witnessed

---

16 Caruth dedicates a chapter to "The Falling Body" (1996, 73–90), falling figures, and figures (also of speech) of falling. In her introduction, she elaborates on the "impact of a fall" and "what it means to fall" (6–7), without, however, referring to the fallen soldier as *Gefallener.*

and endured, but also expressed and communicated in a specific formalized and defined representational genre where form and medium, content and theme meaningfully intersect through the *graphic* in every sense of the word (see footnote 13).

Kollwitz's psychographic work pays tribute to the ethos as well as the pathos of trauma, and to the ethical mandate and creative potential of suffering. Her lithograph *Killed in Action* refers to being killed in war; the image refrains from naming the victim whose pain and death are at stake (who is being killed and hence in English referred to in the passive voice), in addition to evoking the pain suffered by those who survive him. Pathos, however, may turn into agency, "making" may follow "unmaking," as suggested in Scarry's subtitle *The Making and Unmaking of the World*. The term *trauma* refers to the event of violent infliction, while it also indicates the injury's mnemonic persistence in the lives of the living. It is the trauma or wound of death that Kollwitz not only experienced when her son was killed a few weeks after the outset of World War I, but that she had uncannily imagined, actively and creatively so, in a chilling intimation of mortality in *Woman with Dead Child* which anticipated future pain and mourning, and reflected the very wound that was "experienced too soon" (in Caruth's wording cited above). While Freud described mourning's "peculiar painfulness" (1957a, "Appendix C," 169), Scarry classifies "pain and the imagination" as "each other's missing intentional counterpart," stressing the fact that the word "work" is "at once a near synonym for pain, and a near synonym for created object" (169–170) – as in: labor and artwork. Anchored in her empathic imagination (in Margulies's notion of empathy as projection and inscape, as imaginative and creative), Kollwitz's art of mourning clearly falls into Freud's and Scarry's psycho-aesthetic categories.

Generally informed by her deep knowledge of historical wars and their numerous artistic and literary representations, and by her home front experience of World War I in particular, Kollwitz's oeuvre aligns itself with the realm of representations of mourning as sites of trauma. What issues do Kollwitz's art and aesthetic raise in relation to the practical and ethical consequences of objectifying mourning in visible images? And how can the de-objectifying labor of mourning, in turn, challenge the boundaries of visual traditions? Freud's 1917 description of the differences between mourning and melancholia places mourning in the position of a temporally limited process with a liberating and life-affirming outcome (Freud 1957b, 245). It is enlightening to revisit his dichotomy when considering Kollwitz's art and trying to understand what makes hers an art of mourning rather than of melancholia. Her art of mourning challenges Freud's conviction of the lost object as replaceable, for the lost object in Kollwitz is never given up.[17] As her mnemonic art of mourning tirelessly demonstrates, the artist acquires a quantitatively darker and a qualitatively deviant psychic position in heart and mind, both as a mourner who remembers and as an artist who memorializes.

DIE ÜBERLEBENDEN   KRIEG DEM KRIEGE!
HERAUSGEGEBEN VOM INTERNATIONALEN GEWERKSCHAFTSBUND AMSTERDAM

Figure 4: Käthe Kollwitz: *Those Who Survived (Die Überlebenden)*, crayon and brush lithograph 1923, © Käthe Kollwitz Museum Cologne, Germany

Along with Kollwitz's *War* cycle (*Krieg*, 1922–1923), the 1923 poster *Those Who Survived* (*Die Überlebenden*; see figure 4) remembers the physically and mentally injured through its depiction of physical wounds such as loss of sight and mental wounds such as shock, horror, and fear. This work is reminis-

---

17 The term *object* is used in the psychoanalytic sense here, meaning object of desire or love object (which in common usage is a person, or subject). In other words, object here means a living human being of affective interest to another living human being (e. g., lovers, or mothers and children).

cent of Munch's woodcut *Angst* (1915). It does not directly show the dead, but the surviving woman's face at the center more likely resembles a skull than the countenance of a living human being. The children's orbits are hollow and their expressions apparitional, the men's eyes bandaged. The survivors memorialized here are ruined and resemble the dead; they mimic death, and foreshadow further premature dying. The figures portrayed in this work are likely a widowed mother too consumed to fully acknowledge those around her, her own and other mothers' children, and blinded and maimed veterans and invalids whose wounds have come to define them, and who contribute their share to a visualized memory of the innumerous martial atrocities committed during World War I. Appropriately, other titles in Kollwitz's *War* cycle remember survivors who, in turn, remember those they have lost, the fallen, as indicated by titles such as *The Widow* (*Die Witwe*) and *Mothers* (*Mütter*).

Just as the lithograph *Those Who Survived*, the two granite sculptures titled *Mourning Parents* (*Die trauernden Eltern*, 1932; see figure 5), too, refrain from concretely or demonstratively representing the dead. Instead, their absence is powerfully conjured, as the work focuses on the aftermath of war, on the martyred existence of surviving, grieving parents. In a field near Vladslo, Belgium, lay the graves of hundreds of soldiers killed in the early days of World War I, among them Peter Kollwitz. Upon hearing the news of his death near Diksmuide in 1914, Kollwitz decided to create a memorial. This process started with the idea of a body stretched out (as Liebknecht's, perhaps), the father at the head and the mother at the feet.[18] She also thought of a number of other scenarios, but, dissatisfied with them, decided then to put the project aside for a spell. It was nearly two decades after Peter's death that Kollwitz completed this set of sculptures, excluding the presence of a corpse in favor of an eloquent gap that cuts between these helpless survivors paralyzed by their overwhelming pain.

The path to the creation of this memorial was aesthetically challenging and psychologically painstaking. Kollwitz struggled with the preceding stages of this monument and eighteen years later, in 1932, her memorial for the fallen, *Mourning Parents* was eventually erected in her presence at the Belgian cemetery in Roggevelde. In 1955, the graves and the monument were moved to the German War Cemetery in Vladslo. Her sculptures depict the mourning of war victims as a solitary endeavor, even though the two surviving mourners are placed side by side. In her portrayal of both parents, Kollwitz turned away from sensu-

---

18 "The monument shall have Peter's figure [...] the father at his head, the mother at his feet." ("Das Denkmal soll Peters Gestalt haben [...] den Vater zu Häupten, die Mutter zu Füssen" [Kollwitz 1989, 177].)

Figure 5: Käthe Kollwitz: *The Mourning Parents (Die trauernden Eltern)*, war memorial on the soldiers' cemetary in Vladslo, Belgium, granite 1914–32, © Käthe Kollwitz Museum Cologne, Germany / Photo: Lothar Schnepf

ousness and expressive emotion, focusing instead on the gesture of prayer reminiscent of works by Constantin Brancusi.

This late work's stoic, repressed, and emotionally minimal and introverted quality is diametrically opposed to the earlier pre-World-War-I depiction in *Woman with Dead Child*, especially in comparison with the latter's vehement pathos and its all-encompassing gesture of strong physical impact and emotional maximum. It is also rather different from *Battlefield* – in medium, genre, and expression. The mother figure in Kollwitz's memorial bends and kneels, curls in, and is thoroughly separated from the outside world by a large shawl that almost entirely covers her, whereas the father's posture is suspiciously strict and painfully straight, as if in uniform. These survivors almost mimic a burial they did not have a chance to witness, in that the mother's shawl shrouds her, while the father's garb shares similarities with the rigidity of a casket. The geniality of this composition lies in the empty space between the parents, a gap that intensifies the sense of grief, loss, pain and isolation, and addresses, *ex negativo*, their expression. The gesture of withdrawal and restraint, combined with the literal making of space for death *post factum*, conveys the surviving parents' grief in a striking sculptural portrait that acknowledges, represents, and identifies with absence, whereas Kollwitz's first attempts to design a monument not only included, but began with and focused on Peter's body.

Kollwitz was extremely aware of how uncannily repetitive deaths in action are: always pointing backwards to previous wars and hence always "secretly familiar" (to recall Freud's definition cited earlier), and, as ongoing repetitions, all the more horrendous. She recognized and represented these traumatic events in general, less interested in the specificity of one war alone, even though the 22 October 1914 indubitably marked the moment of her greatest personal loss, a caesura from which she never recovered. Her focus lies rather on various kinds of repetition: first, the repetition of history that in repeating its tragedies renders itself cruder (as Karl Marx claimed in his essay on the *18th Brumaire of Louis Bonaparte*, 1852); and then the artist's own repetitive insistence on one major theme and its most prominent corresponding figure: the horror of war, the trauma embodied in the fallen soldier, and the ensuing haunting profiles of his absence.

Kollwitz's insistent portrayal of mourning as a dark and painful emotion and its expression as an attempt to give voice to the wound of the fallen (the dead) and the injured and vulnerable survivors predated World War I – the two etchings discussed above, *Woman with Dead Child* of 1903 and *Battlefield* of 1907, are only two poignant examples. Her commitment to articulating and exhibiting the wounds of war, evisceration, ruin, and death, her own wounds and those of others, and to acknowledging the labor of mourning, remembering, and witnessing, her own and those of others, persisted throughout her life as an artist. The loss of her son may have intensified this commitment, but it did not create it. Nor are the *Mourning Parents* on the Belgian cemetery meant to show the subjective suffering of Käthe and Karl Kollwitz alone. These sculptures are intended to transcend the artist's and her husband's personal suffering in ways that are representative of a lost generation, of parental and other survivors, their traumata, and their testimonies. They are placed publically and invite communal remembrance.

Kollwitz's encompassing humanistic angle is a crucial criterion, since in spite of her overall popularity, she seems suspended between two World Wars as a Weimar artist, understudied in terms of her psychologically informed aesthetic that affectively and graphically focuses on war and catastrophe. As a woman who suffered and who movingly depicted her own joys and sorrows, and with them, those of others, she is certainly well known. Her lighter graphic scenes of mothers and toddlers, for instance, tend to appear on popular calendars. The reception of Kollwitz's artistic genius, however, seems guided by, if not limited to, the stigma of gender, and as a result, her aesthetic achievement tends to be out of the focus to the degree that even museums seem to place greater emphasis on Kollwitz's individual motherhood and personal emotions, than on her aesthetically successful and artistically and universally representative expressions of the traumatic loss of war that marked (and continues to mark) entire generations of mothers and fathers, sons and daughters. Pain and testimony were her genres.

As quasi-contemporaries, Freud and Kollwitz each lost a son in World War I. Freud's son Hermann was killed in action in 1917, the same year that his father published his essay on mourning and melancholia. Kollwitz died only weeks before the end of World War II, whereas Freud died six years earlier in exile, at the outset of the war. Freud's work during World War I, like Kollwitz's, is embedded in his earlier and later thoughts rather than reflecting World War I in isolation. In other words, concerns were present well before the war and gathered momentum and took up a renewed acuity as a result of the war, but had not originally been spurred by it. Although Freud's "Mourning and Melancholia" (1917) was published during World War I, he had already presented his comprehension of these phenomena in a letter to Wilhelm Fließ in 1895, and had elaborated on his comparative approach as early as January 1914, in a lecture at Vienna's Psychoanalytic Society. Freud's process thus runs parallel to Kollwitz's anticipatory, perhaps vatic stances on mourning, a theme that not only never left her, but that was reinforced and reconfirmed in all its might by impending martial catastrophes.[19]

In Freud's assessment, both mourning and melancholia cause pain as a consequence of loss. He deems mourning the normal, and melancholia the pathological form of a comparable affective phenomenon (Freud 1957b, 243). Although Freud comparatively analyzed both affective states, he did express his surprise at

---

19 In the context of his deliberations on the ego and the superego, Freud elaborated on mourning and melancholia six years after the essay on mourning and melancholia, in "The Ego and the Id" (1961, 28), once again relying on the notions of identification and incorporation, while adding a dimension to what one may call imitation (in that the lost object is imitated and incorporated by the one who lost it and identifies with it). Freud's elaboration is interesting in the context of Kollwitz as an artist who repeatedly represents scenes of loss (who imitates, repeats, and reproduces the images of those who died). As an artist of the early twentieth century she cannot simply be classified as a mimetic (or imitative) artist. However, in spite of her work's proximity to Munch's, for example, she was opposed to being categorized as an expressionist artist, an era, or a movement, in German modernist art of which she could historically have been a part. Her art tends to be more imitative than that of her expressionist contemporaries in both literature and the visual arts, most of whom were men, and many were killed in action in World War I.

the fact that unlike a melancholic, a mourner is not diagnosed as a patient, even if mourning can cause grave psychological deviations (1957b, 243–244).

Kollwitz's *Woman with Dead Child* has more than once been read as a pathological image. In Freud's terms, pathology would equal the melancholic rather than the mourner. Freud classified pathology quantitatively, not qualitatively. To phrase it differently, the melancholic and the mourner are qualitatively similar, if not the same, and it is only a matter of degree, according to Freud, that separates pathology from normalcy.

Was Kollwitz an early mourner or a pathological melancholic? Her wounds of war were traumatic; they cried out, preceded, in Caruth's sense, their impact; they were clearly not healed by time, even though Kollwitz continuously struggled to endow them with the power of expression (by "making" that followed "unmaking," in Scarry's sense), just as she endued her artistic expression with the power and the voice of the wound. But can Kollwitz's art really be classified as an art marked by melancholy (and hence pathology), as Uwe Schneede did (1981, 7)? Was she not rather caught in a phase of mourning that as a result of the war simply could not end, in what Freud called "the work of mourning" (1957b, 245), which runs parallel to *dream work* as the labor of mourning, dreaming, and creating? Freud writes that the mourner is, at some point, relieved, in that after going through the work of mourning the loss of a person, the individual is once again "free and uninhibited" (245), whereas the loss in pathological melancholia is not that of a person, but of a capacity (244). In the case of mourning, the world becomes empty, says Freud, and in the case of melancholia, the self.[20] Kollwitz, then, does not so much emerge as a pathological case of melancholia; rather, her world before, during, and after World War I was itself pathological. Her "lifetime among wars" is poetically remembered by Muriel Rukeyser, in a biographical poem titled "Käthe Kollwitz," with Kollwitz as the speaker (or "witness voice," to recall Rukeyser's other poem cited earlier):

> Held between wars
> my lifetime
> among wars, the big hands of the world of death
> my lifetime
> listens to yours.

---

20 While Freud contrastively compares mourning and melancholia in 1917, more recent psychoanalytic research points to "melancholia" as one of three faces of mourning (the other two being "manic defense" and "moving on" (Akthar 2001, 103–104 and 109). In this taxonomy, Kollwitz's art would likely fall into the category of mourning as melancholia. Further, Freud's later thoughts on mourning and melancholia somewhat relax the tension between these two states of mind.

The faces of the sufferers
in the street, [...]
their lives showing
through their bodies
[...] my lifetime is to love to endure to suffer the music
to set its portrait
up as a sheet of the world [...]
and the child alive within the living woman [...]
and death holding my lifetime between great hands
the hands of enduring life
that suffers [...]

Held among wars, watching
all of them
all these people [...]

Looking at
all of them
death, the children
[...] the corpse with the baby

[...] all streaming to one son killed, Peter;
even the son left living; repeated
[...]; the grandson
another Peter killed in another war [...]

What would happen if one woman told the truth about her life?
The world would split open.
(2005, 460 – 463)

Käthe Kollwitz was traumatized by acts of violence in/and historical wars preceding her time. She was committed to "witness[ing these] in the second degree," to repeat Felman's phrase cited earlier. Kollwitz was also traumatized
by the World Wars during her lifetime, as a witness at the home front who
time and again reaffirmed the humanity of those who were dehumanized,
maimed, and killed. Rather than a pathological melancholic, she was a mourning artist and witness who created graphic testimonies. She did not lose the capacity for engaged affect and empathy, and even before losing her son had imaginatively turned to previous cases of painful catastrophic loss, ranging from
Christian iconography such as the *pietà* (as *the* formula for the pathos of motherly mourning), to farming mothers losing their sons in the Peasants' War that
predated her own loss by centuries. That said, Kollwitz's art of mourning is explicitly ongoing (not finite, as Freud suggested mourning was). Interestingly,
Freud placed great emphasis on the painfulness of mourning, observing that
pain can be the actual reaction to a real or imagined loss of a loved object
(1957a, 170). It is, I submit, this imaginative potential that can be diagnosed in

Kollwitz's anticipation of loss in *Woman with Dead Child*. That this potential should have assumed actuality about a decade later, clearly intensifies the situation (in that her intimation of mortality came true).

Freud approached mourning and melancholia comparatively, and deployed the word "incorporation" (1957b, 249), which encompasses both the living and the dead body. What Kollwitz's mother figure emphatically strives for as early as 1903, seven years after her son's birth and eleven years prior to his death, seems to be an incorporation, or rather a re-incorporation, so as to try and return the child to the womb rather than give it away to the tomb. Her World War I cemetery statues of mother and father are, by contrast, an externalization into gesture rather than immediately reflecting the basic grounds of parental affect. The work of mourning is envisioned by Freud as transitional, as located between a life and an art, at once narcissistic and self-therapeutic. Kollwitz confirms Freud's vision, but also transcends it, as her work of mourning is at the same time historically immersed, ethically engaged, and politically committed. Mourning, as Roland Barthes wrote in his *Mourning Diary*, composed over a span of two years after his mother's death, is ultimately "a susceptibility to emotion" (2009, 43), a potentially endless painful emotion, one may add, which at the same time harbors a desire to overcome itself by way of expression. Kollwitz seeks such expression of emotion in her artwork, in an attempt to let the wounds of the fallen and those of survivors speak as witnesses, to claim their memory and their experience – to split the world (and wound) open, as "[m]emory is, achingly, the only relation we can have with the dead" (Sontag 2003, 103).

Works Cited

Akhtar, Salman. "From Mental Pain through Manic Defense to Mourning." *Three Faces of Mourning: Melancholia, Manic Defense, and Moving on*, edited by Akhtar (Aronson, 2001), pp. 95–113.

Barthes, Roland. *Mourning Diary*. Translated by Richard Howard (Hill and Wang, 2009).

Bonus-Jeep, Beate. *Sechzig Jahre Freundschaft mit Käthe Kollwitz* (Boppard, 1948).

Caruth, Cathy. *Listening to Trauma: Conversations with Leaders in the Theory and Treatment of Catastrophic Experience: Interviews and Photography by Cathy Caruth* (Johns Hopkins UP, 2014).

Caruth, Cathy. *Unclaimed Experience: Trauma, Narrative, and History* (Johns Hopkins UP, 1996).

Freud, Sigmund. "The Ego and the Id." *The Standard Edition of the Complete Psychological Works of Sigmund Freud*. Vol. XIX. Translated and edited by James Strachey (The Hogarth Press and the Institute of Psychoanalysis, 1961), pp. 3–66.

Freud, Sigmund. "Inhibition, Symptom, and Anxiety." *The Standard Edition of the Complete Psychological Works of Sigmund Freud.* Vol. X. Translated and edited by James Strachey (The Hogarth Press and the Institute of Psychoanalysis, 1957a), pp. 77–179.

Freud, Sigmund. "Mourning and Melancholia." *The Standard Edition of the Complete Psychological Works of Sigmund Freud.* Vol. XIV. Translated and edited by James Strachey (The Hogarth Press and the Institute of Psychoanalysis, 1957b), pp. 237–258.

Freud, Sigmund. "The Uncanny." *The Standard Edition of the Complete Psychological Works of Sigmund Freud.* Vol. XVII. Translated and edited by James Strachey (The Hogarth Press and the Institute of Psychoanalysis, 1957c), pp. 217–256.

Friedrichsmeyer, Sara. "'Seeds for the Sowing': The Diary of Käthe Kollwitz." *Arms and the Woman: War, Gender, and Literary Representation,* edited by Helen M. Cooper, et al. (U of North Carolina P, 1989), pp. 205–224.

Hammerstein, Katharina von. "'Meine unhaltbar widerspruchsvolle Stellung zum Kriege': Käthe Kollwitz von Kriegsbefürwortung zu Kriegsgegnerschaft, 1914–1918." *Acta Germanica,* vol. 43 (2015), pp. 165–176.

Hammerstein, Katharina von. "'...die zusehende Frau, die aber alles empfindet': Humanitäre Zeugenschaft in Käthe Kollwitz' Tagebüchern und ausgewählten Kunstwerken." *Auf dem Weg in die Moderne: Deutsche und österreichische Literatur und Kultur,* edited by Roswitha Burwick, et al. (Walter de Gruyter, 2013), pp. 215–242.

Herman, Judith. *Trauma and Recovery: The Aftermath of Violence* (Basic Books, 1992).

Jünger, Ernst. *In Stahlgewittern: Historisch-kritische Ausgabe.* Edited by Helmuth Kiesel (Klett-Cotta, 2014).

Kacandes, Irene. *Talk Fiction: Literature and the Talk Explosion* (U of Nebraska P, 2001).

Kollwitz, Käthe. *The Diary and Letters.* Edited by Hans Kollwitz, translated by Richard and Clara Winston (Northwestern UP, 1955).

Kollwitz, Käthe. *Die Tagebücher.* Edited by Jutta Bohnke-Kollwitz (Akademie, 1989).

Margulies, Alfred. *The Empathic Imagination* (W. W. Norton & Co., 1989).

Marx, Karl. *The 18th Brumaire of Louis Bonaparte.* Translated by Daniel De Leon (Mondial, 2005).

Rukeyser, Muriel. *The Collected Poems.* Edited by Janet E. Kaufman, et al. (U of Pittsburgh P, 2005).

Scarry, Elaine. *The Body in Pain: The Making and Unmaking of the World* (Oxford UP, 1985).

Schneede, Uwe. "Melancholie und Aufruhr: Zum Werk von Käthe Kollwitz." *Käthe Kollwitz: Die Zeichnerin,* edited by Kunstverein Hamburg (Selbstverlag, 1981), pp. 7–10.

Sharp, Ingrid. "Käthe Kollwitz's Witness to War: Gender, Authority, and Reception." *Women in German Yearbook,* vol. 27 (2011), pp. 87–107.

Siebrecht, Claudia. "The Mater Dolorosa on the Battlefield – Mourning Mothers in German Women's Art of the First World War." *Untold War: New Perspectives in First World War Studies,* edited by Heather Jones, et al. (Brill, 2008), pp. 259–291.

Sontag, Susan. *Regarding the Pain of Others* (Penguin, 2003).

Notes on Authors

Marianne Bechhaus-Gerst is an Africanist at the University of Cologne, Germany, specializing in German colonial history, the history of Africans in Germany, constructions of Africa in German popular culture and postcolonial and critical whiteness studies. Her body of academic work includes books about the role of German and African women in German colonialism, people of African descent in Nazi Germany and the history of Cologne as a colonial metropolis. She also works as a curator of historical/cultural historical exhibitions, conducts workshops and gives lectures in her fields of expertise in and outside academia.

Cindy Patey Brewer holds a doctorate degree in German Literature from the University of Utah and studied as a Fulbright scholar at the Humboldt University in Berlin. She is currently an Associate Professor of German Studies at Brigham Young University. She serves as the Associate Director of "Sophie: a Digital Library of Works by German-Speaking Women" (http://sophie.byu.edu/). Her past research focused on German-speaking women writers of the eighteenth and nineteenth centuries. Currently she is working on mission literature written during Germany's colonial period and is writing a book entitled "The Missionary Imagination." Brewer also does personal research on bilingual parenting, raising her eleven multiracial children in German and English.

Maureen O. Gallagher holds an M.A. in Modern Languages from the University of Nebraska–Lincoln and a Ph.D. in German Studies from the University of Massachusetts Amherst. Her research and teaching interests include German colonialism, gender, children's and young adult literature, critical race theory and critical whiteness studies. She currently holds a Max Kade Berlin Postdoctoral Fellowship to the Berlin Program for Advanced German and European Studies at the Freie Universität Berlin where she is writing a book manuscript about whiteness in Wilhelmine Germany based on her dissertation, which won the 2015 Women in German Dissertation Prize.

Katharina von Hammerstein (Ph.D., University of California, Los Angeles/UCLA) is Professor of German Studies at the University of Connecticut. Her books and articles have focused on: literature and art in relation to human rights and war; representations of Blacks in German-language literature and Blacks' perspectives on Germany around 1900; women's self-(re)presentations as political practice in *Sich MitSprache erschreiben: Selbstzeugnisse als politische Praxis schreibender Frauen, Deutschland 1840–1919* (2013); and gender in literary, social and political discourses from the late 1700s to the early 1900s. She published extensively on Romantic Sophie Mereau(-Brentano) (1994, 1997, 2008), colonialist Frieda von Bülow (2012), impressionist Peter Altenberg (2007), furthermore on writers like Friedrich Hölderlin, Bettine von Arnim, Louise Aston, Hedwig Dohm and Franziska zu Reventlow, artist Käthe Kollwitz and WWI, and diverse testimonies on the German-Herero Colonial War of 1904–1908.

Margaret R. Higonnet, Emeritus Professor at the University of Connecticut, has also taught at the Universities of Munich, Santiago de Compostela, and George Washington. President of FILLM and President emeritus of the American Comparative Literature Association and the American Conference on Romanticism, she has also been president of the Gender Studies

https://doi.org/10.1515/9783110572001-016

Committee of the ICLA, and the ICLA publications committee on Comparative History of Literatures in European Languages.

Her theoretical interests range from children's literature to the romantic roots of modern literary theories, and center on the intersection of feminist theory with comparative literature, as
in the volumes *Borderwork* (1995), *Gender in Literary History, CCS* 6.2 (2009), and *Comparatively Queer* (2010). She has edited four volumes on World War I: *Behind the Lines: Gender
and the Two World Wars* (1987), *Lines of Fire* (1999), *Nurses at the Front* (2001), and *Margaret
Hall's Letters and Photographs from the Battle Country, 1918–1919* (2014). Her articles on the
topic address women's war poetry, the transformation of gender and identity in wartime,
women at the front, writings for children, and problems of voice in nursing accounts.

Barbara Kosta received her Ph.D. in German from the University of California, Berkeley and is
Head of the Department of German Studies at the University of Arizona. She is the recipient
of Fulbright and DAAD awards for her research on German cinema, twentieth-century autobiographical filming and writing. Her publications include *Recasting Autobiography: Women's
Counterfictions in Contemporary German Literature and Film* (1994) and *Willing Seduction:
The Blue Angel, Marlene Dietrich, Mass Culture* (2009). She is the co-editor of *Writing Against
Boundaries: Gender, Ethnicity and Nationality in the German-speaking Context* (2003). She
has published numerous articles on contemporary German film and literature as well as on
literature, film, and visual culture of the Weimar Republic.

Martina Kolb holds a Ph.D. in Comparative Literature from Yale University and teaches in the
Departments of Modern Languages, Philosophy, and English at Susquehanna University. She
has been the recipient of a number of research fellowships (for example from the American
Psychoanalytic Association, the Psychoanalytic Center of Philadelphia, and the Suhrkamp Archives in Marbach, Germany), and is the author of a variety of articles on a broad range of
writers and artists, including Dante, Goethe, Pound, Brecht, Beckett, and Christa Wolf. Her research concentrates on poetics, aesthetics, psychoanalysis, and the interarts. Kolb's comparative monograph *Nietzsche, Freud, Benn, and the Azure Spell of Liguria* was published in
2013 in the German and European Studies Series by the University of Toronto Press. Currently, she is at work on a book on interartistic representations of pain.

Erika Kuhlman is Professor of History at Idaho State University. Her latest book, *The International Migration of German Great War Veterans*, was published in 2016. Her other books include *Of Little Comfort: War Widows, Fallen Soldiers, and the Remaking of the Nation after
the Great War* (2012) and *Reconstructing Patriarchy after the Great War* (2008).

Erika Quinn is an Associate Professor of History at Eureka College. Her research interests lie
in Central European cultural history, focusing on questions of self-understanding, emotions,
and religion. Her book *Franz Liszt: A Story of Central European Subjectivity* was published by
Brill in 2014. She has also published articles on twentieth-century German war widows in the
Journal of First World War Studies as well as in *Death Representations in Literature*. Her current project is a book based on a German woman's diary from 1939–1948. She earned her
B.A. in History and German Area Studies from Cornell University and her Ph.D. in Modern European History from the University of California, Davis.

Jennifer Redmann (Ph.D., University of Wisconsin-Madison) is Associate Professor of German at Franklin & Marshall College in Lancaster, Pennsylvania. Her research and publications address both German literary and cultural studies of the late nineteenth and early twentieth centuries and foreign language curricula and pedagogy. She has published on the work of Else Lasker-Schüler, the diary *A Woman in Berlin*, and the girls' literature of Else Ury. Her article "Doing Her Bit: German and Anglo-American Girls' Literature of the First World War" appeared in *Girlhood Studies* in 2011. Together with Pennylyn Dykstra-Pruim, she is author of the textbook *Schreiben lernen: A Writing Guide for Learners of German*. Redmann is currently working on a book-length comparative study of German, British, and American girls' novels published during the First World War.

Livia Rigotti studied history, philosophy and journalism (Magister Artium) at the University of Leipzig, Germany. She was a Ph.D. student at the Max Weber Centre for Advanced Cultural and Social Studies, University of Erfurt, Germany and graduated in 2013. The title of her thesis is "Deutsche Frauen in den Südsee-Kolonien des Kaiserreichs. Alltag und Beziehungen zur indigenen Bevölkerung, 1884–1919" (German Women in the South Sea Colonies of the German Empire. Everyday Life and Relationships with the Indigenous Population, 1884–1919). Her research interests are German colonial history, gender history, and mission history. She lives and works in Mainz, Germany.

Shelley E. Rose is Associate Professor of History and Director of Social Studies at Cleveland State University. She has published articles in the *Journal of Urban History* and *Peace & Change*. Rose directs the digital humanities project *Protest Spaces: Peace Movements in the United States and Germany, 1920–2000* (protestspaces.org) and is completing her book manuscript, "Gender and the Politics of Peace: Cooperative Activism and Transnational Networks on the German Left, 1921–1983." She is a founding coordinator of the German Studies Association's Interdisciplinary Digital Humanities Network.

Julie Shoults received her Ph.D. in German Studies from the University of Connecticut in 2015 and is currently a Lecturer in German at Muhlenberg College in Pennsylvania. Her research interests include life writing and women's socialist literature, and her recent projects focus on intersections of gender and violence in the contexts of WWI, WWII, and the GDR. She is currently also collaborating on a volume about women in German Expressionism. Her work has been published in the *Women in German Yearbook* and *Expressionismus*, and she received the Women in German Dissertation Prize in 2016.

James M. Skidmore is Associate Professor of German Studies at the University of Waterloo. Originally from Saskatchewan, where he took a B.A. in French and German and an M.A. in German, he earned his Ph.D. at Princeton University with a dissertation on Ricarda Huch's writing during the Weimar Republic. Skidmore's research focuses on the representation of political and social issues. He has written on contemporary German literature and film, cultural developments in Germany, and comparative literature. He has also published on online teaching and learning, and in 2012 received the national German Academic Exchange Service German Online award for his online teaching. He is co-editor and founder of kultur360.com, an open website providing analysis of contemporary German-speaking society and culture. He has served as a Teaching Fellow at the University of Waterloo and is an Open Educational Resources Fellow at eCampusOntario. Active in academic service, Skidmore has occupied various administrative positions, including founding Chair of Languages and Literatures at Wilfrid Laurier University and Chair of Germanic and Slavic Studies at the University of Waterloo, and is currently director of the Waterloo Centre for German Studies, an endowed research institute at the University of Waterloo.

Cindy Walter-Gensler is a lecturer at Baylor University who received her Ph.D. in Germanic Studies from the University of Texas at Austin in 2016. Her dissertation entitled "Ideologies of Motherhood: Literary Imaginaries and Public Discourses" examines discourses on mothers reflected in twentieth-century novels by Vicki Baum, Ina Seidel, Heinrich Böll, Gabriele Wohmann, and Hera Lind. Cindy's research interests also include representations of war, particularly the intersection of gender, class, and war. She is currently preparing a book manuscript on war novels written by forgotten female authors, seeking to investigate how class and motherhood influenced war-time experiences for women as depicted in popular women's literature. Cindy has presented her research at various conferences, published book reviews, and organized as well as moderated conference panels at the GSA (German Studies Association) and SCMLA (South Central Modern Language Association).

Names Index